"Ken Benau has made a major contribution not only to the understanding of shame and pride, but also to the field of psychotherapy itself. By providing a finely detailed and clearly explained taxonomy of shame and pride feelings and states, this book reveals the pervasiveness of these experiential phenomena, especially amidst the wide domain of relational trauma, and highlights the great clinical value of being able to recognize, differentiate, and work directly with them. As he says about shame, 'to not name shame is to do shame's bidding.' And with great sensitivity and respect, he indicates the challenges that not only patients have in such naming, but also how hard it is for therapists to experience, let alone name, their own shame and/or pride amidst the psychotherapy process. Offering detailed, annotated transcripts of several psychotherapy sessions that he conducted, he brings the conceptual system to life and presents an integrated, multimodal approach to healing the problematic aspects of shame and pride and facilitating the potentials for some forms of these to reflect and enhance well-being and even flourishing. Readers interested in the neuroscientific aspects of shame and pride phenomena will appreciate the detailed exploration of these in the context of one of the therapy session transcripts. This book is a tremendously rich resource that integrates and builds beyond what has come before in this field. It has great conceptual and clinical value and is clearly the fruit of not only a fine and expansive mind but also a warm and open heart."

David S. Elliott, PhD, coauthor of *Attachment Disturbances in Adults: Treatment for Comprehensive Repair*

"This book is the most comprehensive guide to thinking about shame and its treatment written so far! Shame and pride are discussed in all their different guises and presentations, along with somatic, relational, and visualization approaches to treatment. Densely written and theoretical, yet offering practical applications as well."

Janina Fisher, PhD, Assistant Educational Director, Sensorimotor Psychotherapy Institute, and author of *Healing the Fragmented Selves of Trauma Survivors* and *Transforming the Living Legacy of Trauma*

"A marvelous book! Benau introduces an integrated view of traumatic shame states and its neglected counterpart, pride states. Accessible and erudite, he presents a bridge from theory/concepts to the treatment of patients suffering from maladaptive shame and pride. Therapists learn to navigate ruptures and impasses, creating golden opportunities for transformation. This is a must read for anyone dealing with shame with relational trauma in psychotherapy."

Hanna Levenson, PhD, Professor at the Wright Institute in California, U.S.A

"Clinical and scientific progress oftentimes depends on a useful differentiation and integration of concepts. Ken Benau's present text is a noteworthy and admirable instance of this. He starts by carefully distinguishing and analyzing several kinds of shame and pride. From there, he details how grasping the proposed subtypes helps clinicians to affectively, empathically, and cognitively meet individuals who suffer from the problematic forms of these social emotions. His case examples serve as a major inspiration for therapists who aspire to help people develop more efficient and effective ways of relating to themselves and others. Recommended!"

Ellert Nijenhuis, PhD, independent psychologist and psychotherapist in The Netherlands and Portugal

Shame, Pride, and Relational Trauma

Shame, Pride, and Relational Trauma is a guide to recognizing the many ways shame and pride lie at the heart of psychotherapy with survivors of relational trauma. In these pages, readers will learn how to differentiate shame and pride as emotional processes and traumatic mind/body states. They will also discover how psychodynamic and phenomenological relationships between shame, pride, and dissociation benefit psychotherapy. Therapists will learn about ways to conceptualize and successfully navigate complex, patient-therapist shame dynamics and apply neuroscientific findings to this challenging work. Finally, readers will discover how the concept and phenomena of pro-being pride, that is delighting in one's own and others' unique aliveness, helps patients transcend maladaptive shame and pride and experience greater unity within, with others, and with the world beyond.

Ken Benau, PhD, has a private practice in psychotherapy, consultation, and training in the San Francisco Bay Area.

Shame, Pride, and Relational Trauma

Concepts and Psychotherapy

Ken Benau

NEW YORK AND LONDON

First published 2022
by Routledge
605 Third Avenue, New York, NY 10158

and by Routledge
2 Park Square, Milton Park, Abingdon, Oxon, OX14 4RN

Routledge is an imprint of the Taylor & Francis Group, an informa business

© 2022 Ken Benau

The right of Ken Benau to be identified as author of this work has been asserted in accordance with sections 77 and 78 of the Copyright, Designs and Patents Act 1988.

All rights reserved. No part of this book may be reprinted or reproduced or utilised in any form or by any electronic, mechanical, or other means, now known or hereafter invented, including photocopying and recording, or in any information storage or retrieval system, without permission in writing from the publishers.

Trademark notice: Product or corporate names may be trademarks or registered trademarks and are used only for identification and explanation without intent to infringe.

Library of Congress Cataloging-in-Publication Data
Names: Benau, Ken, author.
Title: Shame, pride, and relational trauma : concepts and
psychotherapy / Ken Benau.
Description: New York, NY : Routledge, 2022. |
Includes bibliographical references and index.
Identifiers: LCCN 2021048019 (print) | LCCN 2021048020 (ebook) |
ISBN 9781138362376 (hardback) | ISBN 9781138362383 (paperback) |
ISBN 9780429425943 (ebook)
Subjects: LCSH: Psychotherapy.
Classification: LCC RC480 .B3587 2022 (print) |
LCC RC480 (ebook) | DDC 616.89/14–dc23/eng/20211109
LC record available at https://lccn.loc.gov/2021048019
LC ebook record available at https://lccn.loc.gov/2021048020

ISBN: 978-1-138-36237-6 (hbk)
ISBN: 978-1-138-36238-3 (pbk)
ISBN: 978-0-429-42594-3 (ebk)

DOI: 10.4324/9780429425943

Typeset in Bembo
by Newgen Publishing UK

With all my love to Tami, Hannah, and Shira. For being.

Contents

List of Tables   x
Foreword by Martin J. Dorahy   xi
Acknowledgments and Credits   xiv
List of Abbreviations   xix

Introduction   1

1 Shame, Pride, and Relational Trauma: What Are They and Why Do They Matter in Psychotherapy?   9

2 Shame and Pride: Subtypes and Processes   36

3 Shame, Pride, Mind/Body Leave Taking, and Structural Dissociation: Psychodynamics, Phenomenology, and Psychotherapy   73

4 Setting the Stage: Transtheoretical Attitudes, Principles, and Concepts When Working with Shame and Pride in Psychotherapy with Relational Trauma   112

5 Psychotherapy with Patient, Therapist, and Dyadic Shame States: Traumatic Reactions, Therapeutic Responses, and Transformation   142

6 From Shame to Pride: Psychotherapy, Neuroscience, and Applications—Three Perspectives   174

7 Shame State to a Core Way of Being: Beyond Pro-being Pride to Radiant Joy, Grief, Integration, and Oneness   214

Index   249

Tables

1.1	Shame and Guilt: Focus of Emotional/Relational Attention	19
2.1	Shame Subtypes	39
2.2	Pride Subtypes	45
2.3	Window of Optimal Arousal and Tolerance	58
3.1	Psychodynamic Relationships Between Shame, Pride, Mind/Body Leave Taking (LT), and Structural Dissociation (SD)	78

Foreword

The stories of those exposed to relational trauma are multilayered. One can tune into the narrative of events: who did what, where, and for how long. The details are more often than not harrowing, and one is forced to confront the reality of a world where the vulnerable (however defined) are intentionally mistreated and hurt rather than protected and respected. Tuning into this narrative layer is important, if not essential, in the therapeutic space, as it offers opportunities to bear witness to the lived external experience of the person seeking assistance. Yet, the work of therapy lies more pressingly in the narrative layer that speaks to the impact of the experience on the person's internal world. Some areas in this exploration are much more palatable than others. For example, exploring symptom manifestations is typically less emotionally arduous than exploring the wounds and developmental arrests experienced in the felt sense that are brought about by relational trauma. This narrative layer brings the therapist face-to-face with a person defeated, humiliated, powerless, shamed, and broken, along with the various ways they have adapted to such internal attack. Ken Benau, PhD has spent years tuning his ear in the therapeutic space to this narrative layer and this area of focus, noting, formulating, and reformulating the various manifestations of, and adaptations to, defeat, shame, and stifled pride in those who were violated. This careful honing, along with countless episodes exploring rupture and repair, with the shame and reconnection they bring, provided a potent tool and active laboratory for Benau's conceptual framework. This foundation was further built upon and crafted by an astute and cultivated knowledge of the theoretical, empirical, and clinical literatures associated with self-conscious emotions, most notably shame and pride.

Few emotions feel so foreign to survivors of relational trauma as pride and few feel so familiar as shame. But as Benau shows in his deeply engaging and richly textured book, such a statement, which on the face of it has clinical, conceptual, and experiential merit, is far too simplistic. It does not capture the complexity of shame and pride as self-conscious emotions integral to healthy development, and how they are molded, reshaped, and manifest in those presenting with a history of relational trauma. The movement from adaptive to maladaptive shame and pride for Benau brings with it a shift from fluid affective experiences that guide immediate adaptation to the world, to ways of being that are more solidified states. These states characterize more universal and rigid views of the self and the other. They also provide a limited repertoire of predictable ways of being, engaging, and being engaged. The states of shame and pride Benau proposes and elaborates in those suffering in the aftermath of relational trauma become more potent and more state-like when dissociation operates to partition experience and reduces fluid and integrated adaptation to the environment.

While complex, often misunderstood, and routinely avoided, shame has become somewhat of a mainstay in the trauma literature, particularly over the past decade. Pride, however, has been largely neglected. The visibility of shame and relative invisibility of pride in the relational trauma literature may parallel their affective salience for the survivor of intentional harm. Yet, Benau not only brings pride firmly and centrally into the therapeutic space, for both therapist and patient, he also unpacks the complexity of pride in its visible and defensive manifestations along with its growth-inducing whispers that he works to transform into self-acknowledged and owned triumphs.

Beyond authentic pride associated with the hard-earned successes of the patient and therapist, there is another manifestation of pride Benau terms "pro-being pride." Pro-being pride, an enduring mind/body state rather than emotional process, is integral to transformative psychotherapy and a core, unique contribution of Benau's work and this book. It reflects the ability of a person to feel joy and celebrate being themselves, in their own skin, in the presence of another who experiences joy and celebrates being who they are. It is a deeply connecting experience, one which profoundly erodes rigid shame states while lubricating flexible ways of being oneself in the presence of oneself and in the presence of another. It is not reserved for the patient. It is also a developmental achievement for the therapist, but can be precarious and prone to erosion or loss in our work with traumatized individuals. Pro-being pride is one of Benau's central axes in the treatment of relational trauma, and it and the pathways which bring it about represent critical contributions to therapy, that is not only relevant to trauma treatment but to living a fully-engaged, relational life.

The therapist is never forgotten in this book, and neither is the importance of solid theoretical maps to guide our journey with relationally traumatized people. The map Benau provides brings with it a multitude of interventions and technical innovations for successful therapy, along with key signposts that support more productive directions for when we are stuck. In Benau's framing, shame and pride are intimately linked to each other, each reliant on the relationship milieu. This book provides a secure base from which we can explore the manifestations of shame and pride in those living with the ravages of relational trauma. Absorbing Benau's framework and key messages allows us to have a guide when working with highly traumatized, shame-filled, and shame-fueled patients. It also provides a way of avoiding, arresting, or liberating ourselves from the slide into our own shame-filled and shame-fueled places. Authentic pride, and even more so pro-being pride, are the reward for our patients and ourselves.

Martin J. Dorahy, PhD, Professor of Clinical Psychology,
University of Canterbury, New Zealand

Acknowledgments and Credits

Acknowledgments

It takes a village to raise a child. So too a book. As with shame and pride, this creation has always been relational. I could not have written this book without the help of many encouraging, stimulating, and loving "relations."

Several people generously read draft chapters of this book. Each offered comments that expanded, deepened, and clarified my thinking. I alone am responsible for the final product, but they helped make this book better: Peter August, Frank Corrigan, Martin Dorahy, Peter Goetz, Fredlee Kaplan, Debbie Liner, Mark Ludwig, and Onno van der Hart.

Beside myself, only four people read the entire book before its launch. These readers generously gave their time and expertise to review this text and write an endorsement. I was comforted knowing my book was in the wise hands of David Elliot, Janina Fisher, Hanna Levenson, and Ellert Nijenhuis.

Frank Corrigan graciously engaged in conversation with me about the neuroscience that correlates with the process of my psychotherapy session with a relational trauma survivor recounted in Chapter 6. Frank is a master psychotherapist and erudite neuroscientist who possesses the remarkable ability to describe what is going on in the brain, moment-to-moment, during a psychotherapy session. Knowledgeable and creative, Frank's humility is perhaps his finest gift.

Books grow out of the rich soil of conversation. There is no such thing as "my idea." However, many ideas I shared with colleagues benefited greatly from our exchanges.

Peter August: Our treasured, weekly walks helped me forge the central ideas of this book while deepening our friendship. Unlike sleeping dogs, you never let any of my ideas simply lie. I am especially grateful for your regular reminders that what mattered most in this book was pro-being pride.

Rich Chefetz: You helped nurture and challenge my ideas about shame and psychotherapy early in their development. You also believed I had a book within me that called to be written.

Martin Dorahy: You were always interested in my ideas about shame and trauma. You repeatedly taught me how much I knew that I did not know

I knew, and what I did not know that I had never considered. Your genius wrapped in humility and kindness is inspiring.

Janina Fisher: Years ago, when I told you I hoped to write a book about shame and psychotherapy, your affirmation was strikingly matter of fact. I safeguarded that memory for several years and, now, here we are.

Ellert Nijenhuis: Your keen, scholarly mind always left me excited and full of questions. I am grateful for your teaching me about Spinoza and his relevance in understanding the interrelationship between mind, body, and nature in psychotherapy.

Adriano Schimmenti: Our many emails about shame and dissociation stretched and sharpened my thinking. I am grateful for your introducing me to the *Mediterranean Journal of Clinical Psychology*, where two of my articles about shame, pride, and dissociation were published.

Onno van der Hart: From the beginning, your friendship and colleagueship showed abiding faith in me and my passions about our shared work. Accompanying me as a first-time book author was always reassuring. Your fine-tuned review of Chapter 3 helped me think and write with greater precision and coherence about structural dissociation and shame. Thank you, too, for deepening my appreciation of Pierre Janet, whose phenomenological approach to psychotherapy and trauma inspires me.

Several people encouraged me to write and publish my thoughts about shame and pride in psychotherapy with relational trauma. Each one of you helped me carry on in ways that led to this book:

Matthew Dahlitz and Richard Hill, editors extraordinaire, thank you for regularly asking me to write about shame, pride, relational trauma, and psychotherapy for *The Neuropsychotherapist*, now *Science of Psychotherapy*, and interviewing me for your podcast. You graciously offered a welcoming forum to hone ideas about our shared interests.

Orit Badouk Epstein, editor of the journal *Attachment: New Directions in Psychotherapy and Relational Psychoanalysis*. You invited me to write an article after my hiatus of eight years, affording me a platform that introduced many to my thoughts about shame, attachment, and trauma.

Elizabeth Lehmann, 15 years ago you suggested I create an online forum to share with colleagues my emergent ideas about shame, pride, and psychotherapy. That germ found its fuller flowering in this book.

Jenny Rydberg, for inviting me to write an article for *The European Journal of Trauma and Dissociation*. You gave me my first platform to share with others how adaptive pride, particularly pro-being pride, pertains to our work as trauma-informed psychotherapists.

Professor Cyril Tarquinio and co-editor Salvatore Settineri of the *Mediterranean Journal of Clinical Psychology*, for your interest in my earliest formulation about shame, pride, dissociation, and relational trauma.

Several special friends have loved, accepted, and played with me over many years. I have no words for the depth of my gratitude and love:

Peter August, when asked what we talk about, I can honestly say I have no idea. I have never learned or laughed more in a state of delightful confusion.

Peter Kassen, our more than 50-year friendship continues to amaze and bless me. Thank you for being the first person who taught me life is an embodied expression of creativity and joy—pure, pro-being pride.

Debbie Liner, you have always been solidly there when I needed you. We have shared much nachas and sorrow. From our earliest days in graduate school, you showed me how deep love and wisdom are two sides of the same coin.

Alan Schnee, graduate school partner-in-crime, you are and always will be family. Thank you for being my bud.

Terry Trotter and Peter Goetz, fellow peer group consultants, cheerleaders, and co-conspirators in unfettered, sarcastic riffs, with you my ideas were bathed in a sea of fun. You also nourished me when I needed it most. You are my forever "shugahs."

Onno van der Hart, our newer friendship has such depth it feels surprisingly old and assured. Thank you for your gentle, steady accompaniment of mind and heart.

I have been blessed with superb co-presenters at two annual conferences of the International Society for the Study of Trauma and Dissociation. You taught me much about shame and dissociation that greatly enriched this book: Frank Corrigan, Rick Hohfeler, Sarah Krakauer, and Ulrich Lanius.

Sue Elkind, consultant for many years, my deepest gratitude for your steadfast, affirming presence and wisdom whenever my patients and I were gripped by shame storms. You gently guided me when my hope waned, and were always ready to welcome me back by reminding me of who I have always been.

In order to understand shame, you have to live it from the inside out. Bruce Ecker, you were the first therapist who helped me realize shame lay at the heart of my suffering, without ever shaming me. Your ability to listen deeply with love, compassion, and unwavering respect, "coherently," nurtured my faith that no matter how much I doubted myself, together we would find "meaning" within "madness." Thank you for countless sessions ending with my feeling better and wiser than when we began. Finally, for your unwavering belief that I could make this book authentically mine.

To all my patients present and past, you continue to teach me how to be a better therapist and person. Special thanks to those who graciously gave permission to share our work so that other therapists and patients might benefit. I am humbled by your generosity.

To Priya Sharma, helping with publishing technicalities, I could not have navigated this on my own.

To my editor, Anna Moore, who, out of nowhere, reached out and suggested I had a book within me. Thanks, too, for patiently shepherding this newbie through the maze of publishing.

Acknowledgments and Credits xvii

To my mother, Freya Benau, who taught me that I was meant to be a therapist, and my father, Bondi Benau, who showed me the importance of hard work and finding time for beauty.

Finally, to my wife Tami, for your love, affirmation, and unwavering patience as this book demanded so much of my attention, and to our remarkable daughters, Hannah and Shira, who live each day with kindness and integrity. My unbounded gratitude and love for you and our family.

Credits

To **Casey Horner**, for generous permission to use your beautiful photograph, "Morning Mystic," for the book cover.

To **Glen Hansard** and **Alfred Music**, for gracious permission to use an evocative lyric from Glen Hansard's song, "Just to Be the One":

JUST TO BE THE ONE
Words and Music by GLEN HANSARD
© 2015 PLATEAU RECORDS LIMITED
All Rights Administered by WC MUSIC CORP.
Exclusive Worldwide Print Rights Administered by ALFRED MUSIC All Rights Reserved Used by Permission of ALFRED MUSIC

To **Matthew Dahlitz**, editor-in-chief at *The Science of Psychotherapy*, for permission to reprint portions of my article:
Benau, K. (2020). From Shame State to Pro-being Pride in a Single "Session." *The Science of Psychotherapy*, March 2020, pp. 20–39.

To **Pascal Léger**, executive publisher, STM Journals—*Health and Medical Sciences*—France, and **Elsevier Masson**, for permission to reprint portions of my article:
Benau, K. (2018). Pride in the Psychotherapy of Relational Trauma: Conceptualization and Treatment Considerations. *European Journal of Trauma and Dissociation*, 2, 131–146. https://doi.org/10.1016/j.ejtd.2018.03.002.
© 2018 Elsevier Masson SAS. All rights reserved. With permission.

To **Kate Pearce**, publisher at **Phoenix Publishing House Ltd**, and **Orit Badouk Epstein**, editor, for permission to reprint portions of my article:
Benau, K. (2017). Shame, Attachment, and Psychotherapy. Phenomenology, Neurophysiology, Relational Trauma and Harbingers of Healing. *Attachment: New Directions in Psychotherapy and Relational Psychoanalysis*, 11(1), 1–27. https://doi.org/10.33212/att.v11n1.2017.1.

To **Salvator Settineri**, editor-in-chief, and **Emanuele Maria Merlo**, journal manager at the *Mediterranean Journal of Clinical Psychology*, for permission to reprint portions of my two articles:

Benau, K. (2020a). Shame, Pride and Dissociation: Estranged Bedfellows, Close Cousins and Some Implications for Psychotherapy with Relational Trauma Part I: Phenomenology and Conceptualization. *Mediterranean Journal of Clinical Psychology*, 8(1), 1–35. Doi: https://doi.org/10.6092/2282-1619/mjcp-2154.

Benau, K. (2020b). Shame, Pride and Dissociation: Estranged Bedfellows, Close Cousins and Some Implications for Psychotherapy with Relational Trauma Part II: Psychotherapeutic Applications. *Mediterranean Journal of Clinical Psychology*, 8(1), 1–29. Doi: https://doi.org/10.6092/2282-1619/mjcp-2155.

Abbreviations

ABS	Alternating Bilateral Stimulation
ADHD	Attention-deficit Hyperactivity Disorder
AEDP	Accelerated Experiential Dynamic Psychotherapy
aIAT	autobiographical Implicit Association Test
ANP	Apparently Normal Part of the Personality
ASP	Anti-Symptom Position
CBT	Cognitive Behavioral Therapy
CRM	Comprehensive Resource Model
CT	Coherence Therapy
C-PTSD	Complex Post-traumatic Stress Disorder
DBR	Deep Brain Reorienting
DID	Dissociative Identity Disorder
DNMS	Developmental Needs Meeting Strategy
DP	Depersonalization
DP/DR	Depersonalization/Derealization
DR	Derealization
DVC	Dorsal Vagal Complex
EMDR	Eye Movement Desensitization and Reprocessing
EP	Emotional Part of the Personality
FC	Functional Coherence
LT	Leave Taking
MDMA	3,4-Methylenedioxymethamphetamine
MR	Memory Reconsolidation
PAG	Periaqueductal Gray
PNS	Parasympathetic Nervous System
PSP	Pro-Symptom Position
Pt	Patient
PTSD	Post-traumatic Stress Disorder
RIGs	Representations of interactions that have been generalized
RT	Relational Trauma
SAS	Self as pervasively experiencing shame
SC	Superior Colliculi
SD	Structural Dissociation

SE	Somatic Experiencing
SES	Social Engagement System
SP	Sensorimotor Psychotherapy
SUDS	Subjective Units of Distress
Th	Therapist

Introduction

Human beings are seekers. Beginning in utero, we are driven to discover ourselves, perhaps before we are drawn to make sense of the external world. From the beginning, our movements, sensory experience, and feelings tell us who we are and who we are becoming. It has been observed that the fetus in utero and later newborn show a motoric intentionality, that is, "movements … guided by anticipation of future events" (Delafield-Butt & Gangopadhyay, 2013, p. 399). Likewise, Damasio (1999) described a "protoself" developing in utero, adding "primordial feelings occur regardless of whether the protoself is engaged by objects and events external to the brain. *They need to be related to the living body and nothing else*" (p. 323, my emphasis).

Human brains are also wired to be social (Brothers, 1990; Firth, 2007). We are relational beings. Learning who we are at any moment in time always involves discovering who we are *with* others and *in relation to* ourselves. These social-emotional knowings begin well before we have language to describe our experience.

Comparing and contrasting who we are in relationship with others and with ourselves help forge our identity. We develop our psychosocial identity, in part, by valuing and devaluing specific qualities in ourselves and others. Valuing and devaluing lie at the heart of pride and shame. Reflect upon these contrasts and you will hear the echoes of pride and shame: in/out, above/below, accepted/rejected, noticed/ignored, welcomed/dismissed, loveable/unlovable, and so on.

Our earliest, most important relationships with caregivers implicitly teach us to value and devalue different ways of being and relating. Some ways are deemed "in" while others are "out." According to developmental researcher Trevarthen (2005), these valuations begin in the first year of life: "*Infants are born with a bold self-consciousness … [and] may … feel pleasure and pride in the approval of others, and shame at failure before them*" (p. 56, my emphasis). Shame and pride, then, are basic to our shared humanity and central to our neurobiological, psychological, and social-emotional heritage.

As part of our genetic heritage, humans can be altruistic and selfish, empathic and dismissive, kind and cruel (Sapolsky, 2017). We both help and harm others. Relational Trauma (RT) refers to enduring harm caused by one or more persons overwhelming and/or underwhelming another person's mind/body. Referring to RT, Schore (2001) wrote:

> Instead of modulating [the infant's neurophysiological arousal], she [the caregiver] induces extreme levels of stimulation and arousal, either too high in abuse or too low in neglect, and because she provides no interactive repair, the infant's intense negative emotional states last for long periods of time.
>
> (p. 205)

RT that is overwhelming is seen in abuse—physical, sexual, interpersonal, emotional, and psychological—repeatedly inflicted upon a child, with no adult helping the child survivor understand these experiences or held accountable. RT that is underwhelming may refer to neglect, but just as often speaks to the impact of the child's needs to be seen, felt, known, and recognized (Bromberg, 2011a, 2011b) going unmet.

RT profoundly damages the child and later adult survivor's sense of self in relationship with others and themselves. Shame developed in relationship with those we love and who are meant to love us but fail, repeatedly, is not a feeling. To *feel* shame, what I refer to as "shame as an emotional process," is not the same as *being* shame, indicative of traumatic "shame states." Shame states excise those qualities of the caregiver, who is loved and trusted but not trustworthy, deemed unacceptable or worse, of no value. Shame states ablate parts of who we are or our entire "being" in order to salvage a bond with those we depend upon and, over time, with ourselves. Similarly, traumatic "pride states" deny a person basic pleasure in what they do, achieve, and, fundamentally, who they are.

For being and relating to flourish following RT, the roots of traumatic, shame and pride states must be unearthed, processed, and transformed. Psychotherapists working with adult survivors of childhood RT quickly learn maladaptive shame and pride emotions and more so traumatic states are pervasive, impede therapeutic progress, and are often extremely difficult to ameliorate. It can be shocking for a therapist to sit with a patient who, by all accounts, is successful in work and love, yet insists they are worthless and a fraud. The therapist who tries to convince their patient that is simply not true will be met with confusion at best and vehement resistance at worst. To the extent a therapist misunderstands the RT survivor's subjective experience of self and relationship, they will unwittingly contribute to greater shame and place authentic pride further out of reach.

Although there have been several books describing shame in psychotherapy, some explicitly with RT survivors, few speak about pride in RT. In addition, shame and pride are typically viewed as maladaptive or pathological, and rarely described as adaptive and benefiting therapy with RT survivors.

Once a therapist knows how to listen for the echoes of shame and pride, they soon discover these emotions and traumatic states everywhere. Shame hides itself in subtle gestures of self-loathing, in what is said and most perniciously what is not said. Shame, hidden in plain sight, is revealed in how a person cannot look you in the eye, even when you have shown them genuine interest and kindness for years. While appearing to trust you, the therapist senses not all of their patient is on board.

While shame is hidden and at the same time ever present, pride is often quite visible yet conceals what is missing. Pride displays, like the peacock. Hubristic pride looks downward at others just as the shamed person looks down on themselves. The person whose pride is authentic and adaptive gently gazes ahead and slightly upward toward hope on the horizon. This is the pride of genuine achievement following concerted effort. Like a magician's sleight of hand, maladaptive pride displays arrogance and occludes vulnerability. Traumatic pride states leave patients no room for positive attributes their caregivers never affirmed and, painfully, sometimes just for being.

Since RT deeply wounds a person's sense of self and worth, how do therapists help restore a patient's belief in their own competence and value? Although answers to that question are complex, I offer a few words here.

Successful psychotherapy generally and specifically with RT survivors must alleviate traumatic shame and pride states and restore authentic pride. As part of this process, Pierre Janet (1935) identified acts of triumph. An act of triumph following trauma processing "requires effort and results in a sense of pride that is a form of joy and heals shame" (Barral & Meares, 2019, p. 121). In my view, psychotherapy with RT survivors also goes beyond a patient's pride in achieving therapy goals, helping them reclaim or connect with for the first time a universal experience I call "pro-being pride."

The word origin of "proud" is derived from the Latinate "prodesse" (Proud, word origin). "Prod" means "for" and "esse" "to be." I think of prodesse as "for being," for one's essence or essential self. Pro-being pride, then, is not about authentic pride, the pride in accomplishing what matters to the person and others who matter to them. Rather, pro-being pride is the quiet joy and effervescent aliveness proclaiming, without words, "*I am*, my unique, organismic self."

Pro-being pride is a birthright taking nascent form in utero. Later, when a parent delights upon their newborn as they enter into the world, the infant not only takes their first physical breath but also their first psychological and relational breath. Parent and newborn each light up the other. This is quintessential, pro-being pride.

Pro-being pride is an intersubjective and intrasubjective experience. Organismic pleasure in being oneself with others is one way we identify pro-being pride. No matter how great a patient's suffering, when their authentic being seeps out without them noticing, I come alive. My whole body vibrates, my pro-being pride welcoming their pro-beingness [*sic*] into our shared world.

By definition, it is not possible to be "for being" and not be "for" others discovering and embodying their pro-being pride. Pro-being pride is always interrelational, self with others, and intrarelational, self with self. My short definition of pro-being pride is, "I delight in being me, delighting in you delighting in being yourself, with me" (self with others); and "I delight in being me, delighting in me delighting in being myself, with me" (self with self).

Though I use the words "joy," "delight," and "enlivenment" throughout this book when describing the experience of pro-being pride, being one's true self (Winnicott, 1965) does not necessarily mean "happy." When people gather to mourn the death of a loved one, sharing memories that accompany loss and grief, pro-being pride is present within and between the mourners.

Pro-being pride is discovered in the smallest, idiosyncratic ways a patient turns their head, in their unique, often private interests and capacities that survive unspeakable maltreatment, and especially in moments of genuine aliveness within patient and therapist and between the dyad. While pro-being pride is embodied and observable in the moment, it also resides in the imagination of the psychotherapist who "sees" their patient's essential self as an infant, pre-trauma and to-be-realized future incarnation, post-trauma transformation. The therapist's understanding and knowing how to access and work with a patient's pro-being pride, and their own for that matter, is most needed when their patient is gripped by trauma and least aware of their authentic aliveness.

Genuine pride can, under the right interrelational and intrarelational conditions, soften the edges of shame. Pro-being pride is of another order. It does not counteract maladaptive shame and pride. Rather, it bursts through leaving them no room. It is not possible to negate and celebrate being at the same time.

Pro-being pride in patient and therapist transcends and is also the most powerful antidote for traumatic shame and pride, the inescapable legacy of RT. Understanding the concept and most importantly the intersubjective and intrasubjective experience that is pro-being pride guides psychotherapy with RT survivors, and is the life-affirming blood coursing through the veins of this book.

In order to heal shame and pride states, the RT survivor ("survivor") must come to appreciate their genuine accomplishments, often at first because the therapist sees what they have achieved and who they are. During the course of successful, depth psychotherapy, the survivor's authentic self will emerge. When a patient's true being is noticed and celebrated, they gradually, despite many impediments along the way, embrace and embody their pro-being pride. When that occurs the patient comes alive, often for the first time they can recall.

This book is about shame, pride, and most importantly pro-being pride in those who have suffered and endured RT, the deep wounds and scars of being treated as unworthy of being themselves. This book is about one therapist working with survivors to help them bear witness to shame and shaming, uncover their secret machinations, and vanquish them with genuine pride and pro-being pride. This book describes how patients, after much hard work with a trusted therapist who is shame, pride, and RT-informed, together nurture the patient's growing embodiment of enlivened being and being with.

…

Those people who know the most about shame and pride have lived it, and I am no exception. Without knowing, I had lived for years with the effects of shame that accompanies RT. Early in my own therapy, I became intermittently aware of feeling "sad" without identifying anything to be sad about. Over time and with the help of my therapist, I realized my "sadness" was, in fact, existential shame, the grief I suffered whenever I was not being true to myself.

I am compelled to write this book because I have learned about shame the hard way, from the inside out, and from the outside in, studying the literature of intrepid shame explorers who preceded me. Everything I know about shame and pride comes from my experience as psychotherapist, patient, student of literature both clinical and creative, and simply as a human being.

We all suffer and cause others to suffer. At the same time, we each hold within us the seeds of creativity, love, and pro-being pride. My greatest wish is that this book benefits you as psychotherapist working with survivors of RT, as patient if that be part of your story, and as human being with other human beings most of whom live with the effects of shame and pride. If this book helps you, your patients, and/or loved ones endure less debilitating shame, relish more authentic pride, and embrace animating, pro-being pride, then, with gratitude, I will join you there.

The first two chapters of this book (Chapter 1 and 2) orient the reader to shame and pride and their importance in psychotherapy with survivors of RT. Chapter 1 defines RT and describes observable behavior and subjective experiences characteristic of shame and pride. This includes differentiating shame and guilt, as well as shame and humiliation. It discusses why understanding and working with shame and pride, both as emotional processes and traumatic mind/body states, are central to psychotherapy in general and with RT survivors specifically.

Chapter 2 continues the discussion of Chapter 1 by differentiating shame and pride as acute, short-lived emotional processes, taking both adaptive and maladaptive forms, and always maladaptive, traumatic shame and pride mind/body states (shame and pride states). The discussion of shame and pride *subtypes* from a "macro," experience-distant perspective, then moves on to a "micro," experience-near description of shame and pride *processes*. Being able to conceptualize shame and pride subtypes and processes is especially important for therapists working with RT survivors, as the emotional storms both within patient and therapist and between the therapy pair are often disorienting and disorganizing.

Shame and pride states are, by definition, traumatic mind/body states that involve different degrees of dissociation. Chapter 3 extends the discussion about shame and pride subtypes and processes to an exploration of the relationships between shame and pride as emotions and traumatic states, mind/body leave taking (LT), elsewhere conceptualized as dissociation as *process*, and *structural* dissociation (SD). Chapter 3 first describes the complex, often confusing *psychodynamic* relationships between shame, pride, LT, and SD. It then delineates specific *phenomenological* features, including attention, gaze, and mind/body organization, shared by and distinguishing shame, pride, LT, and SD. Various psychotherapeutic applications of these psychodynamic and phenomenological understandings when working with RT survivors are presented throughout Chapter 3.

As a gateway into psychotherapy with RT survivors, Chapter 4 proposes 15 attitudes, principles, and concepts that inform this work. Specific psychotherapeutic practices and clinical vignettes bring to life these guiding attitudes, principles, and concepts. While this chapter and the three that follow describe several different approaches to shame and pride-informed psychotherapy with RT, the stance I adopt is transtheoretical and not wed to one therapy modality.

Chapters 5, 6, and 7 take us more directly into the intersubjective and intrasubjective experience of shame and pride-informed psychotherapy with survivors of RT. Chapter 5 outlines a conceptual model that helps therapists differentiate traumatic shame and pride *reactivity* as contrasted with transformative, *reflective responsivity*. This integrative model is informed by Nathanson's (1992) compass of shame defenses, Fisher's (2017) survival strategies/parts model, and Karpman's (2014, 1968) drama triangle and its understanding of trauma-reactive roles. This conceptual roadmap is intended to help therapists navigate the often disorienting and disorganizing experience of shame and pride states within patient and therapist, respectively, and between the therapy dyad. Chapter 5 closes with an application of this model to a challenging enactment in my psychotherapy with a RT survivor. The clinical vignette documents how shame and pride states significantly disrupt therapeutic progress and how the model can serve as a guide into, through, and beyond inevitable impasses.

Chapter 6 offers three perspectives on a single psychotherapy session with "Isaac," an adult survivor of childhood RT, including abuse and neglect. The first view presents a fully transcribed psychotherapy session that documents Isaac's movement from traumatic shame states to authentic pride and pro-being pride, offering my reflections on the therapeutic process. The second vantage point is based upon a conversation between Frank Corrigan, MD, and myself. Dr. Corrigan is a psychiatrist and psychotherapist with expertise in the neuroscience of psychotherapy with RT. He provides the reader a rich understanding of the neuroscientific or brain-based foundations of moment-to-moment, clinical phenomena in my session with Isaac. In this section, Dr. Corrigan and I compare and contrast our respective understandings. The final, third perspective endeavors to answer this question: How might a neuroscientific understanding of psychotherapy with RT survivors inform and enhance our work?

Chapter 7 goes "beyond pro-being pride," continuing my work with Isaac by studying complete transcripts of two psychotherapy sessions and excerpts from two more. I was surprised to discover metatherapeutically processing (Fosha, 2000) pro-being pride takes some relational survivors to joyful states of oneness or unity consciousness, followed by grief that comes with recognizing the lifelong costs of RT, and ultimately deeper, psychological integration and oneness within and with the world.

Now that you have some ideas about where we are going, let us begin.

References

Barral, C. & Meares, R. (2019). The Holistic Project of Pierre Janet: Part Two: Oscillations and Becomings: From Disintegration to Integration. In G. Craparo, F. Ortu, & O. Van der Hart. Eds., *Rediscovering Pierre Janet: Trauma, Dissociation, and a New Context for Psychoanalysis* (pp. 116–129). New York: Routledge. https://doi.org/10.4324/9780429201875.

Bromberg, P. M. (2011a). *Awakening the Dreamer: Clinical Journeys.* New York: Routledge. https://doi.org/10.4324/9780203759981.

Bromberg, P. M. (2011b). *The Shadow of the Tsunami and the Growth of the Relational Mind.* New York: Routledge. https://doi.org/10.4324/9780203834954.

Brothers, L. (1990). The Social Brain: A Project for Integrating Primate Behavior and Neurophysiology in a New Domain. *Concepts in Neuroscience,* 1, 27–51. https://doi.org/10.1007/BF00991637.

Craparo, G., Ortu, F., & Van der Hart, O., Eds. (2019). *Rediscovering Pierre Janet: Trauma, Dissociation, and a New Context for Psychoanalysis.* New York: Routledge. https://doi.org/10.4324/9780203759981.

Damasio, A. (1999). *The Feeling of What Happens: Body and Emotion in the Making of Consciousness.* New York: Harcourt Press. 10.1353/jsp.2001.0038.

Delafield-Butt, J. T. & Gangopadhyay, N. (2013). Sensorimotor Intentionality: The Origins of Intentionality in Prospective Agent Action. *Developmental Review,* 33, 399–425. https://doi.org/10.1016/j.dr.2013.09.001.

Fisher, J. (2017). *Healing the Fragmented Selves of Trauma Survivors: Overcoming Internal Self-alienation.* New York: Routledge. https://doi.org/10.4324/9781315886169.

Fosha, D. (2000). *The Transforming Power of Affect: A Model for Accelerated Change.* New York: Basic Behavioral Science.

Frith, C. D. (2007). *The Social Brain? Philosophical Transactions of the Royal Society: Biological Sciences,* 362, 671–678. Doi: 10.1098/rstb.2006.2003.

Janet, P. (1935). *Les debuts de L'intelligence.* Paris: Flammation.

Karpman, S. B. (2014). *A Game Free Life. The Definitive Book on the Drama Triangle and Compassion Triangle by the Originator and Author: The New Transactional Analysis of Intimacy, Openness, and Happiness.* San Francisco: Drama Triangle.

Karpman, S. B. (1968). Fairy Tales and Script Drama Analysis. *Transactional Analysis Bulletin.*

Nathanson, D. (1992). *Shame, Pride, Affect, Sex and the Birth of the Self.* New York: W.W. Norton. https://doi.org/10.1177/036215379402400207.

Proud, word origin: www.etymonline.com/word/proud. Accessed June 11, 2021.

Sapolsky, R. M. (2017). *Behave: The Biology of Humans at Our Best and Worst.* New York: Penguin Books. https://doi.org/10.1002/ajhb.23336.

Schore, A. N. (2001). The Effects of Relational Trauma on Right Brain Development, Affect Regulation, and Infant Mental Health. *Infant Mental Health Journal,* 22,

201–269. Doi: https://doi.org/10.1002/1097-0355(200101/04)22:1<201::AID-IMHJ8>3.CO;2-9.
Trevarthen, C. (2005). "Stepping Away from the Mirror: Pride and Shame in Adventures of Companionship": Reflections on the Nature and Emotional Needs of Infant Intersubjectivity. In C. S. Carter, L. Ahnert, K. E. Grossman, S. B. Hrdy, S. W. Lamb, S. Porges, & N. Sachser, Eds., *Attachment and Bonding: A New Synthesis*. Cambridge, MA: MIT Press.
Winnicott, D. W. (1965). Ego distortion in terms of true and false self. In *The Maturational Processes and the Facilitating Environment: Studies in the Theory of Emotional Development* (pp. 140–157). New York: International Universities Press.

1 Shame, Pride, and Relational Trauma

What Are They and Why Do They Matter in Psychotherapy?

Introduction

How we think and feel about ourselves, others, and our relationships are basic to being human. It follows that devaluing ourselves, shame, or valuing ourselves and our accomplishments, pride, lie at the heart of who we are and how we relate to ourselves and others. When a person is traumatized by the actions and inactions of others, shame and pride will always be essential features of their intrapersonal, self with self, and interpersonal, self with other, landscape.

How does understanding shame and pride as emotional processes and traumatic mind/body states inform psychotherapy with survivors of relational trauma (RT) (Schore, 2001)? This chapter begins by defining RT, introducing the reader to some of the challenges facing survivors in psychotherapy and life. It then describes concepts and characteristic phenomena of shame and pride that include observable behavior, subjective experience, and differentiating shame and guilt as well as shame and humiliation. This chapter closes with a discussion on why understanding shame and pride is essential to successful psychotherapy generally and specifically with RT survivors.

Because shame and pride are fundamentally about *relationship*, self with other (interrelating) and self with self (intrarelating), survivors of RT best describes the psychotherapy patients with whom I work. RT results from what people do to and do not do for other people. Trauma caused by natural disasters and accidents are not my focus. Although the effects of RT are also seen in patients living with more complex dissociative disorders such as Dissociative Identity Disorder (DID) (Chefetz, 2015), these too are not the patients I describe. While most survivors I work with experience some dissociation (Chapter 3), my patients do not meet the criteria for DID.

Relational Trauma (RT)

Alan Schore (2001) coined the term RT. Schore researched

> the negative impact of traumatic attachments on brain development and infant mental health, the neurobiology of infant trauma, the

DOI: 10.4324/9780429425943-2

neuropsychology of a disorganized/disoriented attachment pattern associated with abuse and neglect, trauma-induced impairments of a regulatory system in the orbitofrontal cortex, the links between orbitofrontal dysfunction and a predisposition to posttraumatic stress disorders, the neurobiology of the dissociative defense, the etiology of dissociation and body-mind psychopathology, the effects of early relational trauma on enduring right hemispheric function, and some implications for models of early intervention.

(p. 201)

Schore (2001) described the nature and effects of a caregiver's abusive and neglectful behavior on the mind/body of the developing child. These effects have significant consequences into adulthood. The child survivor lives with a

caregiver [who] is inaccessible, and reacts to her infant's expressions of emotions and stress inappropriately and/or rejectingly, and shows minimal or unpredictable participation in the various types of arousal regulating processes. *Instead of modulating, she induces extreme levels of stimulation and arousal,* **either too high in abuse or too low in neglect,** *and because she provides no interactive repair, the infant's intense negative emotional states last for long periods of time.*

(Schore, 2001, p. 205, my emphasis)

For our purposes, RT refers to the consequences of the chronic overwhelming and/or underwhelming of a child's developing mind/body experience and behavior. "Overwhelming" refers to abuse—physical, sexual, interpersonal, emotional, and psychological—repeatedly inflicted upon a child, with no adult intervening or helping the child survivor understand these experiences, especially that the caregiver, and not the child, is responsible for the abusive behavior.

"Underwhelming" refers to the impact of repeatedly unmet relational needs. There are many ways needs go unmet, and all involve the child not feeling seen, felt, known, and recognized (Bromberg, 2011a, 2011b) by their caregiver for who they truly are. While "underwhelming" is a consequence of "neglect," its origins can be extreme and/or subtle. Neglect might involve a young boy left alone for days and having to "parent" his younger siblings. Less dramatic forms of underwhelm include a girl never greeted by her father when she comes home from school because others are "more important," or the young boy whose mother dies yet is never asked how he feels.

Underwhelming, then, can reach levels of *traumatic* neglect and abandonment, whereas more subtle forms are characterized by some as *attachment wounds* that exist in relation to trauma (Erozkan, 2016). In my view, both dramatic and subtle forms of neglect reflect RT. Even with subtle yet pervasive neglect, the mind/body registers and remembers patterns of absence as with other trauma. In both dramatic and subtle underwhelm, repeatedly unmet relational needs later play out in relationship, be that through excessive self-reliance, neediness, or both. These patterns persist until, often with the help of psychotherapy, the enduring effects of unmet needs are uncovered and the patient develops new, adaptive ways of relating to their "attachment" needs both within, self with self, and between, self with significant others.

"Trauma" and "Patient"

The word origin of "trauma" is from the Greek, "a wound, a hurt, a defeat," and earlier from the Proto-Indo-European (PIE) "trau-," from the root "tere" with "derivatives referring to twisting, piercing" (Trauma, word origin).

If RT refers to a psychobiological *wounding* as a result of repeatedly overwhelming and/or underwhelming another person, what word best describes the person seeking psychotherapy? I have chosen the word "patient" in lieu of "client" following its word origin from the Latin *patientem*, "suffering" (Patient, word origin). I think of the people I work with as *relational sufferers*, not "customers" or "consumers." To be clear, while I believe all humans are, at times, relational sufferers, not all are survivors of RT.

Patient Confidentiality

Many of the adult patients depicted in this book were psychotherapy patients who graciously gave me permission to describe our work to benefit therapists and patients alike. Some are composites of several patients or my imagined creations. To protect patient privacy, information not required to understand our work has been omitted or altered.

Shame, Pride, and Pro-being Pride: Concepts and Phenomena

Shame and Pride: Introductory Remarks

Many people assume that both shame and pride as emotions are always unwanted or negative. Who wants to feel bad about themselves (shame) and condone behavior treating others as inferior (pride)? As the reader will see, both shame and pride can be adaptive and maladaptive, and both are central to our work with RT survivors.

To be human is to experience shame, although animal behaviorists suggest shame is observed in other mammals and may be a survival adaptation (Bekoff, 2007). When a noisy baby elephant is "reprimanded" by an elder so as not to attract the attention of a predator, "shaming," elephant-style, is at play. Shame or its prototypical, mammalian equivalent, often although not always serves as a powerful downregulator of arousal (Schore, 2003), putting a brake on many emotions (Tomkins, 1963) to preserve individual and species survival. In RT, shame is often activated within an individual whenever thoughts, feelings, and/or behavior are perceived as a threat to vital attachments, self with others and self with self.

Shame as a traumatic mind/body state ("shame state") (Herman, 2012, 2011, 2007, 2006) is more complex and problematic than shame as an emotional process ("shame emotion") (Chapter 2). Shame as emotion *and* traumatic state both put a brake on emotions, thoughts/beliefs, physical sensations, and behavior (Benau, 2021a; 2021b), precipitating states of downregulation and hypoarousal. As with other traumatic reactions, shame states also overactivate the nervous system, precipitating upregulation and hyperarousal that reflect the survivor's self-protective reactions to interrelational and intrarelational threat and/or danger.

Pride is an emotion no less prototypal than shame. Whereas "shame makes us feel small, insignificant and worthless in every respect," "pride, the opposite of shame, gives us a sense of bodily and mental power and worth" (Wille, 2014, p. 697). When feeling proud, we celebrate mastery and achievement (Tracy, 2016).

I have named another adaptive pride subtype "pro-being pride" (Chapter 2). Pro-being pride is not a categorical emotion such as sadness and anger. Pro-being pride is an enduring, mind/body state rooted in the pleasure of being and belonging as one truly is with others experiencing the same. Pro-being pride reflects joyful aliveness shared rather than taking pleasure in one's attribute or achievement. Pro-being pride lies at the heart of psychotherapy generally and specifically with RT survivors. As will become clear, pro-being pride is the guiding light of this book and my work as psychotherapist.

Shame and pride in humans always involve some self-other awareness or consciousness. Without the ability to evaluate oneself, others, and how others are evaluating you, there can be no shame and pride. (See Chapter 3 for more about "*attending*" to self and other as regards shame and pride.)

For the most part, self-consciousness is a uniquely human capacity given the development of the frontal lobe of the neocortex (Sturm et al., 2008, 2006). In the Bible, when Adam and Eve ate from the apple and became aware of their nakedness, self-consciousness and shame banished them from Eden. Hubristic pride got them into trouble with God in the first place. To become aware that one is an object of others' valuation and devaluation is to become self-conscious that one has either met or not met one's own and/or others' expectations. As Mark Twain wrote in *A Connecticut Yankee in King Arthur's Court*, "It shames the average man to be valued below his own estimate of his worth" (Twain, 2011, p. 351). Shame is about self-valuation, others' valuation, and the interaction of these two lived realities. Shame is a peculiarly social emotion that, at its most painful, is rooted in the damaging effects of self- and other-banishment from oneself and one's "tribe"—in effect, Eden.

Pride is also basic to being human. Ancient myths and religious doctrine say much about pride, particularly hubris. The Myth of Icarus memorializes self-destructive conceit, as Icarus had been warned by his father, Daedalus, not to fly too close to the sun. Using the wings Daedalus crafted for his son, Icarus was giddy with the excitement of flight. Flying ever higher until the sun melted the wax that held his feathered wings together, Icarus crashed to his death into the sea now bearing his name.

As early as the New Testament Bible and for the Ancient Greeks, pride is considered dangerous. In Christianity, pride is one of seven deadly sins, the other six being greed, lust, envy, glutton, wrath, and sloth. Each sin represents a natural faculty or passion brought to excess, such as unconstrained anger becoming murderous rage (wrath). The sinfully proud person is excessively self-absorbed such that maladaptive narcissism and arrogance dominate their inner and outer world. Sinful pride, known today by some researchers as hubristic pride (Tracy, 2016; Tangney & Fischer, 1995), is why many people view pride as harmful. The discussion of adaptive pride and shame subtypes (Chapter 2) will show why that is not always true.

General Characteristics of Shame and Pride

Two quotes capture important attributes of shame and pride:

- *On shame*: "In the gaps and clumsy steps in human intercourse, in the misunderstandings and misjudgments, in the blank mocking eyes where empathy should be, in the look of disgust where a smile was anticipated, in the loneliness and disappointment of inarticulate desire that cannot be communicated because the words cannot be found, in the terrible hopeless absence when human connection fails, and in the empty yet rage-filled desolation of abuse—there in these holes and missing bits lies shame. Shame is where we fail" (Mollon, 2018, p. xi).

- *On pride*: "When the mind regards itself and its own power of activity, it feels pleasure: and that pleasure is greater in proportion to the distinctness wherewith it conceives itself and its own power of activity" (Spinoza, 2006/1677, p. 134).

Shame and pride are affects or emotions that are both self and other referential. *Affects* typically refer to nonconscious, neurophysiological reactions, whereas the term *emotion* is often reserved for conscious cognitions or schema, meanings, imagery, somatic experiences, behavioral actions, and interactions (Ekkekakis, 2012). In this book, I use "emotions" and "affects" interchangeably.[1]

Shame and pride refer to a judgment about self in relation to self and other. While *other* usually means other people, it can also refer to families, groups, societies, as well as animate and inanimate objects. Dogs can reassure a trauma survivor they are lovable. When tripping and falling, a person may feel shame, and great pride ascending a mountain peak, even when no one witnesses their actions.

Shame often follows a person failing to master or achieve a desired aim or goal. Shame reflects the difference between "I *failed*" and "I am a *failure*," speaking to a person's lack of worth.

Adaptive pride as emotion is about mastery and/or achievement of a personally or culturally valued goal (Tracy, 2016). Healthy pride includes purposeful, goal-directed action; activity success; and mastery or achievement that brings the person pleasure (Nathanson, 1992; Broucek, 1979). While maladaptive pride may also bring the person pleasure, the hubristic person often confuses their specific attribute (e.g., "I can run fast") with their whole person ("I am better than everyone") (Lewis, 1989, cited by Nathanson, 1992).

Nathanson (1992, p. 317) enumerated several cognitive features of shame that reflect implicit and/or explicit beliefs about self in relation to others, including personal size, strength, ability, and skill (e.g., "I am weak"); dependence/independence (e.g., "I am helpless"); sense of self (e.g., "I am defective"); personal attractiveness (e.g., "I am ugly"); sexuality (e.g., "I am sexually undesirable"); issues of seeing and being seen (e.g., "I am exposed, and want to hide in a hole"); and wishes and fears about closeness (e.g., "I am unlovable"). While Nathanson did not refer to pride here, all of these qualities apply to pride. For example, a person embodying adaptive pride may believe, "I am strong, capable, sufficient, attractive, sexually desirable, happy to show who I am and what I can do. I am worthy of loving and being loved."

Going beyond listing personal characteristics, shame and pride are about almost anything a person attributes to himself in relationship to others. Shame and pride emotions are about devaluing (shame) and valuing (pride), both by the person having these emotions, and by the other person who devalues (shames) or values ("prides") them.

Pride, too, is about self and other valuation. While we may feel proud of an achievement without the other seeing it, as when an infant learns to crawl before the parent observes them, pride is always relational. Pride involves seeing and being seen, prizing and being prized.

In shame, "the other" values or devalues "the *person*" rather than "the person's *behavior*." "The whole person," "being *who* they are, intrinsically, and not *how* they behave," is the object of other-to-self and self-to-self evaluation. Guilt, in contrast, is about the evaluation of one's own actions or inactions (see the section "Shame and Guilt").

A paradox inherent in shame and pride as emotions is that what at first appears *self-focused* is always *relational*. No matter how self-absorbed, socially isolated, disconnected, and/or dissociated the shamed or proud person appears, there are always several *others* lurking in the shadows, externally and/or internally.

Gilbert (1998) also rooted shame in relationality, identifying two types, external shame and internal shame. External shame refers to the perception of self as an object of scorn, contempt or ridicule, whereas internal shame reflects the perception of self as inferior. External and internal shame are both about relationship between (external: self with other) and within (internal: self with self). External and internal shame are not opposites. External shame contains some internal shame projected onto the shaming other who is perceived as gazing back with harsh judgment, and internal shame holds external shame, based upon the internalization or introjection of the shaming other.

Researchers categorize shame and pride, along with guilt, as "self-conscious emotions" (Tracy et al., 2007). The shamed and proud person evaluates themselves in relation to the other's perceived judgment of them, consciously and/or outside of conscious awareness. The reflection and reverberation of shame and pride in relation to self and other is, in fact, even more complex. Experientially, shame and pride are closer to self with self; other with other; self with other with other with self; and self with other with self with other-conscious emotions, ad infinitum, as in a dark hall of mirrors. For our purposes, "self-other conscious and unconscious emotions" suffice, or "self-other conscious emotions," for short.

The traumatized shamed and proud person lives in the past, present, and future, that is, "I was, I am and I will always be 'devalued' (shame) or 'valued' (pride), by myself and others." The evaluative read by the "self" and/or "other" may be accurate, inaccurate, or both. The RT survivor's view of self and other is often distorted, particularly when gripped by a traumatic, mind/body state.

With the exception of highly dissociated RT survivors *some of the time*, the guilty, shamed, or proud person is aware the *spotlight is on them*. "Spotlight" is generated by the other's actual gaze, and/or by the internalized experience and recall of the "guilting," "shaming" or "priding" person and interactional patterns, consistent with Stern's (1985) concept of Representations of Interactions that have been Generalized (RIGs, pp. 97–99), and Bowlby's (1969) internal working model.

Shame and Pride Thoughts/Beliefs, Feelings/Emotions, Physiology, Actions, and Interactions

While shame and pride are usually called "feelings," they are phenomenologically quite complex, comprising thoughts and beliefs; feelings or emotions; physiological activity as evidenced by stereotypical postures and patterns of arousal/energy; and external behavior, including actions and interactions (Benau, 2017).

Shame and Pride Thoughts and Beliefs

Shame and pride beliefs include the person's evaluation of self in relation to others, and associated implicit or explicit meanings. The shame-laden person believes explicitly (consciously) or implicitly (outside awareness yet impacting feelings and behavior) many things about themselves in relationship to themselves and others. As noted, Nathanson (1992) listed several common, maladaptive shame cognitions, such as "I am weak"; "I am helpless"; "I am defective"; and "I am unlovable." For survivors of abuse and neglect, one commonly hears "I am bad," where "bad" refers to inferior, defective, a failure, damaged, unworthy, unlovable, unwanted, disgusting, etc.

16 *Shame, Pride, and Relational Trauma*

An adaptively proud person might legitimately think I am "strong," "capable," "worthy," etc. The maladaptively proud person believes they are superior and are often described by others as cocky, boastful, arrogant, pompous, egotistical, etc. (Tracy, 2016, p. 46).

Shame and Pride Feelings or Emotions

Emotionally, the initial surprise/shock of shame as an emotional process is typically followed by a sinking feeling as though falling into darkness or wanting to crawl into a hole and hide. Defeated, deflated, depressed, collapsed, sinking, invisible, nobody, etc. are words or phrases capturing the shamed person's physical and emotional reality. Shame as emotion "makes us feel small, insignificant and worthless" (Wille, 2014, p. 697). With a traumatic shame *state* rather than emotional *process*, the person's experience may be quite stormy, with both sinking (hypoarousing) and activating (hyperarousing) effects.

"Pride … gives us a sense of bodily and mental power and worth" (Wille, 2014, p. 697). When proud we celebrate mastery and achievement (Tracy, 2016). Healthy pride is about purposeful, intentional actions; activity success; and pleasure in achievement, competence, and efficacy pleasure (Tracy, 2016; Nathanson, 1992; Broucek, 1979). Unlike shame as emotion, pride heightens emotional experience and arousal, giving life greater vividness and meaning, sometimes to the benefit (adaptive pride) or harm (maladaptive pride) of self, others and relationship. As in shame states, pride as traumatic, mind/body state is often much more volatile.

Shame and Pride Physiology

The shamed person may display stereotypical physiological markers familiar to most. Rodin powerfully captured shame in several of his sculptures (Rodin, "shame" sculptures). The shamed person's slumped posture is often slightly collapsed at the chest (i.e., concave, with less breath available), with diminished energy, eyes averted and/or downcast, hands covering head and eyes, and head turned slightly to one side and away from the shaming other. The head turned to one side exposes the shamed person's jugular to the shaming other, consistent with a "submit response." (For more about "submit" reactions and shame, see Chapter 4.) Gazing down and away also embodies the shamed person's subjective and relational reality, as shame usually entails a submission to the other's will and beliefs that the other's authority is privileged. Individuals experiencing traumatic, shame states may alternate between deflated and hypervigilant physiology and postures, at times crushed and other times anxiously watchful for further shaming attacks. (For more about "submit" reactions and shame, see Chapter 4, #15, "Shame and Pride: Prototypical Parts".)

Adaptive pride is often seen in a mildly expansive chest, ease of breath, and eyes looking straight ahead or slightly elevated. A hubristically proud person may have eyes looking down upon others or not seeing them at all, and an overinflated chest combined with overcharged energy and arousal (see Mussolini "hubristic pride" video). Traumatic pride states are experienced at times as hypomanic.

Shame and Pride Actions and Interactions

Shame-based and pride-based beliefs and meanings are given expression in intrapersonal and interpersonal actions and interactions. A shame-ridden person may believe others are more worthy of love. As one consequence of this belief, the shame-ridden are likely to fear and withdraw from social contact, further heightening feelings of shame. They will often keep their true thoughts to themselves and withdraw from intimate relationships where self-disclosure is expected. In contrast, the authentically proud person believing he is worthy seeks and receives love more than their shame-bound counterpart. The hubristically proud person might approach another person to deride or humiliate them, yet avoid intimate relationships that invite vulnerability.

Shame and Guilt

People often confuse shame and guilt. My focus here is on conscious, maladaptive shame and adaptive guilt. Adaptive guilt is reparative guilt, whereas maladaptive guilt is self-punitive, as in survivor guilt. Self-punitive guilt, consistent with Freud's punitive super-ego, may or may not morph into maladaptive shame, pendulate between guilt and shame (sequential), or result in co-occurring guilt and shame (simultaneous). See Table 1.1 for more about the relationship between shame and guilt.

Shame and guilt are self-other conscious emotions that have dysphoric valences. A person can feel adaptive guilt and maladaptive shame simultaneously or alternately. For example, a person may deeply regret hurting a loved one's feelings (adaptive guilt), and then plummet into feeling worthless for hurting anyone (maladaptive shame).

While both shame and pride are self-other conscious emotions, in shame the person's gaze is more on the self (SELF-other) whereas in reparative guilt their focus is more on the other (self-OTHER), specifically on how their behavior hurt another. Not to confuse matters, what I call adaptive, "good enough me shame" (Chapter 2), that is well-regulated shame for not living according to one's values, can be conceived as feeling reparative guilt for having hurt oneself by not being true to oneself. In psychotherapy, working effectively with "*shame can heal the self, while work on guilt can heal relationships, given guilt is about making amends to another while approach behavior in shame is about restoring the self*" (M. Dorahy, personal communication, my emphasis).

The whole person is devalued in shame whereas the guilty *person's behavior*, that is a *part* of the person, is rejected. In shame, "I *am* bad," whereas in guilt "I *did* something I regret." Metaphorically, shame is like a *soul*-ar eclipse (solar eclipse), and guilt like a dark spot on the moon. Shame occludes or eclipses both the self and the other. Feeling guilty, we retain our self (the moon) while recognizing having hurt another (the dark spot).

Shame and guilt are both about connection and disconnection. The shamed person retains an implicit and/or explicit bond with the shaming other, yet remains socially isolated and alienated from themselves. Paradoxically, the shamed person tries to *reject* the shaming other's painful judgment while implicitly *agreeing* with their disapprobation. In contrast, reparative guilt is about association and social inclusion. With Freud (2010/1930), I view guilt as the glue of civilization. Without reparative guilt, there would be no social norms. Shame is a developmentally younger way of maintaining social bonds yet, paradoxically, typically does so by leaving the person painfully alone. When making reparation, both the harmed and guilty person feel less pain.

The shamed person is excluded, banished, rejected, and pushed out by the other, be that an individual or group. The shame-bound person likewise distances from rejected parts of themselves. Nathanson's (1992) "compass of shame" (p. 312) identified four common defensive strategies in response to shame: attack self, attack others, withdrawal from others, and avoidance of painful emotions. All four strategies reflect the shamed person's psychological and/or physical distancing from others and himself. In contrast, the reparative guilty person is drawn toward the injured person to make a relational repair. This person retains empathy and compassion for those they hurt, and for the pain they feel for having caused another's pain. Empathy enables the reparative guilty person to reconnect. In contrast, the shamed person loses contact with the shaming other, with people more generally, with part of themselves, and/or with their entire being.

Shame reinforces the attachment figure's and the social group's norms over the shamed person's values and beliefs about themselves and relationship. Shame is typically conservative and restrictive rather than progressive and expansive. The reparative guilty person's rapprochement supports growth within the person and relationship.

One way to understand the relationship between shame and guilt is to consider two orthogonal characteristics on two continua from "*part-self*" to "*whole-self*" and "*other-focus*" to "*self-focus*" (Table 1.1). "*Part-self*" refers to the person believing their hurtful actions say something about only a part of them, as in "I can be insensitive but that does not make me a bad person." "*Whole self*" means the person believes their hurtful actions say something about them as a whole person, as in "I am insensitive and that makes me a bad person." "*Other-focus*" means the hurtful person is most concerned with the other's welfare, as in "I regret hurting you." "*Self-focus*" means the hurtful person is preoccupied with themselves, as in "My hurting you means I should be punished." Table 1.1 shows "*part-self*" and "*other-focus*" are more associated with "guilt," whereas "*whole-self*" and "*self-focus*" with "shame."

Only guilt" (#1) and "*Only shame*" (#4) are self-explanatory. An example of #1 is, "I regret that my actions hurt you." For #4, "My hurtful actions make me a bad person." These two categories are characterized by unblended or simple emotions.

Table 1.1 Shame and Guilt: Focus of Emotional/Relational Attention

	Other-Focus (Guilt)	*Self-Focus (Shame)*
Part-self (guilt)	#1. Part-self/Other-focus: Only guilt	#3. Part-self/Self-focus: Good enough me shame
		More shame than guilt, More SELF-focused
		Pendulation between shame and guilt
Whole-self (shame)	#2. Whole-self/Other-focus: Self-punitive > reparative guilt	#4. Whole-self/Self-focus: Only shame Not good enough me shame
	More guilt than shame, OTHER-focused	
	Pendulation between guilt and shame	

When considering the blended or complex shame and guilt subtypes, it is important to note that the SELF/OTHER continuum always trumps the part/whole continuum, as the former variable is more about relationship.

#2, "*Whole-self/Other-focus*": When focused on me as a "whole" person, I am living more in shame. Each time I see the other's pain, I am immediately reminded there is something wrong with me. Thinking more about myself as a whole person, my guilt is likely more self-punitive than other-reparative. My attention can easily pendulate between self-punitive guilt and maladaptive shame. My focus on having caused another person pain (self-punitive guilt) then triggers my belief: "This says something about the whole of me and my behavior" (not good enough me shame) (Chapter 2, shame subtypes). Shame/guilt pendulation occurs sequentially and/or simultaneously.

#3, "*Part-self/Self-focus*": When I focus on my specific *action*, I am living more in reparative guilt. However, if I am harshly self-focused on my hurtful actions, I move into self-punitive guilt, as in #2. Alternatively, when my focus shifts to my *self* rather than the *other* person, I am living more in adaptive shame. I call this latter emotional process "good enough me shame" (Chapter 2, shame subtypes). In good enough me shame, I am more concerned with having hurt myself by not being true to myself and my values than hurting the other person. In good enough me shame as contrasted with traumatic shame states (Chapter 2), I observe myself from a mindful, nonjudgmental, and emotionally well-modulated vantage point; I am pained for not being my "best self."

#2 and #3 refer to the relationship between guilt and shame. However, how and why the shift from "guilt" to "shame" and back again occurs is complex. *One way to understand this relationship is to think of guilt as emotional process triggering a traumatic shame state.* Imagine a woman, whom a male friend cares about, says his behavior hurt her, and upon reflection he agrees with his female friend. Now imagine this man is prone to experience both self-punitive guilt and traumatic shame states. For this man, *guilt generally and particularly self-punitive guilt serve as a trauma trigger for a shame state.* This man automatically shifts his emotional/relational attention, or in the language of structural dissociation (SD), "switches" from guilt as an emotional process to a shame state.

Once this switch occurs, the man implicitly believes the woman he hurt must see him as "all bad." In this shame state, the man becomes self-absorbed ("I am a terrible friend, and a terrible human being") and immobilized ("I was, I am, and I will always be incapable of being a friend"). To the extent the man becomes SELF- rather than other-focused and gripped by shame, he will fail to make a genuine repair (reparative guilt). This failure at repair unintentionally causes the man to hurt his friend again, re-activating his guilt-shame cycle and problematic friendship. The man has gone from "I *failed*" to "*I am a failure*, past, present, and future."

In contrast, if this man learned to identify his shame as a traumatic mind/body state, and process the traumatic, relational bonds that generated his shame state, then over time he would experience reparative guilt in lieu of self-punitive guilt and traumatic shame, and more readily make relational repairs. Each time the man does this he will feel better about himself, his friend will feel more cared for, and where once was a shame state there shall reparative guilt be.

Clinical Vignette: "Kristin": From Shame to Guilt

Kristin was a bright, creative, hardworking young woman in her 20s with whom I had worked for several years. In grade school, I identified her as living with high functioning Autism Spectrum Disorder (ASD). Kristin had been an extremely reliable, dedicated, and valued employee at a store for over four years. Pursuing a new career direction, she decided to leave her work. However, Kristin was blocked about giving her two-week notice because she believed that made her "bad." Kristin knew this made no sense logically, confident her boss would not be upset with her.

Kristin's mind was confusing "guilt," that is, "I am doing something I regret; leaving hurts my manager, some, because he has to find a new person," and "shame," "leaving means I am a bad person." Given chronic social exclusion as a child, Kristin was extremely averse to rejecting and being rejected by others. She implicitly believed leaving her job meant she was rejecting others.

In order to help Kristin differentiate "guilt" and "shame," I began by drawing two large circles. "Guilt" was represented by a small dark circle within a large, white circle, and "shame" was depicted as a completely darkened circle. The small dark circle (guilt) represented the one thing Kristin was going to do that she believed hurt her employer (guilt), and the fully dark circle her bad self (shame). I reminded Kristin that one of her mental "superpowers" was her ability to attend to small detail, reminding her that when younger she was the only patient who noticed small changes in my office. I told Kristin her superpower (narrow attending) led her to confuse one regret (giving notice) with a totality (her badness), unconsciously moving from guilt (wide attention) to shame (narrow attention). (See Chapter 3, Attention: Wide and Narrow Lens.) I told Kristin I wanted to help her mind get back to guilt, a more appropriate response to giving notice.

I next reminded Kristin of her many excellent employee attributes as contrasted with her one pending, "hurtful" action. Since Kristin could not list her positive qualities, I did. Kristin was so self-critical that I knew if she endorsed a positive characteristic I named, then she agreed it was true. Kirsten accepted all these attributes: loyal, hardworking, producing high-quality work, getting along with co-workers, a "good enough" teacher of new workers, creative, and honest. I then listed the one thing she did that was "hurtful": leaving. Finally, I asked Kristin how long she had demonstrated the positive behavior—"Four years each." And the hurtful behavior?—"Two weeks notice." By the end of the session, Kristin had gone from visibly depressed and shamed (i.e., head down, flattened affect, and halted speech) to at ease (i.e., head up, even affect, with freer communication).

Kristin's movement from "shame" to "guilt" began with psychoeducation about guilt and shame, followed by an intentional shift in attention from "narrow" to "wide." While this approach would not work for all, it suited well Kristin's neurocognitive gifts, that is, superior attention to small, visual detail and intelligence, and challenges, that is, inflexibility and self-criticism.

Shame and Humiliation

Shame and humiliation are sometimes viewed as two sides of the same coin, with humiliation characterized as an extreme form of shame. While shame and humiliation bear many similarities, particularly with regard to one person causing another to feel less than or worthless, differentiating the two can help therapists get closer to the RT survivor's lived experience and help them feel more understood and less ashamed.

The word origin of shame is the Proto-Indo-European (PIE) "kem," "to cover" (Shame, word origin). Humiliation, in contrast, is rooted in the word "humble." The earliest derivation of "humble" is from the PIE "dhegem" meaning earth, and later "lowly" (Humiliation and Humble, word origins). If the function of shame is to cover and hide, to humiliate is to openly debase the other by making them bow to your will.

The humiliator proclaims their dominance and control by repeatedly demonstrating they can inflict harm on the humiliated with impunity. In so doing, they enforce their preeminent status in the social/psychological hierarchy. When a person humiliates another, they metaphorically "ground" the other into the "earth." The humiliator makes sure the humiliated always know who dominates whom.

The humiliator needs the humiliated much as the master needs the slave. The raison d'être of the humiliator, that is the way they psychologically sustain themselves and, in the extreme, justify their existence, is by finding victims to humiliate. While within every shamed person is also a relationship, be that relationship between the shamer and the shamed, or between two dissociative parts of the shamed person, the relationship between humiliator and humiliated thrives on cruel, public display.

The humiliator takes sadistic pleasure in *exposing* rather than *covering* or obscuring both the humiliating act and the humiliated. Humiliating behavior typically ensures others witness the act in order to powerfully communicate to the entire group who is dominant. At minimum, the humiliated person is forced to bear witness to their own degradation and "know their place." The humiliated is in a chronic state of rebellion thwarted externally, via a power differential, and internally, with dissociative parts reflecting the traumatic adaptation to and internalization of this form of psychological torture.

Leask (2013) argues humiliation, unlike shame, is not a feeling but an act. He writes:

> *humiliation is an act that causes a change for the worse in the position of the victim and in the victim's feelings about himself and the world.* Since power is central to humiliation, the victim of an act of humiliation can be described not as *feeling* but as *being* humiliated, as a victim of an act of power … It is a demonstration of the capacity to use power unjustly with apparent impunity.
>
> (p. 131, first line my emphasis)

Leask (2013) continues: Humiliation consists of several elements, including "stripping of status; rejection or exclusion; unpredictability or arbitrariness; and a personal sense of injustice matched by the lack of any sense for the injustice suffered" (p. 131). And finally, "The therapist will recognise humiliation for what it is: *an exercise of power that is demeaning, arbitrary, excluding and unjust and which can never be made not to have happened*" (p. 141, my emphasis).

In my view, an important distinction between humiliation and shame is that the humiliator intentionally uses power to force another human being to submit to their will, to maintain their social dominance, and to exert total control by perceiving and treating the other as subhuman. The humiliator makes of the other dirt, ensuring the humiliated stays "under foot" and never forgets their lowly status. The shamer, in contrast, repeatedly discards the shamed as worthless.

A related distinction between shame and humiliation is *how* they each exert social control. Both shame and humiliation maintain the dominant social order by "othering" the other. Shame and humiliation both act to crush the other's will and unique way of being alive, that is, their pro-being pride (Chapter 2). Leask (2013) argued "excluding" (p. 141) was one important humiliating action. Rather, exclusion and banishment are what shaming and the shamer do best. Alternatively, humiliation and the humiliator control the other by ensuring they not move. While both shame and humiliation use the threat of social death to maintain social compliance, shame does so by making the other "leave" whereas humiliation makes the other "stay."

Again, in contrast with Leask (2013), I contend humiliation is also a feeling, or more accurately a complex mélange of feelings. The humiliator consciously feels pleasure in using power and rage to dominate, control, force into submission, and make suffer the humiliated. The humiliator feels hubristic, "better me pride" (Chapter 2, pride subtypes), in the extreme. They are less aware or not conscious of dissociative parts characterized by shame, specifically "not me shame" (Chapter 2). The humiliator's "not me shame" likely developed in reaction to having been repeatedly humiliated by someone they depended upon, such as a parent or more powerful caregiver. The humiliator knows implicitly that they are always psychologically on thin ice, living on the edge of anxiety. Given their dog-eat-dog belief system, the humiliator knows that while they are "doing the eating," now, at any moment they can "be eaten" by someone more powerful and cruel. Lurking behind the humiliator's sadistic pleasure, then, is fear or terror that they will be humiliated, again.

For the humiliated, humiliation embodies feelings of being debased, the unbearable agony of being "sub-humaned" or "no-thinged" (*sic*). The humiliated also feels utter powerlessness and gripped by suppressed rage. The humiliated fantasizes retaliation in order to proclaim, "I am human!"; to crush and destroy the humiliator; and/or to force the humiliator to feel the humiliated person's pain and thus restore their dignity (Hicks, 2011). Humiliation, then, contains within its interpersonal and intrapersonal dynamic potent rage (humiliator) and impotent rage (humiliated).

Just as humiliation is an act of power (humiliator) and powerlessness (humiliated), *and* a complex set of emotions, so too is shame characterized by acts and feelings. The act of shame is memorialized in being treated as having no worth, actively and overtly, and/or passively and covertly by failing to acknowledge the shamed person's existence. Shame is also felt, the unutterable pain that if spoken might say, "You are right. Because I think, feel, and/or do 'x,' I am worthless" (Chapter 2: "not me shame"); or "My very being is worthless. I don't exist" (Chapter 2: "no me shame," the shame of existing [Wille, 2014]).

In sum, what differentiates humiliation and shame is that the former reflects a willful, conscious, apparently arbitrary but in fact calculated abuse of power to maintain power and avoid dissociated feelings of powerlessness, shame, and humiliation. Further, the humiliator acts to ensure the humiliated person and often others bear witness to their degradation and dehumanization. In this regard, humiliation enforces life imprisonment with the humiliator as jailer. The shamer also treats the other as worthless, actively and/or passively, yet unlike humiliation the shaming act and shame emotions often go unnamed and unacknowledged. The abuse of power that is shame results in a covering over and a turning away. However, were the shamer to make their secret truth known, they might say, "I, shamer, deem you, shamed, worthless, past, present, and forever into the future." Furthermore, unlike humiliation, shame threatens permanent social banishment, replacing entrapment with the desert or void.

Finally, given the complexity of human experience and RT, survivors often experience both humiliation and traumatic shame. For example, one research study (Negrao et al., 2005) with adult survivors of childhood sexual abuse showed verbal humiliation was significantly associated with nonverbal displays of shame.

Why Shame and Pride Matter in Psychotherapy

Why is understanding shame and pride important? How does our understanding these emotions and traumatic states inform psychotherapy generally, and specifically in psychotherapy with survivors of RT?

Why Shame and Pride Matter in Psychotherapy, Generally

- Shame and pride are emotions basic to being human, developing in the first year of life (Trevarthen, 2005). Shame and pride are about self, other, and relationship, and thus have direct bearing on psychotherapy in general. Shame helps us navigate the interpersonal world:

    Under ordinary conditions of peace, I would suggest that shame is one of the primary regulators of social relations. Fear is the primary regulator only in circumstances where social structures for maintaining peace have broken down and social relations are ruled by violence.
    (Herman, 2012, p. 157, my emphasis)

- Pride helps regulate social interactions by establishing and maintaining social status (Tracy, 2016). Shame and pride lie at the heart of universal attachment dilemmas, such as "connected versus disconnected," "us versus them," "good (moral) versus bad (immoral)," "valued (pride) versus devalued (shame)," and especially "included" (pride) versus "excluded" (shame). Shame offers one route, however painful and flawed, toward restoring the attachment bond and the social/moral order. So, too, does pride. Just as shame signals trouble in relationship (Scheff & Retzinger, 2000), adaptive pride communicates well-being in relationship with self and others.

- Extensive research into maladaptive shame, which includes shame as emotional process and traumatic state (Chapter 2), has been associated with lowered self-esteem; lowered empathy; greater inhibition and a failure to initiate, pursue, and/or sustain efforts toward shared goals, as in psychotherapy; increased depression, suicidal ideation, anger, hostility, aggressive behavior, anxiety, eating disorders, maladaptive daydreaming, substance abuse, Borderline Personality Disorder (BPD), and Post-traumatic Stress Disorder (PTSD) (Ferrante et al., 2020; Scheff, In press; Tangney & Fischer, 1995; Buchman-Wildbaum et al., 2021).

- Nonclinical research shows hubristic, "better me pride" (Chapter 2) correlated with grandiosity and arrogance rather than healthy self-esteem, vulnerability to bouts of shame, clinical depression, and aggressive, hostile, manipulative, and controlling behavior. Hubristically proud people are more impulsive and find it harder to regulate their attention and behavior. They also attribute success to their personality rather than their effort (Tracy, 2016).

- Nonclinical research with people demonstrating authentic, "good enough me pride" (Chapter 2) shows correlations with caring, friendly, calm, anxiety-free, outgoing, creative behavior, and popularity. These individuals show self-control rather than other-controlling behavior. Authentically proud people attribute success to effort rather than identity. Adaptive pride also enhances intrinsic motivation and perseverance in the face of hardship, in order to achieve one's goals and life satisfaction (Tracy, 2016).

- Little has been written about the benefits of directly addressing adaptive pride in psychotherapy. (See Benau, 2020a, 2020b, 2020c, 2019a, 2019b, 2018 for some exceptions.) Nonclinical research suggests adaptive pride likely strengthens a patient's drive to work hard and improve their psychological and interpersonal functioning. This is consistent with clinical observations of Pierre Janet (1935), whose concept of act of triumph following trauma processing (cited by Barral & Meares, in Craparo et al., 2019), "requires effort and results in a sense of pride that is a form of joy and heals shame" (p. 121).

- The patient's, therapist's, and patient's-therapist's shared shame and pride often determine the success or failure of psychotherapy (Dearing & Tangney, 2011). When therapists fail to address shame, patients are prone to feeling misunderstood, terminate prematurely, remain emotionally distant, and convinced the therapist will reject them once they discover who they "really" are (Dearing & Tangney, 2011).

- It is equally problematic when adaptive, "good enough me pride," and especially "pro-being pride" (Chapter 2) are neither noticed nor worked with psychotherapeutically. Therapy is not strictly about the amelioration of psychiatric symptoms. It also involves cultivating the patient's well-being and thriving. Addressing the emotional and relational effects of achievement-oriented, "good enough me pride," the pride of doing, and more importantly "pro-being pride," the pride of being and being with (Chapter 2), helps patients celebrate their true self-in-relationship. Working with both forms of adaptive pride helps patients appreciate their progress, persevere in the difficult work of psychotherapy, and experience a deeper, more integrated sense of self that expresses and fosters personal transformation.

Why Shame and Pride Matter in Psychotherapy with Relational Trauma (RT), *Specifically*

- Working with shame and pride has special import in psychotherapy with RT. Both abuse and neglect are inherently shaming, as the person is not seen, valued, or treated with dignity (Hicks, 2011), and even more not delighted in or cherished for who they are (Chapter 2, pro-being pride). Whether overtly shamed (e.g., "You disgust me!") or covertly shamed (e.g., lacking attunement and reciprocal responsiveness), shame is always present in RT. So, too, is the dearth of adaptive pride.

- Traumatic shame and pride states are often confusing, overwhelming, and disorganizing for the patient, therapist, and their relationship. The patient's shame and shaming of the therapist evokes shame in and countershaming of the patient by the therapist (Dalenberg, 2000), and/or alternatively withdrawing from the patient, and/or dissociating. In complex trauma, shame is often hidden within various psychological problems (Zhu et al., 2020). There are times when a person gripped by a traumatic shame state cannot think, feel, speak, act, or adaptively interact.

- RT is characterized by dysregulation, with dramatic shifts between states of hyperarousal (e.g., emotional activation, high arousal "freeze" states of immobilization, terror, rage, etc.), hypoarousal (e.g., emotional shutdown, low arousal "freeze" states of immobilization, numbing, depression, etc.) (Porges, 2011), or their co-occurrence (Lanius, 2018, personal communication). In shame, a person feels *small* when emotions are *too big* for them and their relationships to hold. Whenever there is marked dysregulation of affect and behavior in RT survivors, we are likely encounter implicit and/or explicit shame. Shame in RT is both cause and consequence of self-perpetuating, emotional storms. Adding insult to injury, survivors often feel shame for feeling shame.

- Survivors often dissociate when enduring overwhelming emotional and neurophysiological dysregulation. Complex, psychodynamic, and phenomenological relationships exist between traumatic shame and pride states, on the one hand, and mind/body leave taking (LT), described by some as dissociation as process (Schimmenti, 2018; Schimmenti & Caretti, 2016), and/or structural dissociation (SD), on the other. (See Chapter 3 for distinguishing characteristics of LT versus SD.) Therapists benefit from understanding that when gripped by shame and pride states, RT survivors also experience at minimum acute or chronic LT and, under chronically adverse conditions, SD.

- Many people in an adult survivor's life will not understand dissociation (SD). This also applies to therapists not trained in RT and dissociative disorders. Being misunderstood by professionals and laypeople reinforce, in the survivor, both maladaptive shame and pride as emotions and traumatic states, which in turn contribute to further SD.

- While working with RT survivors requires specialized training, traumatic shame and pride states are particularly disturbing because they force patient and therapist to feel and believe things about themselves and the other person they would rather not. These may include beliefs such as "I am not worthy of your care" (patient) and "I am not worthy of caring for you" (therapist); "There is nothing good about me and/or your" (patient) and "There is nothing good about me and/or you" (therapist); "There is nothing I nor you can do to change how I feel about myself" (patient) and "There is nothing I nor you can do to change how you feel about yourself" (therapist). Shame and pride states confront patient and therapist with profound existential realities, such as "Does my life and/or your life have meaning," calling into question the entire therapeutic enterprise.

- Survivors of Complex PTSD (C-PTSD), comparable to RT, often seek therapy for help with a damaged sense of self and relationship (Herman, 2011), wounds consistent with the effects of traumatic shame and pride states.

- One study (Alix et al., 2020) of 100 adolescent girls who had been sexually abused found shame predicted PTSD symptoms, self-blame predicted depressive symptoms, and depressive symptoms and avoidance predicted suicidal ideation. In my view, self-blame, depression, and avoidance following sexual abuse all reflect unprocessed, traumatic shame. Likewise, traumatic shame states have been associated with various dissociative disorders, and likewise intrapersonal alienation and social isolation worsen depersonalization (DP), derealization (DR), and dissociation (DePrince et al., 2015; Dorahy et al., 2015, 2013, 2010; Tangney & Fischer, 1995).

- To seek psychotherapy is to acknowledge implicitly having relational needs. To the survivor, depending upon others, including their therapist, means risking once again being hurt, abused, rejected, ignored, manipulated, controlled, and never seen, felt, nor understood. Survivors often experience traumatic shame, pride, and/or dissociative states when interpersonal longings conflict with unconscious prohibitions against dependency needs.

- RT survivors typically struggle to develop secure attachments. When relationships are problematic, that is, too close, distant, conflictual, conflict-avoidant, etc., explicit and/or implicit shame are likely at play (Dorahy et al., 2013; Dorahy, 2010).

- Shame states without repair lie at the heart of disorganized attachment:

    Where no corrective relational experiences take place, pathological variations in the attachment system can develop. In particular, we see disorganized attachment where the primary attachment figure is a source of fear. *I would argue that we also see disorganized attachment where the primary attachment figure is a source of unremitting shame. In this case, the child is torn between need for emotional attunement and fear of rejection or ridicule. She forms an internal working model where her basic needs are inherently shameful.*

    (Herman, 2012, p. 158, my emphasis)

- Traumatic shame states more so than shame as an emotional process are endemic to abusive relationships. "When methods of coercive control are used within primary attachment relationships, as occurs *in the case of child abuse, the developing child learns nothing of ordinary social shame. Rather, the child is overwhelmed with extreme shame states*" (Herman, 2012, p. 163, my emphasis). Not surprisingly, shame states are also associated with suicidality (Dutra et al., 2008).

- Shame bonds the RT survivor to the perpetrator (Cloitre et al., 2006). When a perpetrator repeatedly shames a child, the survivor learns to explicitly and implicitly "agree" with their devaluation. As the child seeks both physical and psychological closeness, the latter by internalizing the caregiver's punishing and/or neglecting "message," the trauma bond is strengthened. Shaming often prevents child and adult survivors from getting close enough to healthy relationships, and distant enough from destructive relationships.

- Clinical observation and research have shown a mother's repeated self-criticism and self-shaming contribute to later self-shaming by their infant or young child (Kaminer et al., 2007). Observational research (Beebe & Lachmann, 2017) of four-month-old infant/mother dyads showed the mother's self-critical display resulted in her diminished attention and lessened mutual gaze, emotional (facial) coordination and touch, including the infant reaching out less often for the mother's touch. In my view, these observed child and parent behaviors are consistent with mind/body leave taking (LT) and possibly structural dissociation (SD) (Chapter 3).

- Research showed a mother's psychological absence, for example, as the result of chronic depression, LT, and SD, resulted in the child developing an overly responsible style of relating (Lyons-Ruth, 2020, personal communication). Overly responsible children often become shame-prone adults. These children chronically "fail" to make the mother (caregiver) psychologically and emotionally available. For the young child, "repeatedly failing to elicit their mother's attention and care" = "being a failure" = "traumatic shame states."

- I would expect that when a parent/caregiver of an infant/young child experiences traumatic shame states, then by definition shame, LT, and/or SD co-occur, and the parent's LT and/or SD further contribute to the infant's/young child's LT and/or SD, and self-shaming. How this parent/infant intrapersonal and interpersonal dynamic might present, follows: Shame state, LT, and/or SD in parent→ the parent is nonattuned/nonresponsive and/or critical of their infant→increases the likelihood the infant develops a traumatic shame state, LT, and/or SD→increasing infant (later young child) nonresponsiveness, LT, and/or SD withdrawal→intensifying the parent's feelings of inadequacy, shame states, LT, and/or SD, and so on, recursively. This is one possible pathway of intergenerational transmission of shame states and RT.

- I know of no comparable research into pride as emotion nor traumatic pride states as relates to infant-parent interaction. Given the hypothesized dynamic proposed, the parent, infant, and later developing child would likely develop maladaptive pride, as in "better me pride" as emotional process, and/or more importantly "not me" and "no me" pride as traumatic states (Chapter 2). People experiencing early RT who feel hated, not seen, and/or not reciprocally responded to are often deprived of pro-being pride experiences, a basic building block of emotional and relational well-being. Survivors of RT, chronic LT, and/or SD typically show a paucity or absence of adaptive pride.

- When shame dominates the survivor's intrapersonal and interpersonal landscape, pride-in-self is largely occluded. Adult RT patients are often self-critical and self-shaming when failing to meet harsh, intrapersonal expectations (Howell, 2020), and have difficulty receiving genuine praise. In contrast, some RT survivors are more other-shaming. Clinical observations describe how malignant narcissism harms individuals, other people, and relationships (Bach, 1977; Ellison et al., 2013; Kernberg, 2014; Kohut, 1972; Middleton et al., 2017; Shaw, 2014; Steiner, 2006).

- Adaptive pride enhances a patient's self-worth and the development of secure attachment. In contrast, when a child's positive personal attributes are ignored and/or dismissed by their primary caregiver, an insecure-avoidant or insecure-preoccupied attachment style likely develops. The avoidant child who rarely or never receives a caregiver's genuine acknowledgment feels little personal pride, with little incentive to seek recognition. In contrast, the insecure-preoccupied patient may anxiously seek praise yet feel chronically unfulfilled or empty.

- Since adaptive pride grows out of mastery, RT and dissociative disorders cut at the heart of adaptive pride reflecting "mastery" of one's mind, body, and behavior, and achieving personal and interpersonal goals. In RT and dissociative disorders, pride is often hidden, lurking in the shadows of dissociation (Chapters 2 and 3). As patients develop and embody adaptive pride, they discover therapy not only relieves symptoms but also enhances personal growth.

- Adaptive pride grows out of accomplishments in therapy (e.g., "I did it!"), strengthening the patient's determination to persevere in the face of psychosocial challenges. Likewise, adaptive pride, that is, "good enough me pride" and "pro-being pride" (Chapter 2), is neurophysiologically energizing and well-regulated. Adaptive pride helps people living with chronic depression, depersonalization/derealization (DP/DR), etc. "light up" and become mobilized in therapy and beyond. For the RT survivor, lacking adaptive pride makes it difficult for patients to process trauma, cope in everyday life, and recognize therapeutic progress.

- Finally, the ACES research (Felitti et al., 1998) demonstrated chronic adverse stress as a result of childhood trauma was significantly correlated with negative physical and psychological health outcomes in adults. We might predict, then, shame and pride states would contribute to various psychosomatic symptoms, for example, traumatic memories held in the body (Van der Kolk, 2014a, 2014b; Scaer, 2001). Likewise, since pride is about mastery in relation to something that matters to the person and their social group (Tracy, 2016), it follows shame emerges out of a failure to master, that is, to adaptively affect what matters to the person and their group. A person who loses control of their mind/body and experiences chronic physical and psychological ailments often feels misunderstood and shamed by themselves—"What's wrong with *me*?" and others—"What's wrong with *you*?". In both physical and psychological illness or health, learning to work psychotherapeutically with shame and pride in RT survivors must go beyond chronic suffering toward enduring healing and growth.

Note

1 While I use "affect" and "emotion" interchangeably, most researchers do not. Russell and Barrett (1999) define "core affect" as a "neurophysiological state consciously accessible as a simple primitive non-reflective feeling most evident in mood and emotion but always available to consciousness" (p. 104), whereas they define "emotion" as a "complex set of interrelated sub-events concerned with a specific object" (p. 806), such as a person, an event, or a thing, whether past, present, future, real, or imagined. According to Ekkekakis (2012), the co-occurring elements that compose a prototypical emotional episode include (1) core affect; (2) overt behavior congruent with the emotion (e.g., a smile or a facial expression of fear); (3) attention directed toward the eliciting stimulus; (4) cognitive appraisal of the meaning and possible implications of the stimulus; (5) attribution of the genesis of the episode to the stimulus; (6) the experience of the particular emotion; and (7) neural (peripheral and central) and endocrine changes consistent with the particular emotion. In my view, emotions or affects include underlying neurophysiological processes that may or may not reach consciousness, as well as associated, conscious cognitions or schema, meanings, imagery, somatic experiences, and behavior.

References

Alix, S., Cosette, L., Cyr, M., Frappier, J., Caron, P., & Hebert, M. (2020). Self-blame, Shame, Avoidance, and Suicidal Ideation in Sexually Abused Adolescent Girls: A Longitudinal Study. *Journal of Child Sexual Abuse*, 29(4), 432–447. https://doi.org/10.1080/10538712.2019.1678543.

Bach, S. (1977). *Narcissistic States and the Therapeutic Process*. Lanham, MD: Rowman & Littlefield.

Barral, C. & Meares, R. (2019). The Holistic Project of Pierre Janet: Part Two: Oscillations and Becomings: From Disintegration to Integration. In G. Craparo, F. Ortu, & O. Van der Hart, Eds., *Rediscovering Pierre Janet: Trauma, Dissociation, and a New Context for Psychoanalysis* (pp. 116–129). New York: Routledge. https://doi.org/10.4324/9780429201875.

Beebe, B. & Lachmann, F. (2017). Maternal Self-critical and Dependent Personality Styles and Mother-Infant Communication. *Journal of the American Psychoanalytic Association*, 65(3), 1–18. https://doi.org/10.1177/0003065117709004.

Bekoff, M. (2007). *The Emotional Life of Animals: A Leading Scientist Explores Animal Joy, Sorrow and Empathy—And Why They Matter*. Novato, CA: New World Library.

Benau, K. (2021a). Shame to Pride Following Sexual Molestation: Part 1: From Traumatic Immobilization to Triumphant Movement. *European Journal of Trauma and Dissociation*, 5(4), 100198. https://doi.org/10.1016/j.ejtd.2020.100194.

Benau, K. (2021b). Shame to Pride Following Sexual Molestation: Part 2: From Pro-being Pride to Retaliatory Rage, Adaptive Anger, and Integration. *European Journal of Trauma and Dissociation*, 5(4), 100194. https://doi.org/10.1016/j.ejtd.2020.100194.

Benau, K. (2020a). Shame, Pride and Dissociation: Estranged Bedfellows, Close Cousins and Some Implications for Psychotherapy with Relational Trauma Part I: Phenomenology and Conceptualization. *Mediterranean Journal of Clinical Psychology*, 8(1), 1–35. Doi: https://doi.org/10.6092/2282-1619/mjcp-2154.

Benau, K. (2020b). Shame, Pride and Dissociation: Estranged Bedfellows, Close Cousins and Some Implications for Psychotherapy with Relational Trauma-Part 2: Part II: Psychotherapeutic Applications. *Mediterranean Journal of Clinical Psychology*, 8(1), 1–29. Doi: https://doi.org/10.6092/2282-1619/mjcp-2155.

Benau, K. (2020c). Shame to Pride in a Single "Session." *The Science of Psychotherapy*, March, 20–39.

Benau, K. (2019a). Catching the Wave. *The Neuropsychotherapist*, 7(4), 4–13.

Benau, K. (January 28, 2019b). Ken Benau Talks about Shame and Pride. Podcast. *Science of Psychotherapy*. www.thescienceofpsychotherapy.com/the-science-of-psychotherapy-podcast/.

Benau, K. (2018). Pride in the Psychotherapy of Relational Trauma: Conceptualization and Treatment Considerations. *European Journal of Trauma and Dissociation*, 2(3), 131–146. https://doi.org/10.1016/j.ejtd.2018.03.002.

Benau, K. (2017). Shame, Attachment, and Psychotherapy: Phenomenology, Neurophysiology, Relational Trauma, and Harbingers of Healing. *Attachment: New Directions in Psychotherapy and Relational Psychoanalysis*, 11(1), 1–27. https://doi.org/10.33212/att.v11n1.2017.1.

Bowlby, J. (1969). *Attachment: Attachment and Loss, Vol. 1: Loss*. New York: Basic Books.

Bromberg, P. M. (2011a). *Awakening the Dreamer: Clinical Journeys*. New York: Routledge. https://doi.org/10.4324/9780203759981.

Bromberg, P. M. (2011b). *The Shadow of the Tsunami and the Growth of the Relational Mind*. New York: Routledge. https://doi.org/10.4324/9780203834954.

Broucek, F. J. (1979). Efficacy in Infancy. *International Journal of Psychoanalysis*, 60, 311–316.

Buchman-Wildbaum, T., Unoka, Z., Dudas, R., Vizin, G., Demetrovics, Z., & Richman, M. J. (2021). Shame in Borderline Personality Disorder: Meta-analysis. *Journal of Personality Disorders*, 35, Supplement A, 149–161 https://doi.org/10.1521/pedi_2021_35_515.

Chefetz, R. (2015). *Intensive Psychotherapy for Persistent Dissociative Disorders: The Fear of Feeling Real*. New York: W.W. Norton. Doi: 10.1080/00332747.2016.1237710.

Cloitre, M., Cohen, L. R., & Koenen, K. C. (2006). *Treating Survivors of Childhood Abuse: Psychotherapy for the Interrupted Life*. New York: Guilford Press. https://doi.org/10.1037/e517322011-039.

Craparo, G., Ortu, F., & O.Van der Hart, Eds. (2019). *Rediscovering Pierre Janet: Trauma, Dissociation, and a New Context for Psychoanalysis.* New York: Routledge. https://doi.org/10.4324/9780203759981.

Dalenberg, C. J. (2000). It's Not Your Fault: Countertransference Struggles with Blame and Shame. In *Countertransference and the Treatment of Trauma* (pp. 115–144). Washington, DC: American Psychological Association. Doi: https://doi.org/10.1037/10380-005.

Dearing, R. L. & Tangney, J. P., Eds. (2011). *Shame in the Therapy Hour.* Washington, DC: American Psychological Association. https://doi.org/10.1037/12326-000.

DePrince, A. P., Huntjens, R. J. C., & Dorahy, M. J. (2015). Alienation Appraisals Distinguish Adults Diagnosed with DID from PTSD. *Psychological Trauma: Theory, Research, Practice, and Policy,* 7(6), 578–582. Doi: https://doi.org/10.1037/tra0000069.

Dorahy, M. J. (Personal communication, June 14, 2020). *Differentiating Shame and Guilt.*

Dorahy, M. J. (2010). The Impact of Dissociation, Shame, and Guilt on Interpersonal Relationships in Chronically Traumatized Individuals: A Pilot Study. *Journal of Traumatic Stress,* 23(5), 653–656. Doi: https://doi.org/10.1037/tra0000069.Dorahy, M. J., Middleton, W., Seager, L., McGurrin, P., Williams, M., & Chambers, R. (2015). Dissociation, Shame, Complex PTSD, Child Maltreatment and Intimate Relationship Self-concept in Dissociative Disorder, Chronic PTSD and Mixed Psychiatric Groups. *Journal of Affective Disorders,* 172, 195–203. Doi: https://doi.org/10.1016/j.jad.2014.10.008.

Dorahy, M. J., Corry, M., Shannon, M., Webb, K., McDermott, B., Ryan, M., & Dyer, K. F. W. (2013). Complex Trauma and Intimate Relationships: The Impact of Shame, Guilt and Dissociation. *Journal of Affective Disorders,* 147(1), 72–79. Doi: https://doi.org/10.1016/j.jad.2012.10.010.

Dutra, L., Callahan, K., Forman, E., Mendelsohn, M., & Herman, J. L. (2008). Core Schemas and Suicidality in a Chronically Traumatized Population. *Journal of Nervous and Mental Disease,* 196(1), 71–74. https://doi.org/10.1097/NMD.0b013e31815fa4c1.

Ekkekakis, P. (2012). Affect, Mood, and Emotion. In G. Tenenbaum, R. C. Eklund, & A. Kamata, Eds., *Measurement in Sport Psychology.* Champaign, IL: Human Kinetics. https://doi.org/10.5040/9781492596332.ch-028.

Ellison, W. D., Levy, K. N., Cain, N. M., Ansell, E. B., & Pincus, A. L. (2013). The Impact of Pathological Narcissism on Psychotherapy Utilization, Initial Symptom Severity, and Early-Treatment Symptom Change: A Naturalistic Investigation. *Journal of Personality Assessment,* 95(3), 291–300. https://doi.org/10.1080/00223891.2012.742904.

Erozkan, A. (2016). The Link between Types of Attachment and Childhood Trauma. *Universal Journal of Educational Research,* 4(5), 1071–1079. https://doi.org/10.13189/ujer.2016.040517.

Felitti, V., Anda, R. F., Nordenberg, D., Williamson, D. F., Spitz, A. M., Edwards, V., Koss, M. P., & Marks, J. S. (1998). Relationship of Childhood Abuse and Household Dysfunction to Many of the Leading Causes of Death in Adults: The Adverse Childhood Experiences (ACE) Study. *American Journal of Preventive Medicine,* 14(4), 245–258. https://doi.org/10.1016/S0749-3797(98)00017-8.

Ferrante, E., Marino, A., Guglielmucci, F., & Schimmenti, A. (2020). The Mediating Role of Dissociation and Shame in the Relationship between Emotional Trauma and Maladaptive Daydreaming. *Psychology of Consciousness: Theory, Research, and Practice,* 1–13. http://dx.doi.org/10.1037/cns0000253.

Freud, S. (2010/1930). *Civilization and Its Discontents.* New York: W.W. Norton.

Gilbert, P. (1998). What Is Shame: Some Core Issues and Controversies. In P. Gilbert & B. Andrews, Eds., *Shame: Interpersonal Behavior, Psychopathology, and Culture*. New York: Oxford Press.

Herman, J. L. (2012). Shattered Shame States and Their Repair. In J. Yellin & K. White, Eds., *Shattered States: Disorganised Attachment and Its Repair* (pp. 157–170). London: Karnac Books.

Herman, J. L. (2011). PTSD as a Shame Disorder. In R. L. Dearing & J. P. Tangney, Eds., *Shame in the Therapy Hour* (pp. 261–275). Washington, DC: American Psychological Association. https://doi.org/10.1037/12326-000.

Herman, J. L. (2007). *Shattered Shame States and Their Repair*. Somerville, MA: Harvard Medical School.

Herman, J. L. (2006). *PTSD as a Shame Disorder*. Somerville, MA: Harvard Medical School.

Hicks, D. (2011). *Dignity: Its Essential Role in Resolving Conflict*. New Haven: Yale University Press.

Howell, E. (2020). *Trauma and Dissociation-Informed Psychotherapy: Relational Healing and the Therapeutic Connection*. New York: W.W. Norton. Doi: 10.4324/9780203888261.

Humble, word origin: www.etymonline.com/search?q=humble&ref=searchbar_searchhint. Accessed June 9, 2021.

Humiliation, word origin: www.etymonline.com/search?q=humiliation. Accessed June 9, 2021.

Janet, P. (1935). *Les Debuts de L'Intelligence*. Paris: Flammation.

Kaminer, T., Beebe, B., Jaffe, J., Kelly, K., & Marquette, I. (2007). Mothers' Dependent and Self-critical Depressive Experience Is Related to Speech Content with Infants. *Journal of Early Childhood & Infant Psychology*, 3, 163–184.

Kernberg, O. (2014). *Aggressivity, Narcissism and Self-destructiveness in the Psychotherapeutic Relationship*. New Haven Yale University Press.

Kohut, H. (1972). Thoughts on Narcissism and Narcissistic Rage. *The Psychoanalytic Study of the Child*, 27(1), 360–400. https://doi.org/10.1080/00797308.1972.11822721.

Lanius, U. (March 22, 2018). *Personal Communication*, ISSTD Annual Conference, Chicago, IL.

Leask, P. (2013). Losing Trust in the World: Humiliation and Its Consequences. *Psychodynamic Practice: Individuals, Groups and Organisations*, 19(2), 129–142. https://doi.org/10.1080/14753634.2013.778485.

Lewis, M. (1989). Presentation at Institute of Pennsylvania Hospital.

Lyons-Ruth, K. (June 5, 2020). *Personal Communication*.

Middleton, W., Sachs, A., & Dorahy, M. (2017). The Abused and the Abuser: Victim-Perpetrator Dynamics. *Journal of Trauma and Dissociation*, 18(3), 249–258. https://doi.org/10.1080/15299732.2017.1295373.

Mollon, P. (2018). *Shame and Jealousy: The Hidden Turmoils*. New York: Routledge. https://doi.org/10.4324/9780429480102.

Mussolini, B. "hubristic pride" video: www.youtube.com/watch?v=CfS8AulsYRk. Accessed July 26, 2021.

Nathanson, D. (1992). *Shame, Pride, Affect, Sex and the Birth of the Self*. New York: W.W. Norton. https://doi.org/10.1177/03621537940240027.

Negrao, C., Bonanno, G. A., Noll, J. G., Putnam, F. W., & Trickett, P. K. (2005). Shame, Humiliation, and Childhood Sexual Abuse: Distinct Contributions and Emotional Coherence. *Child Maltreatment*, 10(4), 350–363. Doi: 10.1177/ 1077559505279366.

"Patient," word origin: www.etymonline.com/word/patient. Accessed January 24, 2021.

Porges, S. W. (2011). *The Polyvagal Theory: Neurophysiological Foundations of Emotions, Attachment, Communication, and Self-regulation.* New York: W.W. Norton.

Rodin, A. "shame" sculptures: www.google.com/search?q=shame+rodin&rlz= 1C5CHFA_enUS806US806&so urce=lnms&tbm=isch&sa=X&ved=2ahUKE wjFx5igtt3tAhWSFTQIHQIkBugQ_AUoAX oECA8QAw&biw=1368&bih= 737#imgrc=MVXJXq2foyj3vM. Accessed July 26, 2021.

Russell, J. A. & Barrett, L. F. (1999). Core Affect, Prototypical Emotional Episodes, and Other Things Called Emotion: Dissecting the Elephant. *Journal of Personality and Social Psychology*, 76(5), 805–819. Doi: https://doi.org/10.1037/ 0022-3514.76.5.805.

Scaer, R. C. (2001). *The Body Bears the Burden: Trauma, Dissociation, and Disease.* Binghamton: Haworth Press.

Scheff, T. J. (In press). *A Social Theory and Treatment of Depression.* http://scheff.faculty. soc.ucsb.edu/main.php?id=62.html. Accessed December 28, 2019.

Scheff, T. J. & Retzinger, S. M. (2000). Shame as the Master Emotion of Everyday Life. *Journal of Mundane Behavior*, 1(3), 303–324.

Schimmenti, A. (September 8, 2018). *Personal Communication*, originally posted on the Dissociative Disorders Listserv (DISSOC). Quoted with permission.

Schimmenti, A. & Caretti,V. (2016). Linking the Overwhelming with the Unbearable: Developmental Trauma, Dissociation, and the Disconnected Self. *Psychoanalytic Psychology*, 33(1), 106–128. https://doi.org/10.1037/a0038019.

Schore, A. N. (2003). *Affect Regulation and Repair of the Self.* New York: W.W. Norton.

Schore, A. N. (2001). The Effects of Relational Trauma on Right Brain Development, Affect Regulation, and Infant Mental Health. *Infant Mental Health Journal*, 22(1–2), 201–269. Doi: https://doi.org/10.1002/1097-0355(200101/ 04)22:1<201::AID-IMHJ8>3.0.CO;2–9.

Shame, word origin: www.etymonline.com/word/shame. Accessed June 9, 2021.

Shaw, D. (2014). *Traumatic Narcissism: Relational Systems of Subjugation.* New York: Routledge.

Spinoza, B. (R. H. M. Elwes, Ed.). (2006/1677). The Ethics (Ethica Ordine Geometrico Demonstrata): Parts 1–5: *On the Origins and Nature of the Emotions, Proposition 53.* Charleston, South Carolina: Bibliobazaar. https://doi.org/10.1524/9783050050 218.1.

Steiner, J. (2006). Seeing and Being Seen: Narcissistic Pride and Narcissistic Humiliation. *International Journal of Psychoanalysis*, 87(4), 939–951. https://doi. org/10.1516/AL5W-9RVJ-WKG2-B0CK.

Stern, D. (1985). *The Interpersonal World of the Infant: A View from Psychoanalysis and Developmental Psychology.* New York: Basic Books.

Sturm, V. E., Ascher, E. A., Miller, B. L., & Levenson, R. W. (2008). Diminished Self-conscious Emotional Responding in Frontotemporal Lobar Degeneration Patients. *Emotion*, 8(6), 861–869. https://doi.org/10.1037/a0013765.

Sturm, V. E., Rosen, H. J., Allison, S., Miller, B. L., & Levenson, R. W. (2006). Self-conscious Emotion Deficits in Frontotemporal Lobar Degeneration. *Brain*, 129(9), 2508–2516. https://doi.org/10.1093/brain/awl145.

Tangney, J. P. & Fischer, K. W., Eds. (1995). *Self-conscious Emotions: The Psychology of Shame, Guilt, Embarrassment, and Pride.* New York: Guilford Press.

Tomkins, S. (1963). *Affect, Imagery and Consciousness: The Negative Affects, Vol. 2.* New York: Springer.

Tracy, J. (2016). *Take Pride: Why the Deadliest Sin Holds the Secret to Human Success.* New York: Houghton Mifflin Harcourt.

Tracy, J., Robins, R. W., & Tangney, J. P., Eds. (2007). *The Self-conscious Emotions: Theory and Practice.* New York: Guilford. Trauma, word origin: www.etymonline.com/word/trauma.

Trevarthen, C. (2005). Stepping Away from the Mirror: Pride and Shame in Adventures in Companionship—Reflections on the Nature and Emotional Needs of Infant Intersubjectivity. In L. Carter, K. E. Ahnert, S. B. Grossman, M. E. Hrdy, S. W. Lamb, S. Porges, & N. Sachser, Eds., *Attachment and Bonding: A New Synthesis* (pp. 55–84). Cambridge, MA: MIT Press.

Twain, M. (2011). *A Connecticut Yankee in King Arthur's Court.* Berkeley: U. C. Press. https://doi.org/10.1525/9780520948075. Accessed January 30, 2017 through EBRARY.

Van der Kolk, B. A. (2014a). *The Body Keeps the Score: Brain, Mind, and Body in the Healing of Trauma.* New York: Viking.

Van der Kolk, B. A. (2014b). *The Body Keeps the Score.* http://bessel.kajabi.com/fe/72501-the-body-keeps-the-score. PESI. Accessed January 31, 2017.

Wille, R. (2014). The Shame of Existing: An Extreme Form of Shame. *International Journal of Psychoanalysis,* 95(4), 695–717. Doi: 10.1111/1745-8315.12208.

Zhu, P., Lau, J., & Navlta, C. P. (2020). An Ecological Approach to Understanding Pervasive and Hidden Shame in Complex Trauma. *Journal of Mental Health Counseling,* 42(2), 155–169. Doi: 10.17744/mehc.42.2.05.

2 Shame and Pride

Subtypes and Processes

Introduction

Chapter 1 described several phenomenological features of shame and pride, and why understanding shame and pride is crucial for therapists working with survivors of relational trauma (RT) (Schore, 2001). Chapter 2 continues this discussion by differentiating shame and pride *subtypes* and *processes*. First adopting a "macro," experience-distant perspective, several shame and pride subtypes are described. These subtypes include acute shame and pride emotional processes ("shame and pride emotions"), taking both adaptive and maladaptive forms, and chronic, always maladaptive, traumatic shame and pride mind/body states ("shame and pride states"). This chapter moves on to a "micro," experience-near description of adaptive and maladaptive shame and pride *processes*. Here, processes refer to how a person's experience shifts from every day, "going-on-being" (Winnicott, 1960, p. 586) to shame and pride emotions and/or traumatic states.

Being able to conceptualize shame and pride subtypes and processes is especially important for therapists working with RT survivors, as the emotional storms both within patient and therapist and between the therapy pair can be overwhelming. Traumatic, shame and pride states are often so confusing, disorganizing, and, depending upon the degree of dissociation, hidden from patients and therapists that they call upon us to refine further our conceptualization. The more therapists have different ways of thinking about and observing shame and pride, the more they will be able to help patients therapeutically process these complex experiences of self, other, and relationship. (For more on patient-therapist shame dynamics, see Chapter 5.)

Shame and Pride "Macro" (Subtypes) and "Micro" (Processes) Perspectives

Chapter 2 observes shame and pride from two perspectives, "macro" and "micro." Imagine the flora and fauna of the woods as representing life experience in all its complexity. Next, consider the trees in the forest as representing "the emotional life of humans." From a "macro" perspective, distinct yet related subspecies of trees represent adaptive and maladaptive shame and pride subtypes. In contrast, a "micro" perspective describes underlying processes that enable shame and pride "trees" to develop and grow.

Just as "subspecies of trees" and "growth processes of trees" are two of many ways we think about trees, shame and pride subtypes and processes are two ways of organizing infinitely complex phenomena and experiences. As social and cultural constructions (Gergen, 2015) of subjective and interpersonal experience, these subtypes and processes should not be confused with the real thing, just as a map is not the same as the terrain, much less how it feels to live with others within that terrain. These constructions are useful to the extent they help therapists think about and give meaning to experience in ways that benefit patient, therapist, and the therapeutic process.

Shame Subtypes: Adaptive versus Maladaptive, Emotional Process versus Traumatic Mind/Body State

Before describing shame and pride subtypes, a few words about the relationship between shame and pride. Given that shame and pride are considered opposites, one might expect a person feeling shame would not feel pride, and vice versa. Subjective experience is more complex. For example, a person can feel ashamed for not living up to their values ("good enough me shame") while retaining pride in their scholarship ("good enough me pride"). Likewise, a RT survivor gripped by a traumatic pride state may dissociate in lieu of feeling proud when self-assertive, yet never be overtaken by a traumatic shame state when angry. While a shame and pride often co-occur as point/counterpoint, that need not be the case.

Adaptive versus Maladaptive Shame

Shame has been conceptualized from many perspectives. Some authors differentiate "good" (adaptive) and "bad" (maladaptive or toxic) shame (Greenberg & Iwakabe, 2011), while others argue there is no such thing as healthy shame (Tangney & Dearing, 2011). I contend shame can sometimes be very adaptive. While some categorize shame according to its content (e.g., sexual, financial, work, etc.; Nathanson, 1992), I do not find listing what patients feel shame about clinically useful. People experience shame about almost everything, including shame. The same is true for pride.

Conceptualizing shame and pride as "adaptive" or "maladaptive" adopts an ecological perspective where shame and pride are embedded within an intrarelational and interrelational context. The major disadvantage of these terms is that "maladaptive" is often equated with "pathological." A better way of understanding "maladaptive" shame and pride is to recognize these self-other conscious emotions or states were once adaptive within specific attachment bonds but no longer serve in present-day relationships. One example would be the sexually abused person who believed as a child they were disgusting and unlovable because they were treated as worthless (i.e., adaptive), yet as an adult continue to believe the same despite their loving spouse and friends (i.e., maladaptive). Thus, I use "maladaptive" as shorthand for "no longer adaptive."

When working with RT survivors, I recommend retaining only a few phenomenological categories. Too many ideas interfere with the therapist's capacity to follow what is going on within themselves and between them and the patient. From a macro perspective, there are four shame subtypes (Table 2.1). Given the multiplicity of mind where within any individual reside several mental states (Putnam, 2016; Schwartz, 1995) or dissociative parts (Van der Hart et al., 2006), patients can and often do experience more than one shame subtype. Most patients experience the effects of at least one type of shame, although some psychopaths may not *feel* shame.

For heuristic purposes, two attributes of both shame and pride subtypes are highlighted: levels of organization and self-reflective capacity, and "shame and pride as emotional processes" versus "shame and pride as traumatic, mind/body states."

Levels of Self-organization and Self-reflective Capacity

The four shame subtypes and five pride subtypes—that is, "good enough me shame," "not good enough me shame," "not me shame," "no me shame," "good enough me pride," "better me pride," "not me pride," "no me pride," and "pro-being pride"—are situated conceptually on a hierarchical continuum from most to least complex and most to least integrated self-organization. Likewise, patients experiencing these subtypes can be identified as having the most to least capacity for nonjudgmental, mindful self-awareness. The one exception is pro-being pride, which is the most complex, integrated, and experientially mindful of all subtypes.

For example, while the person experiencing "good enough me shame" or "good enough me pride" hold feelings of shame or pride alongside attitudes and beliefs about their "good enough" self, the person living with "not me shame" and "not me pride" dissociates, unconsciously placing outside awareness self-aspects deemed unacceptable. Likewise, while the person living with "not good enough me shame" or "better me pride" are more "*in*" maladaptive shame or "*in*" maladaptive pride" than "*reflect upon*" their shame or pride experience, they both retain greater self-reflective capacity than the person experiencing "no me shame" or "no me pride."

Shame as Emotional Process versus Traumatic, Mind/Body State

This section differentiates "shame as an emotional process" ("shame emotion") and "shame as traumatic mind/body state" ("shame state"). Broadly speaking, the same can be said when differentiating "pride as an emotional process" ("pride emotion") and "pride as traumatic, mind/body state" ("pride state"). While these shame subtypes are discussed separately for heuristic purposes, within a patient's subjective reality they often co-occur and even trigger each other. Likewise, adaptive guilt (other-reparative) or maladaptive guilt (self-punitive) and/or shame or pride emotions can, for many RT survivors, trigger traumatic shame and pride states (Chapter 1).

Shame as an emotional process is related to but not the same as shame as a recurring, traumatic, shame state (Herman, 2012, 2011, 2007, 2006). Although bearing a family resemblance, shame as emotion versus mind/body state is neither the same nor treated the same psychotherapeutically. Broadly speaking, shame as an emotional process refers to temporarily *feeling* shame. In contrast, shame as a long-lasting, traumatic, mind/body state refers to *being* shame, or more accurately *nonbeing* an aspect of self or one's entire self as an expression of shame.

Shame as emotional process has a few features significantly affecting therapy with RT survivors. An emotional process is ever-changing, as seen in the Latinate word origin of "emotion," from an assimilated form of ex "out" + *movere* "to move" (Emotion, word origin). Shame as emotion is a transient experience of "part self with shaming part self" (intrarelational), and/or "self with shaming other" (interrelational). Two shame subtypes as emotional processes are "good enough me shame" and "not good enough me shame" (formerly "bad me shame"; Benau, 2017, pp. 11–12).

Shame states (Herman, 2012, 2011, 2007, 2006) are subtypes of relational, traumatic mind/body states and by definition include different degrees of structural dissociation (SD). Shame states are conceptualized as features of dissociated parts of self (Van der Hart et al., 2006) preoccupied with shame-related matters. Conceptually, mind/body "states" are characterized by a lowered degree of complexity than "parts" (Moskowitz & Van der Hart, 2020).

DeYoung's (2015) description of shame points toward dissociative states: "Shame is the experience of one's felt sense of self disintegrating in relation to a dysregulating other" (p. 18). As with dissociated parts of self, shame states represent triggered reactions developed in the face of overwhelming, emotional and/or physical abuse, and/or underwhelming, emotional and interpersonal neglect. Two shame state subtypes are described, "not me shame" and "no me shame" (see Table 2.1).

Table 2.1 Shame Subtypes

	Adaptive	*Maladaptive*
Shame as emotional process (acute)	Good enough me shame	Not good enough me shame
Shame as traumatic state (chronic)	None	Not me shame No me shame

Shame as Emotional Process: "Good Enough Me Shame" and "Not Good Enough Me Shame"

Good Enough Me Shame

Within shame as a conscious, emotional process there are two subtypes, "good enough me shame" (also known as "self-righting shame") and "not good enough me shame," also known as pathogenic or toxic shame (Bradshaw, 1988). My terms echo Winnicott's (1984/1956) "good enough mother" (p. 300). The person experiencing good enough me shame does not think of themselves as "good" but rather "good enough." From an evolutionary perspective this shame subtype is "adaptive," supporting individual and group survival (Greenberg & Iwakabe, 2011, p. 72). Good enough me shame is consistent with Schore's (2003) discussion of a securely attached toddler who feels shame when their parent abruptly exclaims "Careful!" to not break something. This parent repairs the bond by following this rupture with a hug, telling the child they love them and want them safe.

In good enough me shame the person recognizes from a nonreactive, self-accepting place they have not been true to themselves. This shame subtype is "self-righting" as it helps the person return to living according to their values.

Good enough me shame is neurophysiologically well-regulated. Following Ogden et al.'s (2006) window of optimal arousal model, optimal arousal occurs between two parallel lines, where above the upper line represents "hyperarousal," as in rage and terror, and below the bottom line "hypoarousal," as in despair and emotional shutdown. (See also Siegel's [1999] window of tolerance.) In good enough me shame, the person remains between the two lines, typically toward the bottom line. The person experiencing good enough me shame feels, deals, and relates effectively with themselves and others.

Clinical Vignette of Good Enough Me Shame: "Laura" and the Value of Shame

Laura was a patient highly prone to experience "not good enough me shame," "not me shame," and even "no me shame." Laura's history included profound emotional nonattunement and neglect by both parents. Laura taught me about good enough me shame when she shared: "I didn't live up to what I know I am capable of, and how I want to be with others. I don't feel crushed or like I don't deserve to exist [as she felt when gripped by punishing 'not good enough me shame' or annihilating 'no me shame'], but I do feel shame nonetheless. I want to be better next time."

Not Good Enough Me Shame

Previously named "bad me shame" (Benau, 2017) is now "not good enough me shame," as feelings of "inadequacy" rather than "badness" predominate. Not good enough me shame and its associated internal working model (Bowlby, 1969) develop in response to what a caregiver *does* (active or presence shaming) and *does not do* (passive or absence shaming), both disrupting optimal development. Active/presence shaming is exemplified by a latency age child returning home from school excited to share their day and their parent responding harshly, "Don't bother me you idiot! I'm on the phone!". Passive/absence shaming occurs when a caregiver repeatedly fails to meet their child's developmental needs, as when they ignore their child's desire to share their day.

Clinical Vignette: From Not Good Enough Me Shame to Good Enough Me Shame and Reparative Guilt

"Frieda" was prone to feeling not good enough me shame after behaving in ways that harmed a job she loved and a close friend. In this session, Frieda moved from not good enough me shame to good enough me shame and reparative guilt.

Frieda felt "bad" about her current job situation, but too ashamed to share these feelings with her close friend whom she had hurt. As I helped Frieda regulate her not good enough me shame, she was able to recall how her work still engendered good enough me pride. As Frieda began to feel sad about the changes at work, her self-protective reactions quickly took her away from grief and back into not good enough me shame.

We next uncovered Frieda's implicit belief that she must shame herself to ensure she never "mess up" again. I think of this as "shame as a primitive, punitive parent," like a teen might "parent" their younger sibling. Frieda's now conscious awareness of this previously implicit belief helped her realize she could learn from her mistakes without plummeting into not good enough me shame. By the session's end, Frieda returned to feeling good enough me shame and adaptive, reparative guilt, motivated to speak with her friend about the changes at work and her regrets for hurting them.

From an attachment perspective, good enough me shame enabled Frieda to reconnect with her better self, making it possible to feel reparative guilt and reconnect with her friend. This not uncommon pattern involves moving from a repair with the self (i.e., not good enough shame blended with self-punitive guilt to good enough me shame), to a repair with the other (i.e., good enough me shame to reparative guilt). When the repair is well-received by the hurt other, both guilt and shame are assuaged.

Shame as Traumatic Mind/Body State: "Not Me Shame" and "No Me Shame"

Two traumatic "shame states" reflect predictable reactions to RT, that is, "not me shame" and "no me shame." Shame states are conceptualized as dissociated parts of self (Van der Hart et al., 2006) ("not me shame") or one's entire being ("no me shame") preoccupied with shame-related matters, especially experiences of inadequacy and defectiveness. Unlike shame as emotional process, shame states represent the survivor's mostly unconscious, dissociated relationship with shame.

Not Me Shame

The person living with not me shame has one or more dissociative parts of self (Van der Hart, 2006) primarily characterized by the relationally traumatic effects of shame. This person dissociates from those self-aspects the primary caregiver could not tolerate and deemed inadequate or defective, and develops a structurally dissociated part of self retaining this relational knowing. For example, a person growing up with an angry, emotionally abusive, and shaming parent may disconnect unconsciously from self-aspects, such as anger, reminiscent of the abusive parent. Likewise, a child growing up with a needy parent might dissociate from normal dependency needs and view themselves as "weak." The patient gripped by not me shame often projects unconsciously onto others nonrecognized, shamed attributes that are enacted in the patient-therapist relationship.

Not me shame refers to dissociative parts of self outside conscious awareness. Not me shame manifests behaviorally in clinical enactments (see Bromberg, 2011a, 2011b), and/or symptoms such as chronic anxiety, depression, pain, troubled eating, addictions, etc. Depending upon a person's interpersonal history, subtle and dramatic stimuli can trigger not me shame. For example, if a shame-prone person says hello to a friend and the friend fails to respond, that person could, given a history of being raised by a nonresponsive, depressed parent, plummet into a not me shame state, for example, "I'm unworthy of attention, especially when I seek it," while consciously believing, "My friend did not see me."

Shame states like other trauma states are recursive. The person living with shame states internalizes the shaming attachment figure and habitually replays self-shaming (Scheff, In press), often outside awareness. A perfectionist might brutally attack themselves for a small social gaffe. In this instance, the "not me" self-aspect reflects a reaction to the adaptive desire to rely upon others and learn from mistakes.

Whenever a person recursively shames themselves and their mind/brain/body is painfully overwhelmed, they react automatically by what I call "leaving the scene of the crime." Shame that triggers mind/body leave taking (LT) is not consciously "felt" as is shame as emotion. (See Chapter 3, for more on LT versus structural dissociation [SD].)

Clinical Vignette of Not Me Shame: "If Not Depressed, Rage?"

"Karl" grew up with a depressed father and a sometimes rageful emotionally and physically abusive mother. As a young adult, Karl sought therapy to cope with cyclical depression and anxiety. Karl was unaware that underlying his agitated depression was "not me shame," for years misconstrued as "sadness." Karl's inability to express adaptive anger and set healthy boundaries also reflected dissociated "not me shame." Not wanting to be like his mother, Karl projected anger onto authority figures, viewing them as punitive and shaming. Likewise, he compulsively appeased others "to calm them down." In therapy, Karl processed several layers of shame linked with bullying by his mother and older sibling (active/presence shaming), and abandonment by his depressed father (passive/absence shaming). Over time, Karl was able to feel and express adaptive anger without becoming self-punitive or abusive like his mother.

No Me Shame

As in not me shame, no me shame refers to a dissociative part of self (Van der Hart, 2006) primarily characterized by shame or relationally traumatic effects of shame. Unlike not me shame, the person experiencing no me shame lives in a chronic state of dissociation because the bond with the primary caregiver(s) could not tolerate their very being. This person has a structurally dissociated part of self retaining the relational knowing that they, as a whole person, never existed in the mind and heart of their caregiver(s). This dissociative part has no experience other than shame, so the term "part" does not capture, experientially, the totality of no me shame.

No me shame is one predictable response to chronic, absent parenting, that is, a psychologically and physically withdrawn parent not attuned to their child. It can also be the consequence of being hated and wanted dead by the caregiver. A caregiver's "absence" and "presence" can co-occur. No me shame develops in response to not being seen, recognized, or felt. If "no me shame" could speak, it might say, "You're not here, you don't exist, and I'm not here, I don't exist. The more I'm not here, the more I do not recognize and feel myself (i.e., self-alienated); the more you're not here, the more I do not feel you nor anyone with me (i.e., socially isolated)."

"No me shame" is the most pernicious, destructive, and hardest to detect shame subtype. No me shame is difficult to depict with experience-near language, developing no later than 9 and 18 months and sometimes in utero or at birth, before the child can verbalize their profoundly dysregulating experience.

Wille's (2014) shame of existing captures my view of no me shame:

> By the "shame of existing" I mean shame at the fact that we as a person exist as we are and principally the very fact that we exist. This concerns not an aspect or aspects of who or what we are [i.e., my not me shame], but our entire person, our being [i.e., my no me shame]. It is not shame about "who I am" but about "the fact that I am." Whereas shame is usually characterized by the urge to hide and conceal, the shame of existing impels the subject to disappear or dissolve.
>
> (p. 701)

Wille's (2014) patient described debilitating beliefs accompanying no me shame:

> *My very foundations are bad—that's the way I was born.* When I get something, I don't deserve it because *I'm not rooted in good soil.* The only way I'm allowed to exist is by taking care of others. *It is impossible to exist,*

> *And it feels as if I don't exist*, but just slip in between things. *I could just vanish without anyone noticing.* That would be best, just to disappear ... *I'm not allowed to exist the way I am. I'm ashamed of being alive. I'm so terribly ashamed of being.*
>
> (p. 702, my emphasis)

No me shame is one effect of implicitly perceived annihilation. Annihilation can be physical, psychological, or both. As Wille (2014) observed, "the shame of existing may [represent] the internalization by the baby of the rejecting, hating and perhaps even murderous mother" (p. 712).

Infants seek proximity with attachment figures to survive physically and psychologically. To exist psychologically, the infant learns they live in the heart and mind of their caregiver. To dwell in another is to be seen, felt, and at the deepest level "recognized," that is, "to [be] perceive[d] as existing or true" (Recognize, definition). For a dependent infant or child to exist psychologically, they must be recognized, remembered, and reembodied by their caregiver and later themselves.

> A child not being touched and not being allowed to touch play an important part in this situation. Touching and being touched, as the earliest forms of communication, are of great importance for the development of awareness of the boundaries of the self and self-cohesion.
>
> (Wille, 2014, p. 712)

How a caregiver touches the child powerfully affects the child's developing self-worth. Touch that is attuned, reassuring, and protective is experienced by the child very differently from touch that is disconnected from the child and the caregiver. When a mother sees, feels, touches, and delights in their child's being their true self (Winnicott, 1965), reciprocally responding with matching vitality affects (Stern, 1985), the child knows experientially, "I exist" and "I am good enough, worthy of an enlivening response."

No me shame develops in the presence of unbearable relational absence. Absent caregiving may result from parents with severe depression, dissociative disorders, psychosis, and institutional caregivers who may meet the child's physical needs yet fail to respond to their unique way of being and ever-changing psychological, social, emotional, and relational needs (Spitz, 1946).

The child and later adult who endures chronic, no me shame states may experience death terror and panic quickly supplanted by neurophysiological shutdown (Porges, 2011). Shutdown is seen in chronic emotional numbing, depression, depersonalization/derealization (DP/DR), detachment, and more severe forms of dissociation, including SD (Van der Hart et al., 2006). No me shame fills the void of nonbeing. The person gripped by no me shame, however, is often not conscious of their terror of dissolution nor *feeling* shame: "The shame of existing is thus often concealed and largely, if not wholly, unconscious" (Wille, 2014, p. 703).

Clinical Vignette of No Me Shame: Ceasing to Be

"Laura" was a RT survivor of profound psychological nonattunement and absence. In addition to experiencing good enough me shame, not good enough me shame, and not me shame, Laura was intermittently taken over by no me shame. As Wille (2014) observed, "where the shame of existing is involved, less intense shame is never absent" (p. 714).

Laura grew up with a father who was psychotic and/or highly dissociative. Laura said her father was always "looking right through me, as if I weren't there," an experience Laura's husband attested to when meeting Laura's father. While Wille (2014) said his no me shame patient had "intense intolerance of my looking at him," Laura was pained by others *not* gazing at her with genuine interest

Laura shared a fantasy of becoming enraged when a woman standing behind her in line was served first. In session, Laura calmed after imagining knocking the woman down and threatening to hurt her. Although Laura would never act on this fantasy, it vividly captured one reaction to no me shame. *Now* she had the woman's attention and *proof she existed*.

Laura loved to fly. She began therapy seeking help for intermittently feeling overcome by a terrifying, kinesthetic sensation that the plane's floor would drop out beneath her. Laura did not see herself falling to her death but rather ceasing to exist, the terror of disintegration. I now understand Laura's fear of falling into no-being as giving words to a dreaded dissociative future based in a traumatic body memory (Van der Kolk, 2014a, 2014b) of her father's chronically absent parenting. In addition to the "mothers of patients with such problems seemingly not only reject[ing] their children but even wish[ing] to deny their existence" (Wille, 2014, p. 712), Laura's father was utterly incapable of seeing and responding to his daughter. Winnicott (1960) might say Laura's father never truly "held" (p. 589) Laura, nor recognized her subjective reality.

There are five pride subtypes, two conscious and adaptive, "good enough me pride" and "pro-being pride," one conscious and maladaptive, "better me pride," and two less conscious and dissociated, "not me pride" and "no me pride." The most important addition is the enduring, transformative mind/body state I call "pro-being pride" (Table 2.2).

Table 2.2 Pride Subtypes

	Adaptive	*Maladaptive*
Pride as emotional process (acute)	Good enough me pride	Better me pride
Pride as transformative state (enduring)	Pro-being pride	
Pride as traumatic state (chronic)	None	Not me pride No me pride

Pride as an Emotional Process

Good Enough Me Pride

"Good enough me pride," elsewhere named authentic pride (Tracy, 2016), is best compared with "good enough me shame." Good enough me pride is an adaptive, short-lived emotional process rather than a maladaptive, chronic, traumatic, dissociated mind/body state.

Since "better me pride" or hubristic pride (Tracy, 2016) elevates the person above others to the point of self- and other-harm, can pride ever be adaptive? Extensive, nonclinical research suggests yes (Tracy, 2016). Good enough me pride reflects positive feelings of self-regard in response to genuine achievement, accomplishment, mastery, and/or triumph.

When a young child walks for the first time, they appear elated and proud. If they could speak, they might exclaim, "Look at me! I did it!" Authentic pride accompanying mastery and triumph may be genetically hardwired, as evidenced by the stereotypical pride display (i.e., arms and fists extended up and over the head) seen in congenitally blind athletes who never saw nor were taught this gesture (Tracy, 2016).

Good enough me pride refers to an emotion many agree is socially acceptable and adaptive. Good enough me pride statements include "I am proud of myself" for working hard to achieve a personally valued goal, and a parent beaming "I'm proud of you" when honoring their child's accomplishment.

While the importance of good enough pride is largely absent from the psychotherapy literature, good enough me pride is seen in patients who confront their trauma and, with considerable effort, vanquish inner and interpersonal demons. Good enough me pride fits with Janet's description of an act of triumph. Janet (1932) wrote that when "there is success and a triumph, all our functions are better" (p. 36), and that an act of triumph following trauma processing "requires effort and *results in a sense of pride that is a form of joy and heals shame*" (Janet, 1935, cited in Barral & Meares, 2019, p. 121, my emphasis).

The pride that follows a patient's mastery of debilitating psychological symptoms is vital not merely because it feels good, but because it strengthens the patient's faith in himself, the therapist, the therapeutic process, and resolve to face life challenges. Good enough me pride motivates patients to persevere and achieve their psychotherapy goals.

Clinical Vignette of Good Enough Me Pride: "I Can't Believe I Feel Good about Myself Again"

"Kristina" sought therapy to address cyclical depression and anxiety. Intermittently, Kristina began sessions feeling ashamed of herself for many things, including minor work errors and not pleasing her narcissistically vulnerable parents.

Kristina's therapist worked from a Coherence Therapy (CT) perspective (Ecker et al., 2012). The CT practitioner adopts a functionally coherent perspective (Chapter 4, #9, Functional Coherence [FC]), whereby all psychological and behavioral symptoms make sense at one level of experience. Kristina's reacting sarcastically when criticized made sense given Kristina's history of being bullied by her older sibling, where quick, verbal comebacks were her only defense.

Kristina frequently began sessions believing there was something fundamentally wrong with her, and left feeling understood and accepted by her therapist and proud of her achievements in therapy and life. This reflected Kristina's good enough me pride.

Better Me Pride

"Better me pride" has been called hubristic pride by some researchers (Tangney & Fischer, 1995; Tracy, 2016) and in more extreme forms malignant narcissism (Shaw, 2014; Steiner, 2006). Hubris and malignant narcissism refer to excessive pride, arrogance, looking down upon, and shaming others. Better me pride is best contrasted with not good enough me shame, in that this pride is also a maladaptive, emotional process rather than a traumatic, mind/body state. The hubristic person often finds others prone to not good enough me shame, like a hand in glove.

The Myth of Icarus, where Icarus's hubris led him to fly too close to the sun, reveals several aspects of the phenomenology of better me pride and good enough me pride. First, pride is "up," adaptive in the up-regulation of energy and arousal, and maladaptively "up" as in above others. Adaptive pride is about being "out" or "exposed," pleasurably sharing one's genuine capacities, or maladaptively showing off. Adaptive pride goes toward the light as in the light of day, but when excessive, as with Icarus, results in getting burned by hubris. Adaptive pride is light and buoyant as contrasted with dark, heavy, and burdened with shame. In contrast, maladaptive pride is ungrounded and above it all, including all others. Finally, the better me proud person is mobilized from a place of implicitly neuroceived danger or life threat (Porges, 2011), rather than the relational safety of good enough me pride.

Clinical Vignette of Better Me Pride: "Listening to You Is Like Watching Paint Dry"

In couple therapy, it is not uncommon one spouse criticizes the other spouse and seeks the therapist's endorsement. "Mary" regularly found fault in "Jack," including how he played with their children. Jack absorbed Mary's harsh judgment, rarely countering her. Mary insisted I give my professional validation: "The way he plays with the kids is terrible, right?" I did not agree with Mary, but nor did I know how to acknowledge her frustration without denigrating Jack. Given my own RT history, I felt overwhelmed by her overt shaming, fearing it would be directed my way. I froze, not able to think or speak for 30 seconds. Mary could not tolerate my silence and contemptuously blurted, "Listening to you is like watching paint dry." An example of "better me pride" that stayed with me for years.

Pride as a Traumatic Mind/Body State: "Not Me Pride" and "No Me Pride"

As with traumatic shame states, two traumatic "pride states" reflect predictable reactions to RT, that is, "not me pride" and "no me pride." Pride states are conceptualized as dissociated parts of self (Van der Hart et al., 2006) ("not me pride") or one's entire being ("no me pride") preoccupied with pride-related matters, especially the absence of authentic pride. Unlike pride as emotional process, pride states represent the survivor's mostly unconscious, dissociated relationship with pride.

"Not Me Pride"

The person living with not me pride has one or more dissociative parts of self primarily characterized by pride, or more precisely the relationally traumatic effects of the lack of pride-in-self. This person dissociates from positive self-aspects that the bond with the primary caregiver could not tolerate, and develops a structurally dissociated part of self that retains this relational knowing. Therapists discover a patient's dissociated pride indirectly; to paraphrase Bromberg (2011b), in the shadows. Pride states play out in interpersonal enactments in psychotherapy, and intrarelationally when a patient's dissociative barriers weaken and these pride-preoccupied parts erupt emotionally and/or somatically.

In not me pride, a survivor dissociates from at least one positive attribute, unconsciously projecting onto others self-aspects that would otherwise engender good enough me pride and pro-being pride. Not me pride is seen when a patient envies others' positive attributes they are convinced they lack. Not me pride develops in relationships where the other person cannot tolerate the survivor's pleasure in nor display of aliveness, particularly in relation to something that would bring them genuine pride. The caregiver's intolerance may be active, openly attacking or dismissing the survivor's pride, or passive, neither noticing nor responding to their adaptive pride. Not me pride may or may not be accompanied by maladaptive, not good enough me shame, not me shame, and no me shame.

Clinical Vignette of Not Me Pride: "I Wish I Were Him"

"Kara" was convinced she was not creative while insisting others were, particularly male artists. Kara was a RT survivor, bullied by an older sister whenever Kara expressed pleasure in something she created. After several years of psychotherapy, Kara came to realize, first with her trusted therapist and later with others, that although not artistic she was creative in her own way. During the course of therapy, Kara learned that what she previously located in admired friends and professionals were qualities she too uniquely possessed. Experiencing good enough pride when interacting creatively enabled Kara to lessen her envy and idealization of others.

"No Me Pride"

The person living with no me pride has a dissociative part of self (Van der Hart, 2006) primarily characterized by the relationally traumatic effects of absent pride. The person living with no me pride developed a structurally dissociated part of self that retained the relational knowing that they, as a whole person, never existed in the mind and heart of their caregiver, and more fundamentally were never enjoyed for simply being. This dissociative "part" has no experience other than the absence of pride, so the term "part" does not capture, experientially, the totality of no me pride.

No me pride is one predictable response to chronic absent parenting, that is, a psychologically and physically withdrawn parent not attuned to their child. It can also be the consequence of being hated and wanted dead by the caregiver. Caregiver "absence" (i.e., "My life never includes the child") and "presence" ("I wish the child were never born") can co-occur. No me pride is a consequence of a person not being seen, recognized, or felt for anything they achieve, and more so for who they are.

I still find it difficult imagining how a person profoundly neglected, dismissed, not seen, felt, or held, and/or hated by a caregiver, experiences pride. When a person feels invisible, there is no one to "contain" or "feel" pride about anything they do, or even take pleasure in activities and interests that would otherwise engender pride. The no me proud person often lives "as if," dissociated and disembodied, lacking a well-developed sense of self. No matter how successful they might appear, and no matter how much others enjoy them, this person lacks an embodied self that is capable of feeling pride in their actions and being.

Clinical Vignette of No Me Pride: "I Don't Know the Person You Know"

As previously described, "Laura," a survivor of RT marked by chronic nonattunement, was living with no me shame and all other shame subtypes. Laura was a bright, capable woman who achieved considerable professional success and, despite her barren childhood, worked diligently in therapy to build a mutually trusting and satisfying marriage.

Despite Laura's many successes in love and work, whenever I appreciated her achievements she deflected, for example, by attributing her progress to me. Despite great gains during our 10-year psychotherapy, Laura rarely acknowledged her genuine accomplishments (i.e., good enough pride), nor took delight in being the remarkable woman she was (i.e., pro-being pride).

I often marveled aloud how Laura discovered her own creative pathways out of chronic mental anguish. Whenever I praised Laura, she retorted, "I had to."

Laura had nowhere to place my positive regard, still living under the influence of an internalized father who failed to recognize her existence, and a "weak" mother who offered Laura nothing more. Laura's therapy was also constrained by her having difficulty embodying pro-being pride, for example, enjoying herself being genuinely enjoyed by me and others. Were Laura to return to therapy, we would continue to work on diminishing the dominance of specific life-negating, internalized beliefs, and help her reconnect with her pro-being pride.

Pride as Transformative, Mind/Body State: Pro-being Pride

Pro-being Pride: Concept and Phenomena

Pro-being pride ("pro-being" for short) is discussed last for several reasons. First, although pro-being pride is adaptive, it is not an emotional process. Pro-being pride is an enduring mind/body state, a potential living within us at all times, neither trauma-based nor byproduct of post-traumatic growth (Calhoun & Tedeschi, 2006). I have chosen the word "enduring" rather than "chronic" to avoid any pathological connotations. Pro-being refers to discovering, rediscovering, and taking deep pleasure in being and becoming who we truly are, in who others truly are, and in relating authentically. Pro-being pride lies at the heart of transformation in psychotherapy generally and specifically guides my work with RT survivors.

The term "pro-being pride" comes from the word origin of "proud" (Proud, word origin). "Proud" is derived from the Latinate "prodesse," where "prod" means "for" and "esse" translates as "to be" or, in my view, a person's "essence" or "being."

Though good enough me pride and pro-being pride are both adaptive pride subtypes, they are not identical. Good enough me pride focuses on one or more aspects of self, such as a person's valued achievements (Tracy, 2016) or attributes. Pro-being is closer to Bergson's (1911) elan vital and Rogers' (1961) description of "the quiet joy in being one's self ... a spontaneous relaxed enjoyment, a primitive *joie de vivre*" (pp. 87–88, author's emphasis). Transcending achievement, pro-being enters the realm of existential and organismic aliveness.

Aspects of pro-being pride phenomena have been described by philosophers, poets, psychologists, and neuroscientists before me. In *The Ethics*, 17th-century philosopher Baruch Spinoza (2006/1677) wrote about the pleasure derived from developing a relationship with the unique workings of one's own mind. Spinoza viewed mind and body as two attributes of a singular substance he called Nature or God, so when referring to the activity of "mind," he was also describing the activity of the body, emotions, etc. (Nijenhuis, March 21, 2020, personal communication):

> When the mind regards itself and its own power of activity, it feels pleasure: and *that pleasure is greater in proportion to the distinctness wherewith it conceives itself and its own power of activity.*
>
> (Spinoza, 2006/1677, p. 134, my emphasis)

My conceptualization of pro-being pride began with an *inter*relational perspective (self with others), then drew inward toward an *intra*relational connection (self with self), and finally back toward the *extra*relational realm, when one feels connected with all things, a unity consciousness (Goleman, 1972; Weil, 1986; Wilber, 1998).

The following poem by psychoanalyst Marion Woodman (1998, p. 437) speaks to the intrarelational, interrelational, and extrarelational aspects of pro-being pride and its healing potential. Where I use the term "being," Woodman refers to "soul":

Abandoned Souls

Abandoned souls
bring themselves forth
whether we work
with ourselves or not.
They seem insatiable because we fail
to understand their language.

When we connect with our souls,
we connect with the soul
of every human being.
We resonate with all living things.
That's where healing is.
(p. 437, my emphasis)

Attachment-oriented psychologists Daniel Brown and David Elliott describe five major conditions that promote secure attachment (Brown & Elliott, 2016). The first three include security and protection, attunement, and comfort/soothing. The fourth aligns well with what I mean by pro-being pride and is called expressed delight. Referring to parenting, Brown characterized expressed delight this way: "Imagine … parents being openly expressive of everything, taking joy in everything you do, but *more importantly their joy and delight in your being*, because 'expressed delight' is the source of healthy self-esteem" (Van Nuys, 2019, my emphasis). The fifth condition refers to unconditional support of the child's best self, congruent with radical acceptance (Chapter 4, #8, Radical inquiry, radical empathy, radical acceptance, and radical reflection), a requisite ingredient of "self with self" and "self with other" delight. Intrasubjective and intersubjective delight is founded in a deep acceptance of one's unique personhood.

Now, to my abbreviated definition of pro-being pride, embodying interrelational, intrarelational, and extrarelational qualities of delight:

> "I delight in being me, delighting in you delighting in being yourself, with me" (self with other); "I delight in being me, delighting in me delighting in being myself, with me" (self with self); and "I delight in being me, delighting in me delighting in being myself, with all that is" (self with world).

While pro-being pride expresses pleasure in being, belonging, and connecting with all things, it also incorporates embodied activity and agency. Following Spinoza (2006/1677), pro-being pride is reflected in the mind's "own [unique] power of activity" (p. 134). Nijenhuis (2017) added that sorrow emerges when our "being" is thwarted by ourselves or others, and when enduring the effects of RT. I conceive of this sorrow as existential grief and shame for life unlived (Chapter 7). In contrast, joy emerges within ourselves and between ourselves and others when we are active and effective in the world:

> I propose and illustrate several principles for the progression from passions to actions. Individuals engage in passions and experience sorrow the more they are mostly acted on, that is, influenced by external causes. *The more they are their own master, and the more they act, the more they experience joy.*
> (Nijenhuis, 2017, p. 66, my emphasis)

The freedom to act embodies quintessential pro-being pride and is evidenced in spontaneity, improvisation, creativity, humor, and nonstructured play.

Protoself and Pro-being Pride

While not considered from the perspective of pro-being pride, select researchers and neuroscientists have identified specific changes in the growing fetus and newborn that point toward the earliest markers of a unique, protoself. The concept of a protoself suggests each person has an idiosyncratic, organismic way of being and relating that is first observable in utero. Under optimal conditions as Brown (Van Nuys, 2019) described, the intersubjective and intrasubjective experience of pro-being pride refers to the infant's nascent "self" celebrated first by the infant's caregivers and later by the young child with themselves.

Delafield-Butt and Gangopadhyay (2013) argued the fetus and young infant show a motoric intentionality consistent with the concept of primitive "self":

> *Efficient prospective motor control, evident in human activity from birth, reveals an adaptive intentionality of a primary, pre-reflective, and pre-conceptual nature that we identify here as sensorimotor intentionality. We identify a structural continuity between the emergence of this earliest form of prospective movement and the structure of mental states as intentional or content-directed in more*

advanced forms. We base our proposal on motor control studies, from fetal observations through infancy. These studies reveal movements are guided by anticipations of future effects, even from before birth. This implies that *these movements*, even if they are simple and discrete, *are the actions of an intentional agent.*

(p. 399, my emphasis)

Damasio (1999) offered another description of specific "feelings," again in the fetus in utero, that constitute a "protoself": "In theory, primordial feelings occur regardless of whether the protoself is engaged by objects and events external to the brain. *They need to be related to the living body and nothing else*" (p. 323, my emphasis).

Select neuroscientists further suggested a protoself develops when the brain's superior colliculi (SC), located in the midbrain of the brainstem, comes online. The SC orient the fetus and later developing infant to their external environment, determining if stimuli are safe or unsafe. The SC sends neuronal messages to the periaqueductal gray (PAG), also located in the midbrain. The PAG of the fetus and newborn, in turn, show primitive, preaffective forms of active and passive defensive responding (Corrigan & Christie-Sands, 2020).

According to the neuroscientist Panksepp (1998), "The superior colliculus is especially interesting because it is here that we begin to get a glimmer of the first evolutionary appearance of a sophisticated representation of self" (p. 77). Following Panksepp, Solms (2021, p. 139) wrote:

> The superior colliculi … represent in distilled form the moment-by-moment state of the *objective* (sensory and motor) body, in much the same way as the PAG monitors its *subjective* (need) state. Merker calls this affective/sensory/motor interface between the PAG, the superior colliculi and the midbrain locomotor region the brain's "decision triangle." Panksepp calls it the primal SELF, the very source of our sentient being.
>
> (p. 139)

These neuroscientific observations and theories suggest each person embodies a unique protoself typically predating RT. One exception is that there can be trauma before conception that harms, epigenetically, the child-to-be (Yehuda & Bierer, 2009). This protoself can be observed in the growing fetus' sensorimotor orienting and activity, out of which primordial feelings emerge. Further, I would argue a fetus' nascent orienting, intentionality, and feelings mark the earliest expression of their organismic "interest." Following birth, the growing child's interest continues to reveal essential truths about their way of being and relating to their internal and external worlds.

If indeed each person embodies an idiosyncratic protoself, then by observing them with curiosity and acceptance, their unique ways of being and relating come into focus. When these unique ways of being and relating are celebrated, self with self and self with other, pro-being pride experiences are born and develop. The concept of pro-being pride adds to that of a protoself the experience of self-reflected and other-reflected organismic pleasure that grows into a joyful expression of self-in-relationship.

Pro-being Pride, RT, and Psychotherapy: "Antidote" to Shame and Pride States

Early psychologists and psychotherapists described clinical phenomena consistent with pro-being pride when working with patients we now think of as RT survivors. Janet's (1935) description of an "act of triumph" presaged my understanding of pro-being pride as an intersubjective and intrasubjective experience. "Janet expanded even further to include a similar reciprocal of the self and the culture it exists in, with ceremonies and rituals *bringing people together in an experience of shared joy*, 'a good antidote to depression'" (Barral & Meares, 2019, p. 122, my emphasis).

While I use "delight" and "joy" to denote pro-being pride, it should not be equated with "feeling happy." Pro-being pride is about sharing our truer selves (Winnicott, 1965) with ourselves and inviting others to do the same with us. Pro-being is where personal and collective aliveness are valued and nourished. For example, pro-being is shared when grieving deeply with others who grieve with us.

Pro-being pride is an organismic and somatic experience. I experience my patient's and my own pro-being as a full-bodied tingling sensation, resonating with the patient's authentic, albeit sometimes preconscious aliveness. I have patients who likewise describe their body tingling, sometimes throughout their body, when embodying their truth, coupled with an easing or relaxing of tension in their gut and/or chest.

I believe strongly psychotherapy with RT survivors should privilege pro-being pride. In session, I chance upon a patient's pro-being pride in the smallest of ways, for example, when they smile, speak, and/or move in ways that strike me as particular to them. I also become energized when my patient describes one of their passions, regardless of whether the topic interests me. When my patient experiences prolonged suffering, I sometimes hold the patient's pain in mind and heart while "seeing" and feeling into their pro-being pride, for example, picturing their baby or future adult selves, free of traumatic self-negation.

Pro-being is the most powerful antidote to maladaptive shame and pride as emotional processes and traumatic states. As regards maladaptive shame and pride emotions, a person cannot be "pro" being and "anti" one's own being (not good enough me shame) nor another's being (better me pride). Pro-being pride champions dignity for all (Hicks, 2011). Pro-being never countenances one person over another, nor one part-of-self dominating another part-of-self.

Within traumatic mind/body states, the patient gripped by "not me" and "no me" shame and pride lives with an implicit and often explicit belief that "I am not worthy" or worse, "I am not." In contrast, the patient experiencing pro-being pride embodies implicit and explicit beliefs that, spoken, might proclaim, "I am as worthy of being and celebrating my unique self with you, as you are worthy of being and celebrating your unique self with me."

Maladaptive shame and pride as traumatic mind/body states are fundamentally about dissociation or "dis-association," disconnecting from aspects of self (not good enough me shame) and others (better me pride), and one's essential aliveness (not me shame, no me shame, not me pride, and no me pride). Pro-being pride embodies joyful association: "I am" and "We are." When embodying pro-being, a person is never egocentric, moving naturally toward discovering the intrinsic value of others with enlivened interest.

Living within the expansiveness that is pro-being pride, a person invariably feels deeply connected not only with themselves and others, but with all that is, including the animate and inanimate world. This experience of oneness (Goleman, 1972; Weil, 1986; Wilber, 1998) naturally follows deepening into pro-being pride. (See Chapter 7, on the relationship between pro-being pride and unity consciousness.)

Pro-being pride also rises above seemingly inescapable binds within the trauma bond. For example, a survivor of sexual abuse may believe, with their perpetrator, that they are "special" *and* "disgusting." Gripped by these subjective "realities," the survivor's identity ping pongs between hubristic pride (e.g., "I am special") and not good enough me shame, not me shame and/or no me shame (e.g., "Parts or all of me are disgusting"). Pro-being pride transcends this Gordian knot, replacing "I am special" and "I am disgusting" with "I am."

Clinical Vignette: Improvisational Humor and Pro-being Pride

I worked with "Greg" for 10-years prior to this session. Greg was a bright, self-reflective, and funny man in his mid-20s. For more than the first five years of therapy, Greg lived with debilitating social anxiety and shame that led to marked immobilization when pursuing relationships and employment.

A survivor of RT, Greg's family history was complex. Greg was raised by his mother and father but learned, in his late teens, that the man his mother took him to visit regularly starting when he was two years old was in fact his biological father. Greg's birth father was very narcissistic and for years tried yet failed to turn Greg against his father, whom Greg loved. A sensitive, empathic boy, we learned over time that Greg carried several dissociated parts of his mother's chronic shame and anxiety. For example, whenever his mother felt anxious and inadequate, Greg believed he both caused her suffering and failed miserably to relieve her pain.

Greg and I had worked intensively with his deepest layer of shame, no me shame. We discovered Greg held an implicit belief that his very existence painfully reminded his mother of her own traumatic shame. Greg froze when he learned his beloved older brother did not share the same biological father. By the time of this session, we had disentangled many of these implicit emotions and beliefs, making it possible for Greg to live with less chronic shame and dread.

Greg's self-deprecating wit took many forms. We delighted in our shared absurdist humor that accomplished two things: Speaking with honesty about difficult, shame-evoking topics and making each other laugh with abandon.

Greg and I began this session riffing like improvisational jazz musicians. We found ourselves playing with the word "hypocrite," referring to a "hypo-critical" politician. "Hypocrite" morphed into a fictitious political party I dubbed "the Hypocrats," which led us to "hippo-critics" or "critics of hippos." We agreed "hippo-critics" were a dying breed since hippos charged anyone who criticized them. I suggested "hippocrits" worked in military bungalows from which drones were sent to fly over hippos and criticize them. You get the idea.

After 15 minutes of our riffing, Greg interjected, "Maybe I should talk about something pertaining to therapy." I "reluctantly" agreed. Greg wondered if he should resume dating, recalling how exhausting and time consuming it had previously been. "Maybe I should focus on my college studies," where he now excelled after years of struggle.

Greg off-handedly remarked he was good at flirting. My jaw dropped. For many years, Greg was so frozen in anxiety and shame he never approached attractive girls. In hushed and conspiratorial tones, I suggested, "We probably should keep that dirty little secret to ourselves." Greg laughed, and told me he discovered he was good at quickly reading the women, putting *them* at ease!

Our spontaneous riffing allowed Greg and me to explore his immobilizing anxiety in nonshaming ways. While some see therapeutic play as purposeful, I believe as soon as the therapist becomes intentional it ceases to be play. My play with Greg expressed our mutual delight in being ourselves with each other. Did our riffing enable Greg to be more spontaneous with women? Perhaps, but that was not my plan. We riffed because it was our way of being ourselves with each other and that, an expression of our shared pro-being, enabled Greg to be himself *and* face his debilitating, shame-driven inhibitions.

At my best, I do a form of idiosyncratic, co-riffing with all of my patients. What I call "serious play" is to delight in each other and "be" pro-being pride. Play "works" because it embodies several anti-shaming properties. Play co-regulates arousal instead of shame's rush toward hypoarousal, hyperarousal, immobilization, mind/body LT, and/or SD (Chapter 3). Play is collaboratively intrasubjective, the patient freely and dynamically interacting with parts of himself and intersubjective, the patient engaging spontaneously with their therapist. As in improvisation, each member of the dyad adds to but never one-ups their partner. Play nurtures curiosity, possibility, and discovery, as contrasted with shame's rigid and restrictive modes of thinking, feeling, and behaving (Benau, 2021a).

When I delight in being myself with my patient who delights in being and becoming themselves with me, pro-being pride deprives shame its familiar, internal lodging and everything (e.g., hippocritics) and anything (e.g., intimacy) can be fruitfully explored.

Adaptive and Maladaptive Shame and Pride as Micro Process

Shame and pride subtypes offer a "macro," experience-distant view of shame and pride. The following sections are experience-near, describing processes leading to the development of maladaptive shame and pride as emotions and traumatic, mind/body states. This "micro" perspective is crucial because shame and pride emotions and especially chronic, trauma states often seem to have no origin, as though they always were and will be, or suddenly erupt, as if out of nowhere. The more therapists understand and perceive how maladaptive shame and pride come into being, the more they can intervene effectively, helping the patient mindfully observe and, over time, shift their relationship with these anguishing experiences.

A Five-State Shift Model of Shame: From Aliveness to Shame and Dissociation

I first identified a four-step model of shame at the micro level (Benau, 2017), and later described five state shifts from aliveness to shame and dissociation (Benau, 2018). (For a cartoon rendition of this five-step model, see *Coyote Fall* [Anatkramer, 2008]).

The following delineates a sequence of five mind/body states. These state shifts occur as an adaptive or maladaptive emotional process or as a triggered, traumatic state. In both instances, these processes quickly take a person out of "aliveness" into the relative "deadness" of shame, mind/body LT, and/or SD.

Before I describe the five mind-body states associated with shame, a few caveats: While these five mind-body states are numbered 1 through 5, state shifts are often *not* experienced in a linear sequence. Many people with a history of being taken over by shame or shame states when triggered abruptly depart or rarely reside in State 1 ("Going on being" and "Pro-being pride"), spend barely seconds or skip entirely State 2 (Shock) and State 3 (Drop), going directly into State 4 (Shame Proper) and/or State 5 (Shame Self-protective Emotional Responses and Self-protective Traumatic Reactions).

RT survivors often present in a chronic, traumatic shame state with dissociation. When a patient's LT (previously dissociation as process) and especially SD (Van der Hart, 2021) are most prominent, the patient often does not *feel* and therefore is unaware they are living with shame. Further, different mind/body states can co-occur or rapidly switch in succession. One example is when a person gripped by a shame state repeatedly alternates between embodied, "felt" shame, and "not felt" shame-induced LT, including depersonalization/derealization (DP/DR). (See Chapter 3 for more on the relationship between shame, pride, LT, and SD.)

Finally, while I have chosen the word "state," it is important to understand these "states" are never "static." They are always dynamic, changing, and shifting between other states. No matter how iterative, states are never "fixed."

State 1: "Going on Being" and "Pro-being Pride"

For the purposes of this discussion, I situate "going on being" and "pro-being pride" phenomenologically and neurophysiologically in relation to maladaptive shame. "Going-on-being" (Winnicott, 1960, p. 586) refers to a person being themselves, attentive to and engaged with their interests and pursuits, as well as with others, with little to no inhibiting self-consciousness. Pro-being pride is a special variant of going-on-being, the intrinsic delight in being one's true self (Winnicott, 1965) with oneself and others.

State 2: Surprise or Shock

For the purposes of this discussion, *surprise* is associated with shame as an emotional process, and *shock* is linked with shame as a traumatic mind/body state. Surprise and shock both represent an abrupt interruption of a person's aliveness or going-on-being, as well as their pro-being or pleasure in a genuine self, other, and relationship. Both surprise and shock initially result in an increase in arousal.

Following the window of tolerance (Seigel, 1999) and window of optimal arousal (Ogden et al., 2006) models, a "window" is conceived as lying between two parallel lines (see Table 2.3).

The window represents a person's neurophysiologically regulated response to self, others, and environment. Within the window a person feels, deals, and relates effectively to others and themselves. They can be sad, happy, afraid, bored, etc., but their emotional and behavioral responses remain well-regulated.

When a person is *surprised*, their arousal immediately rises, moving toward but not above the top line, or drops, shifting arousal toward but not below the bottom line. Surprise, without triggering body memories of RT may, for example, excite, confuse, or embarrass a person, but will not cause a traumatic, shame state that takes the person outside their window. In psychotherapy, safe surprises (Bromberg, 2011a, 2003) are what therapists seek to engender so that something new and useful emerges for their patients.

In *shock*, the person is either shamed as a result of their own behavior, including thoughts, feelings, and/or actions; or as a consequence of the

Table 2.3 Window of Optimal Arousal and Tolerance

Hyperarousal

Window of Tolerance or Optimal Arousal
"Feel, Deal, and Relate"

Hypoarousal

Sources: Ogden et al. (2006) and Siegel (1999).

response or nonresponse by a significant other; and/or brings to consciousness and/or is traumatically triggered and taken over by a shame-inducing event/memory, thought/belief about self, feeling, physical sensation, action, and/or interaction.

When *shock* occurs, in contrast to surprise, activation rises above the top line into a mind/body state of hyperarousal, and/or below the bottom line, a mind/body state of hypoarousal. The person may experience hyperarousal and hypoarousal at the same time (U. Lanius, March 22, 2018, personal communication), something more common than many realize. When in the zone of hyperarousal, a person experiences overwhelming terror, horror, rage, etc. When associated with traumatic shame states, I have sometimes observed shock accompanied by a holding of the breath, felt in the chest or sternum, followed by physical tensing that can cause shooting pains in the head or upper back. When arousal falls below the bottom line into hypoarousal, emotional and physiological shutdown, numbness, depression, and/or feigned death (Levine, 2010, 1997; Porges, 2011) can occur. When gripped by states of hyperarousal and hypoarousal, the person may be acutely affected or, as with RT survivors, chronically activated and overwhelmed and/or underwhelmed.

Hyperaroused and hypoaroused states move a person outside their window of tolerance, resulting in what I, with others, previously called "dissociation as process" (Benau, 2020, p. 5), and now refer to as an acute or chronic, LT (Chapter 3). LT signifies a shift away from one's thoughts, feelings, and bodily sensations, and is differentiated from SD, a chronic, mind/body organization henceforth used interchangeably with "dissociation" (Van der Hart, 2021). LT is sometimes an adaptive, short-term response, as when a person screens out temporary, "excessive or irrelevant stimuli" (Schimmenti & Caretti, 2016, p. 110), or experiences too little stimuli when bored and spacing out. LT can also be maladaptive, as evidenced in chronic DP/DR. SD develops as a way of adapting to repeated, extreme, overwhelming (abusive), and/or underwhelming (neglectful) interpersonal stress; typically occurs developmentally early; always reflects a "division [that] involves two or more insufficiently integrated dynamic but excessively stable subsystems" (Nijenhuis & Van der Hart, 2011, p. 428); and manifests in states of hyperarousal and hypoarousal.

The shock that rapidly leads to shaming is caused by an active and/or passive, intentional and/or unintentional shaming other (Vogt, 2018). At its worst, shock is experienced as an abrupt "halt" to a person's pro-being pride. Shock results from a consciously perceived or implicitly neuroceived danger or threat (Porges, 2011, 2017) to a person feeling included with others. Shock abruptly interrupts a person's pleasure in being, unexpectedly stopping their flow (Csikszentmihalyi, 1990), their internal and external presence and aliveness. This halt may be perpetrated by an abusive and/or a neglectful other. In each instance, the victim undergoes a rapid, nonvolitional slowing of movement or frozen immobilization in thought, feeling/emotion, physical sensation, energy, action, and interaction (Benau, 2021a, 2021b).

Porges' (2018, 2017, 2011) concept of neuroception can be understood as the implicit, unconscious counterpart of conscious perception that assesses whether the relational environment is safe or not. Porges (2011) focused on safety/unsafety within the external, interrelational environment, but the same principle is beneficially applied to the person's intrarelational landscape. This implicit, automatic assay of the interrelational and/or intrarelational environment results in a rapid, "Yes, safe enough" or "No, not safe enough" reaction. The person's implicit, interrelational readings may or may not be accurate according to others' perception or neuroception of the same interaction. These automatic, safe versus unsafe "reads" are the result of a person's social-emotional history with similar others, as well as other neurophysiological and psychosocial realities, such as age, health, power differentials, social status, etc.

When a person neuroceives safety, they remain within their window of tolerance and operate within what Porges (2011) calls the Social Engagement System (SES), a conscious state of being and being with as described in State 1. When not safe (danger or life threat) is neuroceived, the person automatically engages in various survival strategies that include, often in sequence, fight, flight, and/or high freeze (sympathetic activation), and followed by shutdown (dorsal vagal activation). According to polyvagal theory (Porges, 2011), these hardwired, survival reactions are reflexively engaged in order to restore safe relating.

Fight and/or flight reactions reflect the neuroception of danger and activation of the sympathetic nervous system (SNS) when social engagement (e.g., "Can we talk about this?") fails to restore a felt sense of safety.

At times, fight and flight reactions occur in rapid succession or simultaneously. When a threatening interpersonal experience has been habituated, the person's nervous system may skip fight-flight and go directly to a hyperaroused freeze state, where neither fight nor flight is neuroceived as freeing. *Shock*, State 2, is equivalent to a freeze response in Porges' (2017, 2011) nomenclature. This freeze state reflects hyperarousal rather than hypoarousal, and thus is sometimes called a high freeze state. This should be differentiated from a low freeze state where hypoarousal causes immobilization without safety (see Chapter 4, #15, Shame and Pride: Prototypical Parts).

Porges' (2011) polyvagal theory is but one way of conceptualizing a "shock" phase preceding shame activation. When thinking about fight, flight, and high freeze reactions, we typically refer to activation in the mammalian brain or limbic region. In contrast, some theorists (Corrigan & Christie-Sands, 2018; Corrigan & Elkin-Cleary, 2018) locate in the midbrain of the brainstem the earliest activation of a painful shock that then starts a series of rapid reactions leading to felt shame. According to this midbrain hypothesis, shock activates the superior colliculi (SC), automatically orienting the person toward the shocking stimuli, rapidly followed by activation of the periaqueductal gray (PAG) that prepares the person for active and/or passive defenses. Midbrain activation also initiates affective processing, sending signals up to the limbic brain. The limbic brain then generates an elaborated affective and behavioral response that may ascend to engage the prefrontal cortex and the SES (Porges, 2011), remain in sympathetic activation (mammalian brain), or drop down into Dorsal Vagal Complex (DVC) (reptilian brain) (Porges, 2011).

Whether one views shock as first occurring within the limbic region or midbrain, this activity operates subcortically. These reactions are very rapid and typically, although not always, outside conscious awareness. To bring these phenomena to conscious awareness the patient, often with the therapist's help, must slow things way down so that together they can mindfully observe the patient's physical reactivity with the goal of therapeutic processing of trauma. (For two examples, see Sensorimotor Psychotherapy [SP] [Ogden et al., 2006] and Deep Brain Reorienting [DBR] [Corrigan & Christie-Sands, 2020].)

State 3: Drop (Shame as Emotional Process) versus Drop and Spike (Shame as Traumatic Mind/Body State)

When studying *shame as an acute, emotional process*, in State 3 there is an abrupt drop in arousal. This results from an activation of the parasympathetic nervous system and later what Porges (2011) described as the DVC, yielding neurophysiological shutdown and immobilization with unsafety (Porges, 2011). This rapid drop from normal to lowered arousal, or even from states of hyperarousal to hypoarousal, is commonly described as a sinking feeling. Consistent with Tomkins (1963) affect theory, shame puts a brake on interest and excitement and, in my view, on all unwanted emotions, thoughts, and behavior.

Shame as a chronic, traumatic, mind/body state (shame state), as with other trauma reactions, activates both an increase and decrease in arousal, either simultaneously or in rapid or more prolonged, alternating sequence. Rather than putting a brake on emotion (Tomkins, 1963), a shame state is powerfully endured as both a heightening and shutting down of painful, even anguishing arousal (Corrigan & Elkin-Cleary, 2018). Shame states are intensely confusing and mentally disorganizing, a disorienting somatic and emotional storm consisting in both activation and numbing. When gripped by a shame state, the person's feelings and thoughts take on a global, catastrophic, timeless quality. Feelings of helplessness and powerlessness are accompanied by implicit and explicit beliefs: "I was, I am, and I always be defective, damaged, inferior, etc."

State 4: Shame Proper: Shame as Emotional Process versus Traumatic Mind/Body State

Shame proper, what most people think of as shame, is where the person experiences *shame as an emotional process (acute)* or *shame as a traumatic mind/body state (chronic)*. (See Chapter 1 on the phenomenology of *shame as emotion and traumatic state*, and their characteristic cognitive, emotional, physiological, and behavioral markers.)

Shame as an acute, emotional process typically occurs when the interpersonal threat to a person's aliveness, acceptance, and inclusion is momentary or short-lived, and of mild to moderate intensity. For example, shame as emotion might occur when a person is abruptly told to shut up by someone they respect, or when a person is excited to see someone, says "Hello!", and is ignored.

Neurophysiologically, shame as emotion culminates in a state of hypoarousal, characterized by a loss of energy, motivation, and interest, not unlike when depressed, or a lifelessness akin to feigned death in mammals (Porges, 2011). The shamed person's neurophysiology ("lifeless") matches their self-narrative, moving from "I *feel* worthless" to "I *am* worthless."

In contrast, a *traumatic shame state* typically develops over time as a result of recurrent and/or prolonged shaming events. Shame states are experienced with an intensity and ferocity that Janet (Van der Kolk & Van der Hart, 1989) called vehement emotions. Shame states are repeatedly triggered reactions that overwhelm (in abuse) and/or underwhelm (in neglect) a person's mind/body and nervous system.

Neurophysiologically, hyperarousal and hypoarousal can co-occur or rapidly switch in succession in shame states. As Janet (1930) observed, these traumatic "events … were accompanied by a vehement emotion and a destruction of the psychological system, [that] had left traces" (p. 128). "This initial emotional reaction to the traumatic event ('vehement emotion') accounted for subsequent symptoms: 'Traumas produce their disintegrating effects in proportion to their intensity, duration and repetition'" (Janet, 1909, p. 1558; cited in Van der Kolk & Van der Hart, 1989, p. 1532).

State 5: Shame Self-protective Emotional Responses and Self-protective Traumatic Reactions

Self-protective Responses within Shame as an Emotional Process

Whether an emotional process or traumatic mind/body state, shame is always painful. Consequently, there are a host of self-protective strategies a shamed person employs, typically automatically, to cope with or try to escape their pain. While I acknowledge the contributions of the psychoanalytic literature with regard to defenses (Freud, 1966/1937), I prefer the term "self-protective" as this metaphor is less associated with military action and closer to their function, that is, to protect the person's mind and body from disintegration or destruction.

Since RT survivors often experience shame as emotional process and as a traumatic mind/body state, there are considerable overlaps in self-protective strategies. For heuristic purposes, I am distinguishing two self-protective pathways. For shame as an emotional process, I describe *responses*, and for shame as traumatic mind/body state, I use the term *reactions*. (See Chapter 5 for a differentiation of *responsivity* versus *reactivity*.)

Self-protective responses can be acute or short-lived, or become chronic and habitual. For example, a person can anticipate shaming and failure in specific instances, such as doing poorly on an exam (acute), or always anticipate failure, resulting in depressive thinking and inhibited, withdrawn, and avoidant behavior (chronic).

With respect to *shame as an emotional process*, Nathanson's (1992) compass of shame identified four common defenses (his term) that included fight others, fight self, withdrawal, and avoidance. The protective angry response, or "fight others" activation, is one of several common reactions to shame's rapid downregulation of arousal and emotion. Shame is so deflating, debilitating, and demoralizing that the shamed person often reacts with intense anger in an unconscious attempt to restore feeling alive, empowered, and, from a psychospiritual perspective, to reclaim their soul.

The "fight self" response is one with which most people are familiar. This is consistent with a punitive super-ego or self-punishment, as when a person believes they are worthless, a nobody, etc., or worse, when engaged in bodily self-harm and suicide (Howell, 2020). Self-punitive guilt and/or self-shaming are common responses to being shamed, as the person learns to shame themselves in a conscious or unconscious effort to avoid further shaming.

"Withdrawal" is consistent with the phrase, "I hide my head in shame." The person who withdraws socially tries to avoid further shaming interactions, as in "I exclude myself before you dismiss or reject me." Subtler forms of withdrawal from shame may include reduced eye contact, "forgetting" therapy homework assignments, regularly arriving late, or missing appointments.

Nathanson's (1992) concept of "avoidance" is akin to "withdrawal," but involves avoiding painful emotions more than painful interactions. This can include mind-activating or mind-numbing activities, for example, overworking and other compulsive behavior, such as drug use, sex addiction, eating disorders, and gambling. Avoidance can be understood as compulsive, neurophysiological, and motoric mobilization in an unconscious effort to avoid immobilization and shutting down (Porges, 2011).

Another form of avoidance, not described by Nathanson (1992), I have named mind/body leave taking (LT). LT is consistent with what others referred to as dissociation as *process* (Schimmenti, 2018, personal communication; Schimmenti & Caretti, 2016) or *detachment*. Following Van der Hart (2021), I reserve the term "dissociation" for SD. SD involves "at least rudimentary first-person perspective" of "dissociative part[s] that can interact with other dissociative parts" (Nijenhuis & Van der Hart, 2011, p. 428). In contrast, LT indicates a psychological leaving where the person's attention turns away from emotions as bodily states and feelings, and toward a subjectively detached experience of themselves and others. "Detachment" is defined "as an altered state of consciousness characterized by a sense of separation from aspects of everyday experience; this detachment would especially pertain to depersonalization [DP] and derealization [DR]," (Allen, 2001; Cardeña, 1994; Brown, 2006; Holmes et al., 2005, all cited in Van der Hart, 2021).

LT can be short-lived, non-trauma-induced (e.g., "highway hypnosis"); short-lived, trauma-induced (e.g., when a person being assaulted temporarily "leaves their body" for physical/psychological pain relief); and in depersonalization/derealization (DP/DR) *symptoms* (acute LT) or *disorders* (chronic LT). Within shame as an emotional process, self-protective LT can be trauma- or non-trauma-induced, but is always acute or short-lived. Likewise, when DP/DR are evident, here, they are characterized as *symptoms* not *disorders*.

Other self-protective responses that involve avoidant or inhibited behavior try to keep the person from feeling shame by anticipating being shamed or humiliated. Two common subtypes include anticipatory shaming with increased arousal or decreased arousal. Anticipatory shaming with increased arousal manifests in various anxieties such as social separation or performance anxiety; perfectionism; obsessive-compulsive behavior, etc. Anticipatory shaming with decreased arousal may present as depression or depressive thinking where the person's assumption of failure prevents them from trying.

While less common, seeking closeness is another way people try to mitigate the effects of shame. However, when the patient is a RT survivor, attachment seeking is invariably fraught as closeness was or still is associated with threat or danger. As a result, the patient might freeze when shamed (i.e., high arousal reaction), caught between seeking contact and reassurance and escape, and/or submitting to the will of the shamer (i.e., decreased arousal).

Self-protective Reactions, Including Chronic, LT and/or SD, within Shame as a Traumatic Mind/Body State

Within *shame states,* the most prominent self-protective reactions are chronic LT and SD. To reiterate, LT can be short-lived (acute) or long-lived (chronic), and non-trauma-induced or trauma-induced. Chronic, trauma-induced LT as self-protective reaction applies here, where overwhelming fear and especially shame states precipitate DP/DR as *disorders* rather than *symptoms*.

In SD, a mind/brain/body organization develops where aspects of self are often kept outside the survivor's consciousness, that is, not me shame. For example, a person raised with a violent and shaming parent might develop a dissociated part that is appeasing and submissive, and another part prone to controlling or explosively violent behavior. A more severe form of SD is the shame of existing (Wille, 2014) or "no me shame," so overwhelming the survivor may appear emotionally absent, empty, lost, finding no value in being, and perhaps even in living.

A Five-State Shift Model of Pride: From Aliveness and Adaptive Pride to Maladaptive Pride and Dissociation

Following a close study of shame in patients and myself, the five-state shift model of shame was illuminated. The same was not true for pride. I know of no literature describing the microprocess of pride, both adaptive and maladaptive. The following offers a preliminary formulation. I hope researchers and psychotherapists use this as a starting point to further explore and amend my understanding.

State 1: "Going on Being," "Good Enough Me Pride" and "Pro-being Pride"

State 1 as applies to shame mostly applies here. The person begins with being themselves, going about living their life without significant impediment or disruption. Let us also imagine they are feeling good about themselves, consciously or with little thought, with mastered abilities and achievements valued, that is, good enough me pride. Let us further imagine this person takes pleasure in being their fuller self with themselves and others. This mind/body state is pro-being pride. In both instances, this person enjoys heightened, well-regulated arousal occupying the upper quadrant of their window of optimal arousal (Ogden et al., 2006).

State 2: Surprise or Shock

This follows my description of State 2 shame. In both surprise and shock, the person's pleasure in being experiences an abrupt interruption. This challenges both their good enough me pride and/or pro-being pride, leaving them feeling less sure of their accomplishments and themselves. In good enough me pride, this person might question abilities or achievements they previously prized. In a state of pro-being pride, and depending upon the person's relational history and nature of the interruption, they might experience a painful attack on their being.

As regards adaptive pride, *surprise* might cause a securely attached person with no history of RT to learn, unexpectedly, that they were not doing as well as previously believed. For example, perhaps our protagonist had taken pleasure in their well-developed skiing abilities, yet suddenly falls while traversing familiar terrain. This could precipitate a short-lived blow to their self-esteem. The surprised person might briefly question their self-judgment, evaluate the cause of their fall, and then return to State 1, feeling sobered yet accepting of themselves. If this person had been in a state of pro-being pride, delighting in their embodied aliveness and joyful relationship with their fellow skiers and nature, a surprising interruption might leave them stunned and confused. Even more likely, this person might view their fall as "par for the course," dust themselves off, and continue on with no real threat to their sense of well-being. Their return to State 1 would be readily achieved.

What if a survivor of RT ("survivor") experienced this interruption as a *shock* physically, emotionally, and to their self-worth? What if the survivor's boss, having previously valued the survivor's work and friendship, suddenly turned on them? Worse yet, what if their boss falsely accused the survivor of serious infractions, questioning their integrity? And what if this falsely accused person had been raised by a narcissistic parent who alternately idealized them, ignored all accomplishments less than stellar, and rejected them whenever their parent's self-worth was challenged? Given their traumatic relational history, this survivor would be narcissistically vulnerable.

66 *Shame and Pride: Subtypes and Processes*

They would be triggered by a threat to their self-worth and a valued bond with their boss.

State 3: Drop (Pride as Emotional Process) versus Drop and Spike (Pride as Traumatic Mind/Body State)

Surprised by their fall when skiing, our first protagonist might feel diminished pride or a drop into mild, "good enough me shame," or perhaps "not good enough me shame." While briefly experiencing a drop in arousal, they would remain within their window of tolerance (Siegel, 1999). This drop might be accompanied by a short-lived reduction in self-confidence, readily restored when realizing what had caused the fall and resuming their pleasurable skiing.

Given our second protagonist's early RT, the abrupt loss of their boss' favor would likely be neurophysiologically dysregulating. This *shocked survivor* might experience a rapid drop into hypoarousal and/or be taken over by marked increase into hyperarousal. This dysregulation is consistent with a traumatic pride and perhaps shame state.

State 4: Pride Restored or Threatened: Adaptive Pride as Emotional Process versus Pride as Traumatic Mind/Body State

The *surprised* skier with a history of secure attachment might experience a brief drop in self-worth, that is, good enough me shame, but their resilience would quickly restore adaptive, good enough me pride. They might even laugh at themselves for losing their focus and falling, recognize their error, and quickly return to adaptive, good enough me pride or even exuberant, pro-being pride.

Our second, *shocked* survivor would endure a stormier neurophysiological and psychological reaction to their boss' rejection. Their arousal could suddenly spike, and then drop or enter into simultaneous hyperaroused and hypoaroused mind/body states. Our survivor would experience not me pride states or, worse, no me pride states. They might profoundly question their expertise, doubting whether it was ever real, that is, not me pride. The person living with no me pride might have no feeling at all, believing their relationship with their boss was another expression of their subjective unreality of no-being.

State 5: Self-protective Emotional Responses and Self-protective Traumatic Reactions

Self-protective Responses within Pride as an Emotional Process

As noted under State 4, our well-regulated, securely attached skier's self-protective responses would be relatively mild. Perhaps they would momentarily question their skiing prowess, only to quickly recognize their attention lapsed but skills remained intact. Their good enough me pride would be sustained, with no self-protective measures required. Alternatively, they might have a momentary flash of anger toward themselves (e.g., "How could I be so careless?") or toward the skiing establishment (e.g., "How could they be so negligent with the snow?"). With self-blame, the person would experience not good enough me shame. When momentarily blaming the establishment, they would experience hubristic, better me pride, viewing themselves as a better skier than the owners deserved. Again, these self-protective measures would be short-lived. Our protagonist would quickly return to feeling fine about themselves and the facility owners, a little wiser, and more careful going forward.

Self-protective Reactions, Including Chronic, LT and/or SD, within Pride as a Traumatic Mind/Body State

As described within State 4, our RT survivor would not fare as well. Neurophysiologically, they would experience a rapid drop in arousal and enter into a traumatic not me shame and not me pride state. Our person would likely experience chronic LT, disconnecting from their body and the part that held their sense of competence. In SD, they might retain a sense of their capacities in some areas, for example, as a friend, but lose a sense of their competent work self, questioning entirely their relationship with their boss.

A survivor prone to not me pride states might further react with self-protective rage, directed at themselves, their boss, and/or other people. In self-directed rage, they would likely drop into a shame state, attacking themselves for believing they had value as worker or friend. In other-directed rage, this survivor might verbally and/or physically attack their boss, co-workers, and/or spouse when returning home and discovering dinner is not yet ready.

When the RT survivor was vulnerable to no me pride states, they would likely dissociate, perhaps experience severe DP/DR, and/or enter into a state of unreality where they had no sense of the person who had previously been praised at work. Rather than rage, the no me proud person would be more likely to disconnect from their own feelings and distance themselves from their boss, co-workers, and spouse. They would appear as though they were not really there.

References

Allen, J. G. (2001). *Traumatic Relationships and Serious Mental Disorders*. New York: Wiley. https://doi.org/10.1002/erv.505.

Anatkrama. (2008). *Coyote Fall*. Looney Tunes. www.youtube.com/results?search_query=wile+e+coyote+falls+off+cliff&page=1. Accessed December 12, 2020.

Barral, C. & Meares, R. (2019). The Holistic Project of Pierre Janet: Part Two: Oscillations and Becomings: From Disintegration to Integration. In G. Craparo, F. Ortu, & O. Van der Hart, Eds., *Rediscovering Pierre Janet: Trauma, Dissociation, and a New Context for Psychoanalysis* (pp. 116–129). New York: Routledge. https://doi.org/10.4324/9780429201875.

Benau, K. (2021a). Shame to Pride Following Sexual Molestation: Part 1: From Traumatic Immobilization to Triumphant Movement. *European Journal of Trauma and Dissociation,* 5(4) 100198. https://doi.org/10.1016/j.ejtd.2020.100194.

Benau, K. (2021b). Shame to Pride Following Sexual Molestation: Part 2: From Pro-being Pride to Retaliatory Rage, Adaptive Anger, and Integration. *European Journal of Trauma and Dissociation,* 5(4), 100194. https://doi.org/10.1016/j.ejtd.2020.100194.

Benau, K. (2020). Shame, Pride and Dissociation: Estranged Bedfellows, Close Cousins and Some Implications for Psychotherapy with Relational Trauma Part I: Phenomenology and Conceptualization. *Mediterranean Journal of Clinical Psychology,* 8(1), 1–35. Doi: https://doi.org/10.6092/2282-1619/mjcp-2154.

Benau, K. (2018). Pride in the Psychotherapy of Relational Trauma: Conceptualization and Treatment Considerations. *European Journal of Trauma and Dissociation,* 2(3), 131–146. https://doi.org/10.1016/j.ejtd.2020.100198.

Benau, K. (2017). Shame, Attachment, and Psychotherapy: Phenomenology, Neurophysiology, Relational Trauma, and Harbingers of Healing. *Attachment: New Directions in Psychotherapy and Relational Psychoanalysis,* 11(1), 1–27. https://doi.org/10.33212/att.v11n1.2017.1.

Bergson, H. (1911). *Creative Evolution: Humanity's Natural Creative Impulse* (Arthur Mitchell, Transl.). Mineola, New York: Dover. https://doi.org/10.5962/bhl.title.166289.

Bowlby, J. (1969). *Attachment. Attachment and Loss, Vol. 1:* Loss. New York: Basic Books.

Bradshaw, J. (1988). *Healing the Shame That Binds You.* Deerfield Beach, FL: Health Communications.

Bromberg, P. M. (2003). Something Wicked This Way Comes: Trauma, Dissociation, and Conflict: The Space Where Psychoanalysis, Cognitive Science, and Neuroscience Overlap. *Psychoanalytic Psychology,* 20(3), 558–574. https://doi.org/10.1037/0736-9735.20.3.558.

Bromberg, P. M. (2011a). *Awakening the Dreamer: Clinical Journeys.* New York: Routledge. https://doi.org/10.4324/9780203759981.

Bromberg, P. M. (2011b). *The Shadow of the Tsunami and the Growth of the Relational Mind.* New York: Routledge. https://doi.org/10.4324/9780203834954.

Brown, R. J. (2006). Different Types of "Dissociation" Have Different Psychological Mechanisms. *Journal of Trauma & Dissociation,* 7(4), 7–28. https://doi.org/10.1300/J229v07n04_02.

Brown, D. P. & Elliott, D. S. (2016). *Attachment Disturbances in Adults: Treatment for Comprehensive Repair.* New York: W.W. Norton.

Calhoun, L. G. & Tedeschi, R. G., Eds. (2006). *The Handbook of Post-traumatic Growth: Research and Practice.* New York: Lawrence Erlbaum & Associates.

Cardeña, E. (1994). The Domain of Dissociation. In S. J. Lynn & R. W. Rhue, Eds., *Dissociation: Theoretical, Clinical, and Research Perspectives* (pp. 15–31). New York: Guilford. https://doi.org/10.1080/00029157.1995.10403195.

Corrigan, F. M. & Christie-Sands, J. (2020). An Innate Brainstem Self-Other System Involving Orienting, Affective Responding, and Polyvalent Relational Seeking: Some Clinical Implications for a "Deep Brain Reorienting" Trauma Psychotherapy Approach. *Medical Hypotheses,* 136, 199502. https://doi.org/10.1016/j.mehy.2019.109502.

Corrigan, F. M. & Elkin-Cleary, E. (2018). Shame as an Evolved Basic Affect—Approaches to It within the Comprehensive Resource Model (CRM). *Medical Hypotheses,* 119, 91–97. https://doi.org/10.1016/j.mehy.2018.07.028.

Craparo, G., Ortu, F., & Van der Hart, O., Eds. (2019). *Rediscovering Pierre Janet: Trauma, Dissociation, and a New Context for Psychoanalysis.* New York: Routledge. https://doi.org/10.4324/9780203759981.

Csikszentmihalyi, M. (1990). *Flow: The Psychology of Optimal Experience.* New York: Harper & Row.

Damasio, A. (1999). *The Feeling of What Happens: Body and Emotion in the Making of Consciousness.* New York: Harcourt Press. 10.1353/jsp.2001.0038.

Dearing, R. L. & Tangney, J. P., Eds. (2011). *Shame in the Therapy Hour.* Washington, DC: American Psychological Association. https://doi.org/10.1037/12326-000.

Delafield-Butt, J. T. & Gangopadhyay, N. (2013). Sensorimotor Intentionality: The Origins of Intentionality in Prospective Agent Action. *Developmental Review,* 33(4), 399–425. https://doi.org/10.1016/j.dr.2013.09.001.

DeYoung, P. (2015). *Understanding and Treating Chronic Shame: A Relational/Neurobiological Approach.* New York: Routledge. https://doi.org/10.4324/9781315734415.

Ecker, B., Ticic, R., & Hulley, L. (2012). *Unlocking the Emotional Brain: Eliminating Symptoms at Their Roots Using Memory Reconsolidation.* New York: Routledge. https://doi.org/10.4324/9780203804377.

"Emotion," word origin: www.etymonline.com/word/emotion. Accessed January 22, 2021.

Freud, A. (1966/1937). *The Ego and the Mechanisms of Defence.* London: Routledge. https://doi.org/10.4324/9780429481550.

Gergen, K. (2015). *An Invitation to Social Construction (3rd Edition).* Thousand Oaks, CA: Sage. https://doi.org/10.4135/9781473921276.

Goleman, D. (1972). The Buddha on Meditation and States of Consciousness Part 1: A Typology of Meditation Techniques. *Journal of Transpersonal Psychology,* 4(1), 151–210.

Greenberg, L. S. & Iwakabe, S. (2011). Emotion-Focused Therapy and Shame. In R. L. Dearing & J. P. Tangney, Eds., *Shame in the Therapy Hour* (pp. 69–90). Washington, DC: American Psychological Association. https://doi.org/10.1037/12326-000.

Herman, J. L. (2012). Shattered Shame States and Their Repair. In J. Yellin, & K. White, Eds., *Shattered States: Disorganised Attachment and its Repair* (pp. 157–170). London: Karnac Books.

Herman, J. L. (2011). PTSD as a Shame Disorder. In R. L. Dearing & J. P. Tangney Eds., *Shame in the Therapy Hour* (pp. 261–275). Washington, DC: American Psychological Association. https://doi.org/10.1037/12326-000.

Herman, J. L. (2007). *Shattered Shame States and Their Repair.* Somerville, MA: Harvard Medical School.

Herman, J. L. (2006). *PTSD as a Shame Disorder.* Somerville, MA: Harvard Medical School.

Hicks, D. (2011). *Dignity: Its Essential Role in Resolving Conflict.* New Haven: Yale University Press.

Holmes, E. A., Brown, R. J., Mansell, W., Fearon, R. P., Hunter, E. C. M., Frasquilho, F., & Oakley, D. A. (2005). Are There Two Qualitatively Distinct Forms of Dissociation? A Review and Some Clinical Implications. *Clinical Psychology Review,* 25(1), 1–23. https://doi.org/10.1016/j.cpr.2004.08.006.

Howell, E. (2020). *Trauma and Dissociation-Informed Psychotherapy: Relational Healing and the Therapeutic Connection.* New York: W.W. Norton. 0.4324/9780203888261.

Janet, P. (1935). *Les Debuts de L'Intelligence.* Paris: Flammation.

Janet, P. (1932). *La Force et la Faiblesse Psychologiques.* Paris: Maloine.

Janet, P. (1909). Problèmes psychologiques de l'émotion. *Rev. Neurol*, 17, 1551–1687.

Lanius, U. (March 22, 2018). Personal communication, ISSTD Annual Conference, Chicago, IL.

Levine, P. A. (2010). *In an Unspoken Voice: How the Body Releases Trauma and Restores Goodness*. Berkeley, CA: North Atlantic Books.

Levine, P. A. (1997). *Waking the Tiger: Healing Trauma*. Berkeley, CA: North Atlantic Books.

Moskowitz, A. & Van der Hart, O. (2020). Historical and Contemporary Conceptions of Trauma-Related Dissociation: A Neo-Janetian Critique of Models of Divided Personality. *European Journal of Trauma and Dissociation*, 4(2), 1–10. https://doi.org/10.1016/j.ejtd.2019.02.004.

Nathanson, D. (1992). *Shame, Pride, Affect, Sex and the Birth of the Self*. New York: W.W. Norton. https://doi.org/10.1177/036215379402400207.

Nijenhuis, E. R. S. Personal communication, March 21, 2020.

Nijenhuis, E. R. S. (2017). From Passion to Action: A Synopsis of the Theory and Practice of Enactive Trauma Therapy. *Frontiers in the Psychotherapy of Trauma and Dissociation*, 1(1), 65–89.

Nijenhuis, E. R. S. & O. Van der Hart (2011). Dissociation in Trauma: A New Definition and Comparison with Previous Formulations. *Journal of Trauma & Dissociation*, 12(4), 416–445. https://doi.org/10.1080/15299732.2011.570592.

Ogden, P., Minton, K., & Pain, C. (2006). *Trauma and the Body: A Sensorimotor Approach to Psychotherapy*. New York: W.W. Norton.

Panksepp, J. (1998). *Affective Neuroscience: The Foundations of Human and Animal Emotions*. New York: Oxford University Press.

Porges, S. (2017). Polyvagal Theory: Basic Principles, Experiential Learning and Clinical Applications Workshop (September 23–24, 2017). Berkeley, CA: Somatic Psychology Events.

Porges, S. W. (2011). *The Polyvagal Theory: Neurophysiological Foundations of Emotions, Attachment, Communication, and Self-regulation*. New York: W.W. Norton.

"Proud," word origin: www.etymonline.com/word/proud. Accessed January 25, 2021.

Putnam, F. W. (2016). *The Way We Are: How States of Mind Influence Our Identities, Personality and Potential for Change*. New York: International Psychoanalytic Books.

"Recognize," definition: www.dictionary.com/browse/recognize. Accessed January 25, 2021.

Rogers, C. R. (1961). *On Becoming a Person: A Therapist's View of Psychotherapy*. Boston: Houghton Mifflin.

Scheff, T. J. (In press). *A Social Theory and Treatment of Depression*. http://scheff.faculty.soc.ucsb.edu/main.php?id=62.html. Accessed December 28, 2019.

Schimmenti, A. (September 8, 2018). Personal communication, originally posted on the Dissociative Disorders Listserve (DISSOC). Quoted with permission.

Schimmenti, A. & Caretti, V. (2016). Linking the Overwhelming with the Unbearable: Developmental Trauma, Dissociation, and the Disconnected Self. *Psychoanalytic Psychology*, 33(1), 106–128. https://doi.org/10.1037/a0038019.

Schore, A. N. (2003). *Affect Regulation and Repair of the Self*. New York: W.W. Norton.

Schore, A. N. (2001). Effects of Relational Trauma on Right Brain Development, Affect Regulation, and Infant Mental Health. *Infant Mental Health Journal*, 22(1–2), 201–269. Doi: https://doi.org/10.1002/1097-0355(200101/04)22:1<201::AID-IMHJ8>3.0.CO;2-9.

Schwartz, R. C. (1995). *Internal Family Systems Therapy*. New York: Guilford Press.

Shaw, D. (2014). *Traumatic Narcissism: Relational Systems of Subjugation*. New York: Routledge. https://doi.org/10.4324/9781315883618.

Scheff, T. J. (In press). *A Social Theory and Treatment of Depression*. http://scheff.faculty.soc.ucsb.edu/main.php?id=62.html. Accessed December 28, 2019.

Siegel, D. J. (1999). *The Developing Mind: How Relationships and the Brain Interact to Shape Who We Are*. New York: Guilford Press.

Solms, M. (2021). *The Hidden Spring: A Journey to the Source of Consciousness*. New York: W.W. W.W. Norton.

Spinoza, B. (R. H. M. Elwes, Ed.). (2006/1677). *The Ethics (Ethica Ordine Geometrico Demonstrata): Parts 1–5: On the Origins and Nature of the Emotions, Proposition 53*. Charleston, SC: Bibliobazaar. https://doi.org/10.1524/9783050050218.1.

Spitz, R. (1946). Hospitalism: A Follow-Up Report on Investigation Described in Volume I, 1945. *The Psychoanalytic Study of the Child*, 2(1), 113–117. https://doi.org/10.1080/00797308.1946.11823540.

Steiner, J. (2006). Seeing and Being Seen: Narcissistic Pride and Narcissistic Humiliation. *International Journal of Psychoanalysis*, 87(4), 939–951. https://doi.org/10.1516/AL5W-9RVJ-WKG2-B0CK.

Stern, D. (1985). *The Interpersonal World of the Infant: A View from Psychoanalysis and Developmental Psychology*. New York: Basic Books.

Tangney, J. P. & Dearing, R. L. (2011). Working with Shame in the Therapy Hour: Summary and Integration. In R. L. Dearing & J. P. Tangey, Eds., *Shame in the Therapy Hour* (pp. 365–404). Washington: American Psychological Association. https://doi.org/10.1037/12326-000.

Tangney, J. P., & Fischer, K. W. (Eds.). (1995). *Self-conscious Emotions: The Psychology of Shame, Guilt, Embarrassment, and Pride*. New York: The Guilford Press.

Tomkins, S. (1963). *Affect, Imagery and Consciousness: The Negative Affects, Vol. 2*. New York: Springer.

Tracy, J. (2016). *Take Pride: Why the Deadliest Sin Holds the Secret to Human Success*. New York: Houghton Mifflin Harcourt.

Van der Hart, O. (2021). Trauma-Related Dissociation: An Analysis of Two Conflicting Models. *European Journal of Trauma & Dissociation*, 5(4), 100210. https://doi.org/10.1016/j.ejtd.2021.100210.

Van der Hart, O., Nijenhuis, E. R. S., & Steele, K. (2006). *The Haunted Self: Structural Dissociation and the Treatment of Chronic Traumatization*. New York: W.W. Norton.

Van der Kolk, B. A. (2014a). *The Body Keeps the Score: Brain, Mind, and Body in the Healing of Trauma*. New York: Viking.

Van der Kolk, B. A. (2014b). *The Body Keeps the Score*. http://bessel.kajabi.com/fe/72501-the-body-keeps-the-score. PESI. Accessed January 31, 2017.

Van der Kolk, B. & Van der Hart, O. (1989). Pierre Janet and the Breakdown of Adaptation in Psychological Trauma. *American Journal of Psychiatry*, 146(12), 1530–1540. https://doi.org/10.1176/ajp.146.12.1530.

Van Nuys, D. (July 5, 2019). Working with Attachment and Trauma with Daniel Brown (Shrink Rap Radio #649). www.thescienceofpsychotherapy.com/shrink-rap-radio-649-working-with-attachment-and-trauma-with-daniel-brown/. Accessed July 2, 2021.

Vogt, R. (2018). Trauma Severity: Parallels between SPIM 30 and Polyvagal Theory. In S. W. Porges & D. Dana, Eds., *Clinical Applications of the Polyvagal Theory: The Emergence of Polyvagal-Informed Therapies*. New York: W.W. Norton.

Weil, A. (1986). *The Natural Mind: An Investigation of Drugs and Higher Consciousness (Revised Edition)*. Boston: Houghton Mifflin.

Wilber, K. (1998). *The Essential Ken Wilber*. Boston: Shambhala.

Wille, R. (2014). The Shame of Existing: An Extreme Form of Shame. *International Journal of Psychoanalysis*, 95, 695–717. Doi: 10.1111/1745-8315.12208.

Winnicott, D. W. (1965). Ego Distortion in Terms of True and False Self. In *The Maturational Processes and the Facilitating Environment: Studies in the Theory of Emotional Development*. New York: International Universities Press.

Winnicott, D. W. (1960). The Theory of the Parent-Infant Relationship. *International Journal of Psycho-Analysis*, 41, 585–595.

Winnicott, D. W. (1984/1956). Primary Maternal Preoccupation. In D. W. Winnicott, Ed., *Through Paediatrics to Psychoanalysis: Collected Papers*. London: Karnac Books, 300—305.

Woodman, M. (1998). "Abandoned Souls." In M. Woodman & J. Melnick, Eds., *Coming Home to Myself: Reflections for Nurturing a Woman's Body and Soul* (p. 247). Berkeley: Conari Press.

Yehuda, R. & Bierer, L. M. (2009). The Relevance of Epigenetics to PTSD: Implications for the DSM-V. *Journal of Traumatic Stress*, 22(5), 427–434. https://doi.org/10.1002/jts.20448.

3 Shame, Pride, Mind/Body Leave Taking, and Structural Dissociation

Psychodynamics, Phenomenology, and Psychotherapy

Introduction

Shame and pride states are, by definition, traumatic mind/body states that involve different degrees of dissociation. Chapter 3 extends and deepens the description of shame and pride subtypes and processes (Chapter 2) to explore the relationships between shame and pride as emotions and traumatic states, leave taking (LT), previously conceptualized as dissociation as *process* and structural dissociation (SD). This chapter first describes the complex, often confusing *psychodynamic* relationships between shame, pride, LT, and SD. It then delineates specific *phenomenological* features, including attention, gaze, and mind/body organization, shared by and distinguishing shame, pride, LT, and SD. Various psychotherapeutic applications of these psychodynamic and phenomenological understandings when working with relational trauma (RT) survivors are presented throughout this chapter.

Introduction of Terms: Shame, Pride, Emotion or Affect, Structural Dissociation (SD), and Mind/Body Leave Taking (LT)

Shame and pride are emotions or affects that have both adaptive and maladaptive expressions (Chapter 2). Shame is often associated with the phrase "I *am* inadequate," as contrasted with guilt where "I *did* something that hurt another that I regret and want to make amends" ("reparative guilt"), or punish myself for harming another ("punitive guilt") (Howell, 2020; Steiner, 2006). Adaptive pride accompanies mastery, achievement, and includes what I call "pro-being pride." Pro-being pride is an enduring mind/body state rather than short-lived emotional process, delighting in one's authentic self in relation to another's authentic self (self with other) and one's own self (self with self).

Throughout this book, "affect" and "emotion" are used interchangeably, although some researchers do not (Ekkekakis, 2012; Chapter 1, note 1). Emotions include thoughts, beliefs, and/or meanings, explicit and implicit; conscious feelings; neurophysiological and somatic phenomena; and behavior, including actions and interactions. Short-lived, emotional processes

DOI: 10.4324/9780429425943-4

("emotions" for short) are differentiated from chronic, traumatic mind/body states that always involve dissociative parts (Van der Hart, 2006).

Dissociation is neither emotion nor affect. For some, dissociation includes an acute, mind/body *process* and an enduring mind/body *structure* or organization (Schimmenti & Caretti, 2006), the latter evidenced in SD. Others reserve the term "dissociation" for SD in response to trauma (Van der Hart, 2021; Van der Hart et al., 2006), a view I also adopt.

SD refers to a mental

> division [that] involves two or more insufficiently integrated dynamic but excessively stable subsystems. These subsystems exert functions, and can encompass any number of different mental and behavioral actions and implied states. These subsystems and states can be latent, or activated in a sequence or in parallel. Each dissociative subsystem, that is, dissociative part of the personality, minimally includes its own, at least rudimentary first-person perspective. As each dissociative part, the individual can interact with other dissociative parts and other individuals, at least in principle. Dissociative parts maintain particular psychobiological boundaries that keep them divided, but that they can in principle dissolve.
> (Nijenhuis & Van der Hart, 2011, p. 428)

Dissociative parts of the personality are either trauma avoidant, carrying out everyday life functions and labeled Apparently Normal Parts of the Personality (ANP), or trauma fixated, called Emotional Parts of the Personality (EP) (Van der Hart & Rydberg, 2019; Van der Hart et al., 2006).

In Chapter 2, I introduced the term LT to replace the concepts of *dissociation as process* and *detachment*. Unlike SD, LT does *not* involve "at least rudimentary first-person perspective" of "dissociative part[s] that can interact with other dissociative parts" (Nijenhuis & Van der Hart, 2011, p. 428). LT indicates psychological leaving where the person's consciousness automatically turns away from overwhelming and/or underwhelming emotions as bodily states and feelings, and toward a subjectively detached experience of self, others, and the environment.

LT can be trauma-induced or not, and short-lived (acute) or long-lived (chronic). An example of trauma-induced, acute LT is when a person during sexual assault temporarily "leaves" their body, as though viewing the event from above. Non-trauma-induced, acute LT occurs when a person "spaces out" during temporary sensory overload (e.g., excessive noise) or underload (e.g., boredom). LT may result in a person subjectively experiencing themselves as unreal (depersonalization [DP]) and the world subjectively experienced as unreal (derealization [DR]) (Simeon & Abujel, 2006). Acute LT is seen in *symptoms* of DP/DR, whereas DP/DR *disorders* are consistent with chronic LT. DP/DR symptoms and disorder may or may not be trauma-induced.

Shame and dissociation, particularly in RT (Schore, 2003) and Dissociative Identity Disorder (DID), have been shown in research and clinically to co-occur, to negatively impact interpersonal functioning, and contribute to psychopathology (Chefetz, 2015; DePrince et al., 2015; Dorahy, 2010, 2014; Dorahy & Clearwater, 2012; Dorahy et al., 2013, 2015, 2017a, 2017b; Dyer et al., 2017; Tangney & Fischer, 1995). The relationship between shame, pride, LT, and SD has rarely been discussed (Benau, 2020a, 2020b).

Research into the Relationship Between Shame, Dissociation, Psychopathology, and Treatment

Research by Dorahy and colleagues examined the relationship between shame and dissociation in clinical populations, including Complex PTSD (C-PTSD) and DID, and in nonclinical populations. Research findings most directly related to this chapter showed:

- Increased shame was significantly correlated with increased dissociation, whether the shame was generally experienced or related to internal or external cues, both for student samples and psychotherapy patients (Dorahy et al., 2017b). Induced dissociative detachment (i.e., acute LT) in clinical (i.e., childhood sexual abuse) and nonclinical populations was associated with greater acute shame. In the clinical group, shame following detachment was most due to feeling flawed and exposed (Dorahy et al., 2021). In general population adults, shame activated dissociation and dissociation with a close other evoked shame (McKeogh et al., 2018).

These findings are important from the psychodynamic perspective elaborated below. I argue shame and dissociation co-occur because shame attempts "to solve" or attenuate the distress of chronic LT and SD. Shame brings the person back into their body, perhaps giving them a sense of greater agency when LT proves unbearable, and when dissociative parts threaten intrarelational and/or interrelational stability. LT and SD temporarily "solve" the problem of parts dominated by the unbearable pain of traumatic shame states, and I would add pride states, by leaving the mind/body (LT) or switching to a disembodied part not sharing consciousness with the shame or pride state (SD).

- Shame and dissociation were linked to problems in intimate relationships in C-PSTD, and dissociation predicted relationship depression (Dorahy et al., 2015). Shame mediated between dissociation and relationship difficulties (Dorahy et al., 2013). Dissociation more than shame had severing effects on interpersonal relationships (Dorahy, 2010). Contrasted with a general psychiatric group, patients with a dissociative disorder experienced more severe symptoms including greater shame, guilt, and withdrawal due to shame.
- People diagnosed with DID reported more alienation than those with PTSD. Statements of alienation included: "There is a huge void inside me ... I am disconnected from people" (DePrince et al., 2015, p. 580).

76 *Shame, Pride, and Dissociation*

In my view, statements of "alienation" could be due to dissociative parts characterized by shame, that is, "shame states."

- Studying DID patients, C-PTSD patients, and a nonclinical sample (Dorahy et al., 2017a), it was found that the DID group showed significantly higher "attack self," "withdrawal," and "avoidance" behavior than C-PTSD and healthy controls (Dyer et al., 2017). DID patients experienced significantly more shame and pathological dissociation than the other groups. Shame directly contributed to relationship anxiety, and pathological dissociation correlated with relationship anxiety and relationship depression. In C-PTSD, shame and dissociation indirectly negatively affected all relationship variables.

The relationships between shame, dissociation, "attack self," "withdrawal," and "avoidance" are complex. While this research showed pathological dissociation directly affected relationship anxiety and depression, these co-occurrences are likely multidirectional. Relationship anxiety and depression could contribute to both withdrawal and avoidant behavior that, in turn, lead to greater social isolation and self-alienation, further exacerbating shame and dissociation. Another multidirectional, psychodynamic perspective of shame, pride, and dissociation is discussed below.

The points mentioned in the list above and research on shame as an emotional process (Tangney & Fischer, 1995) demonstrate maladaptive shame and dissociation negatively impacted interrelational (self with others) and intrarelational (self with self) functioning, both important in psychotherapy with RT survivors.

- Adult men sexually abused as children (n= 7) experienced more self as pervasively experiencing shame (SAS), fears of further exposure, and only short-lived benefit from positive connections before shame and withdrawal returned (Dorahy & Clearwater, 2012).

In my view, SAS is consistent with traumatic shame as contrasted with shame as emotional process. Given a RT history, close, positive relating with others, including the psychotherapist, may intensify shame and social anxiety, further exacerbating anxiety, withdrawal, and shame.

- Using the autobiographical Implicit Association Test (aIAT), DID participants experienced implicit, episodic self-referential memory (e.g., "embarrassment") across identities, even when they reported *no conscious awareness of feeling* embarrassed. This suggested some people with DID may live with the *effects* of chronic shame without consciously *feeling* and *reporting* shame, measured by statements such as: "No shower can wash away how dirty I felt … I feel disgust. I feel ashamed" (DePrince et al.,

2015, p. 580). Marsh et al. (2018) showed similar, unconscious effects of shame in DID patients.

These results fit with my clinical experience that dissociative parts with predominantly shame states and traumatic LT may not be "felt" as shame. The same holds for dissociative parts gripped by pride states.

- When responding to a shame script, both dissociative disorder patients and a comparison psychiatric population found these interventions helpful: focusing on feelings, cognitions, and previous shame experiences (Dorahy et al., 2017a).

These interventions likely helped as none avoided exploring shame, countering shame's tendency to hide, and *widened* the shamed person's focus in *nonevaluative ways*. (See the section on "wide lens.")

Psychodynamic Relationships Between Shame, Pride, LT, and SD

This section explores complex, psychodynamic relationships between four domains of experience ("domains"), all in relation to pro-being pride. Having a map of these relationships enables therapists to better navigate the challenging terrain of psychotherapy with RT survivors:

1. Disembodied SD and chronic, disembodied LT.
2. Embodied, dissociative parts characterized by shame and pride (i.e., shame and pride states: not me shame, no me shame, not me pride, and no me pride).
3. Embodied, maladaptive shame and pride as emotional processes (i.e., not good enough me shame and better me pride).
4. Embodied, adaptive shame and pride as emotional processes (i.e., good enough me shame and good enough me pride).

The four domains are described in relation to each other and all in relationship with pro-being pride. Each domain is conceptualized as posing a psychobiological "problem" that its partner domain attempts to "solve." These solutions are always incomplete, sometimes unconscious, and to different degrees adaptive or maladaptive in relationship with self and others. While mapped sequentially, with each domain contiguous to its closest counterpart, patients can experience one or more domain at any time, and/or "skip over" domains.

A visual map (Table 3.1) summarizes these psychodynamic relationships that are then further elaborated. In this model, "←→" signifies a bidirectional, psychodynamic relationship between specific domains experientially and phenomenologically most similar to its contiguous partner. The vertical "…" refers to relationships between all domains and pro-being pride.

78 *Shame, Pride, and Dissociation*

Table 3.1 Psychodynamic Relationships Between Shame, Pride, Mind/Body Leave Taking (LT), and Structural Dissociation (SD)

Pro-being Pride
1. Disembodied SD and Chronic, Disembodied LT ←→ 2. Embodied Shame and Pride States ←→ 3. Embodied, Maladaptive Shame and Pride Emotional Processes ←→ 4. Embodied, Adaptive Shame and Pride Emotional Processes

Psychodynamic Relationship Between Disembodied SD and Chronic, Disembodied LT

We begin with #1 (Table 3.1), disembodied, dissociative parts within SD and chronic LT. When a person endures overwhelming or underwhelming stress, they face the threat of psychological disintegration or madness, and sometimes physical death.

Chronic, disembodied LT, for example, DP/DR as disorder, and SD, reveal distinct mind/body attempts "to solve" the problem of madness or physical death. They each do so by temporarily withdrawing attention from overwhelming fear and terror held in the body, LT without a first-person perspective, and SD with a first-person perspective. These strategies prove unsustainable as chronic disconnection from others and a person's emotional and somatic reality leave them unbearably self-alienated and socially isolated (DePrince et al., 2015), and feeling more deadened than enlivened. Even acute LT is associated with greater shame, feeling flawed, and exposed (Dorahy et al., 2021). In addition, overwhelmingly painful affect intermittently breaks through, as when dissociative barriers weaken in SD.

In sum, chronic disembodied LT and disembodied, dissociative parts within SD seek to "solve" the problem of psychological disintegration or death awareness via distinct ways of withdrawing consciousness. Still, fears of dissolution, self-alienation, social isolation, shame, and deadening lurk in the shadows, threatening to draw the person back into states of overwhelming affect, death anxiety, and/or madness.

Embodied Shame and Pride States

Continuing to #2 (Table 3.1), a person may become painfully embodied in lieu of disembodied LT or SD by plummeting into shame and/or pride states. Shame and pride states, that is, not me shame, no me shame, not me pride, and no me pride (Chapter 2), are features of dissociated parts of self (Van der Hart et al., 2006) expressing shame or pride-related matters, respectively.

In shame and pride states, the child and later adult survivor intermittently "feel" something. However, shame states are excruciatingly painful (hyperarousal) and/or numbing (hypoarousal) (Corrigan & Elkin-Cleary,

2018). Although traumatic pride states are often less painful than shame states, they remain disturbing as disconnection from one's true self (Winnicott, 1965) prevents authentic relating.

Metaphorically, shame states hold a person in the grip of a black hole as condensed and constricted ways of meaning-making, feeling, sensing, and behaving. In pride states, the person cannot tolerate their own and others' complexity and vulnerabilities. This results in their becoming detached from themselves and others, as though floating in space, untethered. In both shame and pride states, the person experiences parts of self (not me shame) and/or parts experiencing existence as shameful (no me shame; Wille [2014]), and/or lacks psychological space to hold authentic pride in attributes (not me pride) or their being (no me pride). When a survivor's enlivened self-expression threatens attachment bonds, overwhelming fears of losing connection often pull the survivor back into chronic LT and/or SD.

In sum, dissociative parts dominated by shame and pride states temporarily "solve" the problem of chronic, disembodied LT and disembodied SD, by giving the child and later adult RT survivor a short-lived, "felt" subjective experience. When the pain of shame and pride states proves unbearable, disembodied LT and disembodied SD may beckon the survivor's return. This often leads to a psychodynamic movement between intrusive and unbearably painful parts characterized by shame and pride states, and chronic, disembodied LT and/or SD.

Embodied, Maladaptive Shame and Pride Emotional Processes

Moving next to #3 (Table 3.1), embodied, maladaptive shame and pride as emotional processes, that is, not good enough me shame and better me pride (Chapter 2), offer different psychodynamic "solutions" to the problem of shame and pride states. This shift toward more modulated embodiment and self-awareness is possible only with sufficient intrapersonal and interpersonal resourcing (Chapter 4, #11, Intrarelational and interrelational resourcing: Lived, imagined, felt, and embodied).

While not good enough me shame and better me pride do not involve LT nor SD, they remain painful experiences of self as inadequate (maladaptive shame) or superior (maladaptive pride). When shame and pride emotions occur repeatedly, as in RT, shame and pride states develop.

There is also a psychodynamic relationship between maladaptive pride and shame. Better me pride may temporarily replace not good enough me shame, shifting the person's belief from "I am worthless and less than others" to "You are worthless and less than me." However, when feelings of superiority cannot sustain the better me proud person's fragile sense of self, they are prone to returning to not good enough me shame, and back again.

In sum, despite personal and interpersonal pain accompanying not good enough me shame and better me pride, both reflect additional ways RT survivors unconsciously seek to reduce suffering caused by traumatic shame and pride states, and avoid more chronic, disembodied LT and SD. Further, better me pride seeks to solve the problem of not good enough me shame and vice versa, switching one to the other.

Embodied, Adaptive Shame and Pride Emotional Processes

Continuing to #4 (Table 3.1), preferred pathways toward transforming not good enough me shame and better me pride include adaptive good enough me shame and good enough me pride. Good enough me shame permits survivors to live according to their values. Good enough me pride accompanies mastery and achievement. Consistent with Janet's (1935) act of triumph (Barral & Meares, 2019, p. 121; Ogden, 2019), this adaptive pride enables the person to conquer, often with psychotherapy, previously intractable problems in living and make meaningful contributions to self, others, and community.

In sum, adaptive, good enough me shame and pride offer the RT survivor preferred "solutions" to the problems of not good enough me shame and better me pride. Often with the benefit of psychotherapy, the ability to feel shame that returns a person to their true values (i.e., good enough me shame) and pride in genuine achievements (i.e., good enough me pride) augur acts of triumph, motivating a survivor's perseverance when pursuing personal and relational growth.

Pro-being Pride in Relationship With Maladaptive Shame and Pride, LT, and SD

Pro-being pride is a powerful, sustaining way of transforming maladaptive and adaptive shame and pride, dissociative parts characterized by shame and pride states, and even chronic LT and SD. Pro-being pride is the enduring, embodied celebration of being (self with self) and relating (self with other).

Maladaptive forms of shame and pride, chronic LT and SD in different ways, each reflect a muting or deadening of a person's aliveness. In contrast, pro-being pride expresses full-bodied enlivenment while remaining poignantly aware no one is immune from psychological disintegration or mortality. Pro-being pride offers inspired, creative responses to knowing we are all vulnerable. For many RT survivors, grief for life unlived accompanies pro-being pride, auguring further opportunities for psychobiological integration and growth (Chapter 7).

As observed, the lived experience of good enough me shame and good enough me pride give RT survivors more sustainable pathways out of maladaptive shame and pride as emotional processes, traumatic states, and more severe forms of traumatic LT and SD. As a celebration of life, pro-being pride never loses sight of our shared vulnerability and mortality. At the same time, pro-being pride represents a portal transcending the other "solutions" available to us all.

Psychodynamic Relationships between Shame, Pride, LT, and SD: A Psychotherapeutic Application

Clinical Vignette: "Carla" Lost and Found

Carla was a RT survivor who witnessed physical violence, emotional abuse, and shaming by her mother toward her older sister; shaming and bullying of

Carla by her older sister; shaming by her mother and father, blaming Carla for not relieving her father's chronic, psychological suffering; and Carla's father not protecting her from her mother's and older sister's violence and shaming.

Prior to the time period described, Carla and I had been working in weekly psychotherapy for over 10-years. Although making considerable progress alleviating her cyclical depression and anxiety, Carla remained vulnerable to intermittent eruptions of dissociative parts colored by traumatic shame and pride states. For two years prior, Carla experienced much success personally and professionally. Relationships with her husband, adult child, and close friends enhanced Carla's adaptive good enough me pride and pro-being pride.

Prior to a traumatic setback, Carla worked for months on a professional presentation. After her presentation, a known colleague critiqued Carla's presentation as "too abstract." The next day, another close colleague told Carla several esteemed colleagues found her enthusiasm off-putting. A few weeks later at a workshop requiring some self-disclosure, another participant told Carla she had "a lot of work to do" regarding her relationship with her father.

Carla initially viewed each person's feedback as intended to be helpful. Several months later she realized these remarks were also self-serving. Given her cumulative stress preceding these incidents and RT vulnerability, Carla precipitously dropped into painful shame and pride states which lasted six months. Gripped by states of pervasive dread and anxiety interrupted by acute, mind/body LT, Carla lost confidence she could do her work and believed her personal relationships were fraudulent.

During the final month of her ordeal, Carla feared she was "going crazy." Carla's fear of losing her mind suggested her acute LT was shifting into chronic LT. Carla's torment also suggested dissociative parts ruled by shame states had overtaken her consciousness.

Several therapeutic approaches helped Carla restore her sense of well-being, more integrated and confident than ever. These included:

- Stabilizing medication.
- Somatic psychotherapy facilitating neurophysiological downregulation and gradual mind/body "returning" rather than "leaving" (LT and SD).
- Working with Carla's young parts from an SD (Van der Hart et al., 2006) and functionally coherent perspective (Chapter 4, #9, Functional Coherence [FC]; Ecker et al., [2012]; Coherence Therapy [CT]).
- Helping Carla process early, subcortical and preverbal roots of her RT (Corrigan & Elkin-Cleary, 2018; Deep Brain Reorienting [DBR]).

The chaotic, emotional-relational storm consuming Carla's life and therapy required I maintain my emotional equilibrium and therapeutic focus. This was difficult as Carla's state worsened over several months. With considerable consultation, I maintained my therapeutic stance by understanding the relationship between Carla's pervasive dread, mind/body LT, mental disorganization, and SD. Carla and I slowly realized she was rapidly switching between mental "disorganization" and more "organized" shame and pride states that convinced Carla one false move with patients and loved ones would result in losing them all, simply for "being."

Things slowly improved as we processed therapeutically Carla's rage at her mother and sister for bullying and shaming her; her anger toward and grief about her father for never protecting her from the abuse; and feeling repeatedly unseen and unfelt by family members.

Gradually, Carla felt more integrated intrarelationally and content in her relationships. Former triggers of Carla's shame and pride states, as when people did not respond promptly to her communications, were less activating. Carla's defensive anger as reaction to critical feedback was markedly reduced. These and related transformations strengthened Carla's good enough me pride and pro-being pride and deepened the integration of previously dissociated parts of self held in shame states. Carla's decompensation reflected her descent into the dark night of the soul. With our shared hard work, Carla "returned" stronger and wiser.

Phenomenology of Shame, Pride, LT, and SD: Shared and Distinct Features and Psychotherapeutic Applications with RT Survivors

We turn our attention to the relationship between the phenomenology of shame and pride, on the one hand, and LT and SD on the other. Although psychodynamic and phenomenological relationships with these phenomena are described separately, they are experientially parts of a whole. For example, when a survivor shifts from maladaptive to adaptive shame and pride, these psychodynamic transitions go hand-in-hand with changes in the phenomenology of gazing at themselves and being gazed at by others (see below).

Shames, pride, LT, and SD share cognitive and somatic features and show important differences. The qualitative features described are founded in my clinical observations and not derived from a formal phenomenological analysis (Giorgi, 2012, 1997). These qualities were selected as understanding each benefit psychotherapy with RT survivors. Relevant clinical vignettes and therapeutic applications follow the description of each phenomenological category.

Three categories explored include *attention, gaze,* and *organization of mind/body* as related to shame, pride, LT, and SD:

1. ***Attention***
    a. Directionality
    b. Quality
    c. Wide and Narrow Lens

This section describes *where attention is directed* (i.e., self, other, self-other, and self-other-self); the *quality* of *attending* (i.e., accepting, delighting, attacking, and absenting); and *the focus of attention* (i.e., narrow, wide, and moving flexibly between the two).

2. **Gaze**
   a. "Heart" and "slant" versus "eyeing" and "goal-oriented"
   b. Mindful, celebratory, evaluative, disintegrative and destructive, and absenting

The *quality of gazing* includes looking at the other from a heart-centered, indirect, and "slant" versus goal-oriented, direct, "eyeing" perspective. Differential effects of being gazed at by self or other in mindful, celebratory, evaluative, disintegrative and destructive, and absenting ways are explored.

3. **Organization of Mind/Body**
   a. Coalescing/connecting versus breaking apart/disconnecting
   b. On the preservation of being in "shards of light," known today as dissociative parts holding specific mind/body states

This final section considers universal processes of *connecting and disconnecting* in relation to shame, pride, LT, and SD. This discussion closes with a Hasidic myth about a person's essence held in a shard of light, and how this bears upon understanding dissociative parts characterized by specific, mind/body states in relationship with shame, pride, chronic LT, and SD.

While discussed separately, "attention," "gaze," and "organization of mind/body" are not entirely distinct capacities. When and how a person *attends* to self and other includes the quality of their *gazing* at self and other, and impacts how, over time, their mind/body becomes *organized*.

Attention

Where and how we place our attention are vital to all aspects of human functioning. Attention conveys interest and interest lives on a continuum from interest to excitement (Tomkins, 1963, 1962). Without attention there is no interest, desire, or embodied aliveness.

Neurocognitively, attention determines what problems need to be engaged. Attention facilitates learning, as when focused attention helps solve math problems and relaxed attention opens us to creative possibilities. Attending to some things and not others reveal what a person values, devalues, and desires. The Premack Principle (Premack, 1959) showed that observers can determine what a nonverbal child finds rewarding by paying attention to what they do when free to choose. Attention coupled with interest reveals essential qualities of a person's *being* and *being with*.

Directionality of Attention: Self, Other, Other's View of Self, and Self's View of Other's View of Self

At first glance, as regards shame and pride, *what* a person attends to is "the self." A closer look reveals *what* the shamed or proud person attends to is "quadri-furcated" (i.e., four-directional), attending to self, other, other's viewing of self, and self's viewing the other's viewing of self. While the emphasis here is on *inter*relationships, this applies equally to *intra*relationships. This is particularly important in understanding SD, as therapeutic attention is often on the patient's internal landscape.

Consider a pre-school-aged child playing with blocks: First, the child attends to themselves and concludes, "I'm good with blocks!" This is attending to SELF, exemplifying good enough me pride. Second, the child sees their parent looking at them with disgust, shouting, "What a slob!" As the parent's tone and gestures implicitly mobilize their shared relational history, the child's attention shifts to a perceived or implicitly neuroceived (Porges, 2011) interpersonal threat. Attending to the OTHER, the child moves out of adaptive pride and toward not good enough me shame. Third, immediately and outside conscious awareness, the child interprets their parent's look and implicitly agrees with them, that is, "I'm disgusting!" If despite the parent's disgust the child retains a positive view of themselves, then good enough me pride persists, for example, "My teacher says I'm good with blocks." This is OTHER viewing SELF. Fourth, the child sees themselves through their parent's eyes internalizing their parent's disgusted, shaming eyes. The proud child looks inward, having internalized their teacher's positive attention and rejecting their parent's judgment. In shame and pride, this child attends to SELF with internalized OTHER viewing SELF, consistent with infant-mother research into mutual gazing (Beebe & Lachmann, 1988).

Direction of attention as relates to LT is quite different from the development of shame and pride as emotional processes. LT tends to *unfocus*, particularly away from physical and emotional pain. This unfocusing of attention in LT is one way the RT survivor temporarily leaves her body, emotions, and relational field to "solve" the problem of shame and pride states.

As regards attentional directionality, SD is more complex than both *LT* and shame/pride as emotions. In SD, *extreme unfocusing and/or withdrawing of attention is followed by a narrow refocusing of attention aggregated within individual parts*. While both LT and SD involve unfocusing and refocusing of attention, they are phenomenologically distinct as only in SD do dissociative parts develop, each with a first-person perspective (Nijenhuis & Van der Hart, 2011).

Imagine an RT survivor of physical assault approached from behind by a stranger. Living with SD, this person copes by withdrawing attention away from a complex experience of self in relation to a stranger and refocusing within distinct, dissociative parts. For example, the person may unconsciously segregate their fight part's way of attending to self and other (e.g., yelling) from their submit part's way of attending (e.g., going along). (Chapter 4, #15, Shame and Pride: Prototypical Parts.) In addition, one dissociated part of the survivor's attention may orient toward external threats (e.g., specific aspects of the perpetrator's behavior) while another part hyperfocuses on internal threat (e.g., specific thoughts, feelings, and/or actions), rather than flexibly shift between self, other, relationship, and environment.

Quality of Attention: Accepting, Delighting, Attacking, and Absenting

Attending to self, other, and the relationship between self→other, other→self and self↔self is not merely a neurocognitive activity. Focusing attention on self-other perceptions and relationships is necessary for normal socialization and the development of RT (Schimmenti, 2012).

What matters most when studying shame, pride, LT, and SD is not the *direction* but rather *the quality of attentional focus* contributing to the development of an internal working model (Bowlby, 1969). The relational qualities described include *accepting, delighting, attacking,* and *absenting*.

Does the caregiver turn their attention toward the infant/child with acceptance? In contrast, does the caregiver attend to the infant/child with contempt or worse, unable to empathically imagine their inner life? Equally important, does the child and later adult receive or reject the other's attention? Do they fail to register genuine acceptance, having learned repeatedly "closeness" heralds "betrayal"? In sum, *the quality of the attentional focus given and received impacts the ways an infant/child and later adult internalize attention or its lack*.

What *quality of the caregiver's attention* toward their child fosters adaptive pride or shame? In pride, the caregiver's attention and accompanying non-verbal cues are *accepting*, valuing the child for what they have done or achieved. A young child hands their parent a toy, the parent smiles, saying "Thank you." In that moment, the child experiences a small dose of good enough me pride. The parent who responds sternly when their child throws a toy, "No throwing!" shames their child. A prompt repair—the parent gently and warmly saying, "I'm sorry I yelled" and "Throwing hurts"—transforms shame of feeling unwanted and excluded into loved and included. This exemplifies *accepting attention* shifting not good enough me shame toward good enough me shame.

The proud child attends to themselves when achieving something they set their mind to, irrespective of their parent's approval. While self-valuation and other-valuation may occur simultaneously, I believe the child standing for the first time would feel pride even if no one witnessed them.

More powerful than *accepting* attention is *delight*. Attentional delight embodies pro-being pride. When the parent's attention lights upon their infant who has only gurgled, the infant experiences their parent shining their love upon them. Over time, the parent's delighting attention is laid down as a somatic/emotional memory state rather than episodic "event." Their de-light activates a quintessential form of inter- and intrasubjective pro-being pride.

When the quality of attention a shamed person experiences is *attacking*, it is as though the shamer remarked, "*You* are bad" rather than "I don't like what *you did*." The "shamer" can be another person or the person themselves. *Absenting* shaming attention results when a caregiver fails to attend to essential aspects of the child's being, as when they never notice their child's grief.

The *qualities of attending* fostering not me shame and not me pride (i.e., *attacking*) are different from those contributing to no me shame and no me pride (i.e., *absenting*). Specific aspects of self *chronically attacked and/or absented* by a caregiver develop, over time, into dissociated parts of the child and later adult survivor. At times, these dissociative parts become unavailable for the survivor to think about, feel, and relate to. Thus, *caregiver attacking and/or absenting* in response to specific child attributes contribute to the development of not me shame and not me pride. *Chronic, "whole person," caregiver attacking (e.g., hating), and even more so absenting attention* lead to no me shame and no me pride. *Chronic, unpredictable and simultaneous accepting, attacking, and absenting attention* contribute to the development of disorganized attachment (Liotti, 2004) and SD parts gripped by shame and pride states.

Wide and Narrow Lens Attention

Wide lens attending is holistic, giving the observing self a felt sense (Gendlin, 2007/1978) of the observed person. Wide lens is a more right than left brain perception (McGilchrist, 2009), attending more to whole than part.

Wide lens perspectives hold complexity within awareness, engendering good enough me pride and pro-being pride. As Walt Whitman's (1855/1965) "Song of Myself" exclaimed:

> Do I contradict myself? Very well then I contradict myself, (I am large, I contain multitudes).
>
> (p. 88)

Alternatively, wide lens attending may overlook unique qualities of the observed.

Most adaptive is flexible alternation between wide and narrow lens perspectives, as needed. As psychotherapist, sometimes it is best to lean into one aspect of the patient's experience, and elsewhere allow the patient's subjective reality to wash over the therapist until something beckons their focused, narrow lens.

Narrow lens perspectives hone in on one quality in the self or other and enhance pride, for example, "You are so smart!" or denigrate and shame, for example, "You dummy!" Sometimes narrowing ameliorates maladaptive shame and pride, as when the therapist brings to the patient's attention a pattern of self-deprecation. Too narrow a focus may miss the patient's self-affirmation despite habitual self-criticism, blinded by the problem-saturated story (White & Epston, 1990).

Janet (1901) presaged my view of narrowing attention. Meares & Barral (2019) argue that for Janet, disintegration reflected states of unconsciousness where "diminution of personal synthesis" occurred via a "*contraction* of consciousness" (p. 111, my emphasis). Janet (1907) described "hysteria," now dissociative disorders, as "a form of mental depression characterized by the *retraction* of the field of personal consciousness" (p. 332, my emphasis). Whether *contraction* or *retraction* of consciousness, each aligns with a narrow lens perspective.

RT often activates the survivor's acute and later chronic, hypervigilant narrowing of attention coupled with an intense judging and searing gaze toward the self (Gazing, see below), and immobilization of mind, emotion, and body (Benau, 2021a, 2021b). These alterations in the survivor's attention reflect differential effects of overwhelming/abusive and/or underwhelming/neglectful caregiver behavior. What differentiates RT *generally* from traumatic shame and pride mind/body states *specifically* is that the latter focuses on one's value as a human being in relation to the abusive/neglectful other. In SD, dissociative parts of self may hold the presence of withering shame or absence of genuine pride. In RT, the survivor sees themselves, the perpetrator, the survivor-perpetrator relationship, and all relationships as reaction to abuse and neglect in narrow, rigid ways consistent with Janet's fixed ideas (Van der Hart & Friedman, 2019).

Maladaptive shame and pride emerge out of *inflexible ways of attending*, rigidly alternating from a narrow to wide lens. The person gripped by maladaptive shame and pride makes too much of too little, and then believes they know the whole truth! For example, the wife who discovers her husband had an affair takes one instance of "being fooled" (narrow lens) and makes it the totality of her relational capacities, "I am a fool" (wide lens).

Likewise, the hubristically proud person's narrow lens view of one personal attribute (e.g., physical attractiveness) widens to conclude, "My attractiveness proves I'm special and you're not." This better me proud person may have been raised by caregivers using a very narrow lens, privileging their child's beauty. The child and later adult learns implicitly to *focus narrowly* on physical appearance in a desperate attempt to retain self-worth and bond with their narcissistic parents.

LT and SD parallel the inflexible, narrow to wide lens perspective seen in chronic LT and with dissociative parts held as not me shame and not me pride. Each reflects a narrow lens excising and disowning (in shame) or privileging (in pride) parts of the whole person to preserve what is left of self and relationship. Not me shame is analogous to a surgeon cutting out cells mistakenly perceived as cancerous to save the patient's lungs. In not me pride, the person narrowly notices thriving cells (e.g., "I'm revered by my work colleagues") while dismissing damaged cells (e.g., "My wife's upset proves she's histrionic"). In the first instance, "cancer cells" represent personal attributes perceived as "unwanted" (e.g., sensitive), when neither toxic nor undesired in other relationships. Likewise, "non-thriving cells" (e.g., the spouse's upset) may teach the person something important about their excelling in some relationships (e.g., work) but not others (e.g., wife).

In chronic LT and SD, a narrow lens view teaches the child specific aspects of their "being" explicitly and/or implicitly threaten the attachment bond. For example, the not me shamed child and later adult may remain connected with their parent by never displaying cleverness, being taught they must not compete with their "smart sibling" whom their parent prefers. Likewise, the better me proud person narrowly focuses on being praised while dismissing feedback that could help them heal wounds they caused loved ones.

When dissociative parts have little to no awareness of other parts, the mind/body automatically, outside awareness, narrows the attentional field. As with maladaptive shame and pride emotions, in SD what is first seen within a narrow lens later expands whereby that "part" becomes "the whole." For example, the structurally dissociated patient's "attach part," longing to be nurtured, may remain unaware that their "flight part" breaks off relationship whenever close. (See Chapter 4, #15, Shame and Pride: Prototypical Parts.) The critical variable is *the inflexibility* of a narrow to wide lens perspective, reflecting SD's compartmentalization when exposed to chronic, relational threat.

Clinical Applications of the Phenomenology of Attention: Directionality, Quality, and Wide versus Narrow

General principles demonstrating how the phenomenology of attention guides psychotherapy with RT survivors are followed by three clinical vignettes illustrating these principles.

Attentional Directionality in Psychotherapy

- There is always at least one interrelational and/or intrarelational "other," from the past and/or present, contributing to a shame and/or pride state. This remains true even when the patient feels utterly alone and far removed from past, traumatizing relationships.
- An intrarelational "other" typically involves the introjection of the "absent" (neglecting) parent and the "present" (abusing) parent. The "other" also includes parts mimicking the abuser or neglecter (Schmidt, 2009), also called perpetrator imitating parts (Van der Hart et al., 2006), and still other parts that learned to cope with the abuser/neglecter and perpetrator mimicking/imitating part(s).
- When working with shame and pride states, the therapist must determine whether there are present-day abusive/neglecting "others" in the patient's life, including childhood traumatizing figures and/or others whose behavior is reminiscent of the RT. Before focusing primarily on the patient's intrarelational landscape, the therapist must help the patient

establish safety in relationships, now. Since intrarelational work may help patients find their way out of traumatizing relationships, this principle refers to relative rather than absolute therapeutic foci.

Attentional Quality in Psychotherapy

- With respect to accepting, delighting, attacking, and absenting attending, the therapist helps their patient identify *how* each part of the patient "attends to" the other parts, and *how* the part receiving that attention react. The therapist accepts the whole person, particularly less likable parts that attack other parts and/or the therapist, helping the patient learn to attend with interest and acceptance. Delighting attention is essential when therapist and patient marvel at the patient's creative capacity to survive and thrive in the face of RT. To clarify, the therapist delights in their patient well before the RT survivor can receive it, and then only after considerable work.

Attention Wide and/or Narrow Lens in Psychotherapy

As regards SD and attention, the sine qua non of shame and pride states is inflexibility, where dissociative parts are fixed in excessively wide or narrow attending. *Attentional* fixedness is one *specific attribute* of Janet's idees fixes (Van der Hart & Friedman, 2019). The therapist's goal is to help patients move from narrow to wide attention and back again, with situation specific freedom of psychological movement. This may be accomplished therapeutically by:

- First, joining rather than agreeing with the patient's narrow or wide lens view, understanding the patient's self-perception from a functionally coherent perspective (Ecker et al., 2012; Chapter 4, #9, Functional Coherence [FC]). Next, helping the patient gripped by mind/body states slowly develop greater complexity (narrow to wide) or specificity (wide to narrow).
- Following therapeutic Memory Reconsolidation (MR) (Ecker et al., 2012), facilitating an experiential juxtaposition between the patient's dominant shamed/prided part and another way of being subjectively true *and* incompatible with the RT-derived belief. (Chapter 4, #10, Memory Reconsolidation [MR].)
- Adopting a narrative therapy stance (White & Epston, 1990), noticing adaptive exceptions to implicit shaming and/or priding, and inviting the patient to give meaning to these anomalies.
- Mindfully observing the physical, imagistic, and/or cognitive features of parts dominated by shame or pride, and slowly introducing one new element. For example, attending to somatic manifestations of maladaptive shame or pride, and helping the patient shift their attention "one inch" away from that physical sensation. Using imagery, inviting the patient to

alter the size, shape, color, tone of voice, etc. of the part characterized by the shame or pride state (e.g., Schmidt's [2009] "switching the dominance" [p. 62]), cognitively, introducing one new thought that helps the patient view himself slightly differently, as in "Are there parts besides the shaming part that haven't yet spoken?" (narrow to wide) or "I understand that is true, but has that ever not been true about you, however briefly?" (wide to narrow).
- In SD, speaking to dissociative parts holding shame or pride that listen rather than front in-session; inviting patient-therapist curiosity about motivations of parts complying with the shamer/prider; and inviting curiosity about the RT conditions fostering the patient's internal working model (Bowlby, 1973).

Clinical Vignette: "Isaac": Who Attends to Whom and How?

Chapters 6 and 7 present several sessions with Isaac, an RT survivor. Here, I describe Isaac's attentional directionality and quality discovered in the first three years of therapy and later how, in one session, his attention moved from inflexibly narrow to wide, open, and free.

Isaac was happily married for over 30 years, with two young adult children, in recovery from alcoholism for 35 years, and an active meditator for 10 years. Isaac was a survivor of a single incident of sexual molestation by a stranger in a park (age six), and of recurrent RT within his family of origin. Isaac's RT included emotional abuse, particularly shaming by his father and older brother; physical abuse by his older brother, including assaults and threats that humiliated and terrorized Isaac; and emotional neglect and nonattunement by both parents, including his mother's collapse after the death of Isaac's beloved younger sister, when Isaac was seven.

During the first three years of therapy, Isaac and I discovered and worked with several dissociative parts. Although not initially conscious of these parts, he lived with their longstanding effects. These younger parts included a 4-year-old, pre-trauma part who loved to sing, dance, and be in nature; a 6-year-old sexually abused by a stranger, carrying unbearable shame; a 7-year-old grieving the loss of his younger sister; a 12-year-old who shamed younger parts for being "weak" and trusting; an enraged 15-year-old who shamed Isaac and pushed him to physical extremes; and a suspicious 20-year-old who feared showing weakness and used anger as self-protection. Together we uncovered his father's "installation" (Isaac's term for introjection) that he could only be weak and subordinate (shameful) or strong and dominant (hubristically prideful). Isaac's self-raging 15-year-old and other-raging 20-year-old parts mimicked (Schmidt, 2009; Van der Hart, 2006) his father's and brother's worldviews and behavior.

Regarding attentional direction and quality, Isaac's 4-year-old was self-accepting and delighting; 6-year-old attacking of the four-year-old for letting his guard down, activating the 4-year-old's not me shame state whenever enlivened; the 7-year-old's internalized, absenting attention of parents who *never* acknowledged Isaac's grieving the death of his beloved sister, leading to the 7-year-old's not me shame (i.e., grief denied) and no me shame (i.e., aliveness unseen); 12-year-old Isaac attacking the 4-, 6-, and 7-year-old parts for any feelings revealing weakness; 12-year-old mimicking his father's and brother's attacking, shaming (father and brother), and terrorizing and humiliating (brother) behavior; 15-year-old part ragefully attacking all younger parts, mimicking his father's directives to endure pain; and Isaac's 20-year-old father-imitating part attacking all younger parts, and feeling enraged with colleagues who challenged Isaac's ideas.

Clinical Vignette: "Sarah": From Inflexible to Flexible Narrow and Wide Lens Attending

As a child, Sarah bonded with her self-absorbed father sharing in his excitement about projects *he* valued. Sarah's excitement was always mixed with anxiety, given her tenuous, "strings attached" relationship with her father. As an adult in couple therapy, Sarah learned her excitement sometimes failed to attune emotionally to her narcissistically wounded husband. Sarah's narrow lens (e.g., excitement about a germ of an idea) to wide lens (e.g., "This idea will bring me and my husband closer!") left her vulnerable. Whenever Sarah's husband did not share her enthusiasm, she dropped from "inflation" (in her words, "a helium balloon whose string I excitedly grabbed onto") to "deflation" ("a pin bursting my balloon"). As Sarah became aware of her inflexible, narrow to wide lens responding, she modified her attentional style, widening her lens to include her husband's interests and seeking shared pleasures.

Clinical Vignette: "Isaac": "Staying with" Somatic Markers of Shame States: From Pinpoint Inflexibility to Wide and Flexible Attending

This session occurred four years, seven months into weekly psychotherapy with Isaac, (introduced above), conducted via Zoom given COVID restrictions. We followed an approach to working with RT called Deep Brain Reorienting (DBR) (Corrigan & Christie-Sands, 2020). DBR was chosen to help Isaac process therapeutically preverbal or not yet verbalized aspects of his shame state. In DBR, the patient observes somatic markers of activation purportedly originating within the brainstem's midbrain structures, particularly superior colliculi (SC) and periaqueductal gray (PAG). SC orients the patient toward or away from stimuli associated with RT. PAG assays danger versus safety of relational stimuli, and initiates active and passive defensive responding. When successful, DBR enables the patient to process midbrain/brainstem effects of RT, that then clear "upstream" traumatic reactivity associated with limbic and neocortical structures.

At the start of DBR sessions, the patient gets comfortable, releases face and neck tensions, and orients in space. The patient then attends to and intermittently describes physical sensations associated with automatic, orienting responses to relational threat, particularly in and around their neck and eyes. In DBR, the RT survivor's orienting response is activated by a prompt encapsulating a core, relational theme. Isaac's prompt was "I've been terrorized my whole life," referring to his older brother. Following the prompt, somatic tracking ensued, in Isaac's case eyes closed.

This transcribed session presents excerpts pertaining to Isaac's narrow and wide attending. As tracking began, Isaac observed "huge energy" in his quadriceps and groin, associated with his sexual molestation, quickly followed by "pulsing" sensations in and around his right eye. (Well before my DBR training, Isaac and I noticed he always held RT activation on the right side, particularly behind his right eye.) While "relaxed," Isaac's "whole body" "told" him what he "fear[ed]" was that he was "gonna be killed" by his older brother. Soon after, Isaac described "a right-side tightening" while his "eyes were watering," holding in his "heart, grief, sorrow, for my childhood."

Isaac next observed physical sensations behind his right eye, associated with "fury, anger," responding to repeated shaming and humiliating messages, "what they [father and brother] told about me, internalized."

In the transcript, "Th" refers to therapist, me, and "Pt" the patient, Isaac. All *emphases* are mine. Note that what seems brief took place over an hour, with long pauses while Isaac observed somatic sensations:

I instructed Isaac to notice "physical sensations" associated with "fury," a year earlier identified as reactive rage toward the sexual perpetrator (Benau, 2021b), father, and now brother:

Pt: "*Tight, right eye focus, in my forehead, pin-pointed.*"
Th: "Right eye, pin-pointed, what is the physical sensation?"
[Isaac's head tilted toward his right side and faced slightly down.]
Pt: "*Laser coming out of my right eye. Energy.* On the right side of my chest, neck, into the eye. Cutting out."
Th: "Good tracking, stay with that."
[Isaac's eyes fluttered, slightly.]
Pt: "*It hurts, my right eye. There's a different feeling, above, my focus is more open, above the right eye and eyebrow.*"
Th: "Hurt on the right side?"
Pt: "It lessened a bit. I sat very still. Less energy coming out. *Different energy in the right eye. Less focused, less laser-like. More open, disparate.*"
[Isaac turned his whole body toward his right. He visage lightened, now facing center, head up, and mouth opened slightly.]
Pt: "*Much lighter, much less focused.* Curved above, the whole area where there was darkness, the stress there, more benign. *Recovering so much, feeling so much anger, grief, now I'm not alone. It feels better.*"
Th: "Stay with it."

[Several minutes passed.]
Th: "What are you noticing?"
Pt: "*Both eyes, pulsing with energy, circular patterns, sometimes colors. My adult self to the time when I was little.* I'm [Adult Isaac] *being with my younger selves, in a circle, 4-, 5-, 6-, 8-, 12-, 15-year-old. I'm talking to myself. What happened was real.*"
Th: "All that terror, chest, going to your neck?"
Pt: "Still some fear, anxiety. On my right side. *My eyes, chest, arms. Much lighter. 'I can do this.' Stepping out of that fear.* I'm tracking, it's really hard, *and* I can do it. I am doing it. *I've got space, freedom, areas of my whole body.*"
Th: "What are the physical sensations that go with, 'I can do this'?"
Pt: "Deeper letting go, relaxation in my arms, shoulders."
Th: "On your right side?"
Pt: "*Hot, my whole body, just relaxation.*"
[Coming to the end of our session:]
Th: "Come back here, when you're ready."
[Isaac opened his eyes, and I asked what the session meant to him.]
Pt: "A couple of things. *Feeling in my eyes, like a wiper. Like losing scales in front of my eyes. Helping me see what actually happened. My eyes.*"
Th: "What are you wiping away?"
Pt: "Denial. Wishing I could be other."
Th: "You can see more clearly."
Pt: To be able to go toward tremendous fear, anxiety. *To sit with it, process it. Eyes forward.* It feels good to do it."
Th: "You did it."
Pt: "It's where I live."
[I thought Isaac was integrating past trauma, held on his right side, and present experience, held on his left side.]
Th: "*Now, [you have] both sides. So freeing. To know the truth.*"
[End of session.]

When a patient mindfully observes, in Isaac's case with the benefit of years of meditation practice and a trusting, therapeutic relationship, significant somatic, emotional, and psychological transformation can be achieved. Isaac's attention went from an activated, tense, narrowed, "pinpointed," "laser" focus, to "less focused, less laser-like," "more open and disparate," and "much lighter." This marked Isaac processing and integrating traumatic reactions to his brother terrorizing him throughout childhood into early adulthood. Isaac described "recovering so much, feeling so much anger, grief, now I'm not alone. It feels better." Isaac's Adult Self collaborated with previously dissociated parts age 4 through 15.

Beginning with "pinpointed" attention, Isaac's eyes were wiped clearer, free and open to "see what actually happened." By the end, Isaac showed psychological and somatic integration, remarking "Now, [I have] both sides. So freeing. To know the truth."

Quality of Gazing

"Heart" and "Slant" versus "Eye" and "Goal-Oriented" Gazing

The quality of gazing accompanying adaptive, good enough me pride and good enough me shame has several features. These include *heart focus* and *looking slant*, and gazing that is *wide, flexible,* and/or *mindful*. We begin with *heart focus* and *looking slant* and contrast these with *eyeing* in a *goal-oriented* way.

Bill Bowen (Bowen website), developer of Psycho-Physical Therapy, taught students to differentiate "seeing from the heart" and "seeing with the eyes." For me, the "heart gaze" is a gentle, receptive, and mildly diffuse way of looking. Seeing with the eyes is "head on" with intense, active, "goal oriented" purposefulness. When you experiment with looking "from the heart" and then "with the eyes," you will experience your version of this distinction.

Gazing from the heart, we discover the other in unexpected ways. When "eyeing," we search for something in the other, implicitly discerning whether they are safe/unsafe, liked/not liked, etc. Heart gazing is accepting, even when the person does something disliked; goal-oriented eyeing is more evaluative (see Evaluative Gazing). Heart gazing is less likely to shame or pride the other, embodying nonjudgmental observation. While "eyeing" is not always evaluative, it is often experienced that way when an RT patient senses the therapist is trying to get something. Who amongst us has *not* had a patient ask what we are looking for by our line of questioning? This exemplifies the difference between looking with an agenda versus looking from the heart, with openness and curiosity.

Looking "slant" also gazes without judgment. In slant gazing, we look out of the corner of our eyes rather than directly, straight ahead. RT patients prone to maladaptive shame and pride often benefit from slant gazing. Direct, face-to-face peering may feel too exposing of vulnerabilities, increasing patient suspiciousness, shaming, priding, LT, and/or activate SD parts. An RT survivor may likewise benefit from looking at the therapist slant, gazing at the edges of the therapist's body rather than making eye contact.

The poet Emily Dickinson (1960/1868, pp. 506–507) valued telling the truth slant, offering a poetic analogy to the benefits of slant gazing:

> Tell all the truth but tell it slant—(1129)

> Tell all the truth but tell it slant—
> Success in Circuit lies
> Too bright for our infirm Delight
> The Truth's superb surprise
> As Lightning to the Children eased
> With explanation kind
> The Truth must dazzle gradually
> Or every man be blind—

"Goal-oriented" gazing can be experienced as less accepting, narrowly focused, missing the whole person in context, and activate maladaptive shame, pride, and LT, and contribute to developing SD. For many survivors, direct eye contact feels so invasive they automatically "leave" to escape perceived or implicitly neuroceived (Porges, 2011) interpersonal threat and judgment. When a person experiences LT, their vision and mental acuity blurs. When a patient leaves the embodied, relational field, they unconsciously seek less feeling and pain. Unfortunately, the survivor's capacity to situationally adjust their gaze and avoid retraumatization is impaired (DePrince et al., 2015; Dorahy, 2010; Dorahy et al., 2013, 2015).

Perceiving interpersonal threats demand goal-oriented gazing "looking for trouble." Looking for trouble is adaptive when failing to detect relational threat is dangerous. Alternatively, some cultural traditions identify certain kinds of gazing as threatening, as when a person curses another by giving the evil eye (Ross, 2010).

One paradox of an RT survivor's gaze is that they can look diffusely or not at all and elsewhere gaze intently to detect perceived threat. The survivor who learns early that people are predictably and unpredictably dangerous, having been repeatedly attacked and/or abandoned, rather than "leave" may vigilantly "eye" others to locate threat in facial expressions, tone of voice, etc., even when no threat presents. To complicate matters, SD patients may have parts with unfocused or absenting attention while other parts with fierce, goal-orienting gaze, "finding trouble before trouble finds them."

In sum, in RT a child repeatedly endures interactions with no safe passage. As adult survivor in psychotherapy, the patient leaves psychologically (LT), seeing without precision or not at all. Alternatively, the same survivor may peer with pinpoint acuity, accurately *and* inaccurately, fending off anticipated threat and/or neglectful caregiving. Therapist "heart gazing" and "looking slant" may engender a patient's adaptive pride and shame, or simply self-acceptance, whereas "goal-oriented eyeing" may activate pride and shame states, evoke acute and/or chronic LT, SD, unfocused gazing, and/or threatening, eyeing back.

Mindful, Celebratory, Evaluative, Disintegrative and Destructive, and Absenting Gazing

Mindful Gazing

It takes considerable practice to view others and oneself nonjudgmentally. Self-acceptance and other-acceptance are ideals not easily achieved, or more accurately gained, lost, and regained. Brach (2003) wrote about the challenges and rewards of radical self-acceptance and comparable difficulties and benefits accrue with radical other-acceptance.

Adults admonish misbehaving children saying, "I accept you but not your behavior." This simple statement references a complex, psychological process. To reject someone's behavior is straightforward: "I do not condone how your behavior impacts me and others." The person who rejects someone's behavior but not their person sees, thinks, feels, and gazes upon the other in two contrasting ways, simultaneously rejecting the person's harmful actions while retaining an image of their better self. At best, therapists maintain a Janus-like consciousness, holding the patient's problematic behavior, including toward their therapist, within a larger frame, understanding and accepting the patient's suffering and archaic ways of coping, while imagining their preferred way of being.

Celebratory Gazing

A person celebrating their pro-being pride extends beyond mindful nonjudgment toward discovering joy in their truer self. Pro-being pride is not only *accepting* but also *delighting in* the person's unique way of expressing their aliveness. A state of pro-being pride does not evaluate others *and at the same time* embodies the highest form of valuing of being, relating, and life.

When the therapist imagines a patient as an infant (pre-trauma), and simultaneously in the future after successful therapy (post-healing), therapist and patient contact their shared, pro-being pride. I intentionally envision this past/future person when struggling with a survivor who is also struggling. Holding two or more discrete entities in thought (Janusian thinking) that occupy the same visualized space (homospatial thinking) underlies creative process (Rothenberg, 1979).

Evaluative Gazing

Evaluative gazing is a more common way of looking. Evaluatively seeing and being with others or oneself identifies good/bad, accepted/rejected, and valued/devalued ways of being. Evaluative gazing is part of our mammalian heritage, perceiving and implicitly neuroceiving (Porges, 2011) when it is safe to socially engage versus when danger/threat necessitates fighting, fleeing, and/or submitting.

Since dissociative parts emerge out of chronic relational conditions of unsafety, it follows traumatic shame and pride states are also rooted in threat. Shame and pride states are held in dissociative parts implicitly and/or explicitly about good and bad, as in "I am bad/inferior and you and your reality are good/superior" (traumatic shame), and "I am good/superior and you and your reality are bad/inferior" (traumatic pride). Evaluative gazing contributes to deflation and inflation of self, respectively.

Approaching RT patients from an evaluative stance, as is sometimes unavoidable, we risk harming survivors raised in evaluative family systems and much worse. The best way out of this bind recognizes the functional coherence (FC) of behavior (Chapter 4; Ecker et al., 2012). FC means the patient's behavior always makes sense within an inter- and/or intrarelational context, past and present. For example, a better me proud person might have learned as a child that dismissiveness kept humiliation outside awareness, although it now leaves them feeling empty and alone. Finding function in dysfunction and meaning in madness adds no further indignities to the patient's shaming themselves and/or others.

Disintegrative and Destructive Gazing

Disintegrative and destructive gazing trigger traumatic, chronic LT and, over time, the development of SD. Disintegrative gazing keeps aspects of self-other experience outside of awareness. Disintegrative gazing results in not me shame and not me pride, as when in SD a person's fight part and attach part never communicate, as anger threatened early bonds. Alternatively, disintegrative gazing may reflect the survivor's unconscious attempt to preserve parts of self that cannot be expressed safely in relationship. SD used unconsciously to hide and preserve parts of self is evidenced when a survivor envies others' creativity and denies their own, having been repeatedly humiliated when displaying creativity. (See Chapter 2, Not Me Pride Vignette.)

Destructive gazing destroys, annihilates, or prevents the development of the person's *entire being* or sense of *an integrated self*. As with absenting gazing, destructive gazing also leads to the development of no me shame and no me pride. Destructive gazing, seen in overt hatred and sadism, intends to kill the person psychologically (cf., Shengold's [1989] soul murder). When internalized by the hated person, this results in an incohesive identity. When destructive gazing predominates intrarelationally, a sense of self either never develops or, when an enlivened self emerges, is shame-attacked by internalized perpetrators.

Absenting Gazing

As with absenting attention, absenting gazing is intrinsically shaming. This occurs when a parent fails to attend to essential aspects of the child's being, for example, their grief, contributing to not me shame and not me pride. In the extreme, absenting gazing contributes to no me shame and no me pride. "Laura," an RT survivor discussed in Chapter 2, said her father "looked right through" her as though she did not exist.

Clinical Applications of the Phenomenology of Gazing: Qualities of Gazing

"Heart" and "Slant" versus "Eyeing" and "Goal-Oriented" Gazing

My habit is to look intently into people's eyes. Some patients experience this as keen interest and presence. My intense gaze helps these patients feel accompanied, diminishing feelings of unbearable aloneness (Fosha, 2000), and mitigating activation of LT, shame and pride states, and SD more generally. In contrast, my gaze intensity causes some to feel I am invasively "eyeing" them or demanding specific responses. These survivors are prone to dropping into shame and/or pride states, LT, and/or SD activation, especially of fight, flight, freeze, and submit parts. When I realize my gaze is triggering my patients, I seek at least one of several corrective actions:

- Looking from my heart rather than my eyes.
- Looking at my patient with curiosity, trusting our relationship and process. It helps when I heart gaze toward the young part of me worrying about not quickly helping the patient.
- Alternating patient "eyeing" with gazing outside the window behind the patient where a large tree soothes me, fostering slant and heart gazing.
- Looking out of the corner of my eyes, or looking at the patient's mouth, forehead, or around the periphery of the patient's body. Looking out of the corner of my eyes allows me to gaze inward, inviting patients to do likewise. With over 45 years working with people living with Autism Spectrum Disorder (ASD), I have learned gazing at the "third eye" and inviting them to do the same helps some ASD patients feel more relationally and emotionally safe. This removes the demand they "make eye contact," a shaming message people with ASD often hear from neurotypicals.

Quality of Gazing: Mindful, Celebratory, Evaluative, Disintegrative and Destructive, and Absenting Gazing

Therapists learn to gaze at patients in a mindful, nonevaluative, and sometimes celebratory ways. Still, many RT survivors have internalized evaluative, disintegrative, and destructive gazing. Self and other-shaming and destructive gazing often dominates the RT patient's intrapersonal and interpersonal landscapes. With therapist intentionality and patient practice, the survivor can develop mindful and celebratory gazing in several ways:

- The therapist refuses to adopt the patient's evaluative perspective, gazing with curiosity, seeking functionally coherent meanings (Ecker et al., 2012), and surprising the patient in "safe but not too safe" ways (Bromberg, 2011, p. 189). These ways of seeing help the patient similarly to gaze upon themselves and others.
- The therapist teaches the patient how to think from a parts perspective (Chapter 4, #14, Multiplicity of Parts). This invites mindful, open-hearted gazing, discovering previously shunned aspects of self and others, which is crucial when working with shame and pride states.
- The therapist "catches" the patient viewing themselves in mindful and even celebratory ways, wondering aloud with the patient what intrarelational and interrelational conditions support these developments (White & Epston, 1990).
- The therapist invites the patient to notice how he thinks, feels, and behaves when experiencing his own, another person's, and/or the

therapist's mindful, nonevaluative, and/or celebratory gazing, and to metatherapeutically process (Fosha, 2000, pp. 161–164) these "moments of meeting" and transformation (Stern, 1998, p. 300; 2004, p. 168).
- Most importantly, the therapist notices and celebrates the emergence of the patient's pro-being pride:

Clinical Vignette: "Jacob": Developing Celebratory Gazing

Jacob was an RT survivor growing up with divorced, narcissistically wounded parents. Beginning our session with a nervous laugh, Jacob shared his new car had arrived. Immediately, Jacob dismissively remarked buying this car was "ostentatious" and "frivolous." Wanting to help Jacob connect with pro-being pride, I asked what excited him about his car. Jacob's self-evaluative and critical gaze quickly returned, with anxiety outweighing pleasure, "70/30 out of 100."

Having previously explored Jacob's difficulty celebrating his birthday, I suggested we had reentered familiar terrain. Jacob agreed to explore his anxiety about this purchase.

I invited Jacob to attend to his pleasure in the new car for as long as possible, noticing when excitement was interrupted by other emotions or physical sensations.

Jacob described his car's technology as "cool," cutting edge. His "sleek white car" was aesthetically pleasing. Jacob then bumped into a shaming, evaluative, and disintegrative gaze. Again, his purchase was "frivolous." Upon inquiry, Jacob realized he viewed his mother as "rich but selfish." His mother's behavior was incompatible with his religious values, including giving of time not just money to those less fortunate.

Dreading his becoming selfish, Jacob observed his chest contracting and emotionally shutting down. Jacob had the urge to look away, avoiding his own and anticipating my evaluative gaze.

Attending to his embodiment of pro-being pride, I asked Jacob to notice his somatic and emotional experience when reflecting on "desire." Jacob now had more room to breathe, his chest gently expanding, and smile shifting from tense to ease. Jacob's transition from "contraction" to "expansion" showed movement, in his words, from "shame" to "pride." Jacob realized he "desired" rather than "needed" the car, associating this with his desire to be more intimate with his wife.

In this session, Jacob went from anxious, constricted, critically evaluative, and destructive gazing and shame/shutdown to "desire." Jacob's desire gave expression to his authentic aliveness, expanding toward celebratory gazing and pro-being pride. My accepting and celebratory gazing helped Jacob attenuate his internalized shaming and disintegrative self-gazing. Most importantly, Jacob's genuine delight, not with his car but rather our shared delighting in his delighting, helped Jacob move from maladaptive shame to adaptive, good enough me pride and pro-being pride.

Organization of Mind/Body

Connecting or Coalescing versus Disconnecting or Breaking Apart

Safely in relationship and securely attached (Main, 2000), we are connected. Safely connected, different ways of being are freely expressed in relationship and given inner voice. There is room to be serious and silly, contemplative and playful, and room for enjoying private thoughts without having to hide shameful secrets.

Connecting is observed throughout nature, when mammals bond, and more basically when lichen attaches to rock, and water molecules coalesce. Connecting and coalescing occur at all levels of existence, from the atomic where neutrons, protons, and electrons coalesce to form molecules, to millions of people organizing as nation states. Disconnection or breaking apart are also ubiquitous in nature, be that two people parting in love or hate, or cells dividing and differentiating, with one line developing lungs and another the brain.

Connection and disconnection are not strictly opposed. The securely attached teen leaving for college disconnects (physically) yet remains connected to family (psychologically, financially, etc.). Disconnection serves adaptive goals, as when a young adult grows into greater independence, and maladaptive goals, when disconnection in SD causes self-alienation and social isolation (DePrince et al., 2015; Dorahy, 2010). Psychopathology can be viewed as too much connection and/or too much disconnection. Excessive connecting in family enmeshment (Minuchin, 1974) also reveals profound disconnecting impeding healthy individuation (Bowen, 1978).

In pride and shame, disconnecting and connecting forces are also at play. Pride and shame may disconnect individuals from others, making them stand out (pride) or stand alone (shame). Pride and shame disconnect the individual from aspects of self, when one characteristic (e.g., aggression) is valued and recognized (pride) or devalued and dismissed (shame).

The adaptively proud, victorious athlete disconnects from others by distinguishing themselves, yet remains connected to their fans. The maladaptively proud person disconnects from their peers and affiliative impulses, yet remains deeply connected to others via an implicit agreement that one person remain superior. The person experiencing adaptive, good enough me shame briefly disconnects from their values and, pausing, adjusts their behavior, reconnecting with their truer self. Trapped in a chronic shame state, the RT survivor is profoundly disconnected from their enlivenment, while remaining painfully connected with their shaming caregiver, alive or deceased.

Chronic, trauma-induced LT and SD can be understood as extreme forms of disconnection and connection. The word "dissociation" is rooted in "dis," a Latin prefix meaning "*apart*," "asunder," and "away" (Dissociation, definition), and "association," "the fact of being *involved with* or *connected to* someone or something" (Association, definition, my emphasis). Dis-association or dissociation refers to a person psychologically and sometimes physically disconnecting from connection, both within (intrarelationally) and between (interrelationally).

Traumatic shame and pride states making up dissociative parts, chronic LT, and SD more generally are, paradoxically, also about connection. In chronic LT, a sexual trauma survivor tries to find ways to connect with their partner, knowing that behaving sexually would humiliate and enrage them.

SD also retains elements of disconnection and connection. Intrapersonally, SD renders separate whole swaths of human experience, for example, meanings, memories, images, sensations, etc. Each may be held in different, dissociative parts outside the person's awareness and functioning (Van der Hart, 2006). Interpersonally, the person living with SD may disconnect from others, not realizing they seek (attach part) when in the grips of rage (fight part).

Connection is less apparent in SD, often operating outside awareness, intrarelationally, when the physically abused child attaches with the abusive parent by complying (submit part), convinced they are never angry (fight part, dissociated). SD allows the child to maintain some psychological equilibrium, however unstable. Interrelationally, SD allows certain parts of personality to maintain some contact with abusive or neglectful caregivers. In contrast, the survivor of violence may become aggressive when others get too close, maintaining distance so as not to hurt and be hurt, again.

Nonclinical Vignette: John: Coalescing and Connecting: Shame State to Pro-being Pride in a Single "Session"

The following describes a colleague's one-day transformation from shame state to pro-being pride (Benau, 2020b).

John Walker, a psychotherapist from Edmonton, Alberta Canada, graciously gave me permission to share this vignette. All quotations are from John's written narrative:

> When I was 10 I joined a Peewee league hockey team ... The other boys on the team had been playing hockey for three to four years whereas I was a beginner. It did not go well. I could skate forward but I could not turn or stop. My puck handling and shooting skills were abysmal. I was relegated to the fourth line at best, and more often the bench. I was ridiculed even by my own teammates. Being a sensitive, introverted, and socially insecure boy I experienced this as a deeply humiliating and shameful torture. Previously I had been extensively bullied in elementary school and so this added to the pain of it all. I wanted to quit but my mother, who is a fighter (who at age eight clubbed a 11-year-old boy over the head with a shovel who was beating on her older brother), wouldn't hear of it and so the sad affair dragged out over five months.

I did not play organized hockey again. I did not speak of how painful this ongoing public shaming was … a private misery.

35 years later I live in a… neighborhood with an outdoor ice rink. I would take my young daughters skating there and occasionally we would shoot a puck around. I have become a much better ice skater.

One night there is a pickup game at the rink with a bunch of 20-year-old guys. I decide to join in. Most of the guys are faster and more skilled than me, so I hang out on defense. They will have to get through me to get to the goalie! The action moves up and down the ice. And then it's just me defending against an opposing player making for our net. Enthusiastically and recklessly I rush him and, still lacking in the braking department, I crash into him, cracking heads together. We tumble to the ice. We are both bloodied, I have an open wound needing stitches on my brow.

I feel fantastic!! I pack up and walk home through that beautiful wintery night elated!! I feel so alive and free!! My wife, my daughters are upset about the blood down my face and I just feel so happy!!

For me this single event resolved those months of childhood misery.

Discussion of John's Vignette

John, a self-described sensitive, introverted, and empathic child, was prone to feeling shame. Children like John are often shame-prone because:

- They experience their own and others' feelings intensely, particularly social nonattunement, whether or not actively shamed and ignored. With a porous stimulus barrier (Freud, 1961/1920), they are prone to feeling more than their mind/body can integrate *alone*. "Alone" is highlighted because "stimuli overload," "alone," and "shame" are a recipe for a shame state. John was alone, in relation to his teammates, coach, and most importantly his "fighter" mother who had difficulty accepting her sensitive son.
- They internalize rather than externalize their own and others' emotions. Rather than fight back, these children typically go inward to manage strong emotions. They are prone to believe their shame says something painfully true about them, rather than the shamer(s).

Coupled with John's introversion, sensitivity, and mother's insisting he fight on, John was "extensively bullied" prior to the shaming event. Left utterly alone "for five months," it is no wonder John "[does] not play organized hockey again." Nor does John "speak of how painful this ongoing public shaming was … a private misery."

John's shame state was reinforced rather than born anew, shame layered upon shame. Lacking a secure attachment to process shaming events with dignity and genuine pride, John endured the shame of being ridiculed, by people (i.e., peers, coach, and mother) with whom he most needed to connect; and alone, his shame painfully, recursively was remembered (Scheff, in press) for 35 years.

Perhaps because John created new, secure attachments within, as a result of personal therapy and becoming a psychotherapist, and between, with his wife and children, John finds the courage to join a pick-up game. What at first looks like shame state redux, John's crashing into his opponent and "cracking heads" is transformative. Why?

John entered immediately into a state of pro-being pride:

> *I feel fantastic!! I pack up and walk home through that beautiful wintery night elated!! I feel so alive and free!! My wife, my daughters are upset about the blood down my face and I just feel so happy!!* [John's inner and outer landscapes were instantly transformed, walking home on a "*beautiful wintery night …*"] (my emphases).

How did John move from a traumatic shame state to pro-being pride, from profound disconnection to reconnection and coalescing in one smashing moment?

John's gets on the ice, attacks his opponent, confronting his potential shamer and not only surviving but also thriving. This is an act of triumph (Janet, 1919, 1925; Ogden, 2019; Van der Hart et al., 1989).

John's transformation reflects the process of memory reconsolidation (MR) (Ecker et al., 2012) within the domains of meaning, emotion, and the body. (Chapter 4, #10, Memory Reconsolidation [MR]).

Within the domain of meaning, John's experience of self, other, and relationship to ice hockey are "updated" (Ecker et al., 2012, p. 33), following an experiential juxtaposition of the original schema and new, incompatible belief. Previously, "fighting" was associated with bullying and disconnection, banished from the circle of his peers,' coach's and mother's love. Now, "fighting" means fighting your way back into the circle of love, connecting with one's own and others' aliveness.

Emotionally, John moves dramatically from a crushing and deadening shame state where he is small, constricted, and excluded by others, to an enlarging, enlivening state of pro-being pride. Rather than "out," blood is literally and metaphorically commingled and shared. John feels connected with his fellow players, family, and nature.

John experiences a somatic juxtaposition, moving from physiological hypoarousal and shame shutdown to an invigorating state of heightened, well-regulated arousal, and finally to a larger, upright body as energy moves through him. John shifts from traumatic immobilization to triumphant movement (Benau, 2021a, 2021b).

While John's transformation seemed to happen in a single, smashing moment, many experiences led to its development, including therapy, his own and as therapist, and earned secure attachment within his family and with his mother (Roisman et al., 2002), as attested to by John's coherent narrative (Main, 1991) and comments after reading my account:

At this time several important developments were co-occurring: I was half way through an intensive six-year training as a psychotherapist and, not unrelated, I was in a 15-year psychological struggle for identity and differentiation with my mother. We went at it hammer and tong for those long years, struggling over who had authorship of my experience as her son. Gradually she came to accept that our different versions of our relationship could co-exist. We went on to enjoy the best years of our relationship as she lived well into her 90s.

Eric Berne, developer of Transactional Analysis, purportedly said, "I can cure anyone in one session. It may, however, take me three years to get to that one session." In John's case, 35 years and a moment in time.

On the Preservation of Being in "Shards of Light," Known Today as Dissociative Parts Holding Specific Mind/Body States

Schimmenti (2018, personal communication) wrote this about SD:

> I also believe that dissociation (SD), as a general function of the mind, protects from attachment disorganization, by compartmentalizing internal states and mental/bodily representations linked to traumatic attachment.

Extreme forms of SD reflect the mind/body's valiant attempt to remain connected with essential aspects of being and relationship. This does not ignore the shattering of the mind's capacity to contain dysregulating emotions and give meaning to experience. At the same time, the idea that SD compartmentalizes to avoid even greater disorganization suggests dissociative parts retain distinct "shards of being" so as not to completely lose one's mind (i.e., madness) or body (i.e., death). The idea that "being" may be viewed as a "shard of light" comes from a creation myth in the Kabbalah, a book of Jewish mysticism:

> In reference to individual acts of repair, the phrase "tikkun olam" (repairing the world) figures prominently in the Lurianic account of creation and its implications: God contracted the divine self to make room for creation. Divine light became contained in special vessels, or kelim, some of which shattered and scattered. While most of the light returned to its divine source, some light attached itself to the broken shards.
>
> (Tikkun olam, meaning)

If each "shard of light" is comparable to a "dissociative part," then Schimmenti's (2018, personal communication) understanding that "dissociation … protects from attachment disorganization" is apt. SD creates and maintains separate, dissociative parts, or shards of light. These shards each hold aspects of a person's thoughts, feelings, sensations, memories, and meanings that could not be held together or perhaps coalesce in the first place, given early traumatic overwhelm (abuse) and underwhelm (neglect). These shards also hold the person's whole self or "being" that, at the same time, has always and never been. Further, shards as dissociative parts are retained separately for safekeeping until the intrarelational and interrelational conditions make it possible for these shards to come together in a larger, welcoming vessel. Here, the vessel refers to the survivor's inner life *and* outer world of life-enhancing relationships.

The conceptualization of parts held separately for safekeeping was derived from a workshop I attended years ago with David Scharff, MD, an object relation psychoanalyst. Scharff suggested some internalized objects (i.e., parts of self) remain hidden for years as a form of self-protection, until the relational environment is safe enough for them to enter awareness. While Scharff focused on the relational environment of the therapist–patient, the same can be applied to the patient's intrarelational environment.

SD represents a profound breaking apart, internally and relationally, in part to preserve *some* psychological organization, however primitive and unstable. The organization of the SD mind serves intrarelational needs, so the trauma survivor may one day be reunited and reintegrated with previously dissociated parts of being. SD also serves interrelational needs, as the person unconsciously and/or consciously seeks relationships with a psychotherapist and/or significant other(s) offering more hospitable conditions for formerly dissociated self-aspects to reappear. The Kabbalistic perspective suggests shards of light sometimes preserve being and being with. Being hides within dissociated shards (parts) until they can be reunited and fully realized in pro-being pride, "delighting in being myself delighting in you delighting in being yourself, with me."

Clinical Vignette: "Kathy": Shards of Light and Tikkun Olam: Repairing Inner and Outer Worlds

Kathy began this session mentioning boyfriend troubles, and then offhandedly her "fear of abandonment." Kathy was placed in a foster home from birth until adoption at one year. Kathy was insecurely attached to both adoptive parents. Her father was mostly absent and overtly shaming, whereas her mother was physically present but never reassuring, unaware of Kathy's emotional-relational needs.

Following a SD model (Van der Hart et al., 2006), I used components of the Comprehensive Resource Model (CRM) (Schwarz et al., 2017) that accesses multisensory resources to help Kathy regulate and process her RT, primarily intrarelationally.

During this session, Kathy contacted for the first time a somatic memory of herself as "a baby," presumably age one to two years. Kathy "remembered," somatically, being held by her mother: "I didn't feel safe." Kathy had never before realized her mother was neither physically nor emotionally soothing.

Kathy's previously dissociated, somatic-emotional-relational memory can be conceptualized as a shard of light, an essential aspect of Kathy's way of being and being with. It contained both her traumatic, body/emotional memory (i.e., "Kathy held but not soothed by her mother") and a previously unmet need (i.e., "Held in a way that feels safe"). This memory and its associated meanings were crucial to our understanding why Kathy felt "abandoned" after fighting with her boyfriend. Now, Kathy's adult self felt sufficiently "held," intrarelationally by an imagined attachment figure accessed using CRM, and interrelationally with me during this session and the prior six months of our work. Kathy visualized her adult self holding her baby self until her baby self felt complete "calmness." Kathy labeled this newly embodied, relational truth, "acceptance" and "strength."

Kathy's "calmness, acceptance, and strength" can be understood as shards of light of her being that had always been there but dissociated, held outside her awareness until new intrarelational and interrelational realities made it safe enough to come forward. Metaphors of "shards of light" and "tikkun olam" (i.e., repair of the world) offer a vision of original union (i.e., self with self, self with others, and the world), disunion, dissociative fragmentation and reorganization in the form of SD, and finally integrative reunion through somatic, affective, trauma, and attachment-informed psychotherapy. From this perspective, isolated, dissociative parts, our contemporary shards of light, retain for safekeeping the hope and possibility of the return, reorganization, and renewal of a more integrated self.

Closing Remarks

Research and clinical observation suggest shame, pride, LT, and SD often co-occur in complex relationships with each other. By exploring these relationships psychodynamically and studying phenomenologically different qualities of attending to, gazing at, disconnecting, and coalescing in relation to shame, pride, LT, and dissociation, several shared and distinctive features were identified. These observations and findings further informed ways of understanding and working psychotherapeutically with RT survivors. Attending, gazing, disconnecting from the familiar, and connecting anew, invite us to discover innovative ways of working psychotherapeutically with shame, pride, LT, and dissociation, particularly with patients who have suffered so much yet their pro-being pride endures and, within optimal conditions, thrives.

References

Association, definition. https://dictionary.cambridge.org/us/dictionary/english/association. Accessed December 4, 2021.

Barral, C. & Meares, R. (2019). The Holistic Project of Pierre Janet: Part Two: Oscillations and Becomings: From Disintegration to Integration. In G. Craparo, F. Ortu, & O. Van der Hart, Eds., *Rediscovering Pierre Janet: Trauma, Dissociation, and*

a New Context for Psychoanalysis (pp. 116–129). New York: Routledge. https://doi.org/10.4324/9780429201875.
Beebe, B. & Lachmann, F. M. (1988). The Contribution of Mother-Infant Mutual Influence to the Origins of Self- and Object Representations. *Psychoanalytic Psychology*, 5(4), Fall, 305–337. Doi: https://doi.org/10.1037/0736-9735.5.4.305.
Benau, K. (2021a). Shame to Pride Following Sexual Molestation: Part 1: From Traumatic Immobilization to Triumphant Movement. *European Journal of Trauma & Dissociation*, 5(4), 100198. https://doi.org/10.1016/j.ejtd.2020.100194.
Benau, K. (2021b). Shame to Pride Following Sexual Molestation: Part 2: From Pro-being Pride to Retaliatory Rage, Adaptive Anger, and Integration. *European Journal of Trauma and Dissociation*, 5(4), 100194. https://doi.org/10.1016/j.ejtd.2020.100194.
Benau, K. (2020a). Shame, Pride and Dissociation: Estranged Bedfellows, Close Cousins and Some Implications for Psychotherapy with Relational Trauma Part I: Phenomenology and Conceptualization. *Mediterranean Journal of Clinical Psychology*, 8(1), 1–35. Doi: https://doi.org/10.6092/2282-1619/mjcp-2154.
Benau, K. (2020b). Shame, Pride and Dissociation: Estranged Bedfellows, Close Cousins and Some Implications for Psychotherapy with Relational Trauma- Part 2: Part II: Psychotherapeutic Applications. *Mediterranean Journal of Clinical Psychology*, 8(1), 1–29. Doi: https://doi.org/10.6092/2282-1619/mjcp-2155.
Bowen, B. website. www.relationalimplicit.com/bowen/. Accessed June 6, 2021.
Bowen, M. (1978). *Family Therapy in Clinical Practice*. New York: Jason Aronson.
Bowlby, J. (1973). *Attachment and Loss, Vol. 2: Separation Anxiety and Anger*. New York: Basic Books.
Bowlby, J. (1969). *Attachment and Loss, Vol. 1: Attachment*. London: Hogarth Press.
Brach, T. (2003). *Radical Acceptance: Embracing Your Life with the Heart of a Buddha*. New York: Bantam.
Bromberg, P. M. (2011). *Awakening the Dreamer: Clinical Journeys*. New York: Routledge. https://doi.org/10.4324/9780203759981.
Chefetz, R. (2015). *Intensive Psychotherapy for Persistent Dissociative Disorders: The Fear of Feeling Real*. New York: W.W. Norton. Doi: 10.1080/00332747.2016.1237710.
Corrigan, F. M. & Christie-Sands, J. (2020). An Innate Brainstem Self-Other System Involving Orienting, Affective Responding, and Polyvalent Relational Seeking: Some Clinical Implications for a "Deep Brain Reorienting" Trauma Psychotherapy Approach. *Medical Hypotheses*, 136, 199502. https://doi.org/10.1016/j.mehy.2018.07.028.
Corrigan, F. M. & Elkin-Cleary, E. (2018). Shame as an Evolved Basic Affect— Approaches to It within the Comprehensive Resource Model (CRM). *Medical Hypotheses*, 119, 91–97. https://doi.org/10.1016/j.mehy.2018.07.028.
Craparo, G., Ortu, F., & Van der Hart, O., Eds. (2019). *Rediscovering Pierre Janet: Trauma, Dissociation, and a New Context for Psychoanalysis*. New York: Routledge. https://doi.org/10.4324/9780203759981.
DePrince, A. P., Huntjens, R. J. C., & Dorahy, M. J. (2015). Alienation Appraisals Distinguish Adults Diagnosed with DID from PTSD. *Psychological Trauma: Theory, Research, Practice, and Policy*, 7(6), 578–582. Doi: https://doi.org/10.1037/tra0000069.
Dickinson, E. (1960/1868). "Tell All the Truth but Tell It Slant" (Poem #1129). In T. H. Johnson, Ed., *The Complete Poems of Emily Dickinson* (pp. 506–507). New York: Back Bay Books.

Dissociation, definition: www.dictionary.com/browse/dis-. Accessed June 3, 2021.
Dorahy, M. J. (2014). Scham und Täterintrojekte [Shame and the Perpetrator Introject]. *Trauma: Zeitschrift für Psychotraumatologie und ihre Anwendungen*, 12(4), 16–25. Kröning: Asanger Verlag.
Dorahy, M. J. (2010). The Impact of Dissociation, Shame, and Guilt on Interpersonal Relationships in Chronically Traumatized Individuals: A Pilot Study. *Journal of Traumatic Stress*, 23(5), 653–656. Doi: https://doi.org/10.1037/tra0000069.
Dorahy, M. J. & Clearwater, K. (2012). Shame and Guilt in Men Exposed to Childhood Sexual Abuse: A Qualitative Investigation. *Journal of Child Sexual Abuse*, 21(2), 155–175. Doi: https://doi.org/10.1080/10538712.2012.659803.Dorahy, M. J., Gorgas, J., Seager, L., & Middleton, W. (2017a). Engendered Responses to, and Interventions for, Shame in Dissociative Disorders: A Survey and Experimental Investigation. *The Journal of Nervous and Mental Disease,* 205(11), 886–892. Doi: 10.1097/NMD.0000000000000740.
Dorahy, M. J., Schultz, A., Wooler, M., Clearwater, K., & Yogeeswaran, K. (2021). Acute Shame in Response to Dissociative Detachment: Evidence from Nonclinical and Traumatised Samples. *Cognition and Emotion*. Doi: 10.1080/02699931.2021.1936461.
Dorahy, M. J., McKendry, H., Scott, A., Yogeeswaran, K., Martens, A., & Hanna, D. (2017b). Reactive Dissociative Experiences in Response to Acute Increases in Shame Feelings. *Behaviour Research and Therapy*, 89, 75–85. Doi: https://doi.org/10.1016/j.brat.2016.11.007.
Dorahy, M. J., Middleton, W., Seager, L., McGurrin, P., Williams, M., & Chambers, R. (2015). Dissociation, Shame, Complex PTSD, Child Maltreatment and Intimate Relationship Self-concept in Dissociative Disorder, Chronic PTSD and Mixed Psychiatric Groups. *Journal of Affective Disorders,* 172, 195–203. Doi: https://doi.org/10.1016/j.jad.2014.10.008.
Dorahy, M. J., Corry, M., Shannon, M., Webb, K., McDermott, B., Ryan, M., & Dyer, K. F. W. (2013). Complex Trauma and Intimate Relationships: The Impact of Shame, Guilt and Dissociation. *Journal of Affective Disorders*, 147(1–3), 72–79. Doi: https://doi.org/10.1016/j.jad.2012.10.010.Dyer, K. F. W., Corry, M., Matheson, L., Coles, H., Curran, D. Dorahy, M. J., Black, R., Lenaire Seager, L., & Middleton, W. (2017). Comparing Shame in Clinical and Nonclinical Populations: Preliminary Findings. *Psychological Trauma: Theory, Research, Practice, and Policy,* 9(2), 173–180. Doi: https://doi.org/10.1037/tra0000158.
Ecker, B., Ticic, R., & Hulley, L. (2012). *Unlocking the Emotional Brain: Eliminating Symptoms at Their Roots Using Memory Reconsolidation.* New York: Routledge. https://doi.org/10.4324/9780203804377.
Ekkekakis, P. (2012). Affect, Mood, and Emotion. In G. Tenenbaum, R. C. Eklund, & A. Kamata, Eds., *Measurement in Sport Psychology* (pp. 321–332, 517–519). Champaign, IL: Human Kinetics. https://doi.org/10.5040/9781492596332.ch-028.
Fosha, D. (2000). *The Transforming Power of Affect: A Model for Accelerated Change.* New York: Basic Behavioral Science.
Freud, S. (1920/1961). *Beyond the Pleasure Principle.* New York: W. W. Norton.
Gendlin, E. T. (2007/1978). *Focusing.* New York: Bantam Dell.
Giorgi, A. (2012). The Descriptive Phenomenological Psychological Method. *Journal of Phenomenological Psychology*, 43(1), 3–12. Doi: https://doi.org/10.1037/10595-013.

Giorgi, A. (1997). The Theory, Practice, and Evaluation of the Phenomenological Method as a Qualitative Research Procedure. *Journal of Phenomenological Psychology*, 28(2), 235–260. Doi: https://doi.org/10.1163/156916297X00103.

Howell, E. (2020). *Trauma and Dissociation-Informed Psychotherapy: Relational Healing and the Therapeutic Connection*. New York: W.W. Norton. 0.4324/9780203888261.

Janet, P. (1935). *Les Debuts de L'Intelligence*. Paris: Flammation.

Janet, P. (1925). *Principles of Psychotherapy*. London: Allen & Unwin. https://doi.org/10.1037/13452-000.

Janet, P. (1919). *Psychological Healing*. New York: Macmillan.

Janet, P. (1907). *The Major Symptoms of Hysteria*. New York: Macmillan. https://doi.org/10.1037/10008-000.

Janet, P. (1901). *The Mental State of Hysteroids*. New York: Putnam & Sons. https://doi.org/10.1037/10597-000.

Liotti, G. (2004). Trauma, Dissociation, and Disorganized Attachment: Three Strands of a Single Braid. *Psychotherapy: Theory, Research, Practice, and Training*, 41(4), 472–486. https://doi.org/10.1037/0033-3204.41.4.472.

Main, M. (2000). The Organized Categories in Infant, Child, and Adult Attachment: Flexible vs. Inflexible Attention under Attachment-Related Stress. *The Journal of American Psychoanalytic Association*, 48(4), 1055–1096. Doi: https://doi.org/10.1177/00030651000480041801.

Main, M. (1991). Metacognitive Knowledge, Metacognitive Monitoring, and Singular (Coherent) vs. Multiple (Incoherent) Models of Attachment. In C. M. Parkes, J. Stevenson-Hinde, & P. Marris, Eds., *Attachment across the Life Cycle*, (pp. 127–159). New York: Routledge. https://doi.org/10.4324/9780203317914.

Marsh, R. J., Dorahy, M. J., Verschuere, B., Butler, C., Middleton, W., & Huntjens, R. J. C. (2018). Transfer of Episodic Self-referential Memory across Amnesic Identities in Dissociative Identity Disorder Using the Autobiographical Implicit Association Test. *Journal of Abnormal Psychology*, 127(8), 751–757. Doi: https://doi.org/10.1037/abn0000377.

McGilchrist, I. (2009). *The Master and the Emissary: The Divided Brain and the Making of the Western World*. New Haven: Yale University Press.

McKeogh, K., Dorahy, M. J., & Yogeeswaran, K. (2018). The Activation of Shame Following Dissociation in the Context of Relationships: A Vignette Study. *Journal of Behavior Therapy and Experimental Psychiatry*, 59, 48–55. Doi: https://doi.org/10.1016/j.jbtep.2017.11.001.

Meares, R. & Barral, C. (2019). The Holistic Project of Pierre Janet: Part 1: Disintegration or Desagregation. In G. Craparo, F. Ortu, & O. Van der Hart, Eds., *Rediscovering Pierre Janet: Trauma, Dissociation, and a New Context for Psychoanalysis* (pp. 106–115). New York: Routledge. https://doi.org/10.4324/9780429201875.

Minuchin, S. (1974). *Families and Family Therapy*. Cambridge, MA: Harvard University Press.

Nijenhuis, E. R. S., & Van der Hart, O. (2011). Dissociation in Trauma: A New Definition and Comparison with Previous Formulations. *Journal of Trauma & Dissociation*, 12(4), 416–45. https://doi.org/10.1080/15299732.2011.570592.

Ogden, P. (2019). Acts of Triumph: An Interpretation of Pierre Janet and the Role of the Body in Trauma Treatment. In G. Craparo, F. Ortu, & O. van der Hart Eds., *Rediscovering Pierre Janet: Trauma, Dissociation, and a New Context for Psychoanalysis* (pp. 200–209). New York: Routledge. https://doi.org/10.4324/9780429W201875.

Porges, S. W. (2011). *The Polyvagal Theory: Neurophysiological Foundations of Emotions, Attachment, Communication, and Self-regulation.* New York: W.W. Norton.

Premack, D. (1959). Toward Empirical Behavior Laws: I. Positive Reinforcement. *Psychological Review,* 66(4), 219–233. https://doi.org/10.1037/h0040891.

Roisman, G. I., Padron, E., Sroufe, A., & Egeland, B. (2002). Earned-Secure Attachment Status in Retrospect and Prospect. *Child Development,* 73(4), 1204–1219. https://doi.org/10.1111/1467-8624.00467.

Ross, C. (2010). Hypothesis: The Electrophysiological Basis of the Evil Eye Belief. *Anthropology of Consciousness,* 21(47), 47–57. Doi: https://doi.org/10.1111/j.1556-3537.2010.01020.x.

Rothenberg, A. (1979). *The Emerging Goddess: The Creative Process in Art, Science and Other Fields.* Chicago: University of Chicago Press.

Scheff, T. S. (In press). *A Social Theory and Treatment of Depression.* http://scheff.faculty.soc.ucsb.edu/main.php?id=62.html. Accessed December 28, 2019.

Schimmenti, A. (September 8, 2018). Personal communication, originally posted on the Dissociative Disorders Listserv (DISSOC). Quoted with permission.

Schimmenti, A. (2012). Unveiling the Hidden Self: Developmental Trauma and Pathological Shame. *Psychodynamic Practice: Individuals, Groups and Organisations,* 18(2), 195–211. Doi: https://doi.org/10.1080/14753634.2012.664873.

Schimmenti, A. & Caretti, V. (2016). Linking the Overwhelming with the Unbearable: Developmental Trauma, Dissociation, and the Disconnected Self. *Psychoanalytic Psychology,* 33(1), 106–128. https://doi.org/10.1037/a0038019.

Schmidt, S. J. (2009). *The Developmental Needs Meeting Strategy: An Ego State Therapy.* San Antonio, TX: DNMS Institute.

Schore, A. N. (2003). The Effects of Relational Trauma on Right Brain Development, Affect Regulation, and Infant Mental Health. *Infant Mental Health Journal,* 22(1–2), 201–269. Doi: https://doi.org/10.1002/1097-0355(200101/04)22:1<201::AID-IMHJ8>3.0.CO;2-9.

Schwarz, L., Corrigan, F., Hull, A., & Raju, R. (2017). *The Comprehensive Resource Model: Effective Therapeutic Techniques for the Healing of Complex Trauma.* New York: Routledge. https://doi.org/10.4324/9781315689906.

Shengold, L. (1989). *Soul Murder: The Effects of Childhood Abuse and Deprivation.* New York: Ballantine. https://doi.org/10.2307/j.ctt1ww3v7x.

Simeon, D. & Abugel, J. (2006). *Feeling Unreal: Depersonalization Disorder and the Loss of the Self.* New York: Oxford University Press.

Steiner, J. (2006). Seeing and Being Seen: Narcissistic Pride and Narcissistic Humiliation. *International Journal of Psychoanalysis,* 87(4), 939–951. https://doi.org/10.1516/AL5W-9RVJ-WKG2-B0CK.

Stern, D. N. (2004). *The Present Moment in Psychotherapy and Everyday Life.* New York: W.W. Norton.

Stern, D. N. (1998). The Process of Therapeutic Change Involving Implicit Knowledge: Some Implications of Developmental Observations for Adult Psychotherapy. *Infant Mental Health Journal,* 19(3), 300–308. https://doi.org/10.1002/(SICI)1097-0355(199823)19:3<300::AID-IMHJ5>3.0.CO;2-P.

Tangney, J. P. & Fischer, K. W., Eds. (1995). *Self-conscious Emotions: The Psychology of Shame, Guilt, Embarrassment, and Pride.* New York: Guilford.

Tikkun olam, meaning: www.myjewishlearning.com/article/tikkun-olam-repairing-the-world. Accessed June 3, 2021.

Tomkins, S. S. (1963). *Affect, Imagery, Consciousness, Vol 2. The Negative Affects.* New York: Springer.

Tomkins, S. S. (1962). *Affect, Imagery, Consciousness, Vol 1. The Positive Affects.* New York: Springer.

Van der Hart, O. (2021). Trauma-Related Dissociation: An Analysis of Two Conflicting Models. *European Journal of Trauma & Dissociation,* 5(4), 100210. https://doi.org/10.1016/j.ejtd.2021.100210.

Van der Hart, O. & Friedman, B. (2019). A Reader's Guide to Pierre Janet. In G. Craparo, F. Ortu, & O. Van der Hart, Eds., *Rediscovering Pierre Janet: Trauma, Dissociation, and a New Context for Psychoanalysis* (pp. 4–27). New York: Routledge. https://doi.org/10.4324/9780203759981.

Van der Hart, O. & Rydberg, J. A. (2019). Vehement Emotions and Trauma-Generated Dissociation: A Janetian Perspective on Integrative Failure. *European Journal of Trauma & Dissociation,* 3(3), 191–201. https://doi.org/10.1016/j.ejtd.2019.06.003.

Van der Hart, O., Brown, P., & Van der Kolk, B. (1989). Pierre Janet's Treatment of Post-traumatic Stress. *Journal of Traumatic Stress,* 2(4), 1–11. Doi: doi.org/10.1007/BF00974597.

Van der Hart, O., Nijenhuis, E. R. S., & Steele, K. (2006). *The Haunted Self: structural Dissociation and the Treatment of Chronic Traumatization.* New York: W.W. Norton.

White, M. & Epston, D. (1990). *Narrative Means to Therapeutic Ends.* New York: W.W. Norton.

Whitman, W. (1965/1855). Song of Myself. In H. W. Blodget & S. Bradley, Eds., *Leaves of Grass* (p. 88). New York: New York University Press.

Wille, R. (2014). The Shame of Existing: An Extreme Form of Shame. *International Journal of Psychoanalysis,* 95(4), 695–717. Doi: 10.1111/1745-8315.12208.

Winnicott, D. W. (1965). Ego Distortion in Terms of True and False Self. In *The Maturational Processes and the Facilitating Environment: Studies in the Theory of Emotional Development* (pp. 140–157). New York: International Universities Press.

4 Setting the Stage

Transtheoretical Attitudes, Principles, and Concepts When Working with Shame and Pride in Psychotherapy with Relational Trauma

Introduction

> Going "meta" theoretically and therapeutically: Not a "shame and pride psychotherapy."

As a gateway into psychotherapy with relational trauma (RT) survivors, this chapter proposes a total of 15 attitudes, principles, and concepts guiding this work. Specific psychotherapeutic practices and clinical vignettes are presented to bring these to life. Although this chapter and the three that follow describe several different approaches to shame and pride-informed psychotherapy with RT (Schore, 2001), the stance adopted is transtheoretical and not wed to one therapy modality.

Regardless of theoretical orientation or preferred treatment approach, therapists benefit from learning and bringing into practice certain understandings of, attitudes toward, and ways of being with patients, and familiarizing themselves with principles and concepts guiding this work. These attitudes, principles, and concepts are a set of assumptions that while at first learned explicitly, over time become implicit ways of being-in-relationship with the patient's and therapist's experience of shame and pride.

Training over many years in several therapeutic modalities has taught me that therapists do best finding ways of working congruent with their values and unique personhood, inviting the patient to do the same, all befitting the concept of pro-being pride (Chapter 2). This "meta" perspective avoids unproductive therapy wars. My hope is that these guiding attitudes, principles, and concepts will be beneficially applied to diverse psychotherapeutic approaches when working with shame and pride in RT survivors.

These include:

1. There are no shame and pride therapy "techniques."
2. Shame and pride are always relational: Self-conscious and self-other conscious emotions.
3. Shame and pride: Adaptive and maladaptive subtypes (macro/experience-distant) and processes (micro/experience-near).

4. Traumatic shame and pride states and dissociation.
5. The evolutionary, survival, and "thrival" functions of shame and pride.
6. Shame and pride develop in the first year of life.
7. Traumatic shame and pride states and the body.
8. Radical inquiry, radical empathy, radical acceptance, and radical reflection.
9. Functional Coherence (FC).
10. Memory Reconsolidation (MR): Transforming maladaptive shame and pride.
11. Intrarelational and interrelational resourcing: Lived, imagined, felt, and embodied.
12. Psychological distance: The capacity to "observe" rather than "become" shame and pride states.
13. Co-consciousness and shared consciousness: Patient's and therapist's mindful, compassionate selves in relation to the patient's shame and pride states.
14. Multiplicity of parts.
15. Shame and pride: Prototypical parts.

Though these attitudes, concepts, and principles are discussed separately, they interrelate in complex and meaningful ways. Though this discussion emphasizes shame states, pride states are implicated throughout. Finally, the abbreviated terms "survivors" or "RT survivors" both refer to "survivors of relational trauma."

1. There Are No Shame and Pride Therapy "Techniques"

Let us begin with a paradox: There are no shame and pride psychotherapy "techniques," yet therapists have developed many ways of working with shame (Dearing & Tangney, 2011; Tangney & Dearing, 2011; Greenberg & Iwakabe, 2011), and to a lesser extent adaptive pride (Benau, 2021a, 2021b, 2020a, 2020b, 2019a, 2019b, 2018) in RT.

Apropos pro-being pride, how could there be a specific "technique" causing "a patient to delight in being themselves, delighting in others delighting in being themselves, with the patient" and "the patient delighting in being themselves while delighting in being themselves, with themselves"? (Chapter 2).

Working with adult psychotherapy patients whose subjective experience as children was dismissed or negated by their caregiver(s), Stern (2019) also rejects "techniques": "In a way, *not having a prescriptive approach is exactly what these patients need* since their core issue is the impingement of others' mental frameworks on the development of their authentic subjectivity" (p. 439, my emphasis). Stern (2019) adds,

> Ultimately, the aims of treatment will need to include the patient separating from the internalized, negating other to free himself or herself for the re-subjectification process at the heart of the work. Usually, this

capacity to separate will depend on the patient forming a sufficiently deep and trusting (selfobject) connection to the analyst, such that the over-whelming affects and realities associated with the early traumas and losses can be recognized, witnessed, reclaimed and worked through (grieved). *But the specific path toward these process[es] aims—the specific needed relationship (Stern, 2017)—is always unique and emergent from the complex evolution of the dyadic system over time.*

(p. 439, my emphasis)

Given Stern's (2019) admonition, how do therapists working with shame and pride proceed? For a patient to become more "real-ized," to embody their authentic way of being and relating, and integrate previously dissociated aspects of self, the therapist must also be real, owning errors without being overtaken by shame, and learning from successes free from hubristic pride (Tracy, 2016).

Carl Whittaker, renowned family therapist, began his career as an experiential psychotherapist doing co-therapy with Tom Malone. They worked successfully with a man with chronic schizophrenia for several years. When "Whitaker asked the [patient] if there was one moment he found particularly helpful," the man replied, "Well, there was one moment when nobody was up to anything" (Barach, 2021, personal communication).

How do we, as therapists, ensure we are not "up to anything"? First, we have to be authentic, replete with many theories and techniques that, in the moment, are put to the side as the therapist shows up, one human being with another. Salvador Minuchin, another family therapy icon, shared at a workshop that therapists ideally engage in "trained spontaneity." Our only "agenda" is to help patients, but without prescribed ways of doing so. In order to help patients discover who they truly are, their pro-being pride, the therapist enters their shared, relational space in a spirit of spontaneity and serious play.

Clinical Vignette: Be Real

Therapists can also be real by being transparent. When confronted by a patient about something not working, the therapist reflects upon and owns their part of the "problem" without shaming themselves or the survivor.

"Dan," a survivor of sexual abuse and violence as a very young boy, shared that my new way of working with him, following the Comprehensive Resource Model (CRM) (Schwarz et al, 2017), was not a good fit. Dan complained he could not speak with me during CRM processing as he had when we used another intrarelational approach (the Developmental Needs Meeting Strategy [DNMS]; Schmidt, 2009). While CRM permits patients to speak, it places greater emphasis on intrarelating (patient with parts of self) than interrelating (patient with therapist). CRM left Dan feeling too alone. While Dan's concerns might have been worked through using CRM, given his severe RT history I chose to privilege his agency and return to his preferred approach. I also took responsibility for my part of this problem, reassuring Dan our relationship was strengthened by his speaking up. I made this explicit in part because Dan's father was caustically shaming, and his mother's behavior dangerous and life threatening toward herself and Dan. Dan needed to know expressing his needs and setting boundaries were welcomed.

For survivors to approach all aspects of their experience with genuine curiosity, the therapist leads by example. The therapist takes responsibility for their misattunement, either changing their behavior or finding a shared understanding benefiting the patient. As the therapist accepts feedback without plummeting into shame, hubristic pride, or defensive countershaming (Dalenberg, 2000; see also Chapter 5), the survivor learns to do the same.

Shame, Pride, Recognition, and Therapy Techniques

> I will recognize you, when you are lost to yourself.
> Glen Hansard, "Just to be the One"
> (Glen Hansard/Warner Chappell Music)

Appreciating the centrality of therapist-patient *recognition*, Bromberg (2011a, 2011b) offered another way of thinking about shame and pride in RT. Recognition refers to the therapist and later patient seeing, feeling, knowing, accepting, and, over time, integrating previously dissociated aspects of self, other, and relationship.

Are there "techniques" helping therapists "recognize" a patient's inherent worth and dignity (Hicks, 2011)? Which techniques attenuate the damaging effects of a caregiver's *misrecognition* (abuse) of a child and help patients heal from *nonrecognition* (neglect)?

Survivors *need* a therapist genuinely engaged and alive in relationship with them. RT survivors have helplessly endured years of unwanted things being done to them, or not done with and for them. Regretfully, technique often connotes something the therapist *does to* a patient. "Doing something to" or "not doing something for" a patient are reasons survivors protest therapists becoming "techniquey." Doing something *to a patient* may trigger traumatic memories of *being done to*, as contrasted with respectfully *being with them* in an "I-Thou" relationship (Buber, 1970).

Since nonrecognition (Bromberg, 2011a, 2011b), that is, not being seen and delighted in for who we are by others and ourselves, lies at the heart of pathogenic shame and pride, it follows recognition might ameliorate these problems. Is there a "recognition therapy" that benefits RT survivors?

Clinical Vignette: RT, Shame, and a Smile

"Kerry", a professional in her 40s, lived with intermittent moderate to severe depression since her teens. When I first met Kerry, she did not know she was a survivor of RT. Her trauma included witnessing physical violence by her mother toward her older sister; her father failing to protect both children from abuse; shaming by her older sister; and her parents explicitly blaming Kerry for causing and failing to relieve her father of chronic anxiety, and implicitly for causing and failing to stop the violence.

Kerry had worked with therapists on and off from her teens until now, and benefited from each therapy. Only in our work did Kerry realize she lived with chronic shame.

Referring to a prior therapist, Kerry shared a story that struck me. At the time, Kerry participated in group therapy and on occasion, when struggling with depression, met individually with one of the group co-therapists. Kerry recalled one time feeling very depressed, and deeply ashamed for feeling depressed.

Within her family of origin, Kerry had been told by her parents she was the "good" child, "unscathed" by her family's strife. Kerry believed no one, including her therapist, would want to be with her when depressed, the opposite of "unscathed." While Dr. Jones, Kerry's therapist, was well-versed in Gestalt Therapy and Bioenergetics, what Kerry recalled about this session were not techniques but rather Dr. Jones' beaming smile as Kerry entered the office. Kerry was stunned Dr. Jones was genuinely happy to see her.

Why had Dr. Jones' warm smile stayed with Kerry 20 years later? Kerry and I came to understand that Dr. Jones' welcoming smile told Kerry, unequivocally, she was liked and perhaps loved by Dr. Jones. Following pro-being pride (Chapter 2), Dr. Jones delighted in Kerry being Kerry despite her depression. Following Glen Hansard's song, Dr. Jones recognized Kerry when she was lost to herself. Her smile proved to Kerry she had worth when she was convinced she had none, and even more that Dr. Jones en-*joy*-ed her. Bathed in Dr. Jones' welcoming smile, Kerry *knew*, despite implicitly believing she was irrevocably damaged, she was more than okay. This experiential juxtaposition between Kerry's belief ("I'm wretched") and Dr. Jones' smile ("I'm enjoyed as I am") is consistent with therapeutic memory reconsolidation (MR) (Ecker et al., 2021; see #10, "Memory Reconsolidation [MR]"). Dr. Jones' spontaneous smile was clearly no technique. Twenty years later, that made a world of difference.

2. Shame and Pride Are Always Relational: Self-conscious and Self-Other Conscious Emotions

A central paradox within shame and pride, particularly the most maladaptive subtypes, is that what appears self-focused is always relational. There is always a "self" and "other" devaluing (shame) or valuing (pride) the "self" or "other." That "other" can include another person or group (interrelational) and another self-aspect (intrarelational).

As noted in Chapter 1, researchers have called shame, pride, and guilt self-conscious emotions (Tracy et al., 2007). In fact, the reflection and reverberation that is the subjective reality of shame and pride is closer to self with self, other with self, self with other with self, and self with self with other with self—although "self-other conscious emotions" suffice (Chapter 3). Therapists working with survivors are reminded that no matter how self-absorbed and disconnected from others the shamed or proud person appears, there is always an "other" lurking in the shadows, externally and/or internally.

3. Shame and Pride: Adaptive and Maladaptive Subtypes (Macro/Experience-Distant) and Processes (Micro/Experience-Near)

Chapter 2 detailed shame and pride adaptive and maladaptive subtypes, and the processes by which they develop. Both micro and macro perspectives are crucial for psychotherapists' understanding RT survivors for several reasons, including that shame especially and pride to a lesser extent often remain hidden from therapist and patient, and can secretly impede or derail therapeutic progress (Bromberg, 2011a; Dearing & Tangney, 2011), and that shame and pride, particularly as traumatic states, are often disorienting and disorganizing for patient and therapist (Chapter 5). Holding both macro and micro perspectives enables the therapist to think more clearly during these emotional and relational storms, and help patients gain psychological distance from, reflect upon, and process these traumatic states.

4. Traumatic Shame and Pride States and Dissociation

Chapter 3 detailed complex, psychodynamic and phenomenological relationships between traumatic shame and pride mind/body states, mind/body leave taking (LT), previously dissociation as *process*, and structural dissociation (SD). The psychodynamic perspective demonstrates how dissociative processes and structures provide the RT survivor a temporary escape from unbearable, dysregulating shame and pride states, and disembodied LT and SD; how shame and pride as emotional processes are experienced as point/counterpoint, each to the other; and how pro-being pride provides an alternate, transformative experience to all these phenomena. These psychodynamic and phenomenological perspectives offer several valuable therapeutic applications.

5. The Evolutionary Survival and "Thrival" Functions of Shame and Pride

The terms "adaptive" and "maladaptive" connote an environment that humans adapt to well or poorly. This evolutionary perspective is profitably applied to emotions and behavior. Assuming all universal emotions served an adaptive function at one time in our human evolution, what are the evolutionary, survival functions of shame?

Some have argued shame evolved to maintain social hierarchies, group cohesion, and social/moral norms (Terrizzi & Shook, 2020). Maintaining the status quo also operates within smaller social groups, for example, familial relations. During early, traumatizing relationships, it often pays to not feel or express certain emotions, nor express one's unique aliveness or pro-being pride.

Clinical Vignette: "Sam" and Terms of Attachment

Sam, a survivor of RT, learned that in order "to be" he had "to be attentive and responsive to the needs of his father" who was severely depressed, in part because he had to father Sam! Shame for Sam, taking the form of the implicit belief "I am never good enough," served two adaptive, psychological functions: First, to give Sam's life meaning, purpose, and hope, for example, "If I learn to be a good enough son, maybe Dad's depression will lift and he will meet my needs." Second, to keep at bay Sam's profound grief for not being loved and the terror of nonbeing (Wille, 2014), a dread Sam experienced when not seen, felt, nor known by his father. Sam provides one of many examples where shame and the suppression of pro-being pride supports group survival at the cost of individual suffering.

…

Contrary to some authors (Tomkins, 1963; Schore, 2003, 1998), shame does not always downregulate arousal. Particularly in traumatic shame states, a heightened state of hyperarousal, hypervigilance, overwhelming fear, and rage may accompany shame affect (Corrigan & Elkin-Cleary, 2018). In these instances, shame serves as a punishing warning, for example, "If I dare be myself, I will lose everything and everyone!" Traumatic shame states may cause people to freeze in terror and pain, emotional and physical, in an effort to avoid social banishment. As one patient shared, "Every time I think or feel something I was taught not to, I get a shooting pain in my head, like an electrical shock screaming, 'Stop! Never allowed!'"

While hardwired to survive as individuals and species, people are also hardwired to thrive (Fosha, 2000). This is observed clinically when some therapy approaches facilitate natural healing processes, with minimal therapist intervention (Corrigan & Christie-Sands, 2020). The "thrival" (my coinage) functions of shame and pride complement and are distinct from their "survival" functions. As described in Chapter 2, in good enough me shame "the person recognizes from a nonreactive, self-accepting place they have not been true to themselves and/or their values. This shame subtype is 'self-righting', helping the person's return to living according to their preferred self." Living according to their values allows a person not only to survive but also to enjoy heightened individual and social well-being.

As noted, shame is highly relational. The shamed person remains implicitly connected to a shaming caregiver (survivor function), sometimes long after the caregiver has died, and/or implicitly and authentically connected to their core values and preferred ways of being and being-in-relationship ("thrivor" function).

Adaptive pride also serves survival and thrival functions. Good enough me pride brings attention to and joyfully reinforces developmentally appropriate achievements. The child learns to stand: "Pride!", walk some more and learns to run, "Pride!", and so on. Likewise, the survivor who overcomes great difficulties, with the help of their therapist, invariably feels good enough pride that encourages them to confront future adversities.

Pro-being pride supports individual and species thrival. With pro-being pride, the person's aliveness is celebrated when they are being and becoming more of who they are and who they are meant to be in relationship.

6. Shame and Pride Develop in the First Year of Life

Several child development researchers situate the onset of the capacity to feel shame between two and a half and three years of age (Tangney & Fischer, 1995). In contrast, Nathanson (1992) observed that "shame affect can be seen in babies long before they can … experience embarrassment" (p. 210). Research (Papousek & Papousek, 1975) with three to four-month-old infants who first learned to elicit interesting light stimuli and then, following researcher manipulation, were unable to do so, showed a loss in muscle tone, slumping, turning their faces away, and increased blood flow to the skin, suggestive of primitive shame (Broucek, 1982; cited in Nathanson, 1992). Likewise, Trevarthen (2005) eloquently described how shame and pride begin in the first year of life: *"Infants are born with a bold self-consciousness … [and] may … feel pleasure and pride in the approval of others, and shame at failure before them"* (p. 56, my emphasis).

If we accept that infants experience at minimum proto-shame and proto-pride in the first year of life, then what becomes available to them is not only "the pleasure and pride in the approval of others" (Trevarthen, 2005, p. 56), nor pride in mastery, accomplishment, and/or achievement (Tracy, 2016), but also pro-being pride, the pride in being and being with.

How might we reconcile these two contrasting views, that shame and pride begin around age three, and my view that prototypical shame and pride begin in the first year of life? The short answer has to do with language and its developmental trajectory. A three-year-old child can tell as well as show a researcher feeling embarrassed about something he did or failed to do. In contrast, the infant at one year or younger can only show the researcher the proto-affects of shame and pride. In addition, when shame is dissociated, the implicit experience of shame will differ from self-reported shame (Marsh et al., 2018).

The still-face research paradigm (Tronick, 2020) provides another window into the infant's preverbal shame and pride experience. In the still face paradigm, a typically relationally responsive mother with her securely attached four to nine-month-old infant is instructed to stop responding for a minute and become "still face." The infant-mother dyad goes from shared delight, a coordinated interest consistent with pro-being pride, to the infant failing to get their nonresponsive mother to come alive so that they, too, can come alive with their mother. The infant cries out in protest and distress and, after less than a minute, collapses into physical and emotional shutdown.

According to developmental researcher Karlen Lyons-Ruth, this shutdown may be an early precursor of shame. Lyons-Ruth (2003) observed infant and child-parent relationships and their developmental consequences. She studied the longitudinal effects of maternal absence, the caregiver's failure to attune and reciprocally respond to their infant's and toddler's relational needs. She noted that caregiver absence is not only "done" to an infant, but rather something the baby struggles against in a valiant effort to engage the caregiver. "The infant tapes also show so poignantly that the baby does not give up but tries and tries again to get something from the caregiver. So, neglect is not just passively experienced but is *an active defeat of all the infant's attempts to attract the involvement of the caregiver, which would be at the heart of shame*" (K. Lyons-Ruth, 2020, personal communication, my emphasis).

Shame and pride are embedded in the attachment system and develop in the first stages of life in response to perceived rejection (shame) or praise and delight (pride) from caregivers. Shame alerts the child to the threat of separation, and that action must be taken to protect the attachment bond. Adaptive pride lets the child know the bond is secure and desirable.

The cycles of attachment, rupture, and repair in the infant/caregiver dyad are essential for emotional regulation. Shame plays an important role in this process (Schore, 1998; Schimmenti, 2012), and so too with pride. When caretakers are not affectively attuned, the infant experiences his affective needs as unworthy and shameful. As the trust in an attachment figure is betrayed, early trauma creates a template for pathological shame (Hahn, 2000; Schimmenti, 2012). I hypothesize research would also show secure attachment bonds strengthened by co-regulated, adaptive pride.

Therapists working from an attachment-informed perspective will be best prepared to work with shame and pride states that often develop preverbally and/or present without words or coherent narratives. For two contemporary approaches, see Fosha (2000) and Brown and Elliott (2016).

7. Traumatic Shame and Pride States and the Body

Shame and pride as emotions and especially traumatic shame and pride states are more of the body than mind, where "mind" refers to verbalized consciousness and meaning-making (Van der Kolk, 2013, 2014a, 2014b). Shame states require that the therapist understand and have ways of working with emotional dysregulation, including reactive terror, rage (Lewis, 1971, 1992), shutdown (Porges, 2011), and/or dissociation (Chapter 3); and track the patient's "window of tolerance" (Siegel, 1999; Ogden et al., 2006), including how dysregulated arousal states manifest somatically within and between patient and therapist (Chapter 5). Likewise, pride states require the therapist find ways to understand and quiet emotional dysregulation, including threats to one's perceived and implicitly neuroceived (Porges, 2011) social status; states of hyperarousal, particularly reactive rage more than terror; emotional detachment (e.g., hubris where shame is either not felt and/or vehemently denied); and dissociation.

As observed, the patient gripped by a shame state often has few if any words to describe their experience. Chapter 2 described how a survivor's shame state takes them outside his window of tolerance (Siegel, 1999), first shocked into a brief state of hyperarousal—high freeze state—such that heightened anxiety, terror, agitation, and/or rage responses are frozen or immobilized (Benau, 2021a, 2021b), followed by a rapid drop into hypoarousal—shutdown, deflation, numbing, dissociation, etc., or in simultaneous hyperaroused and hypoaroused mind/body states. The patient's loss of speech and going mentally blank is common in trauma states generally, and shame states in particular. Rather than narrated, traumatic memories are more likely experienced as emotional and somatic eruptions (Benau, 2009). The somatic and emotional memories that are shame states are often not verbalizable for several reasons, including the person who first experienced these states when they had few if any words; the original, recurrent shaming interactions were overwhelming, as in sexual and physical abuse; the child's language centers went offline; traumatic memories were dissociated (Chapter 3); and/or no one helped the child name their experience and make it real.

The person captured by a pride state may, in contrast with shame states, appear to speak and move freely. However, his words and actions may be detached from embodied experience, distanced from an integrated self-experience, and disconnected emotionally from others. On the basis of my clinical observations, when a pride state is triggered, the patient may be taken over by a recurrent rant imbued with contempt and disgust for certain groups, and are temporarily unavailable for reciprocally responsive communication with the therapist or significant others. These patients are often unaware they have been triggered and how arrogant they sound. As with shame states, the survivor gripped by a pride state typically retains no conscious memory of the relational milieu within which their reactivity developed.

Given these unspeakable aspects of shame and pride states, talk therapy alone will not ameliorate relational "truths" held within implicit beliefs and emotional and somatic memory. The therapist is encouraged to develop capacities to work imaginally and somatically with what the patient's body remembers about their earliest neglect and intrusions.

This takes time. While I do not call myself a somatic psychotherapist, I have 20 years clinical experience and specialized training in this area, and many more years working with developmentally disabled children with little to no language. As regards training in body psychotherapy, my most prominent methods include the Comprehensive Resource Model (CRM) (Schwarz et al., 2017; Corrigan & Elkin-Cleary, 2018), Sensorimotor Psychotherapy (SP) (Ogden et al., 2006; Ogden & Fisher, 2015), and Psycho-Physical Therapy (Bowen, website). One new therapy approach to early, non-verbal RT, Deep Brain Reorienting (DBR) (Corrigan & Christie-Sands, 2020), works primarily with somatic sensations originating in the neck, face, and eyes that purportedly reflect midbrain (brainstem) activation and preaffective, relationally traumatic reactions. Other approaches also work well with implicit, not yet verbalized experience and meanings (e.g., Coherence Therapy [CT]; Ecker et al., 2012), or the emotional-somatic expressions of traumatic attachment (Accelerated Experiential Dynamic Psychotherapy [AEDP]; Fosha, 2000). A therapist will do well to have different ways of working somatically and more broadly with nonverbal phenomena congruent with their conceptualization of psychotherapy with RT generally and shame and pride states specifically.

8. Radical Inquiry, Radical Empathy, Radical Acceptance, and Radical Reflection

Maladaptive shame and pride result from a survivor's conscious and unconscious rejection of or dissociation from aspects of their experience, including thoughts, beliefs, images, memories, feelings, physical sensations, and patterns of action and interaction. Living with maladaptive shame or pride, patients often experience secondary, maladaptive shame or pride in reaction to their original, pathogenic shame or pride. For example, a patient often reacts with further self-shaming and/or hubristic self-priding when made aware of and reexperiencing, with their therapist, maladaptive shame and/or hubristic pride. Therapists must assist patients in cultivating an attitude of interest in and acceptance of thoughts, feelings, sensations, and behavior that generate maladaptive shame or pride and inhibit pro-being pride.

How does a therapist "accept" a patient gripped by pathogenic shame, especially when the patient believes they are not deserving of love? How does a therapist not reprimand the patient whose arrogance drives them to treat others, including the therapist, with dismissiveness and denigration?

At the heart of all psychotherapy, and especially when working with maladaptive shame and pride, the therapist bears witness to and reflects back their deep, nonjudgmental interest in and understanding of the rich tapestry—preferred and nonpreferred threads alike—that is the patient's experience. The shame and pride-informed therapist cultivates and embodies attitudes of and behavior consistent with *radical inquiry*, *radical empathy*, *radical acceptance,* and *radical reflection*.

Radical Inquiry

"Radical" refers to "root," from the Latin "radix" or "root" (Radical, word origin). The therapist's way of inquiring into and engaging with the patient helps patients get at the root of shame or pride and embody those qualities, such as pro-being pride, that transcend maladaptive shame and pride. "Inquiry" refers to seeking information, knowledge, or truth (Inquiry, definition). Thus, the therapist's *radical inquiry* reflects the embodiment of their interest in getting to the root of the patient's emotional and relational truth, minimizing judgment and prejudice.

Radical Empathy

Whereas the therapist's *radical inquiry* reflects their dedicated intention to discover, with the patient, the implicit meanings of the patient's experience, *radical empathy* refers to the therapist imaginatively, emotionally, and somatically *entering into* the patient's experience. As much as possible, the therapist puts their own thoughts, beliefs, feelings, and biases to the side, dwelling in the affective-relational world of the patient. While radical empathy remains an ideal, it is central to the therapeutic enterprise generally and particularly when working with shame and pride states. Since shame and pride states reflect the rejection and dismissing of, or dissociating from, the emotional experience of self, other, and self-in-relation to self and others, healing of RT requires empathy, a gateway to compassion and love (Gilbert, 2010).

Radical Acceptance

Brach (2003) has written eloquently about *radical acceptance*. I emphasize the importance of the therapist listening to and engaging with the patient's experience from a place of not-knowing and nonjudgment. This is easier said than done, as many well-meaning therapists try to talk their patients out of maladaptive shame (e.g., "You can't really believe you're *that* bad!") or hubris (e.g., "How can you be so insensitive?"). Radical acceptance means the therapist neither agrees nor disagrees with their patient feeling inferior (pathogenic shame) or superior (hubristic pride). The therapist accepts that the patient's shame or pride state at this moment is a part but not the whole of their subjective reality. This includes the patient's painful experience *with* their therapist. Oftentimes it is *because* the therapist is caring that shame or pride states intensify, reflecting the survivor's unconscious attempt to emotionally distance from their therapist and not reveal who they fear they "really are." Psychotherapy with shame and pride requires the therapist hold the paradox of accepting what is and discovering what is emerging and changing.

Radical Reflection

Radical reflection is best exemplified by Carl Rogers' groundbreaking work that has been parodied as the therapist repeating back the patient's words. Years ago, a movie was produced with "Gloria," a patient who had one session each with Carl Rogers, Fritz Perls, and Albert Ellis, all therapy giants at that time ("The Gloria Films: Three Approaches to Psychotherapy: All Three Sessions" [1965]). I vividly recall Carl Rogers sweating profusely as he worked intently to enter into Gloria's experience and reflect back his understanding of her phenomenological reality. Rather than parroting Gloria's words, Rogers imaginatively immersed himself in Gloria's world and shared his deep understanding and feeling of being Gloria. Likewise, radical reflection implicitly invites the patient to develop their own self-immersive and self-reflective capacities, so together the dyad discover and express the patient's subjectivity. The therapist assumes their understanding and empathy are always a work in progress. For a therapist to radically reflect their patient's reality, particularly when gripped by a traumatic shame or pride state, without imposing their own reality is, in my view, a radical act of love.

9. Functional Coherence (FC)

The concept of FC posits that no matter how troubling a thought, feeling, and/or behavior is for a patient and others in their life, there is always an implicit way of giving meaning to or making sense of experience. Given how painful and disturbing are traumatic shame and pride, a functionally coherent way of thinking is especially important as the impulse, in therapist and patient, is to view these states as something to be rid of *before* understanding their communication.

FC posits that a meaningful *coherence* exists across domains of consciousness between the problematic behavior and at least one of the patient's underlying "schema"[1]; and that what operates implicitly serves important psychological and/or social-emotional *functions*. This way of thinking is best described in Coherence Therapy (CT), an experiential-constructivist approach to psychotherapy, although FC is evident in many therapeutic approaches (Ecker et al., 2012; Coherence Therapy [CT] website).

Clinical Vignette: There's No Convincing "Karl"

Karl felt inadequate and depressed despite his intellectual prowess and kindness. Whenever Karl was told he was intelligent, he quickly identified people who were smarter. When his therapist or girlfriend, Thea, observed Karl treated someone thoughtfully, Karl countered that his fear of others becoming angry with him "proved" he wasn't "*really* caring." Likewise, when Karl's therapist asked how he made sense of his gratifying, long-term relationship with Thea, Karl shared his darkest fear that when Thea discovered who he *really* was, she would leave him for "someone better." While these beliefs saddened Karl, he was convinced of their verity.

Karl's self-shaming thoughts, feelings, and behavior could be considered by some as irrational, a biochemical imbalance, or a phenotypic marker of a genetic predisposition for depressive and distorted thinking. From a FC perspective, Karl's beliefs made sense within a larger matrix of implicit meanings and ways of relating to himself and others.

In therapy, Karl came to understand that as a child he learned repeatedly from his mother, mostly implicitly, that he "failed his father" by not relieving him of his chronic depression. When Karl failed to please his father in ways his mother demanded, his father became more depressed for which Karl's mother blamed him and intermittently became enraged.

As a result of these repeated childhood experiences, Karl was convinced he was incapable of loving "the right way," and completely responsible for his girlfriend's occasional unhappiness. Despite evidence to the contrary, Karl believed it was just a matter of time before he was replaced by someone better able to secure Thea's happiness.

Adopting a FC perspective, Karl was gripped by an implicit, shame-filled belief system or internal working model (Bowlby, 1969). Karl *not* believing he was selfish would offer further proof of his selfishness. Karl's shame that he was a defective partner, while painful, now made sense.

Maladaptive Shame and Pride from a FC Perspective

Karl's vignette offers one way of understanding the functionally coherent origins of maladaptive shame and pride. No matter how punishing the patient's inner, critical voice (Firestone, 2016), understanding that shame makes sense within a RT history offers the therapy dyad a way of both accepting and working to update early, emotional learnings. Likewise, rather than react critically and withdraw from an arrogant patient's denigration and dismissiveness of their therapist and others, the therapist can ask themselves, where, when, and with whom this behavior makes sense. Over time, the therapist can wonder aloud with their patient, "Who taught you that way of relating? How did that serve you as a child, or now as an adult? Does it come at any cost to your current relationships, perhaps leaving you lonely and unappreciated?"

These and similar explorations emerge naturally once the therapist's FC mindset has been firmly established. FC also helps therapists maintain their intrapersonal and interpersonal equilibrium and approach the shame-filled and hubristically proud person with curiosity and nonshaming behavior of their own (Dalenberg, 2000; Chapter 5).

10. Memory Reconsolidation (MR): Transforming Maladaptive Shame and Pride

Therapeutic applications of MR research findings suggest that implicit, emotional truths about self, other, and relationship can be updated in the brain (Ecker et al., 2012). Updated refers to the fact that while the episodic memory of the RT remains intact, its maladaptive meanings and emotional and interpersonal effects are transformed. Nonclinical, MR research posits that two experiential juxtapositions need to occur for *de-consolidation* (juxtaposition #1) and *reconsolidation* (juxtaposition #2) of traumatic relational learnings to be updated (Ecker et al., 2012).

The first therapeutic juxtaposition (#1) facilitates a de-consolidation or breaking up of original neuronal/synaptic connections that kept the patient's troubling symptoms intact. Employing a FC perspective, this involves the therapist and patient experientially discovering how current problems with thinking, feeling, and/or behaving are consistent with at least one underlying, subjective truth. In order for memory de-consolidation to occur, the patient needs to experience a juxtaposition between their conscious, anti-symptom position (ASP), that is, the symptoms the patient rejects and wants to rid themselves of, and a new, previously implicit pro-symptom position (PSP) (juxtaposition #1). The PSP refers to the implicit schema that contribute to the development of the presenting problems. The second juxtaposition (#2) requires the patient experientially juxtapose their PSP with a subjective and observable reality directly disconfirming the PSP. These concepts are delineated in Coherence Therapy (CT) (Ecker & Hulley, 1985; Ecker et al, 2012) and two non-clinical examples (Benau, 2020c).

Clinical Vignette: "If You're Angry with Me, then I'm Out in the Cold, Forever"

"Kendra" was given up at birth because her teen mother's parents would not let Kendra's mother keep the baby. Kendra was placed in foster care for one year and then adopted by the parents who raised her. Kendra's mother was critical and emotionally unavailable, causing Kendra to feel abandoned, unlovable, and worthless. Her father, while more benign, never protected Kendra from her mother's maltreatment, and his touch always felt detached and never comforting, leaving Kendra implicitly shamed.

Whenever Kendra's teen son, "Ryan," expressed anger toward Kendra for not being emotionally available, Kendra felt abandoned and collapsed. In therapy, we discovered Kendra had unconsciously equated Ryan's anger with her own repeated losses and implicit shaming. Gradually, Kendra realized Ryan wanted more, not less, of his mother.

In order for Kendra to heal her earliest RT and wounds, an "old" and "new and disconfirming" emotional reality would need to be discovered and experientially juxtaposed (juxtaposition #2). Kendra needed to reexperience, in vivid imagination, what it was like to be "abandoned" in utero (i.e., Kendra's teen mother drank alcohol when pregnant), "given up" by her foster parents, and explicitly and implicitly shamed by her adoptive parents. For MR to succeed, Kendra needed to experience simultaneously two relational realities, both of which felt true yet could not be true at the same time: "I am not worthy of being loved" (PSP—original, emotional/relational reality), and "My worth as a person is simply true" (new, emotional/relational reality).

Kendra lived with the shame and helplessness of her earliest abandonment that contributed to not good enough me shame and dissociated, not me shame, fueling her PSP, now brought to consciousness (juxtaposition #1): "I'm unlovable and there's nothing I can do about it." In therapy, Kendra's PSP was repeatedly, experientially juxtaposed (#2) with feeling loved for who she was by several intrarelational resources (e.g., Kendra imagining holding herself as a baby), while at the same feeling secure in our therapeutic relationship. This second juxtaposition (#2) moved Kendra out of shame and helplessness (PSP) toward embodying her intrinsic worth (i.e., new intra- and interrelational reality). This shift from not good enough me shame and not me shame toward reparative guilt helped Kendra acknowledge having hurt Ryan and motivated her to reconnect with her son.

11. Intrarelational and Interrelational Resourcing: Lived, Imagined, Felt, and Embodied

Since traumatic shame and pride reflect mind/body reactions to RT, they are experienced consciously as states of hyperarousal and/or hypoarousal, and less consciously when dissociated. Gripped by these states, the RT survivor is often emotionally and somatically dysregulated, living outside their window of optimal arousal (Siegel, 1999; Ogden et al., 2006), with an impaired ability to feel, deal, and relate adaptively to others and themselves.

The therapist must help the patient better regulate their shame and pride states, in order to better comfort themselves and relate more effectively. Arousal regulation also enables the patient to "observe" rather than "become" their shame and pride state, gradually processing traumatic memories and giving them new meanings. (See #12, Psychological Distance.)

Resourcing is anything that helps a patient cope adaptively with stress, including the traumatic stress of shame and pride states. Resources that are *lived* are ones accessed through some observable action or interaction. *Imagined* resources use imagery of all sense modalities to interact with aspects of the patient's experience, including their thoughts, beliefs, feelings, somatic experience, and/or parts. Resources *felt* include emotionally stimulating or soothing imagery, as needed. *Embodied* resources use somatic experience, for example, mindful attention to micromovements, physical sensations, energy flow, etc., that help the patient restore states of optimal arousal.

For heuristic purposes although these resources are described as distinct, they actually represent different perspectives on unified experience. What is lived is felt, what is felt always embodied and vice versa, and what is vividly imagined is felt, embodied, and therefore lived.

Therapeutic resources are verbal, imaginal, and/or physical activities the patient engages in to regulate their inner life primarily on their own (intrarelational resourcing), or with the help of a trusted other, including their therapist (interrelational resourcing). Therapeutic resources make it possible for patients to create psychological distance between their observing self and those experiences that hold, at the same time, traumatic shame and pride state memories and present-day experiences of relational safety. (See #12, 13 and 14, below.)

Given that shame and pride states are relational, self with self and self with other, healing must always take place within a relational matrix. Following research on MR (Ecker et al., 2012; #10), when a person has been traumatized by other people, healing *must* involve an experiential juxtaposition of abusive and neglectful ways of relating with new, disconfirming, interrelational, and intrarelational experiences. This is another reason why intrarelational and interrelational resources are valuable.

Most resources are *both* intrarelational and interrelational. For example, while praying alone may seem only intrarelational, people typically pray to a

128 *Setting the Stage*

higher power, making prayer interrelational as well. The patient who accesses visual and verbal imagery to compassionately interact with younger parts (#14 and #15, below) reflects intrarelational resourcing. At the same time, patients often do this in the presence of a trusted therapist, an interrelational resource. In fact, the therapy relationship provides the patient a model of acceptance that informs how they intrarelate with their younger parts. Likewise, the therapist's emotional support is a resource enabling the patient to find the courage to face previously devalued (maladaptively shamed) or overvalued (maladaptively "prided") aspects of self.

12. Psychological Distance: The Capacity to "Observe" Rather Than "Become" Shame and Pride States

For a patient to become aware of their shame and pride states, and over time develop new ways of relating to traumatic ways of being, they must develop the capacity to create "psychological distance" between themselves and their maladaptive shame and pride ways of being.

Werner and Kaplan (1963) identified four psychological capacities of symbol formation, each involving psychological distance. These include *differentiating*: (1) the symbolizer (e.g., the observing self) and the object (e.g., parts of self); (2) the self and symbolic vehicle, that is, giving symbolic form to experience in words, drawings, movements, etc.; (3) the symbol and its referent, that is, the experience the symbol represents; and (4) the self and audience, that is, "others."

Applying the concept of psychological distance to therapy with shame and pride states, the patient must learn to *differentiate*: (1) a nontraumatized aspect of self *and* shame and pride states; (2) an aspect of themselves *and* the symbolic form representing their shame or pride state; (3) the representational form of their shame or pride state *and* its meaning; and (4) the self *and* the other with whom the patient verbally and nonverbally communicates about their shame or pride state. "Other" includes aspects of self (intrarelational communication) and/or another person, such as the therapist (interrelational communication).

How do therapists help RT survivors create psychological distance between themselves and their shame and pride states, so that new ways of thinking, feeling, meaning-making, and relating emerge? While specific therapy examples are described in Chapters 5, 6, and 7, the following provides some general guidelines for fostering psychological distance:

- *Name shame, pride, and pro-being pride*: Naming shame gives the survivor a label that allows him to begin to distance psychologically and emotionally from, and reflect upon, the functions and meanings of their shame states. Some argue labeling a patient's emotional experience as "shame" is shaming. In my view, the *experience* of shame states is more debilitating than naming shame. *How* a psychotherapist names shame is key. *When* shame fits with the patient's experience, the patient's feelings are described in a functionally coherent way (#9), given the relational milieu in which these states developed; and the patient is shown shame

Setting the Stage   129

can be worked with, engendering hope, *then* the patient will use the word shame with greater ease, and learn to observe with less judgment their shame emotions and traumatic states.

While I do not name pride as often as shame, I do help patients differentiate adaptive pride (good enough me pride) and hubris (better me pride). As mentioned (Chapter 2), I always privilege my patients' probeing pride, although I rarely use that term with them.

- *Thinking about and reflecting upon traumatic shame states* is essential to work with RT. Distancing helps patient and therapist manage the shame state's often overwhelming affective charge, making these mind/body states more manageable and malleable. Shaw (2019) indicated "there is an educative dimension that is crucial … a direct, psycho-educational way of explaining the toxic identification to the patient, repeatedly as needed, [that] can aid the patient's efforts at self-delineation and disidentification" (p. 464). For our purposes, "self-delineation and disidentification" refer to the maladaptively shamed and/or proud person differentiating themselves from the abusive and/or neglectful other, whether that other lives within the patient's external or inner landscape.

- Following Sensorimotor Psychotherapy (SP) (Ogden & Fisher, 2015; Ogden et al., 2006), *helping the patient differentiate maladaptive, shame and pride implicit and explicit beliefs about self from feelings, physical sensations (e.g., flush face) and movements (e.g., eyes cast down).* As I often tell patients, "Let's mindfully observe what is happening in your body. The meaning will follow."

- Following the work of Levine's Somatic Experiencing (SE) (Levine, 2010; Levine & Frederick, 1997) and Bowen's Psycho-Physical Therapy (Bowen, website), *patients are taught to observe distinct physical sensations and movements associated with "resourced" and "shame or pride states," respectively, and pendulate or alternate attention between each state.* Pendulation enhances psychological distancing, improves arousal regulation, and enhances new meaning-making. The patient gains agency as they are more able to notice when *not* in the grips of maladaptive shame or pride.

- Internal Family Systems (IFS) (Schwartz, 1995) *facilitates psychological distancing by identifying shame and pride states as parts and teaches patients to observe these states interacting with other parts from the perspective of Self.* (See #15, for a different parts model.)

- *Using intrarelational imagery or a quasi-hypnotic approach informed by Eye Movement Desensitization and Reprocessing (EMDR) (Shapiro, 2001), the therapist asks the patient to identify beliefs, emotions, and physical sensations associated with their shame or pride state and "float back in time, as far back as you can go, when you experienced something like this."* Often the patient will "see," at some distance, a younger version of themselves who was maladaptively shamed or "prided" and left alone with these states.

- Several approaches work experientially with the intrarelational effects of RT and dissociation (e.g., Developmental Needs Meeting Strategy

130 Setting the Stage

[DNMS]; Schmidt, 2009; and The Comprehensive Resource Model [CRM]; Schwarz et al., 2017). These therapies use imaginal resources of people, real or imagined (DNMS), or power animals or spirit guides (CRM) to intrarelationally resource the patient while processing shame and pride states. *Human and nonhuman resources provide the patient sufficient psychological distance to approach traumatic memories without becoming dysregulated or retraumatized.*

- *Since shame and pride states overwhelm patients, therapists use imagery and/or hypnosis to foster psychological distance.* For example, the patient is instructed to picture the shaming/priding other on a screen at some distance. Adjusting the size, color, sound, and emotional intensity of the image helps the patient feel greater compassion toward their shamed/prided self. DNMS' "switching the dominance" protocol (Schmidt, 2009, pp. 62–69) identifies negative, introjected others (e.g., a caregiver's contemptuous look), teaching the patient to modify that memory, for example, by shrinking the maladaptively shaming/priding other down to the size of a postage stamp. This creates sufficient psychological space for the survivor to learn how various younger parts react to the introjected caregiver, pointing the way toward healing.

- *Inspired by Coherence Therapy (CT) (Ecker et al., 2012), I developed a way of working with shame/pride states that facilitates MR* (Benau, 2020c, 2019a). The survivor is guided to visualize (or use other, preferred sense modalities) the embodiment of implicit beliefs associated with their shame/pride state to one side (e.g., to their right). Then, after the patient has been helped to discover a positive, disconfirming schema, they picture that to the other side (e.g., to their left). As in Levine's (2010) pendulation, the patient moves back and forth from one experience to the other.

  An example of a patient's shame state schema might be, "I must make myself small and insignificant or I will be attacked, just like when Dad raged at me." A schema that disconfirms this original shame state might be, "I have learned that when I express my authentic self with my boss at work, even when he is angry, I am heard and respected. I am safer and proud of myself, now."

Whether mindfully attending to different aspects of the patient's shame/pride state or creating opportunities to relate to the shamed/prided self in new ways, psychological distance is crucial in these endeavors.

13. Co-consciousness and Shared Consciousness: Patient's and Therapist's Mindful, Compassionate Selves in Relation to the Patient's Shame and Pride States

Working with traumatic states requires *co-consciousness* (patient with patient) and *shared consciousness* (patient with therapist) in order to transform the patient's relationship with their RT. The survivor develops the capacity for *co-consciousness* by accessing two realities simultaneously, for example, "the present," safe "here and now" and "the past," threatening "there and then" that previously invaded the patient's mind. In *shared consciousness*, the therapist serves as an anchor to help the patient differentiate present-day perspectives of self and traumatic states. In both instances, the patient's new experience disconfirms implicit messages of the shame/pride state.

Although co-consciousness and shared consciousness are corollaries to psychological distancing (#12), they are not identical. For example, a patient gripped by a shame state may view their shamed self at some distance (e.g., picture their younger self rejected by their best friend), while not maintaining co-consciousness and shared consciousness sufficiently to transform their relationship to this younger, shame-bound state.

Clinical Vignette: "Shara": Developing Co-consciousness with the Help of Patient-Therapist Shared Consciousness

During this session, Shara described how, as a little girl, she was emotionally abused by her father and emotionally neglected by her mother. In grade school, Shara was teased by peers for her small size. While Shara made significant progress in therapy as an adult, she still struggled with feeling "unworthy." Shara's shame states led her to react with defensive anger when friends corrected her and judged herself for feeling any shame.

With my prompting, Shara readily "saw" her lonely 10-year-old self as distinct from her present-day adult self. Creating psychological distance between her younger and adult self was not difficult for Shara. The clinical challenge rested with *the quality* of Shara's relationship with her younger self. Shara said she was irritated and angry with her 10-year-old self because she hurt her current relationships.

For shame states to be transformed, the patient must learn to feel accepting of previously devalued aspects of herself. For Shara to feel compassion toward her 10-year-old, she first needed empathy for a teen part who expressed disdain for the neglected 10-year-old.

Shara observed her "critical teen" sat behind her. Noticing Shara pulled in both shoulders, I wondered if Shara had experienced threat coming from behind, but she recalled no such memory. I asked Shara to attend mindfully to her back tension. Following an approach borrowed from SP (Ogden & Fisher, 2015; Ogden et al., 2006), I asked Shara, "What movement does your back and shoulders want to make?" Shara's body turned inward, concave, to protect her heart. After a few minutes, Shara's body memory elicited an episodic memory of an older peer standing behind her, harshly criticizing Shara for not helping them. We now realized Shara's teenaged "inner shamer" was trying to protect her from feeling hurt and attacked by peers.

I next invited Shara to imaginally construct a "shield to protect her from the peer." Once Shara did this, she became visibly more relaxed. Asking Shara to imagine a shield, we used our shared consciousness to affirm she was deserving of protection. This helped Shara develop a new co-consciousness and alter her relationship with the inner, teenage shamer.

I then suggested Shara "ask the teen protector to stand down, for a few minutes," while Shara's adult self and I interacted with her "very vulnerable 10-year-old." Shara imagined her inner teen moving far from her back, as Adult Shara interacted with her inner 10-year-old. Again, we used shared consciousness to strengthen Shara's benevolent co-consciousness.

For the first time, Adult Shara felt "warmth" toward her lonely, 10-year-old self. Imagining placing her arm on the 10-year-old's shoulder brought present-day Shara deep relief. The contempt Shara's teen had shown toward her 10-year-old self and the shame within her younger self faded away. If I had asked Shara how she felt about our work, she might have expressed good enough me pride. Together, shared consciousness and co-consciousness made that possible.

14. Multiplicity of Parts

While *radical inquiry* (#8) adopts a stance of not knowing, it is also clinically useful to retain nomothetic understandings of mind/body organization. One concept particularly valuable when working with shame and pride states is multiplicity of parts.

There are several ways multiplicity has been understood and worked with psychotherapeutically (Chefetz, 2015; Putnam, 2016; Schwartz, 1995; Van der Hart et al., 2006; Watkins & Watkins, 1997). In everyday parlance people often say, "There's a part of me that … while another part of me …" These parts include distinct modes of thinking, feeling, and perceiving self, others, and relationship, as well as idiosyncratic physical sensations, movements, and behavior characteristic of that part.

I can be playful and silly as well as serious and studious. I experience both as parts of me. Their differences do not trouble me. Some people, including those living with the effects of RT, may not always experience their different ways of being as part of a cohesive self. In SD (Van der Hart et al., 2006), different parts may not be aware of other parts. Some survivors lack co-consciousness of distinct, dissociative parts.

Dissociative parts are adaptations to the shifting demands of different, everyday social-emotional contexts, as in Van der Hart et al.'s (2006) apparently normal parts of the personality (ANP). In contrast, some parts are developmental adaptations to extreme, traumatic relationships, as in Van der Hart et al.'s (2006) emotional parts of the personality (EP). For example, people growing up with chronic violence often develop a submissive part that learns to lay low and go along to avoid inciting assaults by more powerful caregivers. While a submit part may be adaptive for children living with an abusive parent, this same part is maladaptive when the adult survivor must confront their boss about harassment.

Traumatic, dissociative parts dominated by shame (i.e., shame states) develop within the cauldron of RT such as physical violence, sexual abuse, emotional abuse, recurrent emotional misattunement without repair, and neglect. Traumatic dissociative parts characterized by pride (i.e., pride states) often develop in similar family environments, or where a child's capacities are neither seen nor responded to by the parent in an age-appropriate way. The latter child may be viewed as special in ways that overinflate their abilities, and/or the parent/caregiver/leader manipulates the child's gifts to meet their own narcissistic needs (Miller, 2008; Shaw, 2014).

The concept of multiplicity is useful when working with shame and pride states, helping the patient and therapist see the survivor's maladaptive shame or pride as a part rather than representative of their entire being.

Clinical Vignette: From Shame States to Emergent, Self-acceptance and Pride

"Ellen's" mother and father were very critical of Ellen, her siblings, and others outside the family, calling them "too full of themselves." Ellen's parents were prone to fits of rage and physical violence toward their children. When we first met, Ellen was dominated by a chronic, painful shame state causing debilitating depression. Ellen was convinced she was an abject failure, despite appreciation by her clients and children.

Over the course of psychotherapy, Ellen came to understand her struggles fit with previously undiagnosed depression and Attention-deficit Hyperactivity Disorder (ADHD). After a few years of therapy, Ellen no longer lived under the shadow of chronic depression and knew how to better manage challenges posed by ADHD.

In this session, Ellen and I observed different parts, previously outside her awareness, particularly one associated with self-judgment and self-shaming. This can be thought of as Ellen's "fight toward self" part (see #15). Ellen was working on a project discarding materials from a room she associated with her "failures." Ellen noticed she felt "saturated" with this tedious task that required attention to detail. Rather than forcing herself "to keep doing it," as her parents would have demanded, Ellen realized she needed to stop and work on another, more satisfying project where she quickly made tangible progress.

Ellen then hit another roadblock. She felt increasingly frustrated with and discouraged by a technical problem. Ellen started to fall into a shame state, feeling deflated and mildly depressed. She felt "heaviness" in her body and "darkness" clouding her mind, the latter indicative of LT (Chapter 3). Ellen's shame state made it impossible for her to see how to solve the technical problem. While at first Ellen thought she should "just keep going" as she had been taught by her father, she was able—due to our recent work—to recognize she was gripped by a shame state which prevented her from thinking creatively and problem solving. Ellen understood her reaction, an emotional and somatic childhood memory, was larger than the current impasse. Ellen decided it was best to take a break from what stymied her.

Ellen left the room, showered, ate, just then realizing she was hungry, and took a long walk she reliably enjoyed. Revived and feeling "fine," Ellen realized she almost succumbed to a depressive shame state, but was able to shift her mind/body state so she could creatively solve the previously intractable problem.

Ellen and I attributed her successful psychological shifts from "saturated" to "productive," and later "stuck and ashamed" to "creative problem solver," to three essential features of working with parts: (1) Stepping back and realizing she was gripped by a shame state, reminiscent of her traumatic childhood; (2) distancing from triggers that evoked Ellen's shamed state; and (3) performing meaningful activities that activated enlivened, mind/body states. These activities gave Ellen feelings of adaptive pride, further fueling her success.

15. Shame and Pride: Prototypical Parts

Following the work of Herman (2012, 2007, 2006, 1992) and Schore (2001, 1998), I view RT as both anxiety/fear and shame-based. In addition, RT is often a pride-based disorder, given that shame and pride are two aspects of how a person evaluates self-in-relationship. Following Fisher's (2017) model of multiplicity (#14), therapists working with RT survivors and shame and pride states can identify recurrent survival strategies as prototypical parts. As discussed here, these universal survival strategies include fight, flight, freeze, attach, and submit.

Fight others: This is commonly seen in rage reactions to being shamed or humiliated (Dorahy, 2017; Chapter 1), and in hubristically proud patients who dominate, shame, and/or humiliate more vulnerable others. With respect to maladaptive pride (better me pride), this part presents as a harsh, punitive, contemptuous, other-shaming voice.

Fight self: This represents the self-punitive and self-critical voice directing its judging messages toward other aspects of self (not good enough me shame, not me shame, and no me shame) (see also Firestone, 2016; Howell, 2020, pp. 111–134). This part may attack the patient's attach part that seeks closeness, comfort, and expresses dependency needs, or attack any emotion or behavior the shaming caregiver would not tolerate in the patient. Fight self is less evident in maladaptive pride, but may operate outside awareness when aspects of self, considered weak, are rejected or attacked.

Flight: In shame, this is the part that physically and/or psychologically flees to escape further attack by others or parts of self (i.e., not good enough me shame). In pride, flight occurs when the patient rises above and distances themselves from their authentic, vulnerable self, as well as denigrates others (i.e., better me pride). In better me pride, this part flees and joins fight others by denigrating others and fight self by attacking unwanted self-aspects. In addition to physically and emotionally leaving (i.e., not good enough me shame and better me pride), this part leaves the present moment and relationships with self and others by dissociating from aspects of self (i.e., not me shame and not me pride) and/or from one's entire being and aliveness (i.e., no me shame and no me pride).

Freeze-High: High freeze marks the initial shock of having one's being and being with abruptly interrupted and shamed, and/or in maladaptive pride, having one's status relative to others threatened. In this state of hyperarousal, the patient neither perceives nor implicitly neuroceives (Porges, 2011) a safe passageway escaping from (flight), neither safely reconnecting with (attach), nor defeating (fight) the shaming or maladaptively priding other. In heightened arousal, the person is unable to think, feel, act, deal with, and relate to the shaming and/or priding other or anyone else. This part reflects immobilization with overwhelming anxiety and shame (Benau, 2021a, 2021b) or maladaptive pride (Benau, 2018). Dissociation in response to states of terror, horror, or overwhelming anxiety are common. In shame states, these occur early in the shaming process, when the person anticipates being rejected, ignored, and/or overpowered by an abuser. In pride states, high freeze is activated when the person consciously perceives or implicitly neuroceives (Porges, 2011) a threat to social status, with no immediate means of restoring their stature.

Freeze-Low: This is a state of hypoarousal where the patient neither perceives nor implicitly neuroceives any safe passageway toward escaping (i.e., flight), reconnecting with (i.e., attach), nor defeating (i.e., fight) a shaming or maladaptively priding other. In freeze-low, the patient experiences a state of hypoarousal and shutdown consistent with Porges' (2011) description of the activity of the dorsal vagal complex (DVC) and "feigned death" (p. 16). In shame states, numbness, depression, LT, and SD (Chapter 3) in states of emotional and neurophysiological shutdown or flatness are common. In pride states, the person displays emotionally distant, dismissive, disinterested, detached, cold, and nonempathic behavior toward others or aspects of themselves. This part may or may not blend with or react to a *Submit* part.

Attach: The attach part includes thoughts, feelings, actions, and interactions consistent with the attachment system, seeking proximity in order to receive protection, nurturance, and care. I also include the capacity to nurture and care for others. In shame states, the attach system is either in a state of high alert and hypervigilance, desperately trying to reconnect with the shaming other, or in collapse, resignation, and despair (see *Submit*) over ever being accepted by significant others. Paradoxically, the person gripped by shame state experiences themselves as outside the shaming other's psychological and interpersonal orbit, yet at the same time remains deeply connected to and identified with the shaming other. Over time, this results in the internalization of the shaming other. Self-shaming, then, reflects the activation of both fight self and attach parts. With respect to maladaptive pride, the attach part is activated as described in shame. The individual seeks to reconnect safely, and with shared respect and dignity (Hicks, 2011; Chefetz, 2017). When that fails, the maladaptively proud person withdraws into a state of superiority, denigration, disdain, disgust, contempt, and/or dismissiveness toward the other, individual, or group (better me pride), and/or dissociates from an aspect of self (not me pride), or their entire being (no me pride).

Submit (also known as *Collapse* or *Flag*): In this part, the person accedes psychologically, emotionally, and physically to the will of the shaming other. This includes becoming dominated and taken over by the other's thoughts, beliefs, emotions, and reality. The other could be an inner part, an actual person, or an entire group. (See also Shaw [2014] on the traumatizing narcissist's hegemonic control of the victim's mind and body.) The submit part is seen in states of emotional and somatic shutdown, where resignation, hopelessness, and despair predominate. Shame states also include feeling hopeless and despairing about ever feeling worthy. In hubristic, better me pride, as well as dissociative, not me pride and no me pride states, the person is driven to dominate and control, or acts superior intrarelationally, where one part dominates another part that becomes subservient to the first part's humiliating message. If the submit part further overwhelms the mind/body, severe dissociation and actual death may result (Ross, 2010). Pride states are often dissociated from the submit response, and typically counter submit states with contempt, rage, compulsive behavior (e.g., overwork), addictive behavior, and denial of personal vulnerabilities.

Conclusion

This concludes the discussion of concepts, attitudes, and principles guiding psychotherapy with shame and pride in RT. Together, they provide therapists a comprehensive way of thinking about and working with shame and pride that, while informed by many psychotherapeutic approaches, adopts a transtheoretical approach to this complex work. Chapters 5, 6, and 7 provide detailed accounts of several psychotherapy sessions with RT survivors, so that the reader can better understand how these ideas play out in practice.

Note

1 Depending upon the approach to therapy, these implicit organizing principles have been variously conceptualized as schema (Young, 2003), emotional truths or limbic learnings in CT (Ecker & Hulley, 1996; Ecker et al., 2012); Representations of Interactions that have been Generalized or RIGs (Stern, 1985); internal working model (Bowlby, 1969); pathogenic beliefs in Control Mastery Theory (Weiss & Sampson, 1986); and rackets in Transactional Analysis (Berne, 1964); etc.

References

Barach, P. Personal communication, ISSTD World Listserv, May 1, 2021.
Benau, K. (2021a). Shame to Pride Following Sexual Molestation: Part 1: From Traumatic Immobilization to Triumphant Movement. *European Journal of Trauma and Dissociation,* 5(4), 100198. https://doi.org/10.1016/j.ejtd.2020.100194.

Benau, K. (2021b). Shame to Pride Following Sexual Molestation: Part 2: From Pro-being Pride to Retaliatory Rage, Adaptive Anger, and Integration. *European Journal of Trauma and Dissociation*, 5(4), 100194. https://doi.org/10.1016/j.ejtd.2020.100194.

Benau, K. (2020a). Shame, Pride and Dissociation: Estranged Bedfellows, Close Cousins and Some Implications for Psychotherapy with Relational Trauma Part I: Phenomenology and Conceptualization. *Mediterranean Journal of Clinical Psychology*, 8(1), 1–35. Doi: https://doi.org/10.6092/2282-1619/mjcp-2154.

Benau, K. (2020b). Shame, Pride and Dissociation: Estranged Bedfellows, Close Cousins and Some Implications for Psychotherapy with Relational Trauma-Part 2: Part II: Psychotherapeutic Applications. *Mediterranean Journal of Clinical Psychology*, 8(1), 1–29. Doi: https://doi.org/10.6092/2282-1619/mjcp-2155.

Benau, K. (2020c). From Shame State to Pro-being Pride in a Single "Session." *The Science of Psychotherapy*, March, 20–39.

Benau, K. (2019a). Catching the Wave. *The Neuropsychotherapist*, 7(4), 4–13.

Benau, K. (January 28, 2019b). Ken Benau Talks About Shame and Pride. Podcast. *Science of Psychotherapy*. www.thescienceofpsychotherapy.com/the-science-of-psychotherapy-podcast/.

Benau, K. (2018). Pride in the Psychotherapy of Relational Trauma: Conceptualization and Treatment Considerations. *European Journal of Trauma and Dissociation*, 2(3), 131–146. https://doi.org/10.1016/j.ejtd.2020.100198.

Benau, K. S. (2009). Contrasts, Symbol Formation and Creative Transformation in Art and Life. *Psychoanalytic Review*, 96(1), 83–112. https://doi.org/10.1521/prev.2009.96.1.83.

Berne, E. (1964). *Games People Play: The Psychology of Human Relationships*. New York: Ballantine.

Bowen, B. website: https://relationalimplicit.com/bowen. Accessed July 24, 2021.

Bowlby, J. (1969). *Attachment. Attachment and Loss. Vol. 1: Loss*. New York: Basic Books.

Brach, T. (2003). *Radical Self-acceptance: A Buddhist Guide to Freeing Yourself From Shame*. Boulder, CO: Sounds True.

Bromberg, P. M. (2011a). *Awakening the Dreamer: Clinical Journeys*. New York: Routledge. https://doi.org/10.4324/9780203759981.

Bromberg, P. M. (2011b). *The Shadow of the Tsunami and the Growth of the Relational Mind*. New York: Routledge. https://doi.org/10.4324/9780203834954.

Broucek, F. J. (1982). Efficacy in Infancy. *International Journal of Psychoanalysis*, 60, 311–316.

Brown, D. & Elliott, D. (2016). *Attachment Disturbances in Adults: Treatment for Comprehensive Repair*. New York: W.W. Norton.

Buber, M. (1970). *I and Thou*. New York: Charles Scribner & Sons.

Chefetz, R. A. (2017). Dignity Is the Opposite of Shame and Pride Is the Opposite of Guilt. *Attachment: New Directions in Psychotherapy and Relational Psychoanalysis*, 11(2), 119–133. https://doi.org/10.33212/att.v11n2.2017.119.

Chefetz, R. A. (2015). *Intensive Psychotherapy for Persistent Dissociative Processes: The Fear of Feeling Real*. New York: W.W. Norton. Doi: 10.1080/00332747.2016.1237710.

Coherence Therapy website: www.coherencetherapy.org. Accessed July 24, 2021.

Corrigan, F. M. & Christie-Sands, J. (2020). An Innate Brainstem Self-Other System Involving Orienting, Affective Responding, and Polyvalent Relational Seeking: Some Clinical Implications for a "Deep Brain Reorienting" Trauma Psychotherapy Approach. *Medical Hypotheses*, 136, 109502. https://doi.org/10.1016/j.mehy.2018.07.028.

Corrigan, F. M. & Elkin-Cleary, E. (2018). Shame as an Evolved Basic Affect – Approaches to It within the Comprehensive Resource Model (CRM). *Medical Hypotheses,* 119, 91–97. https://doi.org/10.1016/j.mehy.2018.07.028.

Dalenberg, C. J. (2000). It's Not Your Fault: Countertransference Struggles with Blame and Shame. In *Countertransference and the Treatment of Trauma* (pp. 115–144). Washington: American Psychological Association. https://doi.org/10.1037/10380-000.

Dearing, R. L. & Tangney, J. P., Eds. (2011). *Shame in the Therapy Hour.* Washington, DC: American Psychological Association. https://doi.org/10.1037/12326-000.

Dorahy, M. J. (2017). Shame as a Compromise for Humiliation and Rage in the Internal Representation of Abuse by Loved Ones: Processes, Motivations, and the Role of Dissociation. *Journal of Trauma & Dissociation,* 18(3), 383–396. Doi: 10.1080/15299732.2017.1295422.

Ecker, B. & Hulley, L. (1996). *Depth Oriented Brief Therapy: How to Be Brief When You Were Trained to Be Deep and Vice Versa.* New York: Jossey-Bass.

Ecker, B., Ticic, R., & Hulley, L. (2012). *Unlocking the Emotional Brain: Eliminating Symptoms at Their Roots Using Memory Reconsolidation.* New York: Routledge. https://doi.org/10.4324/9780203804377.

Firestone, R. W. (2016). *Overcoming the Destructive Inner Voice: True Stories of Therapy and Transformation.* Amherst, NY: Prometheus Books.

Fisher, J. (2017). *Healing the Fragmented Selves of Trauma Survivors: Overcoming Internal Self-alienation.* New York: Routledge.

Fosha, D. (2000). *The Transforming Power of Affect: A Model for Accelerated Change.* New York: Basic Behavioral Science.

Gilbert, P. (2010). *Compassion-Focused Therapy.* New York: Routledge. https://doi.org/10.4324/9780203851197.

Greenberg, L. S., & Iwakabe, S. (2011). Emotion-Focused Therapy and Shame. In R. L. Dearing & J. P. Tangney, Eds., *Shame in the Therapy Hour* (pp. 69–90). Washington, DC: American Psychological Association. https://doi.org/10.1037/12326-000.

Hahn, W. K. (2000). Shame: Countertransference Identifications in Individual Psychotherapy. *Psychotherapy,* 37(1), 10–21. https://doi.org/10.1037/h0087670.

Hansard, G. Taken from "Just to be the One." Written by Glen Hansard/Warner Chappell Music. Permission granted June 27, 2021. ("Just to Be the One" song). Listen to on YouTube: www.youtube.com/watch?v=kHRYV692QDc. Accessed June 26, 2021.

Herman, J. L. (2012). Shattered Shame States and Their Repair. In J. Yellin & K. White, Eds., *Shattered States: Disorganised Attachment and Its Repair,* (pp. 157–170). London: Karnac Books.

Herman, J. L. (2007). *Shattered Shame States and Their Repair.* Somerville, MA: Harvard Medical School.

Herman, J. L. (2006). *PTSD as a Shame Disorder.* Somerville, MA: Harvard Medical School.

Herman, J. L. (1992). Complex PTSD: A Syndrome in Survivors of Prolonged and Repeated Trauma. *Journal of Traumatic Stress,* 5(3), 377–391. https://doi.org/10.1002/jts.2490050305.

Hicks, D. (2011). *Dignity: It's Essential Role in Resolving Conflict.* New Haven: Yale University Press.

Howell, E. (2020). *Trauma and Dissociation Informed Psychotherapy: Relational Healing and the Therapeutic Connection.* New York: W. W. Norton. 0.4324/9780203888261.

"Inquiry" definition: www.dictionary.com/browse/inquiry. Accessed April 30, 2021.
Levine, P. (2010). *In an Unspoken Voice: How the Body Releases Trauma and Restores Goodness*. Berkeley, CA: North Atlantic.
Levine, P. & Frederick, A. (1997). *Waking the Tiger: Healing Trauma*. Berkeley: North Atlantic.
Lewis, H. B. (1992). *The Role of Shame in Symptom Formation*. Hillsdale, NJ: Lawrence Earlbaum Associates.
Lewis, H. B. (1971). *Shame and Guilt in Neurosis*. New York: International Universities Press.
Lyons-Ruth, K. Personal communication, June 5, 2020.
Lyons-Ruth, K. (2003). Dissociation and the Parent-Infant Dialogue: A Longitudinal Perspective from Attachment Research. *Journal of American Psychoanalytic Association*, 51(3), 883–911. https://doi.org/10.1177/00030651030510031501.
Marsh, R. J., Dorahy, M. J., Verschuere, B., Butler, C., Middleton, W., & Huntjens, R. J. C. (2018). Transfer of Episodic Self-referential Memory across Amnesic Identities in Dissociative Identity Disorder Using the Autobiographical Implicit Association Test. *Journal of Abnormal Psychology*, 127(8), 751–757. Doi: https://doi.org/10.1037/abn0000377.
Miller, A. (2008). *The Drama of the Gifted Child: The Search for the True Self*. New York: Basic.
Nathanson, D. (1992). *Shame, Pride, Affect, Sex and the Birth of the Self*. New York: W.W. Norton. https://doi.org/10.1177/036215379402400207.
Ogden, P. & Fisher, J. (2015). *Sensorimotor Psychotherapy: Interventions for Trauma and Attachment*. New York: W.W. Norton.
Ogden, P., Minton, K., & Pain, C. (2006). *Trauma and the Body: A Sensorimotor Approach to Psychotherapy*. New York: W.W. Norton.
Papousek, H. & Papousek, M. (1975). Cognitive Aspects of Preverbal Social Interaction between Human Infants and Adults. Ciba Foundation Symposium. *Parent-Infant Interaction*. New York: Association of Scientific Publications.
Porges, S. W. (2011). *The Polyvagal Theory: Neurophysiological Foundations of Emotions, Attachment, Communication, and Self-regulation*. New York: W.W. Norton.
Putnam, F. W. (2016). *The Way We Are: How States of Mind Influence Our Identities, Personality and Potential for Change*. New York: International Psychoanalytic Books.
"Radical," word origin: www.etymonline.com/word/radical. Accessed April 30, 2021.
Ross, C. (2010). Hypothesis: The Electrophysiological Basis of the Evil Eye Belief. *Anthropology of Consciousness*, 21(47), 47–57. Doi: https://doi.org/10.1111/j.1556-3537.2010.01020.x.
Schimmenti, A. (2012). Unveiling the Hidden Self: Developmental Trauma and Pathological Shame. *Psychodynamic Practice*, 18(2), 195–211. https://doi.org/10.1080/14753634.2012.664873.
Schmidt, S. J. (2009). *The Developmental Needs Meeting Strategy: An Ego State Therapy for Healing Adults with Childhood Trauma and Attachment Wounds*. San Antonio, TX: DNMS Institute.
Schore, A. N. (2003). *Affect Regulation and Repair of the Self*. New York: W.W. Norton.
Schore, A. N. (2001). The Effects of Relational Trauma on Right Brain Development, Affect Regulation, and Infant Mental Health. *Infant Mental Health Journal*, 22(1–2), 201–269. https://doi.org/10.1002/1097-0355(200101/04)22:1<201::AID-IMHJ8>3.0.CO;2-9.

Schore, A. N. (1998). Early Shame Experience and Infant Brain Development. In P. Gilbert & B. Andrews, Eds., *Shame: Interpersonal Behaviour, Psychopathology, and Culture*, (pp. 55–77). New York: Oxford University Press.Schwartz, R. C. (1995). *Internal Family Systems Therapy*. New York: Guilford Press.

Schwarz, L., Corrigan, F., Hull, A., & Raju, R. (2017). *The Comprehensive Resource Model: Effective Therapeutic Techniques for the Healing of Complex Trauma*. New York: Routledge. https://doi.org/10.4324/9781315689906.

Shapiro, F. (2001). *Eye Movement Desensitization and Reprocessing (EMDR): Basic Principles, Protocols, and Procedures (2nd Edition)*. New York: Guilford.

Shaw, D. (2019). Double Binds, Unhealing Wounds: Discussion of "Airless Worlds: The Traumatic Sequelae of Identification with Parental Negation." *Psychoanalytic Dialogues*, 29(4), 460–469. https://doi.org/10.1080/10481885.2019.1632658.

Shaw, D. (2014). *Traumatic Narcissism: Relational Systems of Subjugation*. New York: Routledge. https://doi.org/10.4324/9781315883618.

Siegel, D. J. (1999). *The Developing Mind: How Relationships and the Brain Interact to Shape Who We Are*. New York: Guilford.

Stern, D. (1985). *The Interpersonal World of the Infant*. New York: Basic Books.

Stern, S. (2019). Airless Worlds: The Traumatic Sequelae of Identification with Parental Negation. *Psychoanalytic Dialogues*, 29(4), 435–450. https://doi.org/10.1080/10481885.2019.1632660.

Stern, S. (2017). *Needed Relationships and Psychoanalytic Healing: A Holistic Relational Perspective on the Therapeutic Process*. London and New York: Routledge. https://doi.org/10.4324/9781315268316.

Tangney, J. P. & Dearing, R. L (2011). Working with Shame in the Therapy Hour: Summary and Integration. In R. L. Dearing & J. P. Tangney, Eds., *Shame in the Therapy Hour* (pp. 375–404). Washington, DC: American Psychological Association. https://doi.org/10.1037/12326-000.

Tangney, J. P. & Fischer, K. W., Eds. (1995). *Self-conscious Emotions: The Psychology of Shame, Guilt, Embarrassment, and Pride*. New York: Guilford Press.

Terrizzi, Jr., J. A. & Shook, N. J. (2020). On the Origin of Shame: Does Shame Emerge From an Evolved Disease-Avoidance Architecture? *Frontiers in Behavioral Neuroscience*, 14(19), 1–12. Doi: 10.3389/fnbeh.2020.00019.

The Gloria Films: Three Approaches to Psychotherapy: All Three Sessions (1965). www.youtube.com/watch?v=NFT89grAUOI. Accessed July 24, 2021.

Tomkins, S. (1963). *Affect, Imagery and Consciousness: The Negative Affects, Vol. 2*. New York: Springer.

Tracy, J. (2016). *Take Pride: Why the Deadliest Sin Holds the Secret to Human Success*. New York: Houghton Mifflin Harcourt.

Tracy, J., Robins, R. W., & Tangney, J. P., Eds. (2007). *The Self-conscious Emotions: Theory and Practice*. New York: Guilford.

Trevarthen, C. (2005). "Stepping Away from the Mirror: Pride and Shame in Adventures of Companionship": Reflections on the Nature and Emotional Needs of Infant Intersubjectivity. In C. S. Carter, L. Ahnert, K. E. Grossman, S. B. Hrdy, S. W. Lamb, S. Porges, S., & N. Sachser. Eds., *Attachment and Bonding: A New Synthesis* (pp. 55–84). Cambridge, MA: MIT Press.

Tronick, E. (2020). YouTube "Sill Face Paradigm." www.youtube.com/watch?v=apzXGEbZht0. Accessed October 26, 2020.

Van der Hart, O., Nijenjuis, E. S., & Steele, K. (2006). *The Haunted Self: Structural Dissociation and the Treatment of Chronic Traumatization*. New York: W.W. Norton.

Van der Kolk, B. A. (2014a). *The Body Keeps the Score: Brain, Mind, and Body in the Healing of Trauma.* New York: Viking.

Van der Kolk, B. A. (2014b). *The Body Keeps the Score.* http://bessel.kajabi.com/fe/72501-the-body-keeps-the-score. PESI. Accessed January 31, 2017.

Van der Kolk, B. A. (2013). New Frontiers in Trauma Treatment Workshop. *Institute for the Advancement of Human Behavior,* San Francisco, CA, September 19–20.

Watkins, J. & Watkins, H. (1997). *Ego State Theory and Therapy.* New York: W.W. Norton.

Weiss, J. & Sampson, H. (1986). *The Psychoanalytic Process: Theory, Clinical Observations, and Empirical Research.* New York: Guilford.

Werner, H. & Kaplan, B. (1963). *Symbol Formation: An Organismic-Developmental Approach to the Psychology of Language.* San Francisco: Wiley.

Wille, R. (2014). The Shame of Existing: An Extreme Form of Shame. *International Journal of Psychoanalysis,* 95, 695–717. https://doi.org/10.1111/1745-8315.12208.

Young, J. (2003). *Schema Therapy: A Practitioner's Guide.* New York: Guilford.

5 Psychotherapy with Patient, Therapist, and Dyadic Shame States

Traumatic Reactions, Therapeutic Responses, and Transformation

Introduction

This chapter focuses on patient, therapist, and patient-therapist dynamics as seen in defensive reactions and reflective responses to shame in psychotherapy with survivors of relational trauma (RT survivors) (Schore, 2001). It begins by differentiating defensive or self-protective *reactions* as contrasted with reflective *responses* to shame-inducing events. The use of the terms explicit and implicit as contrasted with conscious and unconscious is then described. Next, three factors that contribute to shame proneness in patients and therapists, that is, psychological, temperamental, and developmental, are highlighted. This chapter then identifies several common reactions to trauma generally and traumatic shame states ("shame states") specifically in order to understand these phenomena, integrating models informed by the work of Nathanson (1992), Karpman (2014, 1968), and Fisher (2017). This model is designed to orient and emotionally ground the therapist when working with complex, dysregulating, and psychologically disorganizing traumatic shame states within and between patient and therapist. The presentation of this unified model is followed by a discussion of patient-therapist interrelational and intrarelational, reactive shame dynamics. Next, an overview of a three-phase therapeutic process and specific tasks within each phase of that process is presented, showing how the patient-therapist dyad moves from shame-induced, self-protective reactivity to reflective responsivity. This chapter closes with a clinical vignette describing how my and my patient's shame-based interreactions and intrareactions first propelled us into an intransigent enactment and how, together, we worked toward enhanced awareness, understanding, and collaborative, creative aliveness.

Differentiating Self-protective (Defensive) *Reactions* and Self-reflective (Nondefensive) *Responses* to Shame-Induced Events

This chapter explores what others have characterized as patient-therapist shame transference and countertransference (Dalenberg, 2000), and I prefer to call "self-protective reactions." While I appreciate how the psychoanalytic

DOI: 10.4324/9780429425943-6

literature has contributed much to understanding the complexity of patient with patient, therapist with therapist, and patient with therapist dynamics, I prefer the term "self-protective reactions" to "transference/countertransference defenses" for several reasons, including: (1) "Defenses" uses a military metaphor suggesting the patient and therapist must defend against an internal and/or external attack or assault. "Self-protective" as metaphor brings us closer to a once adaptive survival strategy the patient employs, initially outside conscious awareness, when seeking relative intrarelational and interrelational safety; (2) Self-protective reactions emphasize contributions of the present moment, whereas transference/countertransference has been historically associated with past, relational experiences projected onto the patient or therapist; and (3) Early in the psychoanalytic literature, transference-countertransference phenomena were commonly associated with psychopathology needing to be analyzed so as not to disrupt the therapy and therapist effectiveness. While contemporary, relational psychoanalysis no longer adopts this view, I wanted to avoid any connotations suggesting these phenomena are anything other than normal adaptations to adverse, relational conditions no longer serving the patient.

Shame as Emotional Processes and Traumatic States: Inter-actions and Intra-actions

In this chapter, I focus primarily on shame rather than pride, as more is known about shame in psychotherapy, including how unaddressed shame stalls and impedes therapeutic progress. I explore how shame and associated reactions in the patient can result in similar experiences in the therapist, making work with survivors of relational trauma ("RT" and "survivors") particularly challenging (DeYoung, 2015; Tangney & Dearing, 2011). Good enough me pride and pro-being pride discussed when I show what is on the other side of the therapy dyad's successful processing of individual and shared shame states.

Chapter 1 explores many aspects of the relational nature of shame and pride. Here, I highlight how shame and pride are essentially about devaluing (shame) and valuing (pride) *the person* rather than *actions*, and that these valuations develop in relationship to others, to oneself, and to the relationship. If one accepts that psychotherapy, both its success and failure, is rooted in inter- and intra-"relationships," then shame and pride lie at the heart of social-emotional life and psychotherapy, generally, and psychotherapy with traumatic shame and pride states, specifically.

Given the relational nature of shame "emotions," I address emotional interactions, between patient and therapist, and intra-actions, within patient and within therapist, respectively. As described in Chapter 1, in addition to feelings, emotions refers to thoughts, beliefs, and attendant meanings; physical experience, including bodily sensations, micro- and macro-movements, energy, and arousal; actions and interactions; imagery of all sense modalities; and memories. For the purpose of this discussion, emotions include all those domains of experience, conscious (explicit) and not yet in conscious awareness (implicit), that impact work with RT survivors living with traumatic shame states and their sequelae. These sequelae include several identifiable, self-protective reactions to shame states that will be described.

While emotion refers to shame as an acute, transient emotional *process*, for the purposes of this discussion I emphasize shame as a chronic, traumatic, mind/brain/body *state* or "shame state" (Chapter 2). Shame states rather than shame as emotional processes are highlighted because they are ubiquitous in RT survivors' experiences in psychotherapy, are often difficult to work with, and contribute to various forms of psychopathology (Tangney & Fischer, 1995) and therapeutic impasses (Dearing & Tangney, 2011). Using my shame subtype conceptualization, shame states refer to both not me shame, where a shamed part of self has been dissociated, and no me shame or the shame of existing (Wille, 2014). Both shame state subtypes require an understanding of the relationship between shame states and dissociative processes. (See Chapter 2 for a discussion of shame subtypes, and Chapter 3 on the relationship between shame, pride, and dissociation.)

Therapist, Patient, and Therapist-Patient Shame-Induced Reactions and Responses

Describing patient and therapist "emotions" with respect to patient and therapist shame states, I include two broad categories: (1) self-protective *reactions*, consistent with transference and countertransference reactions and patient-therapist enactments (Dalenberg, 2000; Bromberg, 2011a, 2011b); and (2) self-reflective and other-reflective mindful, nonjudgmental *responses*. The term *responses* is borrowed from a Gestalt Therapy perspective that defines responsibility (response-ability) as a person's *ability to respond* (Binderman, 1974), a conscious, creative choice rather than reaction to the press of internal and external demands. As therapists working with their patient's, their own, and patient-therapist shame dynamics, an overarching goal of therapy is to transform *reactions* into *responses*. How that is achieved is where the greatest challenges and opportunities lie.

Many factors make working with shame states with RT survivors challenging, which is why I developed a model that guides therapists in this work. Since working with shame is fundamentally about self, other, and relationship, it is impossible for therapists to not get confused, at least some of the time, as to whose shame they are reacting. Shame states are so painful that neither patient nor therapist wants to feel and hold shame. I have described this colloquially as "the shame hot potato," where both patient and therapist behavior implicitly insist, "This shame is *yours*, not mine!"

Shame states are by definition traumatic, mind/body states. To the extent patient and therapist traumatic shame reactions are triggered, both members of the dyad can be in a shame state at the same time. It is hard enough for therapists to help the patient when the patient is triggered. At times it can feel near impossible when the therapist is as well.

When therapist and patient are gripped by shame states, they often believe they are failing at their respective roles. To fail at something that matters to a person is to experience shame. What I am describing here are shame reverberations within and between each member of the therapy dyad. At their most painful, shame state intrareactions, that is, reactions within patient and therapist, and interreactions, that is, reactions between patient and therapist, lead the dyad to feel as though they are trapped in a dark hall of mirrors, where neither person can see where they are or how to escape. This experience is analogous to the Chinese finger trap (Chinese finger trap, Wikipedia), where the harder the patient and therapist "pull" to try and get out, the more they remain trapped. This finger trap analogy is apt because the only way "out" of this therapy bind is to go "toward" understanding how shame states operate within and between patient and therapist. My aim in this chapter is to do just that.

Explicit and Implicit versus Conscious and Unconscious Shame Phenomena

The reader will observe that I often use the terms *explicit* and *implicit* rather than *conscious* and *unconscious* when describing shame phenomena arising within and between patient and therapist. I do so to avoid the complexity of how *the unconscious* has been defined in the psychoanalytic literature, be that as occupying a psychological place, part of a mental structure and/or psychodynamic process, made up of past and/or present experience, etc. I recognize there are different levels of awareness of shame and its effects. For my purposes here, *explicit* refers to the patient and/or therapist awareness of *feeling the effects* of shame. When *implicit*, these effects will impact both individuals and the therapy dyad *outside their awareness*. Implicit also means to some degree the effects of shame states are *dissociated and manifested in enactments* (Bromberg, 2011a, 2011b), as will become evident in the clinical vignette. (See Chapter 2 and especially Chapter 3 for more about the relationship between shame, pride, and dissociation.)

Factors Contributing to Shame Proneness: Psychological, Temperamental, and Developmental/Attachment

Several factors contribute to patient and therapist proneness to shame reactivity. These pertain whether or not the person is a RT survivor, but are exacerbated when they do have that history. These include but are not limited to psychological, temperamental, and developmental/attachment factors. The following references therapists but apply equally to patients.

Psychological

One psychological factor contributing to shame proneness involves the therapist's guilt, in response to the patient's suffering, habitually triggering the therapist's maladaptive shame. For example, "I regret not helping the patient as much as I would like" morphs into self-shaming. Instead of the therapist believing, "I am failing to help the patient and have something to learn to be more effective," they conclude, explicitly or implicitly, "I *am* a failure."

Another psychological explanation for the therapist attacking themselves in reaction to the patient's attacking the therapist is *the therapist's reactive anger or rage is experienced as relationally threatening*. The therapist feels anger or reactive rage toward the patient, but implicitly represses their urge to counterattack. Instead, the therapist directs anger/rage, blame, and/or shame toward themselves, fearing they will further harm and shame the patient and their relationship.

A third psychological explanation for therapist self-shaming as reaction to a patient's shaming attack has to do with the trauma-based attachment bond. Once again, the therapist's self-shaming behavior represents an implicit attempt to preserve the bond with a loved other. In the present, this loved other is the patient. In the therapist's history, however, the loved other was often a caregiver and/or perpetrator of abuse and neglect. This other shamed the dependent child who later became the adult therapist.

All three psychological processes that move from patient suffering and/or shaming the therapist to therapist self-shaming play out between patient and therapist and within the therapist. These shame-inducing processes within and between are mutually reinforcing.

Temperamental: Sensitivity, Empathy, and Introversion

Several temperamental factors make the therapist more vulnerable to dropping into a shame state in reaction to the patient's attack. Heightened *sensitivity, empathy, and introversion* exacerbate the therapist's tendency to feel intensely, mirror the patient's experience, and internalize the patient's shame.

As sensitive children and later adult therapists, these individuals experience their own and others' feelings intensely. Thin-skinned, their stimulus barrier is highly porous or permeable (Freud, 1961). Particularly as children but even as adult therapists, they are prone to experience sensory and emotional overload, unable to process and integrate more than their nervous systems can handle. This is particularly true when actively/overtly or passively/covertly shamed by others.

Empathic and introverted children tend to internalize their own and others' emotional experience in an effort to manage strong emotions. They often feel the other person's pain as their own, consistent with shame "contagion" effects (Lewis, 1998, in Gilbert & Andrews, Eds., 1998, p. 136) or mirror neuron activation (Gallese & Goldman, 1998). As introverts these individuals focus on their internal experience, seeking comfort and solace within. When shamed, however, they often believe their shame means something unacceptable about *them* rather than the shaming *other*. Absorbing the patient's shame, these therapists are prone to blaming and shaming themselves for the patient's shame reaction and their own.

Developmental/Attachment

As the concept of wounded healer attests (Nouwen, 1972), therapists often become therapists, in part, because they have been repeatedly psychologically wounded by people they depended upon and later decide, implicitly or otherwise, to heal themselves by healing others. The therapist's developmental history might include being overtly shamed by their caregivers' and loved ones' *presence*, and/or covertly shamed via their loved ones' withdrawal or *absence*. This developmental trajectory often leads to a therapist's habitual self-shaming as an unsuccessful strategy to meet basic, relational needs, having internalized how they were treated in ways they should not have been, and not treated in ways they should have been.

While people with secure and insecure attachment styles will be challenged by working with shame states in psychotherapy, all insecure and particularly disorganized attachment styles face special difficulties. Insecure attachments develop in relationships where the bond does not reliably repair inevitable ruptures, and shame frequently ruptures relationships with others and self. In addition, many disorganized attachments are borne out of RT, adding fuel to the therapeutic fire (Benau, 2017; Bowlby, 1969; Liotti, 2004).

Prototypical Shame-Induced Self-protective Reactions: Three Models

I will describe three models of self-protective reactions that are then integrated into a unified model describing shame reactions. Before describing each model, it is important that the reader understands my *purpose* for developing an integrated model, and how each model *contributes* something of distinct value.

Purpose of an Integrated, Shame Reaction Model

I offer this model to therapists as a way of thinking about and reflecting upon their patients' and their own shame reactivity, and the interrelationship between the two. Shame states are complex, neurophysiologically dysregulating, and psychologically disorganizing. When traumatically triggered, the person's frontal lobe is abruptly hijacked, with logical thought and even speech impaired or shut down. This is evident in high and low freeze states, described in Fisher's (2017) model below, but can also be activated within any of the traumatic reactions. When triggered, the therapist often struggles to know what is going on within the patient, themselves, and their ever-changing relationship. This model may be used to help therapists mindfully think about and reflect upon what is happening during shame states in order to formulate useful responses. This integrated model is analogous to having an air navigation system while flying in turbulent weather.

148 *Patient, Therapist, and Shame States*

Contributions of Each Individual Model

The three models I have selected are Fisher's (2017) trauma-based, survival reactions/parts model; Nathanson's (1992) "compass of shame" (pp. 305–359) model that identifies four defensive reactions to shame; and Karpman's (1968) drama triangle that describes three action roles applicable to interactional patterns during traumatic reactivity. Fisher's (2017) model is useful because it describes common internal reactions to traumatic triggers readily mapped onto traumatic shame states. Nathanson's (1992) description of common shame defenses provides more shame-focused specificity than Fisher's trauma model. While both Fisher's (2017) parts model and Nathanson's (1992) compass of shame pertain to *within*-person phenomena, Karpman's (1968) stereotypical roles occur *between* patient and therapist. These include patterns of "interreaction," that is, reactivity *between* patient and therapist, and an extension of Karpman's triangle (1968) to include patterns of "intrareactions," that is, *between* different parts. In sum, I have chosen a general, *trauma parts* model (Fisher, 2017), a *shame-specific defense* model (Nathanson, 1992), and a *role/interactional* model (Karpman, 1968) that, together, aid therapists in understanding common patterns within and between patient and therapist shame state reactivity.

Three Models: Fisher's Trauma Reaction Parts, Nathanson's Shame Defenses, and Karpman's Trauma Roles

When discussing shame state reactivity in the patient, therapist, and dyad, three conceptual frameworks organize my thinking: Fisher's (2017) parts model, Nathanson's (1992) "compass of shame" (pp. 312–314), and Karpman's (2014, 1968) drama triangle ("triangle").

Fisher's (2017) model describes six survival reactions observed in trauma generally, including fight self, fight other, flight, freeze, attach, and submit. The parts that develop in this model are consistent with structural dissociation (SD) theory (Van der Hart et al., 2006) and represent different degrees of dissociation as contrasted with part-to-part co-consciousness.

Nathanson's (1992) compass of shame focuses on four defensive reactions to shame, including attack self, attack other, avoid, and withdraw. To Nathanson's (1992) model, I add a form of psychological withdrawal others named dissociation as adaptive or maladaptive *process* (Benau, 2020a, 2020b; Schimmenti & Caretti, 2016; Schimmenti, personal communication), that I now call mind/body leave taking (LT). In LT, the person experiences decreased mind/body consciousness and increased detachment in reaction to traumatic or nontraumatic stimuli. (See Chapter 3 for more on differentiating LT and structural dissociation [SD].)

Finally, Karpman's (1968) drama triangle refers to three stereotypical action roles that include victim, persecutor, and rescuer. As will be shown, both patient and therapist can adopt any of these three roles.

Each of these self-protective reactions are outlined and integrated into a single, conceptual framework. This unified framework helps the therapist, first, and then the patient, shift from "defensive reactor" to "reflective responder." Responding reflectively enables the patient-therapist dyad to move out of triggered shame states and enactments and toward adaptive, good enough me pride, pro-being pride, and deep transformation. (See Chapter 2, Shame and Pride Subtypes.)

Fisher's Trauma Survival Reactions Parts Model

Fisher (2017) identified six survival reactions observed in people generally and RT survivors specifically. (See Chapter 4, #15, Shame and Pride: Prototypical Parts, for more about this model as relates to shame and pride states.)

- *Fight Self*: Reactive anger and rage directed at the self, both in external behavior, for example, cutting, and internally, for example, self-punitive guilt (Howell, 2020) and maladaptive shame.
- *Fight Other*: Reactive anger, rage, and shaming directed at others, as in verbally or physical attacking another in reaction to a perceived and/or neuroceived threat or danger. Porges' (2011) concept of neuroception refers to a person's implicit, neurophysiological register of interpersonal safety versus unsafety.
- *Flight*: Physically and/or psychologically fleeing from danger or threat, both interrelationally and intrarelationally.
- *Freeze (High)*: A state of hyperarousal where neither fight nor flight is perceived or neuroceived as available to the survivor. In high-arousal freeze states, LT (transient dissociation, as in loss of body consciousness) and immobilization (Benau, 2021a, 2021b) are common. Colloquially, these are "deer in the headlights" phenomena.
- *Freeze (Low)*: A state of hypoarousal where neither fight nor flight is perceived or neuroceived as available to the survivor. Low arousal, LT, and immobilization (Benau, 2021a, 2021b) apply here. (See LT, below.)
- *Attach*: Following attachment theory (Bowlby, 1969), this involves seeking physical and psychological closeness and care, and/or providing physical and psychological closeness and care.
- *Submit*: Physically and/or psychologically acquiescing to the demands of the threatening/dangerous other. At extremes, this includes a state of neurophysiological and psychological shutdown, hypoarousal, and/or death feigning (Schore, 2009; Porges, 2011; Levine, 1997).

Consistent with SD theory (Van der Hart et al., 2006), these reactions are initially outside the patient's awareness, including consciousness of the other prototypic reactions or parts, and how these reactive parts interrelate. For example, a patient with a disorganized attachment is often unaware that when, at the start of therapy, their *attach* part seeks care their *freeze* part is activated as closeness was historically associated with sexual abuse, and then often followed by *fight self* and *submit* reactions.

Nathanson's Shame Defense Model Expanded

Nathanson's (1992) "compass of shame" model (p. 312) identified four defensive reactions to shame: attack self, attack other, withdraw, and avoid.

"Attack self" (Nathanson, 1992, pp. 326–335) refers to the shamed person turning anger, self-blame, punitive guilt (Howell, 2020), and maladaptive shame toward themselves. This strategy represents the patient's attempt to take charge of being shamed by shaming themselves, turning passive into active and an "other" to "self" locus of control. Attack self can be either a transient or a habitual reaction. The latter is seen in dissociated, self-punitive parts (Van der Hart et al., 2006). Nathanson's attack self is similar to Fisher's (2017) fight self, with the former specifically related to being shamed, and the latter referring to various self-harming reactions, including shame.

"Attack other" (Nathanson, pp. 360–377) refers to the shamed person directing anger, blame, and shame toward the perceived shamer. Attack other is similar to Fisher's (2017) "fight other" part, the former being shame-focused and the latter referring to global survival reactions that also include other ways of "fighting."

"Withdrawal" (Nathanson, 1992, pp. 315–325) refers to the shamed person rapidly, physically withdrawing from the shamer. Withdrawal from shame may entail a patient avoiding eye contact, coming late to appointments, and spending excessive time alone. Social withdrawal that is more chronic often leads to painful social isolation, self-alienation, and greater shame (Dorahy, 2010; DePrince et al., 2015). Nathanson's (1992) withdrawal is similar to Fisher's (2017) flight reaction, where the former is shame-focused and the latter a more general reaction to relational survival threat.

"Avoid" (Nathanson, 1992, pp. 336–359) is a form of withdrawal that tends to be longer term and habitual than withdrawal. Avoid includes psychological and behavioral strategies that keep shame emotion outside one's own and the other's conscious awareness, what Nathanson (1992) called "say no to shame" (p. 339). Acute and chronic psychological avoidance includes a patient not thinking about shame-inducing topics, relationships, and/or feelings. For example, a patient may not share with their therapist feeling angry with loved ones, convinced their anger proves there is something wrong with them as a person. Avoidant styles may include dramatic displays of success that hide one's view of self as defective; pressured, competitive pursuit of new skills that distract the inner critic and deflect others' criticism (p. 345); identifying with highly admired, distant others (p. 346) and, likewise, "borrowed pride" from another's prestige (p. 353); maladaptive narcissism and grandiosity (pp. 348–340); creation and display of a false self (p. 350); and excessive comparison and competition with others (p. 350).

In my view, psychological avoidance also involves LT as differentiated from SD. (See Chapter 3, for more on LT versus SD.) LT can be trauma-induced or not, and acute (short-lived) or chronic (long-lived). An example of trauma-induced, acute LT is when a person being sexually assaulted temporarily "leaves" their body, as though viewing the abuse from above, but never develops dissociative parts (Van der Hart et al., 2006). Non-trauma-induced, acute LT is exemplified by a person "spacing out" during sensory overload (e.g., excessive noise or disturbing emotion) or sensory underload (e.g., boredom) (Schimmenti, 2018; Schimmenti & Caretti, 2016). Depersonalization (DP) and derealization (DR) as *symptoms* reflect acute LT that may be trauma- and/or neglect-induced, whereas DP/DR as *disorders* involve chronic LT (Simeon & Abujel, 2006). Ruth Lanius' (2021) research suggests reduced activation of the flocculus cerebellum of the brainstem or reptilian brain is associated with decreased body consciousness in PTSD with dissociation, consistent with chronic, trauma-induced LT.

Karpman's Drama Role Model

Karpman's (1968) drama triangle includes three action roles that have been usefully applied to interactional patterns during traumatic reactivity, that is, victim (v), persecutor (p), and rescuer (r). With respect to shame reactions, "v" is the person who is shamed, "p" the person who does the shaming, and the "r" seeks to free the "v" from the shaming "p." According to Karpman (1968), a true drama involves switching of roles during the interaction, as will be apparent in the clinical vignette.

Integrating Three Shame Reaction Models

Integrating Fisher's (2017), Nathanson's (1992), and Karpman's (1968) models with the present addition of LT, several shame reactions are identified. The reader will observe there is some overlap between each model. For example, Fisher's (2017) fight self, Nathanson's (1992) attack self, and Karpman's victim share several features. Likewise, Fisher's (2017) fight other, Nathanson's (1992) attack other, and Karpman's persecutor bear similarity. In addition, Fisher's (2017) flight and Nathanson's (1992) withdrawal, and Fisher's (2017) attach and Karpman's (1968) rescuer, respectively, have some qualities in common. As noted, however, the most important distinctions are that Fisher's (2017) model is *trauma*-focused, Nathanson's (1992) *shame*-focused, and Karpman's (1968) *role*-focused.

In order to flesh out patient and/or therapist beliefs that are typically implicit rather than spoken, I offer examples or phrases representing each shame reaction, although these reactions are more typically repeated actions (reactions) rather than verbalizations.

The shame-based reactions I find most useful when working with RT survivors and their shame states are as follows.

- Fight Self, Attack Self, and Victim
  "I'm such an idiot!"
- Fight Other, Attack Other, and Persecutor
  "Once again, he dismisses me, thinks I'm worthless. He's scum to me! Two can play this game!"

- Flight, Withdraw, and Victim
  "I'm a worthless good for nothing. I'm never going to say anything to him again!"
- Freeze and Victim
  "When he called me loser, *again*, my heart raced, I couldn't say a word. I just froze. What's wrong with me? I'm so messed up!"
- LT and Victim
  "Whenever I start to think about how stupid and weak I was my mind goes blank and I feel nothing. I'm such a space cadet."
- Attach and Rescuer
  "Even though he keeps calling me a loser, I know how cruel his mother treated him as a boy. I'm going to prove to him how loveable he truly is."
- Submit and Victim
  "He's right. I'm a nobody—past, present, and future. What's the point? I give up."

Prototypical Patient and Therapist Intrarelational and Patient–Therapist Interrelational Reactive Shame Dynamics

Using these self-protective reactions as entry points, the following describes several prototypical, patient-patient, therapist-therapist, and patient-therapist dynamics encountered in psychotherapy with RT survivors experiencing shame as emotion and, more so, traumatic shame states. While each dyadic, patient-therapist dynamic is discussed separately, several psychodynamic pairings can and often play out between patient-therapist, that is, interrelationally, and part of patient with another part of patient, and part of therapist with another part of therapist, respectively, that is, intrarelationally, at any moment in time and over the course of therapy.

While not exhaustive, the following list of shame-induced dynamic patterns is commonly seen when working with RT survivors. Note that "= =" means an *interrelational* dynamic between patient and significant other, including their therapist. "←→" signifies an *intrarelational* dynamic within, part of patient with part of patient, and part of therapist with part of therapist, respectively.

Patient Attack Self/Fight Self, Victim == Two Therapist Reactions

- Therapist Attach, Rescuer
- Therapist Attack Self/Fight Self, Victim

Patient Attack Self/Fight Self, Victim == Therapist Attach, Rescuer

The patient reacts to an interaction with another person and/or the therapist with self-shaming and self-denigrating. For example, imagine a patient who hurt their loved one's feelings. This patient might say or implicitly believe, "I'm so cruel and mean! I don't deserve happiness, nor any relationship. I'm not loveable!"

In this scenario, the patient's self-shaming is experienced by the therapist as an implicit invitation to draw closer. The therapist's energy and actions go toward the patient in an effort to reassure and comfort him. The therapist might simply say, "You're really a good person. Of course you deserve love." A psychologically more sophisticated but still rescuing reaction would be:

> You were taught to believe you are not deserving of love by your cold, withdrawing mother. But you are with me now, you have a caring wife, and we both have told you that you are loveable. Can't you see that is true?

This therapist's reaction begins as an expression of compassion, empathy, and kindness. Implicitly, it often reflects the therapist's difficulty sitting with the patient's pain and their own, resonant and activated, shame-filled memories. As I learned early in my training, reassurance is almost never reassuring. Therapist "rescue missions" are not helpful because they counter and, in effect, dismiss the patient's experience, which by itself can be shaming, rather than discover with the patient, experientially, the function of their communication (Ecker et al., 2012). For example, a patient who harshly judges and shames himself for hurting his wife may have had an early attachment history with a cold and withdrawing mother, and self-shames in order to cope with powerful, implicit fears of losing his wife's love. In these instances, no amount of well-meaning affirmation can alter the patient's internal working model (Bowlby, 1969) that his wife's distress proves he is utterly worthless and unlovable.

As elaborated below, in these instances the therapist must do two things, in this order: (1) Understand the source and nature of their own rescuing reaction; and (2) Focus on the patient's experience by exploring several questions: Who is involved, past or present; What happened, that is, the actual intra-actions and interactions, past and/or present; When did it happen; and How did it happen, that is, the patient's attendant thoughts/beliefs/meanings, feelings, physical experiences, behavior, etc. The Why question is intentionally omitted as this invites the patient and therapist to intellectualize, moving away from the patient's present, lived, relational experience within themselves and between themselves and others, including their therapist.

Patient Attack Self/Fight Self, Victim == Therapist Attack Self/Fight Self, Victim

Imagine the same patient attacking and shaming himself for hurting their spouse. This time, however, rather than trying to rescue the patient, the therapist also adopts the victim role, attacking and shaming themselves as though saying, "It's not you, it's me. Since I didn't fix your painful marriage, I'm unworthy of your love." In effect, the therapist wears the victim mantle in an unconscious effort to reduce the patient's suffering. This shame dynamic demonstrates how difficult it can be for therapists who identify with the patient's suffering to not react symmetrically.

To the extent the therapist conveys implicitly "This is my pain, not yours," the patient is invalidated and shamed, once again feeling not seen and not understood as they experienced with their emotionally absent parent. This can be confusing for the patient because the therapist, unlike their cold, distant parent, is warm and caring. However, below the surface the patient may feel abandoned by their therapist, left holding their pain alone. Again, in order to move through this patient self-attack == therapist self-attack dynamic, the therapist needs to learn to tolerate their own pain activated by the patient's self-shaming, and remain emotionally present enough so that therapist and patient, together, can better understand what historically and in the present underlies the patient's attack self/fight self, victim position.

Patient Attack Other/Fight Other, Persecutor == Five Therapist Reactions

- Therapist Attack Other/Fight Other, Persecutor
- Therapist Attack Self/Fight Self, Victim
- Therapist Attach, Rescuer
- Therapist Freeze, Victim
- Therapist Withdrawal and LT, Victim

To be held in the grip of a traumatic shame state is unbearably painful, so much so that the shamed person is compelled to escape via one or more reaction, including attacking back, attacking themselves, seeking closeness and care, freezing, and physically and psychologically withdrawing, as in LT.

Patient Attack Other/Fight Other, Persecutor == Therapist Fight Other/Attack Other, Persecutor

The familiar expression, "fight fire with fire," captures well the therapist reacting to being shamefully persecuted by their patient by becoming a withering blamer and shamer in return. In this dynamic, the patient gripped by shame turns their anger and shame against the therapist and the therapist "returns fire." A triggered therapist might say, or at best think and feel, "Who do you think you are? After all these years of my being there for you! How ungrateful can you get? You think *I'm* the failure? It is no wonder your spouse wants to divorce you!"

The therapist's countershaming can be done overtly and unabashedly, as in "I'm not the one who needs help, here!" or covertly, feeling it but not saying anything and/or speaking subtly, as in "Notice how you made this about me, when you've told me how badly you feel." If the patient, in their shame state, turns their ire against another person outside the therapy, the therapist can attack back, as mentioned, or view the shamed person as victim who needs to be rescued. Each therapist reaction prolongs both the patient's and therapist's suffering. The patient is driven to fight back, likely in the same shaming way, and the therapist is drawn repeatedly into attack mode, or drops into shame and withdraws, blaming themselves for losing self-control and behaving badly.

Patient Attack Other/Fight Other, Persecutor == Therapist Attack Self/Fight Self, Victim

The therapist reacts to the patient's attack with virulent, unrelenting attacks on themselves. The therapist's self-shaming behavior suggests three variables are at play: (1) the therapist seeks to achieve something they value, in this case to help their patient. If successful, the therapist experiences a form of adaptive pride I call good enough me pride (Chapter 2); (2) the therapist perceives the patient's shaming as indicating they have not accomplished their desired goal; and (3) the therapist holds their whole self or "being" responsible for their terrible failure.

The shame-prone therapist concludes not being able to help their shamed patient proves they are inadequate as a person, not merely a therapist struggling with a therapeutic impasse. This therapist's "It's all me" reaction would stand in contrast with the therapist who does not yet know how best to respond to their patient's attacks. When a therapist views their not knowing as evidence they have something to learn about working with the patient's shame, for example from further self-reflection, training, consultation, psychotherapy, etc., they will experience no lasting shame.

The therapist's reactive self-shaming reflects their implicitly acceding to the patient's "demands." The therapist implicitly "agrees" in order to remain connected to the patient, at all costs. Submitting to the patient's will is often driven by the therapist's fear that resisting the patient's press, for example by expressing anger back, would make matters worse. After the therapist's harsh self-castigation (e.g., "I deserved that!), the therapist may collapse further into a state of self-shaming isolation (flight), collapse (submit), and/or emotional/somatic numbing (LT). Not infrequently, this spurs on another round of the patient feeling shamed for "harming" and/or "being abandoned by" the therapist, followed by reactive rage and shaming of the therapist, who in turn renews their self-punishment, unintentionally perpetuating the cycle.

Patient Attack Other/Fight Other, Persecutor == Therapist Attach, Rescuer

The expression "kill them with kindness" captures one therapist reaction to a patient reacting to their own shame by attacking the therapist with virulent anger, blame, and shame. That "kill" precedes "kindness" is fitting, as the therapist reaction often involves denial, suppression, and/or implicit projection of the therapist's aggression onto the patient. This approach is familiar to therapists raised in environments where more powerful family members and/or caregivers used explosive rage and shame-attacks to dominate, coerce, and control others. To the extent a therapist tries to appease the "shame-throwing" patient, they may unwittingly communicate several things, including: they cannot handle the patient's nor their own aggression; anger is shameful; the "best" response to being shamed is to submit to the more dominant other and "save yourself"; and the pain underlying the patient's attack is neglected, contributing to more defensive shaming. Clearly, each of these implicit, therapist communications would exacerbate patterned, problematic reactions in RT survivors.

Patient Attack Other/Fight Other, Persecutor == Therapist Freeze, Victim

The patient's shaming, persecutorial attack of the therapist can also place the therapist in an impossible bind, akin to what Liotti (2004) observed in children with a disorganized attachment with an abusive parent. In reaction to being shamed, the therapist has the urge to reconnect with the patient by seeking closeness (attach) and/or attacking back (fight other) *at the same time* as they withdraw (flight). When a therapist can neither go toward the patient, for fear of further attack or abandonment, nor away, for fear of further attack and abandonment, a hyperaroused, freeze state is activated. As shown in the vignette closing this chapter, when I froze initially in the face of my patient's shaming behavior, I could neither speak nor think clearly enough to know what to say.

Patient Attack Other/Fight Other, Persecutor == Therapist Withdrawal and LT, Victim

When under attack by a vehement, shaming patient, a reactive therapist can withdraw in several ways. One is to physically leave, for example, ending the session early or, when the shaming is unremitting, terminate the therapy. Subtler forms of withdrawal by the therapist are displayed when the therapist turns their gaze away from the patient, repeatedly checks the time, etc. Therapist withdrawal often intensifies the patient's feelings of abandonment, and may induce further shame-rage reactions (Lewis, 1971, 1992) directed toward the patient (punitive guilt and shame) and therapist (rage).

When the therapist sees no way to go toward the shame-attacking patient without wounding both patient and therapist, nor away from the patient without further shaming the patient, psychological LT may ensue. This can be thought of as the therapist reflexively "leaving the emotional-relational field." LT can take many forms, but all involve some loss of somatic and emotional awareness.

The therapist's leaving will likely be experienced by the patient in one or more deleterious ways. The RT survivor may view the therapist's LT as passive-aggressive behavior, again feeling abandoned and shamed by the therapist, further enraging the patient who resumes their shaming attack of the therapist. Were this dynamic to persist without the therapist acknowledging their leaving, the shame-prone patient might conclude there is something unspeakably wrong with them for pushing away the therapist.

In contrast, the patient may see the therapist's "checking out" as cold and distant rather than hot and angry. In these instances, the patient may be left feeling uncared for when, for example, the therapist speaks with bland, matter-of-factness, "Let's get back to when we were talking about your mother," and avoids acknowledging the patient's attack. The patient might also leave in reaction to the therapist's checking out (see Patient LT, victim == Therapist LT, victim). The RT survivor might also react to the therapist's LT by feeling abandoned and shamed by, and further enraged with, the therapist. Were this dynamic to persist without the therapist acknowledging leaving, the RT patient would be vulnerable to believing there must be something unspeakably wrong with them for pushing away their therapist.

Patient Withdrawal from the Relational Field

Since the word origin of shame means to cover, as in covering one's head in shame, it is not surprising patients have several ways they can withdraw from the relational field when shamed. Three such patient-withdrawing, self-protective strategies include:

- Patient Flight/Withdraw, Victim
- Patient Freeze, Victim
- Patient LT, Victim

Each withdrawing behavior by the patient elicits common therapist reactions. These patterns can include the following:

Patient Flight/Withdraw, Victim == Therapist Attach, Rescue

Patients physically withdraw in reaction to shame in various ways, including repeatedly arriving late or missing appointments, avoiding eye contact, turning away from the therapist, etc. They may psychologically withdraw by avoiding certain topics that evoke feelings, such as anger toward the therapist, which they fear reflects something shameful about them that will destroy their relationship. The therapist takes it upon themselves "to bring the patient back" and help the patient see they are worthy of respect and love.

There are several problems with the therapist's rescuing behavior. As is true for all rescues, the therapist treatment of the patient as childlike victim disempowers and implicitly shames the patient, as though the therapist had said, "You're not psychologically sturdy enough to face and work with your feelings." In addition, the therapist's attempted rescue would interrupt the patient's understanding the intrapersonal and interpersonal *function* of their withdrawal. For example, if the patient's withdrawal served to keep anger toward their therapist outside awareness, and the patient's anger further protected against their fear of intimacy, then that would remain outside the dyad's shared consciousness and unavailable to work with therapeutically.

Patient Freeze, Victim == Therapist Freeze, Victim

A patient's freeze reaction communicates, nonverbally, that they can neither go toward the therapist, seeking care or expressing anger, nor away from the therapist, seeking safety alone or with another person.[1] Therapists can readily sense a patient's freeze reaction, sometimes by feeling gripped by their own freeze reaction.

A frozen therapist is disconnected from their own mind and body, unable to access words, feelings, physical sensations, and adaptive actions. The therapist knows something is wrong, but does not think clearly enough to understand what is happening or what to do. This renders the therapist immobilized and ineffective, often precipitating further freezing, self-shaming, and overwhelm (Benau, 2021a, 2021b).

The therapist's freezing can result in at least four additional patient reactions, including:

- *Patient Attack Other/Fight Other, Persecutor*: The patient shame attacks the therapist. This may reflect the patient's unconscious attempt to pick a fight and force the therapist to unfreeze and return to their body, feeling, and reengaging with the patient.
- *Patient Attack /Fight Self, Victim*. The patient's shame attacks themselves. This may reflect the patient's attempt to engage the therapist by unconsciously pulling for the therapist to rescue them and/or blaming themselves for the therapist's emotional absence.
- *Patient Withdraw/Flight and LT, Victim*: The patient withdraws and leaves their mind/body, implicitly communicating unbearable pain and perhaps a desire to pull the therapist into an "attach," rescue mission.
- *Patient Attack/Fight Self, Victim ←→ Attack/Fight Other, Persecutor ←→ Freeze, Victim*: The patient experiences simultaneously several irreconcilable emotions, including angry blaming and shaming toward themselves and the therapist. This intensifies both the patient's and therapist's freeze reactions, rendering the dyad immobilized, unable to look backward to understand or move forward to progress in their work.

These repetitive, interrelational dynamics between patient and therapist, and intrarelational cycles within patient and therapist, respectively, are consistent with a series of traumatic reactions. Without new, reflective responses by the therapist, these patterns contribute to prolonged impasses and enactments (Bromberg, 2011a, 2011b).

Patient LT, Victim == Therapist Attach, Rescue

Recurrent and chronic traumatic shame states are often so unbearable that the patient leaves by detaching from their body and emotions. In these instances, the patient no longer feels shame, nor do they feel much of anything. These patients might appear blank, disinterested, detached, disengaged, and to not care about anything, including the therapy. "Losing" the patient in this way can bring up a host of reactions in the therapist, including a powerful surge of empathy and drive to rescue the patient from their isolation. The therapist's reaction may emerge out of several sources, including feeling guilty and/or ashamed for "making the patient leave," and/or feeling abandoned by the patient, panicked, and desperately seeking the patient's assurance that they are "good" and "lovable" rather than "bad" and "unlovable."

Therapist reactions that try to shake the patient out of their LT will always be ineffective, as they fail to consider the patient's implicit motives for leaving. A patient leaves his mind/body when they feel or anticipate feeling too much or too pained. These overwhelming emotions may include the patient's terror or panic when too close; the dread that their rage or sexual feelings will destroy the therapist or therapy relationship; and even more shame. The therapist's job is first to calm their own reactivity so they can see the patient's reaction as a meaningful and historically adaptive coping strategy. The patient, too, needs to understand and accept their role in the drama before they can safely return to the relational field.

Patient LT, Victim == Therapist LT, Victim

Sometimes the only way I know shame is lurking in the shadows is when I feel sleepy or bored with a patient. In these instances, the patient often says things we previously agreed were valuable, yet now seem empty and devoid of meaning. These are times when my "sleepy" LT has "caught" the patient's LT, a form of dissociative attunement (Hoppenwasser, 2008), analogous to yawning uncontrollably when another person yawns. Were the dyad unable to break out of this shame-induced, co-dissociative state, the therapy would stall or fail. When the patient reacts to the therapist's leaving, they might feel abandoned and experience panic/terror, rage, and/or more shame, each more than they could bear alone. The same could be true for the therapist who comes to only find the patient detached. When the therapist recognizes their nonfeeling is indicative of the patient's psychological absence and implicit emotional overwhelm, they can begin to identify an interreactive, dynamic pattern fruitfully brought to their shared attention.

Patient Submit, Victim Reaction

Polyvagal theory (Porges, 2011) predicts that when a RT survivor perceives and/or implicitly neuroceives threat or danger in the therapy relationship, and likewise feelings of shame emerge within the patient or between patient and therapist, then the patient may first respond by trying to talk his way out of his distress, a self-protective strategy Porges (2011) calls social engagement. When the patient's fear/terror and/or shame does not abate, fight, flight, and/or freeze reactions are automatically activated. When these too fail to return the patient-therapist to safe, social engagement, then emotional/behavioral shutdown and submit reactions invariably follow. When a patient submits in reaction to feeling shamed, two therapist reactions are common:

- Therapist Attach, Rescuer
- Therapist Submit, Victim

Patient Submit, Victim == Therapist Attach, Rescuer

Not surprisingly, it can be extremely painful for a therapist to see their patient's chronic shame state precipitate unrelenting shutdown, depression, worthlessness, meaninglessness, and despair. Seeing someone you care about give up on life often leads therapists to feel as despairing as their patient. Feeling incompetent and unable to do their job and help their patient may further elicit in the therapist feelings of resentment toward the patient and shame for being a failure. For many therapists, this too becomes more than they can bear, at times triggering frenetic, rescuing behavior that seeks to counteract the patient's lifelessness and their own helplessness. This therapist behavior is analogous to an infant's desperation when confronted with their mother's blank look during still-faced research (Tronick et al., 1978). This "hyper-active" therapist often fears falling into and never escaping the same dark hole as their patient. Failing to assuage their own panic and despair, the therapist may be driven by a false, implicit belief that "The more I'm energetically *up* the more my patient will be lifted out of their shutdown." These therapist reactions fail for many reasons, including that the patient feels more misunderstood and alone, and even greater shame and guilt that their chronic misery causes the therapist to suffer. The therapist and patient must come to understand that patient shutdown is an extreme but predictable reaction to a perceived, omnipresent internal and/or external threat that, when unaddressed, plagues the patient and therapy dyad.

Patient Submit, Victim == Therapist Submit, Victim

When the therapist repeatedly fails to wake the patient from their stupor, over many months and even years, they may end up feeling as powerless as their patient. Once the therapist drops into their own submit reaction, both patient and therapist will feel dead in the water, a shared state of profound, mind/body immobilization (Benau, 2021a, 2021b). Patient and therapist now suffer alone in their respective, psychological silos. This engenders greater feelings of shame and hopelessness (e.g., Patient: "I'm damaged beyond repair"; Therapist: "I'm of no help nor value").

In my experience, the most helpful therapist response to patient shutdown and submit reactions is to empathically join with the patient so that they feel felt. For example, a therapist working with a chronically shame-ridden, depressed patient must be careful not to dismiss their patient's view of himself as irrevocably damaged. Instead, the therapist feels into their patient's experience so they can say, with genuine empathy, "How could you *not* feel and believe that." Once the patient feels sufficiently accompanied, patient and therapist can begin to understand in what interrelational and intrarelational contexts, past and present, the patient's collapsed reaction made and/or makes sense. The dyad comes to view the patient's deadened reaction as a sign of coping, however problematic, rather than a *failure* to cope. Admittedly, this is easier said than done, as patient absence and appearing deadened is always harder to sit with than patient presence and being enlivened, no matter how provocative.

Shame-Induced Reactivity to Reflective Responsivity: Therapeutic Process and Tasks

Given the complexity and variability of patient and therapist shame-induced intrareactions and interreactions, it is impossible to provide a "how to" protocol when working with traumatic shame states and their sequelae. However, several guiding principles can benefit psychotherapists working with RT survivors. (Chapter 4 details several attitudes, principles, and concepts that inform this transtheoretical approach to psychotherapy with RT survivors.)

A General Therapy Process Working With Shame States: Three Phases and Therapist Tasks

A general therapeutic process when working with shame states can be summarized as having three phases. These three phases are described separately and sequentially when, in fact, they regularly loop back to each other as part of a nonlinear, dynamic system. Within each of the three phases, specific tasks are performed by the therapist to begin with, and later the patient and therapist-patient dyad together, in order to understand and work through shame state reactivity.

Phase 1

The therapist comes to recognize, over time, that a shame dynamic has been activated, within the patient, therapist, and between patient and therapist.

Therapist Tasks

Be It and Be In It

RT is rooted in the patient's relationship with self and other. For shame reactions to emerge in therapy, these relationships must be lived, not merely talked about, by both patient and therapist. Therapists react, in part, because they care enough about the patient and their shared work to have a strong, emotional and behavioral reaction.

At the same time, to live or more accurately to relive in the present RT is to invite becoming *overwhelmed* and *underwhelmed*. Traumatic overwhelm includes being flooded by unbidden thoughts, including beliefs about self, others, and relationship; feelings, including conflicting and chaotic emotions; disturbing somatic experience, including disorienting, often unwanted physical sensations and movements; and behavior, including actions toward oneself and interactions with others that experientially remind or convince the patient and therapist of past, traumatic truths. Reliving trauma also includes being *underwhelmed*, experiencing the pain and grief that accompanies chronically unmet relational needs, embodying and feeling what previously was not felt as a consequence of chronic LT and SD.

Since the trauma we are working with is relational, it follows that healing must likewise be relational. Relational includes patient's self with parts of self, therapist's self with parts of self, and patient with therapist, including previously dissociated patient parts with previously dissociated therapist parts. The material we work with must eventually be embodied by the patient, the therapist, and within their shared mind/body experience. Both patient and therapist must be it and be in it before they can know what it means and how to be in relationship with "it" in new, helpful ways.

Feel It

Feeling it goes hand-in-hand with *being it and being in it*. In the course of therapy, the patient gradually becomes less affect-phobic and starts to feel previously disowned and dissociated aspects of self and relationship. For therapy to work, the therapist has to *feel it* too, which includes empathically entering into the patient's intense emotional experience, and feeling their own feelings and memories evoked by being with the patient.

Phase 2

The therapist helps himself/herself and then their patient to step back and observe the shame dynamic. Over time, they develop a narrative about how patient and therapist co-participated, initially implicitly, in the problematic, shame interaction. This dual capacity, to mindfully observe and be in the experience, first on the part of the therapist, and over time on the patient's part, is an essential feature of all therapy with RT, and shame states, in particular. (See Chapter 4, #13, Co-consciousness and Shared Consciousness.)

Mindful, nonjudgmental, self-other reflection is made possible with the benefit of internal resourcing, such as self-soothing and self-analysis, and external resourcing, such as the therapist seeking professional consultation and personal therapy. (See Chapter 4, #11, Intrarelational and Interrelational Resourcing.)

Therapist Tasks

See It

As discussed in Chapter 4 and as with all trauma, the RT therapist must be close enough to the patient's and their shared experience while psychologically distanced enough so as not to be completely overwhelmed and/or underwhelmed as when the patient was originally traumatized. *Seeing it* requires the participants have at least one foot in the water and one foot on the shore. "Being in the water" encompasses Phase 1 tasks, while "on the shore" refers to Phase 2 tasks, where the therapist, first, and patient and dyad to follow become able to think about and reflect upon their individual and shared relationship with the trauma effects, *now*.

Name It and Share It

Shame, particularly traumatic shame states, cloak therapist, patient, and their relationship. Many therapists do not name the patient's shame, even when they recognize it, for fear of further shaming the patient. This is analogous to the belief that speaking directly about suicide increases the chances a patient will kill themselves. In my experience, to not name shame is to do shame's bidding, a view supported by research that shows avoiding shame stalls or causes the therapy to fail (Dearing & Tangney, 2011). Naming shame helps therapist and patient develop greater psychological distance between the person and the shame state, and in turn enhances their ability to think about, feel, and respond rather than react to shame. (See Chapter 4, #12, Psychological Distance.)

Some common examples of *naming shame* follow the patient exclaiming, "I'm such an idiot," "I just want to crawl in a hole," or "I don't deserve her love." The therapist might ask the patient what he is feeling, and if the patient says "I don't know" or "bad," the therapist might observe, "It sounds like you're feeling shame" or "When you say 'x,' that sounds like shame is talking."

Naming shame is necessary but not sufficient. Traumatic memories are by definition too much, as in abuse, and too little, as in neglect, for the individual to bear alone. The admonition "to share" what the therapy evokes in patient and therapist makes the previously unbearable, bearable. Sharing painful, shame-based feelings and memories serves several functions, including attenuating emotional dysregulation; recognizing shame and shame-inducing events as valid and part of shared, consensual reality; and giving these experiences new, adaptive meanings.

Phase 3

In this phase, the patient-therapist dyad work through their shame dynamic and toward a more flexible, creative, and adaptive pride-enhancing way of being and relating. Ideally, the therapy dyad ultimately experience pro-being pride, defined as "I delight in being me, delighting in me delighting in being myself, with me" (self with self), and "I delight in being me, delighting in you delighting in being yourself, with me" (self with other). (See Chapter 2 on pro-being pride, and all other pride and shame subtypes.)

Therapist Tasks

Move It

Each prior task prepares both patient and therapist to move previously stuck or fixed thoughts, feelings, bodily experience, actions, and interactions toward more adaptive ways of being. I have described this as transforming traumatic immobilization into triumphant movement (Benau, 2021a, 2021b), a form of "un-fixing" what Janet (1911) referred to as "fixed ideas" (Van der Hart & Friedman, 2019 in Craparo et al., Eds., 2019, p. 16), along with unlocking rigid feelings and behavior. *To move it*, then, refers to the patient and therapist accessing and understanding thoughts, feelings, sensations, and behavior in more complex, flexible, and creative ways.

Repeat It, Creatively

The patient's new ways of thinking, feeling, embodying, and behaving must be practiced, both in therapy, patient with themselves and patient with therapist, and outside of therapy, patient with co-workers, acquaintances, and loved ones. Only by practicing emergent ways of being in new and useful ways, the best definition of creativity, can more adaptive ways of thinking, feeling, and doing become integrated within the patient and in their everyday experience.

Clinical Vignette: "Harold": Patient Shame, Therapist Shame, Dyadic Shame, and Finding Our Way Through to Co-created Meanings and Adaptive Pride

Working with traumatic shame states in survivors of complex, RT is never easy, often gets stuck, and sometimes fails. The following vignette with my patient, Harold, first discussed elsewhere (Benau, 2017), provides one example of a challenging yet ultimately successful patient/therapist process that occurred during two months of weekly psychotherapy sessions.

The previous discussion that models patient, therapist, and patient with therapist reactivity and then responsivity grounds these concepts in Harold's and my lived therapy experience. Interspersed throughout the clinical narrative, *prototypical intrarelational and interrelational dynamics are summarized and coded in parentheses and italicized* for clearer differentiation from the clinical narrative. Some readers will find this coding of shame dynamics helpful while others less so. Should the reader choose not to review the coding, the narrative alone will make understandable the complex dynamics described. Pt= patient and Th= therapist or significant other. "←→" refers to an intrareaction between patient parts of self and between therapist parts of self, respectively. "==" denotes an interreaction between patient and therapist.

Harold was a very bright, articulate, psychologically minded, and therapy savvy single young man in his mid-20s, pursuing advanced training in his chosen profession. We met in mostly weekly and occasionally twice-weekly psychotherapy sessions for 18 months prior to the work described.

Harold had never been physically abused, sexually abused, nor neglected. However, he had endured considerable emotional nonattunement by his very anxious and emotionally dependent mother, and emotionally absent, insecure, and intermittently verbally explosive father.

When triggered by unmet relational needs to be seen, felt, and genuinely valued by intimate friends and romantic partners, Harold felt "needy" and psychologically fragmented. Harold coped, reflexively, by switching between feeling hatred and rage toward a "depriving" other; painfully gripped by overwhelming, traumatic shame states when feeling dependent, what Harold called "co-dependent"; and emotionally tormented. *(Pt: attack/fight self, victim ←→ Pt: attach, victim ←→ Pt: attack/fight other, persecutor == Th: attach, persecutor.)*

Harold often found his intrarelational and interrelational landscapes confusing, disturbing, and disorganizing in his closest relationships with friends, girlfriends, and therapist. Harold alternated between shaming himself and shaming the other. Following theories of attachment and SD (Bowlby, 1969; Van der Hart, 2006), Harold's self-shaming part caused other parts to feel unsafe and insecure in relation with himself. Specifically, Harold's struggled to feel accepting and compassionate toward himself, felt ashamed of his powerful, dependency needs, and despairing of his needs ever being met. When these intrarelational dynamics became unbearable, parts of Harold turned the shaming toward me until his fear of losing me and dependency needs going unmet overwhelmed and short-circuited him. *(Pt: submit, victim ←→ Pt: attach, victim ←→ Pt: attach, rescuer ←→ Pt: attack/fight self, victim ←→ Pt: attack/fight other, persecutor == Th: attach, victim ←→ Th: flight/withdraw, victim.)*

These dynamics were further complicated by Harold's mind/body, chronic LT *(Pt: LT, victim)* and SD, such that Harold was not always conscious of different parts contributing to his stormy relationship with himself, his intimate partners, and now me. Harold was aware that he was in great pain and that, at this point in his therapy, I was not helping.

Harold coped with his traumatic shame states, in part, by trying unconsciously to control and shame others. The more insecure Harold felt was his bond with others he loved and depended upon, including his romantic partner and me, the more he tried to control them with anger, blaming, and shaming. Harold's controlling behavior, unwanted by him and others, inevitably left him feeling worse about himself and hopeless that his feelings about himself and his relationships would ever improve. *(Pt: submit, victim ←→ Pt:*

attack/fight self, victim ←→*Pt: attach, victim* ←→*Pt: attack/fight other, persecutor* ←→*Th: attach, victim.)*

During a period of two months following 18 months of deep, beneficial therapeutic work, Harold became angry, controlling, blaming, and shaming of me whenever I made what seemed to me, at least at first, relatively small, empathic errors. Whenever I was misattuned in ways painfully reminiscent of Harold's childhood, for example, when I spoke too much and too authoritatively, Harold was viscerally reminded of feeling helpless in the face of being unseen and patronized by his parents, other adult family members, and an older sibling throughout his latency and teen years. *(Pt: submit, victim* ←→*Pt: attach, victim* ←→*Pt: attack/fight other, persecutor* == *Th: attack/fight other, persecutor* ←→*Th: attach, rescuer* ←→*Th attach, victim* ←→*Th: LT.)*

No matter how challenging his behavior, I never believed Harold's reactions were his fault. I tried to turn my kindness and interest toward Harold and rise above so that we could both see more clearly our shaming interreactivity. *(Both patient and therapist seeking reciprocal responsivity and reflectivity: Pt: attach* == *Th: attach.)* In retrospect, my errors, including my talking too much and too authoritatively, were a consequence of my feeling insecure and anxious because I feared two things: I would become an abusive, shaming, attacking other *(Th: attack/fight other, persecutor* == *Pt: attach, victim)*; and Harold would turn his anger and shaming toward me *(Th: flight, victim* ←→*Th: attach, victim* == *Pt: attack/fight other, persecutor)*. Only after the fact did I realize I wanted to flee first by shaming Harold, and then shame myself for abandoning and attacking Harold. *(Th: flight, victim* ←→*Th Attack/fight self, victim* ←→*Th: attack/fight other, persecutor* == *Pt attack/fight other, persecutor* ←→*Pt: attach, victim.)*

At first, I responded to Harold's confrontations in ways that made things worse. I anxiously froze, feeling helpless, ineffective, and ashamed of myself both for reacting rather than responding thoughtfully, and for being unable to help Harold. I also tried desperately and in vain to understand what was happening within Harold, within me, and between us. *(Pt: attack/fight other, persecutor* == *Th: attach, rescuer* ←→*Th: attack/fight self, persecutor* ←→*Th freeze, victim* ←→*Th: LT, victim* ←→*Th: submit, victim.)*

For over a month, Harold continued to shame me during each session for not helping him, even to the point of telling me he helped members of his peer group, as a layperson, better than I did as his therapist. My first reaction to Harold represented twin impulses, neither verbalized, including angrily pushing back at Harold (e.g., "Don't blame me! I'm trying to help you!") and shaming him (e.g., "There is something wrong with you?!"), while simultaneously blaming and shaming myself (e.g., "What's wrong with me?! Why can't I get us out of this painful, recurrent pattern?!"). With Harold alternating between attacking himself and attacking me, and me wanting to attack back and shaming myself, I repeatedly froze up, immobilized, and speechless in a high arousal, freeze reaction coupled with LT. *(Pt: attack/fight self, victim* ←→*Pt: attack/fight other, persecutor* == *Th:*

attack/fight other, persecutor ⟵⟶ *Th: attack/fight self, victim* ⟵⟶ *Th: freeze, victim* ⟵⟶ *Th: LT, victim.)*

The reader will next see how I *reacted* rather than *responded* to this complex dynamic. I often found myself trying to appease Harold and intellectually explain and interpret his behavior. My reactions predictably left Harold experiencing me as emotionally cold, uncaring, distant, and superior to him, and feeling utterly alone and shamefully judged by me. My failed attempts to appease Harold represented, in retrospect, a remnant of my childhood RT. *(Th: submit, victim* ⟵⟶ *Th: LT, rescuer* == *Pt: attack/fight other, persecutor* ⟵⟶ *Pt: attack/fight self, victim* ⟵⟶ *Pt: attach, victim.)*

It is worth noting, here, the not uncommon connection between unmet attachment needs and self-shaming and other-shaming reactivity. This aspect of my work with Harold provides a clear example of how the patient's RT history and coping patterns interreact with that of the therapist, leading to unintended retraumatization of both. To the extent the therapist knows or senses they are retraumatizing their patient when the therapist is mostly in a young, mind/body state, the therapist's self-punitive guilt and shame will further complicate the patient == therapist interaction. I found myself dreading sessions with Harold, as I anticipated hurting him and being hurt by him, and helpless to ameliorate the situation.

In an effort to respond mindfully rather than react, I tried to quiet my anger and urge to shame Harold. *(Th: reflectivity* ⟵⟶ *Th: attack/fight other, persecutor.)* Repeatedly failing left me feeling frustrated, angry with Harold and wanting to retaliate, and angry toward and ashamed of myself, confused, frozen, and very alone. I imagine Harold felt that he, too, repeatedly lost his better self and me in our unintended yet painful, co-created shame reactivity. *(Pt: attach, victim* ⟵⟶ *Pt: attack/fight other, persecutor* == *Th: attack/fight other, persecutor* ⟵⟶ *Th: freeze, victim* ⟵⟶ *Th: attack/fight self, victim* ⟵⟶ *Th attach, victim.)*

Given the complexity of Harold's and my respective intrarelational and interrelational shame reactions, I needed help to more clearly see and respond to the dynamics that left us stuck and unintentionally harming each other for over a month. I called upon several people whom I trusted to help me "take at least one foot out of the water," observe, and respond more effectively. I needed more eyes, hearts, and minds to help me see my way both into and out of this problematic interreaction, so that I could help Harold and me find our way out, together.

With consultation from several colleagues in a peer consultation group, my longstanding consultant, several sessions with my personal therapist, and ongoing self-reflection, I gradually was able to unfreeze out of my own shame state and reactive self-other shaming.

Kaufman (1992, 1996/1989) described helping shame-bound patients move out of shame by building an interpersonal bridge between the patient and trusted others, beginning with the therapist. In my view, this bridge must be built *interpersonally*, between patient and therapist, and *intrapersonally*, between patient and parts of themselves and therapist and parts of themselves.

Gripped by shame within myself and between Harold and me, I knew I needed to reach out to those who understood complex psychotherapy dynamics and enactments, and also recognized my strengths and vulnerabilities without exacerbating my shame.

By virtue of their interest in and acceptance of me, my consultants helped me reclaim my fuller self, first with them and then with Harold. Their interest in me being myself and reclaiming my adaptive pride, my competence as therapist (good enough me pride) and authentic aliveness (pro-being pride) in lieu of my traumatic shame state pointed me toward an intrapersonal bridge back to myself and helped me reestablish a previously sturdy, secure interpersonal bridge between myself and Harold.

Since traumatic shame states are co-constructed *intrasubjectively*, internalized, shaming self-state with shamed self-state, and *intersubjectively*, shaming other with shamed self, it follows that shame states occlude access to one's embodied, enlivened, authentic self, and capacity to care and be cared for. A diminished self, then, contracts the loved and loving other, and their relationship. Harold's shaming of himself and me, and my reactive shaming of myself and Harold, diminished us both, threatening our therapeutic bond. In contrast, my consultants' capacity to see and feel me as I am, flaws and all, despite the shame state that initially left me feeling unworthy of their care, enabled me to restore my compassion toward my shamed self and, gradually, with Harold.

I came to understand that my complex state of intense, immobilizing fear, helplessness, and shame represented triggered, visceral, and emotional memories of previously dissociated interpersonal trauma in childhood, along with acute, conscious shame emotions in the present. My experience with Harold triggered all three, maladaptive shame subtypes in me (Chapter 2), beginning with not good enough me shame (i.e., failing to help my patient), followed by not me shame (i.e., trying to be "nice" and "instructive" rather than owning my own anger, fear, and shame), and no me shame (i.e., early losses triggering fears of being abandoned by and abandoning Harold). As documented elsewhere (Tauber, 2002), my experience was not uncommon. Present-day traumatic events, therapist with patient, often activate traumatic memories in the form of somatic and emotional flashbacks of the therapist's past, traumatic relationships. Finally, my good enough me shame, good enough pride, and pro-being pride were all evident when, with others' help, my drive to be true to myself and to Harold, professional competence, and restored aliveness augured the recovery of my therapeutic capacities.

Feeling my consultants powerfully with me, in session, while still experiencing shame reactivity, I came to realize how my interactions with Harold evoked painful reminders of my being shamed in the past by loved others. I was increasingly able to unfreeze and reassociate with myself and Harold, to think and feel again in Harold's presence, and reflect upon our dynamic. This helped me *respond* mindfully, with curiosity and kindness toward Harold, whereas previously I could only *react* in ways that exacerbated the chaotic volatility of our interaction.

My consultants also offered me several practical, experiential strategies that helped me remain present and open with both Harold and myself. First, I visually imagined a semipermeable membrane between me and Harold, such that I felt protected from his projected, shame attacks but not walled off, so that I could feel with him and he with me. I used some somatic, self-regulation methods, such as placing my hand on my belly, in order to calm myself enough to remain emotionally present in the room. I was also encouraged to visualize caring for my younger, shamed self in-session, for example, imagining a very "Young Kenny" playing with a sand tray I had in my office, while "Adult Ken" remained Harold's therapist. I also visualized being quietly accompanied by my consultant and therapist, standing to either side of me, while meeting with Harold. As a result of these experiential strategies, I no longer felt alone in session with Harold's shamed and shaming younger self, neither intrarelationally (i.e., experiencing my present-day Adult Self caring for my Younger Self) nor interrelationally (i.e., having my present-day Adult Self cared for by my adult, caring colleagues, consultant, and therapist), and in turn interrelationally with Harold. *(Th: attach, victim ⟵⟶ Th: attach, rescuer == Pt: attach, victim.)*

All of these strategies helped me better self-regulate, allowing me to feel present with Harold in new and helpful ways. I began to describe and explore with Harold our shared enactment in ways that were neither shaming of Harold nor myself. I gently pointed out to Harold how he was shaming himself and me, in words and contemptuous tone. While I feared this might hurt Harold and instigate more shame, he found it relieving. I quickly discovered Harold did not really want to shame me, and had not realized he was doing so until I pointed this out.

Gradually, Harold was able to see how he had been engaged in "co-dependent" behavior (his words) that left him feeling "weak," powerless, and ashamed in my presence. In his not me shame state, Harold both demanded I know how to make him feel better and "fix him," while becoming enraged, blaming, and demeaning when I failed. I can see now, but not at the time, that this was a repeat of a much younger Harold's experience with his parents and older sibling. By observing together our shame interreactivity, Harold and I were more able to think about and respond, rather than react, to our own and the other's suffering. (Harold's increased reflectivity about our shared, shame state dynamic: *Pt attach, victim ⟵⟶ Pt attack/fight self, persecutor ⟵⟶ Pt attack/fight other, persecutor == Th attach, victim).*

Increasingly, Harold and I found ways to avoid falling into our co-created, trauma vortex of self/other shaming and blaming, helpless longing to be rescued, and resignation and despair that our therapeutic relationship would ever be restored. *(Pt: attack/fight self, victim ⟵⟶ Pt: attack/fight other, persecutor ⟵⟶ Pt: attach, victim ⟵⟶ Pt: submit, victim == Th: attack/fight other, persecutor ⟵⟶ Th: attack/fight self, victim ⟵⟶ Th: attach, victim ⟵⟶ Th: submit, victim.)* For example, following a Gestalt Therapy, two-chair approach (Perls, 1992/1969), we agreed to make room for Harold's rage by inviting him to direct it, verbally, toward my empty chair representing his internalized, abandoning mother, while I sat closer to him in a chair to his right. Harold was able to fully embody and express his anger toward its rightful, original source without fear of being abandoned, while also making it possible for me to be more with Harold, at his side rather than becoming self-protective. *(Pt: attack/fight other, persecutor ←→Pt: attach, rescuer == Th: attach, rescuer.)* I was now returning to my previous status as Harold's earned, secure attachment figure (Roisman et al., 2002), in ways I could not achieve when Harold's actions left me immobilized in our respective, shame-filled pasts. (From *Pt: attack/fight other, persecutor == Th: freeze, victim←→ Th: attack/fight other, persecutor* to *Pt: attach, victim == Th: attach, rescuer.)*

These and related strategies, but most importantly my becoming much more somatically and emotionally well-regulated, no longer frozen in shame, fear, and reactive anger, and therefore emotionally present with Harold, gradually freed Harold to utilize his own, already well-developed self-soothing and self-regulatory strategies, the opposite of self-shaming and other-shaming behavior. This further freed me to become more of a resource for and ally to Harold when faced with his disintegration and dissociation, rather than the perceived and actual cause of his feeling abandoned and shamed. *(Pt: attach, victim ←→Pt: attach, rescuer == Th: attach, rescuer.)*

Another way to conceptualize this transformation, from co-traumatizing and traumatized victims to co-realizing and enlivened partners, is that Harold and I found our way back into our respective and shared good enough me pride and pro-being pride. As we made our way through this challenging impasse, we both experienced acts of triumph, consistent with good enough me pride. As Janet (1935) observed, an act of triumph following trauma processing "requires effort and results in a sense of pride that is a form of joy and heals shame" (cited in Barral & Meares, 2019, p. 121). Pro-being pride is not only life affirming. Pro-being pride helps both the individual and those with whom he relates reclaim their creative capacity to play with implicit beliefs, feelings, and somatic experience in new and useful ways. This was exemplified by all my creative strategies, imagined and realized in session, previously unavailable to me while frozen. Likewise, as Harold reclaimed his pro-being pride with me, his well-developed empathic imagination returned, enabling him to resume caring for himself and me.

Harold and I found our way into, through, and out of our co-created shame state and reactivity. In so doing, we learned much about ourselves and our relationship in ways that strengthened each of us and fortified the resilience of our therapy bond. This work demonstrated that shared, traumatic shame cannot only be endured but, with a hard-earned restoration of secure self with self and self with other, transform patient, therapist, and therapy relationship in unexpected and enlivening ways.

Note

1 This discussion of patient-therapist freeze reactions is consistent with Liotti's (2004) description of adult disorganized attachment styles developing out of childhood RT.

References

Barral, C. & Meares, R. (2019). The Holistic Project of Pierre Janet: Part Two: Oscillations and Becomings: From Disintegration to Integration. In G. Craparo, F. Ortu, & O. Van der Hart, Eds., *Rediscovering Pierre Janet: Trauma, Dissociation, and a New Context for Psychoanalysis* (pp. 116–129). New York: Routledge. https://doi.org/10.4324/9780429201875.

Benau, K. (2021a). Shame to Pride Following Sexual Molestation: Part 1: From Traumatic Immobilization to Triumphant Movement. *European Journal of Trauma and Dissociation*, 5(4), 100198. https://doi.org/10.1016/j.ejtd.2020.100194.

Benau, K. (2021b). Shame to Pride Following Sexual Molestation: Part 2: From Pro-being Pride to Retaliatory Rage, Adaptive Anger, and Integration. *European Journal of Trauma and Dissociation*, 5(4), 100194. https://doi.org/10.1016/j.ejtd.2020.100194.

Benau, K. (2020a). Shame, Pride and Dissociation: Estranged Bedfellows, Close Cousins and Some Implications for Psychotherapy with Relational Trauma Part I: Phenomenology and Conceptualization. *Mediterranean Journal of Clinical Psychology*, 8(1), 1–35. Doi: https://doi.org/10.6092/2282-1619/mjcp-2154.

Benau, K. (2020b). Shame, Pride and Dissociation: Estranged Bedfellows, Close Cousins and Some Implications for Psychotherapy with Relational Trauma Part II: Psychotherapeutic Applications. *Mediterranean Journal of Clinical Psychology*, 8(1), 1–2. https://doi.org/10.6092/2282-1619/mjcp-2155.

Benau, K. (2017). Shame, Attachment, and Psychotherapy: Phenomenology, Neurophysiology, Relational Trauma, and Harbingers of Healing. *Attachment: New Directions in Psychotherapy and Relational Psychoanalysis*, 11(1), 1–27. https://doi.org/10.33212/att.v11n1.2017.1.

Binderman, R. M. (1974). The Issue of Responsibility in Gestalt Therapy. *Psychotherapy: Theory, Research & Practice*, 11(3), 287–288. https://doi.org/10.1037/h0086360.

Bowlby, J. (1969). *Attachment: Attachment and Loss Volume One (Basic Books Classics) (Attachment and Loss Series, Vol. 1) (2nd Edition)*. New York: Basic Books.

Bromberg, P. M. (2011a). *Awakening the Dreamer: Clinical Journeys*. New York: Routledge. https://doi.org/10.4324/9780203759981.

Bromberg, P. M. (2011b). *The Shadow of the Tsunami and the Growth of the Relational Mind*. New York: Routledge. https://doi.org/10.4324/9780203834954.

Chinese finger trap, Wikipedia: https://en.m.wikipedia.org/wiki/Chinese_finger_trap. Accessed August 1, 2021.

Craparo, G., Ortu, F., & Van der Hart, O., Eds. (2019). *Rediscovering Pierre Janet: Trauma, Dissociation, and a New Context for Psychoanalysis*. New York: Routledge. https://doi.org/10.4324/9780429201875.

Dalenberg, C. J. (2000). It's Not Your Fault: Countertransference Struggles with Blame and Shame. In *Countertransference and the Treatment of Trauma*. Washington: American Psychological Association (pp. 115–144). https://doi.org/10.1037/10380-000.

Dearing, R. L. & Tangney, J. P., Eds. (2011). *Shame in the Therapy Hour*. Washington, DC: American Psychological Association. https://doi.org/10.1037/12326-000.

DePrince, A. P., Huntjens, R. J. C., Dorahy, M. J. (2015). Alienation Appraisals Distinguish Adults Diagnosed with DID from PTSD. *Psychological Trauma: Theory, Research, Practice, and Policy*, 7(6), 578–582. Doi: https://doi.org/10.1037/tra0000069.

DeYoung, P. (2015). *Understanding and Treating Chronic Shame: A Relational/Neurobiological Approach*. New York: Routledge. https://doi.org/10.4324/9781315734415.

Dorahy, M. J. (2010). The Impact of Dissociation, Shame, and Guilt on Interpersonal Relationships in Chronically Traumatized Individuals: A Pilot Study. *Journal of Traumatic Stress*, 23(5), 653–656. Doi: https://doi.org/10.1037/tra0000069.

Ecker, B., Ticic, R., & Hulley, L. (2012). *Unlocking the Emotional Brain: Eliminating Symptoms at Their Roots Using Memory Reconsolidation*. New York: Routledge. https://doi.org/10.4324/9780203804377.

Fisher, J. (2017). *Healing the Fragmented Selves of Trauma Survivors: Overcoming Internal Self-Alienation*. New York: Routledge. https://doi.org/10.4324/9781315886169.

Freud, S. (1961). *Beyond the Pleasure Principle (transl. J. Strachey)*. New York: W.W. Norton.

Gallese, V. & Goldman, A. (1998). Mirror Neurons and the Simulation Theory of Mind-Reading. *Trends in Cognitive Sciences*, 2(12), 493–501. https://doi.org/10.1016/S1364-6613(98)01262-5.

Gilbert, P. & Andrews, B., Eds. (1998). *Shame: Interpersonal Behavior, Psychopathology, and Culture*. New York: Oxford University Press.

Hopenwasser, K. (2008). Being in Rhythm: Dissociative Attunement in Therapeutic Process. *Journal of Trauma & Dissociation*, 9(3), 349–367. https://doi.org/10.1080/15299730802139212.

Howell, E. (2020). *Trauma and Dissociation-informed Psychotherapy: Relational Healing and the Therapeutic Connection*. New York: W.W. Norton. 0.4324/9780203888261.

Janet, P. (1935). *Les Debuts de L'Intelligence*. Paris: Flammation.

Janet, P. (1911). *L'état Mental de Hystériques*. Paris: Alcan.

Karpman, S. B. (2014). *A Game Free Life. The Definitive Book on the Drama Triangle and Compassion Triangle by the Originator and Author: The New Transactional Analysis of Intimacy, Openness, and Happiness*. San Francisco: Drama Triangle.

Karpman, S. B. (1968). Fairy Tales and Script Drama Analysis. *Transactional Analysis Bulletin*.

Kaufman, G. (1992). *Shame: The Power of Caring (3rd Edition)*. Rochester, VT: Schenkman Books.

Kaufman, G. (1996/1989). *The Psychology of Shame: Theory and Treatment of Shame-based Syndromes (2nd Edition)*. New York: Springer.

Lanius, R. (March 4, 2021). *Trauma, Balance, and Recovery: Restoring Emotion Regulation, Balance, and a Sense of Self in the Aftermath of Developmental Trauma*. Webinar. EEG/Learn.

Levine, P. (1997). *Waking the Tiger: Healing Trauma*. Berkeley: North Atlantic Books.

Lewis, H. B. (1992). *The Role of Shame in Symptom Formation*. Hillsdale, NJ: Lawrence Erlbaum Associates.

Lewis, H. B. (1971). *Shame and Guilt in Neurosis*. New York: International Universities Press.

Lewis, M. (1998). Shame and Stigma. In P. Gilbert & B. Andrews, Eds., *Shame: Interpersonal Behavior, Psychopathology, and Culture*. New York: Oxford University Press.

Liotti, G. (2004). Trauma, Dissociation, and Disorganized Attachment: Three Strands of a Single Braid. *Psychotherapy: Theory, Research, Practice, Training*, 41(4), 472–486. https://doi.org/10.1037/0033-3204.41.4.472.

Nathanson, D. (1992). *Shame, Pride, Affect, Sex and the Birth of the Self*. New York: W.W. Norton. https://doi.org/10.1177/036215379402400207.

Nouwen, H. J. M. (1972). *The Wounded Healer Ministry in Contemporary Society*. New York: Doubleday, Image Books.

Perls, F. S. (1992/1969). *Gestalt Therapy Verbatim.* Gouldsboro, Maine: Gestalt Journal Press.

Porges, S. W. (2011). *The Polyvagal Theory: Neurophysiological Foundations of Emotions, Attachment, Communication, and Self-regulation.* New York: W.W. Norton.

Roisman, G. I., Padron, E., Sroufe, L. A., & Egeland, B. (2002). Earned-Secure Attachment Status in Retrospect and Prospect. *Child Development,* 73(4), 1204–1219. https://doi.org/10.1111/1467-8624.00467.

Schimmenti, A. (September 8, 2018). Personal communication, originally posted on the Dissociative Disorders Listserv (DISSOC). Quoted with permission.

Schimmenti, A. & Caretti, V. (2016). Linking the Overwhelming with the Unbearable: Developmental Trauma, Dissociation, and the Disconnected Self. *Psychoanalytic Psychology,* 33(1), 106–128. https://doi.org/10.1037/a0038019.

Schore, A. N. (2009). Relational Trauma and the Developing Right Brain: An Interface of Psychoanalytic Self Psychology and Neuroscience. Self and Systems: *Annual New York Academy of Science,* 1159(1), 189–203. Doi: 10.1111/j.1749-6632.2009.04474.x.

Schore, A. N. (2001). The Effects of Relational Trauma on Right Brain Development, Affect Regulation, and Infant Mental Health. *Infant Mental Health Journal,* 22, 201–269. Doi: https://doi.org/10.1002/1097-0355(200101/04)22:1<201::AID-IMHJ8>3.CO;2-9.

Simeon, D. & Abujel, J. (2006). *Feeling Unreal.* New York: Oxford University Press.

Tangney, J. P. & Dearing, R. L. (2011). Working with Shame in the Therapy Hour: Summary and Integration. In R. L. Dearing & J. P. Tangney, Eds., *Shame in the Therapy Hour* (pp. 374–404). Washington, DC: American Psychological Association. https://doi.org/10.1037/12326-000.

Tangney, J. P. & Fischer, K. W., Eds. (1995). *Self-conscious Emotions: The Psychology of Shame, Guilt, Embarrassment, and Pride.* New York: Guilford Press.

Tauber, Y. (2002). High Holidays 2000 and Aftermath: Doing Psychotherapy with Holocaust Survivors and the Second Generation in Israel during the Sudden Eruptions of Violence. *American Journal of Psychotherapy,* 56(3), 391–410. https://doi.org/10.1176/appi.psychotherapy.2002.56.3.391.

Tronick, E., Als, H., Adamson, L., Wise, S., & Brazelton, B. (1978). The Infant's Response to Entrapment between Contradictory Messages in Face-to-Face Interaction. *American Academy of Child Psychiatry,* 17(1), 1–13. https://doi.org/10.1016/S0002-7138(09)62273-1.

Van der Hart, O. & Friedman, B. (2019). A Reader's Guide to Pierre Janet. In G. Craparo, F. Ortu, & O. Van der Hart, Eds., *Rediscovering Pierre Janet: Trauma, Dissociation, and a New Context for Psychoanalysis.* New York: Routledge. https://doi.org/10.4324/9780429201875.

Van der Hart, O., Nijenjuis. E. S., & Steele, K. (2006). *The Haunted Self: Structural Dissociation and the Treatment of Chronic Traumatization.* New York: W.W. Norton.

Wille, R. (2014). The Shame of Existing: An Extreme Form of Shame. *International Journal of Psychoanalysis,* 95(4), 695–717. Doi: 10.1111/1745-8315.12208.

6 From Shame to Pride

Psychotherapy, Neuroscience, and Applications—Three Perspectives

Introduction

This chapter presents three perspectives on my psychotherapy session with "Isaac," an adult survivor of relational trauma (RT) (Schore, 2001) and sexual abuse. The first perspective includes a fully transcribed session. In brackets [ ], I share my thoughts during and about the session. The second vantage point is based upon a conversation between Frank Corrigan, M.D. (FMC), and myself (KB). Dr. Corrigan is a psychiatrist and psychotherapist with expertise in the neuroscience of psychotherapy with RT. He provides the reader a rich understanding of the neuroscientific or brain-based correlates of moment-to-moment, clinical phenomena in the session with Isaac. In this section, Dr. Corrigan and I compare and contrast our respective understandings. The final, third perspective endeavors to answer this question: How might a neuroscientific understanding of psychotherapy with RT survivors inform and enhance this work? To better feel the flow of the session, the reader may choose to read first the session transcript, and then return to my discussion with Frank.

This session took place 2 years, 8 months into weekly psychotherapy with Isaac. At the time of this session, Isaac was married for 35 years with two adult children, in recovery from alcoholism for over 30 years, and an active meditator for over 10 years.

Isaac is an adult survivor of RT that included a single incident of sexual molestation at age six by a stranger in a park; a history of chronic emotional abuse and shaming by his father and older brother; emotional and occasional physical neglect by his mother; witnessing his mother's breakdown marked by overwhelming anxiety, depression, and grief following the loss of her two-year-old child; Isaac's loss of this beloved, younger sibling, and the divorce of his parents at age seven; and physical abuse that included physical restraint, humiliation, and psychological terrorizing by the same older brother.

Isaac began this 80-minute session sharing he recently received a surgeon's second opinion about his foot surgery the year prior. Isaac's recovery had not gone well, and was enduring considerable pain when walking. The surgeon said Isaac's pain would not remit without additional surgery. We agreed to

DOI: 10.4324/9780429425943-7

give Isaac a referral for physical therapy (PT), but neither the surgeon nor Isaac believed PT would help.

I suggested Isaac seek a PT "skilled" in understanding his surgery, and "caring" enough for Isaac to trust. I was concerned some of Isaac's younger, dissociative parts (Van der Hart et al., 2006) might "choose" "going solo" and "enduring pain" rather than seeking the best care.

[My insistence that Isaac "not endure pain unnecessarily any longer" stemmed, in part, from my guilt. While I had given Isaac a PT referral several months prior, I had not inquired about his lack of follow-through.]

I suggested to Isaac that we had been lulled into a mild trance state, not registering that his persistent pain required prompt attention. [As part of my dissociative attunement (Hoppenwasser, 2008), I too learned to "endure pain" as a boy.] I noted men in our culture are taught from an early age "to suck it up" and "not to act like a sissy" (Real, 1997).

Isaac observed that while his Adult Self agreed to find the best PT, a younger part did not. We decided to work with this reluctant, younger part. Although Isaac had the money, his younger part did not feel "worth" the cost of his initial PT assessment.

[I now realized Isaac was gripped by another traumatic shame state ("shame state" for short; Chapter 2), a chronic, maladaptive, mind/body state far more harmful than shame as emotional process or "feeling." Isaac was living with not me shame where dissociative parts of self were linked with shame, specifically Isaac's compulsion to "endure pain" and "not being worthy" of spending money on his physical care.]

...

FMC: The worthlessness Isaac feels in himself would likely be a component of the shame residual from the early experiences of humiliation; it leaves him unable to properly value his health and well-being. The powerfully visceral pain and the associated urge to hide have a residual impact on the valence of the self. The brainstem-based view is that the cognitive schema changes are derived from the recurrently distressing shaming.

KB: Your view fits with Scheff's (In press) concept of recursive shaming, where the mind/body replays shaming experiences like a traumatic flashback. The stubborn persistence of shame states is a real challenge in psychotherapy with RT.

The neurobiology of shame helps explain the discrepancy between what Isaac *knows* cortically and implicitly, and subcortically believes. Isaac's subcortical knowing is not amenable to cognitive/verbal disconfirmation necessary to consider more adaptive behavior. Depending upon your neurobiological theory of shame, "subcortical" refers to "limbic" (Ecker et al., 2012) and/or "midbrain/brainstem" (Corrigan & Elkin-Cleary, 2018). When Isaac's subcortical shame state dominated his internal landscape, he knew (cortically) he could afford PT, while also knowing (subcortically) he would never seek treatment. Isaac's negative self-image and shame state developed at a very young age, reinforced by primary attachment relationships with his shaming father (i.e., "Giving in to physical pain is weak") and shamed, fragile mother, both of whom neither saw nor attended to Isaac's emotional pain.

Isaac's internalized working model (Bowlby, 1969) dominated his implicit thoughts/beliefs, feelings, and inaction about his pain. Isaac and I were now awakening from our shared *dis-association*, having previously failed to *associate* "Isaac in pain" with "Isaac taking action to alleviate his pain."

...

[This session followed The Comprehensive Resource Model (CRM) protocol (Schwarz, 2014–2017; Schwarz et al., 2017). CRM is a creative psychotherapeutic approach to chronic RT and dissociation. To facilitate deep trauma processing, the CRM patient is well-resourced neurophysiologically and emotionally well-regulated. CRM uses imagined, nonhuman figures such as animals for intrarelational resourcing to avoid patients becoming triggered by human reminders of RT. CRM's resources also include breathwork; bilateral music; patient toning, that is, chanting or humming nonverbal sounds to express powerful affect and self-regulate; sensory imagery; somatic awareness and building an internal, somatic grid; intrarelationally bonding younger parts with the patient's compassionate adult self; eye positions as used in Brainspotting (Grand, 2013), to anchor, strengthen, and reconnect the patient with transformational mind/body states; and the embodiment of symbolic representations of therapeutic gains, including colors and geometric shapes.]

[Isaac chose not to listen to bilateral music as he usually did. He was able to access his other resources without formal reintroduction.]

Therapist (Th): "Go inside and find the place in your body that holds the memory of 'I'm not worth it.'"

[Isaac's eyes were closed the remainder of the session, until the last few minutes.]

ISAAC (Patient—Pt): "It's in my lower stomach, gut. Fear."

...

FMC: So here we have the activation of the midbrain periaquductal gray (PAG)—with the dread in the gut as described in Mobbs et al. (2007). In standard CRM this would be enough to work with through resourcing the self-state holding the visceral fear and creating the possibility of stepping into the affect (Schwarz et al., 2017).

KB: The co-occurrence of gut dread and shame states is interesting. The "shock" of threat to one's "being" and "being with" is intrinsic to dread (Chapter 2). Shock and dread are phenomenal markers of the abrupt interruption of aliveness and the implicit and/or explicit threat of physical and/or psychological banishment and death. When held by a shame state, the patient makes himself small or invisible, in order to not be perceived as threatening and vulnerable to being destroyed by the shaming other. In effect, shame's "invisibilizing" and attendant dissociation (Chapter 3) *sometimes* quiet this gut dread.

FMC: It is, of course, hypothetical but I have recently argued for a "*preaffective shock*" state that arises through midbrain connections with ascending noradrenergic systems *before* there is an *affective* response mediated by the PAG (Corrigan & Christie-Sands, 2020). According to the anatomy of the brainstem, it is possible for the shock of relational disconnection to activate arousal experienced as shock, before the affective response mediated by the PAG and hypothalamus comes in. Although shame may reduce fear in some circumstances, the visceral pain that can go with it is highly unpleasant; and the urge to be very small is an urge not to be seen when being in the gaze of another is the source of the pain. Being exposed to the direct gaze of another can activate the brainstem areas of the superior colliculi (SC), periaqueductal gray, and locus coeruleus. In complex PTSD, while controls engage in more cortical processing (Steuwe et al., 2014), the brainstem response to the internal or external trigger is fast and precognitive and elicits the visceral sensations.

The functional view of shame, that it is regulating the gut dread, can subtly diminish the importance of the painful shame state itself: the basic affect view of shame avoids that by giving it equal status with fear, rage, and grief.

KB: Frank, your recognition of the gut as implicated in preaffective shame is clinically important as patients often notice gut activation before their felt sense of shame.

From a "micro" perspective, I posit two pathways of shame activation (Chapter 2). The first, "shame as an emotional process," downregulates arousal and affect (Schore, 2003; Tomkins, 1963). The second pathway, "shame as a traumatic mind/body state," is closest to your view, Frank, and like other traumatic states causes dysregulation with alternating or concurrent states of hyperarousal and hypoarousal. Both forms of shame are painful, albeit the latter much more so.

RT survivors may also benefit from understanding different *functions* of shame, for example, shutting down, making oneself small or invisible (i.e., shame as emotional process) and/or freezing, remaining immobile (i.e., shame state). Psychoeducation helps some patients see themselves as less crazy when gripped by a shame state. With psychoeducation, patients feel *more* understood, further diminishing their shame. Finally, psychoeducation fosters "psychological distance" (Chapter 4, #12) between the "mindful observer" (adult self) and "experiencer" (dissociative younger part). As you suggest, Frank, these cortical understandings of shame states cannot replace subcortical processing within the midbrain (Corrigan & Christie-Sands, 2020) and limbic system (Schwarz et al., 2017).

…

Th: "Notice what in your body goes with that fear in your lower gut."

[Instructing Isaac to observe his somatic experience served several purposes: to help Isaac remain embodied and not dissociate; to process somatic and emotional trauma memory; and to help me better track and empathically connect with Isaac.]

Pt: "Lower level, electric nervousness."
Th: "Pulsing? Shaking?"
Pt: "A buzzing vibration."
Th: "Where in your body is that buzzing vibration?"
Pt: "The very bottom of my stomach."
Th: "What is its size?"
Pt: "A thin line. From hip to hip."
Th: "Color?"
Pt: "White. White-ish."
Th: "Texture?"
Pt: "No texture. Smooth."
Th: "Temperature?"
Pt "No. Seems, a lightness, would be warm but doesn't feel warm."
Th: "Quality of vibration?"
Pt: "Low level, buzzing."
Th: "Sound?"
Pt: "No."
Th: "Are there any other physical sensations near or in relation to the buzzing vibration?"
Pt: "No, just the thin line."
Th: "What is your current distress level that goes with the buzzing vibration, with 0= no distress up to 10= most distress?"
Pt: "6."

[Isaac's Subjective Units of Distress (SUDS) was moderate, sufficient to motivate him but not overwhelming, outside his window of tolerance (Siegel, 1999) or optimal arousal (Ogden et al., 2006).]

Th: "Is the buzzing sensation in the front, back, or both?"
Pt: "Front."
Th: "What is the age of the part that holds the memory associated with the buzzing sensation and feeling worthless?"
Pt: "Four or five, maybe younger."
Th: "Before or after the molestation?"
Pt: "Before. It feels *installed*" (my emphasis).
...

["Installed" grabbed my attention. It suggested this "part" came from someone other than Isaac, an "introject" rather than a "younger part of self". (See Schmidt's [2009, p. 26] distinction between "introjects" and younger, reactive parts). Younger parts live in the shadow of introjected caregivers, adopting ways of relating to self and others that mimic the caregiver's ways of relating.]

[One year later, Isaac said his father "installed" in him pernicious beliefs. These included two opposing commands Isaac *must* yet *could not* obey: "You *must* dominate all others or you will be weak, dominated, and shamed"; *and* "You *must* submit to me (father) dominating you (Isaac)." These conflicting demands are common in cult leaders (Shaw, 2014). Given the pervasiveness of contradictory admonitions coming from an attachment figure, that is, father, Isaac loved, feared, and depended upon for survival, liberation from these "installations" took several years of therapy.]

...

Th: "Is the [installed] sensation in or on you?"
Pt: "In me, but not deep. Closer to the surface."

[I thought "closer to the surface" fit with forced "installation." I did not share this as I did not want Isaac to focus on his thoughts and away from processing preverbal, traumatic memory. I also wanted to avoid any young part of Isaac perceiving me as "installing" something.]

Th: "Ask your body, not your mind, can your Adult self be a secure, reliable, attachment figure for five-year-old Isaac?"
Pt: "Yes."
Th: "Now ask five-year-old Isaac, can Adult Isaac be a secure, reliable, attachment figure for you?"
Pt: "Yes."

[Following CRM protocol (Schwarz, 2014–2017), five-year-old Isaac bonded with Adult Isaac by imagining looking deeply into the other's eyes, making physical contact, breathing in rhythm, placing a hand on the other's heart, feeling their hearts beating in rhythm, and "Listening for the message, the teaching, the medicine, and the healing," five-year-old to Adult Isaac. Establishing a secure, intrarelational bond between Young Isaac and compassionate, present-day Adult Isaac facilitated trauma processing.]

...

FMC: CARE/Nurturance is a PAG-based affect (Panksepp, 1998) that is usually experienced as positive. In contrast to the prefrontal cortex (PFC)/PAG axis from prefrontal cortex to periaqueductal gray involved in fear and shame, this PFC/PAG axis confers a positively valenced affect and a positive attachment experience which combine to form a valuable resource.

KB: You are describing a juxtaposition between shame and/or fear-driven bonds and safe/secure relating, each within subcortical, nonverbal domains of experience. Whether viewed from the perspective of Panksepp's CARE system or attachment theory, the most powerful antidote to fear/terror and shame is safe enough relating (Winnicott, 1971). This includes crossing an interpersonal bridge (Kaufman, 1996/1989), for example, patient with therapist, and/or an intrarelational bridge between an adult self and younger part. The power of this bond to dissolve Young Isaac's fear and shame, emboldening him to "stand up" for himself, is unmistakable toward the session's end.

Frank, can you speculate on how shame/fear and CARE might interact, neurophysiologically, at the level of the PAG?

FMC: One affect may displace another when fluctuations in environmental conditions confer altered priority. For example, Panksepp (1998) *described PLAY as being promoted by a secure and warm base for the young mammal and eliminated by fear and hunger* (KB: my emphasis). Young mammals would tend to look for soothing and reassurance from their parents and it is likely that CARE/Nurturance promotes a sense of safety in animals who have felt alone and exposed to threat. The maternal care system has, like other affects, upper-level components in the cingulate cortex, but is largely driven by brainstem and limbic structures and by their associated neurochemicals. The isolated, worthlessness of shame is counteracted by CARE that is validating, in part through the implicit recognition that there is worth in the person being cared for. The associated, but also effective, physiological and neurochemical displacements have yet to be defined but likely involve the oxytocin receptors of the ventro-lateral PAG.

KB: Panksepp's (1998) CARE and PLAY systems as "displacements" of shame states make sense. As Winnicott (1971/1968) observed, play implies trust, and belongs to the potential space between (what was at first) baby and mother-figure, with the baby in a state of near-absolute dependence, and the mother-figure's adaptive function taken for granted by the baby (p. 69). Play takes place in a transitional, holding space where the caregiver's physical and/or psychological presence makes it *safe and enjoyable enough* to play. Pro-being pride is a form of CARE and PLAY, that is, "to delight in being oneself delighting in others delighting in being themselves, with you." Pro-being pride includes playing with one's aliveness within (intrarelationally) and between (interrelationally). Care, play, and pro-being pride are all evolutionary, genetically endowed capacities, and powerful antidotes to shame states (Chapter 2; Benau, 2020).]

...

Th: "Find the eye position where the five-year-old feels the strongest connection with Adult Isaac, and vice versa."

[Following the CRM protocol (Schwarz, 2014–2017), locating and returning to the eye position anchored the bond between Adult Isaac and Young Isaac, serving as another intrarelational resource aiding trauma processing.]

[Isaac nodded when he found his eye position.]

Th: "Be sure to keep your eye on this eye position, maintaining eye contact and physical contact between five-year-old Isaac and Adult Isaac throughout your work today. Feel free to dialogue with five-year-old Isaac, asking questions, stating your thoughts, hopes, fears, and needs. And invite five-year-old Isaac to ask questions of Adult Isaac, stating his thoughts, hopes, fears, and needs."

Pt: "He [five-year-old Isaac] is asking questions of me [Adult Isaac]. He's asking, 'Will you leave me?' [Adult Isaac:] 'No. I'm here, now.'"

Th: "How does five-year-old Isaac feel as he hears that, 'I'm here now'?"

[I sought to strengthen the secure attachment between Young Isaac and Adult Isaac, in contrast to Young Isaac again being left alone with his traumatic experience. This facilitates trauma processing and memory reconsolidation (MR) via an experiential "mismatch" (Ecker et al., 2012, p. 82).]

Pt: "He [five-year-old Isaac] just relaxes. It maintains the connection in a more energetic way."

...

FMC: Feeling connected and attached is allowing Isaac's body to relax as the fear reduces and he gets a sense of safety. It may also feel good because there is an implication of worth, of worthiness to be loved. This sense of his own worth sets up a nice physiological mismatch for both the fear and the shame.

KB: We agree, Frank, there was a physiological mismatch for fear and shame. Please comment on the following: Following Ecker (personal communication) on MR, this mismatch occurs at the level of "memories" experienced neurophysiologically, emotionally, *and* cognitively, and the implicit beliefs and meanings derived from those memories. Isaac felt reduced fear and shame, and an increased sense of relational safety and the physiological correlates of self-worth, that is, good enough me pride and pro-being pride (Chapter 2). Within the domain of implicit memory, belief, and meaning, Isaac moved toward a felt sense of himself as worthy of love as contrasted with his self-experience at the start of this session. Isaac came to know he was loved in part because his physiology changed and was better regulated (i.e., from hyperarousal in fear, and hyper- and hypoarousal in shame states), *and* because he felt, viscerally and emotionally, a secure bond between five-year-old and Adult Isaac. Isaac's knowing "I am loved" became a visualized and felt reality at the same time he experienced his traumatic, father-"installed" memory. In my view, mismatches auguring MR are *physiological* and also include implicit, *emotional*, and later cognitively encoded *memories* and *meanings*. In therapy, we seek to engender an integrated mind/brain/body experience.

FMC: Your belief, Ken, would certainly be representative of the consensus and I have no direct evidence to contradict that. However, if you have horrible wallpaper in your living room that makes you agitated every time you enter it and then you redecorate in your preferred soothing and welcoming colors—you won't need 100 hours of exposure to the new wallpaper and a revised cognitive schema to find that you can enter the room without agitation. Similarly, if the negative affects associated with a memory are completely cleared, resulting in physiological, postural and other body changes, the cognitive schema resolution is secondary to this. Bottom-up, as opposed to top-down, resolution of distress is the basis of body-based trauma therapies that are transformational rather than counteractive (Corrigan & Hull, 2018).

KB: We agree more than disagree. The most powerful transformations occur at the subcortical level of affect (i.e., limbic), as in this session and, as you observe, are also preaffective and precognitive (i.e., brainstem). Limbic to cortical and midbrain/brainstem to limbic to cortical activation each reflects bottom-up processing. When bottom-up processing succeeds, archaic beliefs and meanings about self, other, and relationship are transformed. As the wallpaper changes (i.e., changes in subcortical preaffective and affective activation in response to RT), so do implicit and later explicit beliefs associated with the wallpaper.

Isaac's contrasting old and new beliefs, if spoken, might include "Just as Dad taught me, I implicitly 'remember' (i.e., at the level of physiology, affect, and cognition) and believe all people want to dominate me. I must defeat them before they do me" (old); and "I now have experience and associated memories that teach me some people use their power benevolently. It's not always dog eat dog" (new). Young Isaac embodied this new belief with Adult Isaac, and Adult Isaac with me and trusted others, based upon new experiences and meanings that emerged from physiologically, emotionally, and later cognitively encoded memories.

In our shared view, Frank, bottom-up processing within the domains of neurophysiology (i.e., midbrain/brainstem) and emotion (i.e., limbic) introduce new memories and meanings that alter conscious, verbalized (i.e., cortical) meanings and beliefs about relating, self-with-self and self-with-others. The now transformed conscious, cortical brain then signals the subcortical brain, "Yes, we agree," via top-down processing. Over time, this leads to integration within the mind/brain/body system.

...

Th: "How does relaxed feel in his [five-year-old Isaac's] body?"

Pt: "We have hands on each other's hearts. Relaxation. Hand on heart. Less tension in my shoulders and upper body."

...

FMC: Basic affect system activation is now centered on CARE rather than FEAR.

KB: "CARE" rather than "FEAR" provides the interpersonal bridge that resolves shame (Kaufman, 1996/1989). Treated with kindness within a safe, trusted bond (Panksepp's [1998] CARE versus FEAR systems), the child comes to know, implicitly, "I am worthy of love," a powerful contrast with shame states.

...

[With five-year-old Isaac and Adult Isaac well-bonded, I instructed present-day Isaac to bring his full attention back to the sensation at the bottom of his gut, a "low level, buzzing sensation." This is where Isaac held the traumatic, body memory of worthlessness.]

...

FMC: Returning to the PAG-based activation that goes with the shame to see how strong it is now and whether there is more to be processed in the associated information file.

KB: I wanted to ensure we were processing fear and shame and not counteracting it (Ecker et al., 2012). Your comment about the PAG reminds us that we are working within a deep, subcortical, and often nonverbal domain of experience.

FMC: The basic affects involve cingulate cortex (e.g., Vogt & Laureys, 2009) in addition to subcortical and brainstem structures, so I am always referring to systems rather than individual structures operating in isolation. However, basic affective systems operate when there is no cortex (Merker, 2007).

...

Th: "Keeping your eye on the eye position, eye contact, and physical contact bonding five-year-old Isaac with Adult Isaac, breathe, breathe, breathe into, above, below, around, and through that buzzing sensation at the bottom of your gut, gently using your breath to invite the material to unfold, to move what needs to be healed and known from unconscious to consciousness; inviting the remembering; inviting the body to reveal what needs revealed, what has been hidden, buried, and protected."

[Following the CRM protocol (Schwarz, 2014–2017), Isaac's focused breathing facilitates effective processing of traumatic memory by increasing physiological activation and embodiment while ensuring Isaac remain in his window of optimal arousal (Siegel, 1999; Ogden et al., 2006).]

...

FMC: In Schwarz et al. (2017), it is argued that respiratory patterns are often disrupted by traumatic experience, either in an involuntary attempt to regulate the distress or as an expression of the sympathetic nervous system activation that accompanies the basic affects (Kreibig, 2010). Conscious control of breathing patterns likely brings in prefrontal cortex control of the PAG as it helps to diminish the physiological activation associated with the trauma memory. The physiology is helpfully discussed, with references, in Kozlowska et al. (2015).

KB: As diaphragmatic breathing downregulates arousal, traumatic activation is lessened. Changes in breathing support mindful self-awareness. The patient was experientially in the past, trauma memory and present, secure attachment with himself (Adult Isaac with Young Isaac) and another person (Adult Isaac with me). This facilitated trauma processing *and* MR (Ecker et al., 2012).

...

[After a few minutes of silence, I asked Isaac what he noticed.]

Pt: "The five-year-old. This feeling. It's bullying. Rejected and ground down. With language, and bullying, and action."

Th: "Bullying. From whom?"

Pt: "From my Dad. Some mom, a passive message from Mom, but active message from Dad. 'We're not spending *that* money on *you!*' Not only money, that's just part of the message. The five-year-old feels he's just alone, with whatever pain or feelings or excitement."

[Isaac confirmed what I had conjectured. Money was associated with the pain of not being noticed and cared for. Shaming can be active, Isaac with his father, and passive, Isaac with his mother and father. Passive shaming included Isaac's mother failing to nurture him; Isaac "failing" to relieve his mother's psychological suffering; and both parents never delighting in Isaac's playful spirit, his pro-being pride. As contrasted with active shaming, the effects of passive shaming are harder to transform therapeutically, in part because the patient has no conscious memory of ever having been shamed.]

Th: "Not worth care. You're alone and you're not worthy."

[Notice the link between "not worth care" and Isaac's feeling unworthy of physical therapy and timely medical attention.]

...

FMC: Shame and sadness are two distinct forms of the pain of separation distress (Corrigan & Elkin-Cleary, 2018)—and both are being experienced here.

KB: Isaac's traumatic shame state included both *feeling* shame and the pain of unbearable aloneness (Fosha, 2000).

Therapeutically, five-year-old Isaac received the loving attention, protection, and compassion from Adult Isaac. While not the focus of CRM, Isaac also experienced his adult and younger self cared for by me. Isaac's healing was intrarelational and interrelational, each bond strengthening the other, deep pools reflecting within and between.

FMC: The third aspect might involve the resolution of distressing affects associated with the traumatic experiences and the change in how he sees himself when the hitherto painful memories are no longer disturbing.

KB: You are reminding us changes within the midbrain, that is, "distressing affects" and "hitherto painful memories [that] are no longer disturbing," impacted upstream what Isaac later became aware of consciously.

...

Pt: "Of being accompanied, being given attention. You're a bother."

Th: "Keep breathing, breathing, breathing into, above, around, and through that thin, whitish buzzing sensation at the bottom of your gut. Invite the remembering of the source of feeling worthless. Be sure five-year-old Isaac is connected with Adult Isaac, eye position, eye contact, physical contact."

[These instructions served two purposes, that is, activating Isaac's memory of traumatic shaming and abandonment by his father and other family members, and activating Isaac's five-year-old's secure bond with Adult Isaac. "Traumatic shaming and abandonment" were incompatible with "secure attachment." This experiential juxtaposition of old and new emotional-relational realities leads to MR and "emotional updating" (Ecker et al., 2012, p. 33).].

...

FMC: The aim in CRM is to transform the trauma memory held in the body through stepping into the core of the affect and changing its physiological state by, for example, changing the associated breathing patterns.

KB: CRM focuses on altering the physiology, the basic affect, before conscious meaning. Physiological changes are essential, and later attached to imagery and story.

"Memory" and "meaning" exist within all three domains of the brain (Ecker, personal communication). There are cortical memories and associated meanings, usually conscious thoughts (e.g., Cognitive Behavioral Therapy [CBT]; Beck, 2021); limbic memories and related meanings, explicit and often implicit, emotional truths, or schema (e.g., Coherence Therapy [CT], Ecker et al., 2012); and midbrain/brainstem memories and implicit, physiologically encoded meanings, always unconscious unless when attending to subtle, somatic sensations in and around the neck and eyes (Deep Brain Reorienting [DBR]; Corrigan & Christie-Sands, 2020). "Meaning" includes what we think about, that is, cortical activation, and unconscious patterns of relating, that is, deeper brain responding.

Given my reasoning, Frank: (1) What are your thoughts about both cortical and subcortical brain structures having distinct ways of "remembering" and "giving meaning to" interrelational and intrarelational stimuli?; (2) When we change subcortical physiology, do memories and meanings automatically change at higher levels of the brain?; and (3) Does the focus on neurophysiology alter what psychotherapists do in-session, as contrasted with the view that "memories and associated meanings" occur within all three levels of the brain (i.e., cortical, limbic, and brainstem) and each, in turn, can contribute to therapeutic MR (Ecker et al., 2012)?

FMC: We have a different perspective on the neurophenomenology of healing from emotional distress, Ken. I was very influenced by my early experience of using EMDR (Shapiro, 1995) where I saw that supplying the right conditions was often sufficient to help patients to heal from adverse experiences. Using the standard protocol and providing eye movements or Alternating Bilateral Stimulation (ABS) allowed the emergence of a resolution in a way which I could never have predicted. A single-case neuroimaging study (Richardson et al., 2009) led me to the view that the PFC-PAG axis was being selectively activated by ABS. If that is a sine qua non of EMDR, is that the one and only way to promote the intrinsic healing process? Or may there be others operating at a similarly nonconceptual level (Corrigan & Christie-Sands, 2020)? Your view of the neurophenomenology of healing requires much more input from the therapist in directing the process. With healing, there is a change in the way that deeper brain structures respond to stimuli, including those that funnel down from cortical activations. That could be described as a change in the intrinsic meaning, according to what you write above, in the sense that the change in affective tone or arousal prompted by the stimulus will lead to change in perception and cognition.

KB: I believe "healing requires ... more input from the therapist ... directing the process" *some of the time*, particularly when the RT survivor feels unbearably alone (Fosha, 2000). At other times, the therapist's role in facilitating a healing process is best achieved by bearing witness and "getting out of the patient's way." Every patient and patient-therapist dyad is different, and every moment in time experienced differently. In the sessions with Isaac documented in Chapter 7, sometimes up to four minutes passed in silence, with minimal comments from me following these silences. At their best, therapists discern, moment-to-moment, when their patient needs active versus receptive responding.

...

[Isaac nodded, yes, five-year-old Isaac felt connected with Adult Isaac.]

Th: "Continue to allow the deepest, forgotten material to unfold, inviting the body to remember and feel it fully, keeping your contact of five-year-old with Adult Isaac. Step into the dandelion root of intolerable emotion that happens during the events your father treated you as worthless, BUT BEFORE the defense response kicks in. The mind and body know what we mean by this, just invite it to happen. Remember the split-second moment of intolerable pain or emotion before you split off."

Pt: "Tremendous fear ... Whole body, tight."

...

FMC: The therapist is giving Isaac the opportunity to get into the core of the affective residue of humiliation whether that involves fear, shame, or a compound affect such as shame/fear in which there are somatic features of both (Corrigan & Elkin-Cleary, 2018).

KB: Regarding the compound affect of shame/fear: (1) Phenomenologically, how do psychotherapists know when they are observing both shame and fear?; (2) Can shame ever be free of fear, given that shame includes the fear of loss of self and relationship with an attachment figure?; and (3) Does knowing there is a shame/fear compound alter the therapeutic response in contrast to "pure fear" or "pure shame"?

FMC: In the therapeutic work that I do it is important to identify which affects are activated by nonconceptual stimuli. The affects in their relatively pure states have specific physiological and defensive components. Shame can have a curling-in tendency which is dominant when it is not part of a compound affect but which is counteracted by bracing of the torso if there is simultaneous fear or anger. The breathing pattern with the compound affect of shame and panic is different from that with shame and sadness. These distinctions can be important in the processing of emotionally charged memories.

KB: Knowing specific physiological markers helps therapists understand the patient's experience and focus therapeutic interventions. For example, "shame and fear/panic" presumably show signs of hyperarousal/activation, and "shame and sadness" hypoarousal/de-activation.

...

Th: "Where in your body is the tension?"

Pt: "Arms, legs, mainly my arms, and chest, and head."

[Isaac's arms, legs, head, and chest tension suggested an active defense was initiated (Corrigan & Christie-Sands, 2020; Ogden et al., 2006). Head activation may have indicated orienting toward the perceived threat;

chest tension possibly reflected protection of heart and lungs; and Isaac's arms and legs might have tensed in preparation for the mobilization of a fight/flight response.]

...

FMC: Bandler et al. (2000) describe the active defensive responding arising from stimulation of the lateral and dorsolateral columns of the PAG while passive defensive responding arises from the ventrolateral column of the PAG. Fight and flight are active defensive responses while hypotonic collapse with immobility is a passive response. Tonic immobility (Bovin et al., 2014) is a freeze response that involves both lateral/dorsolateral and ventrolateral columns of the PAG. The PAG and hypothalamus drive the autonomic nervous system changes while the PAG through the thalamus and basal ganglia drives more overt defensive responding. Preliminary tension in the muscles can be elicited by the deep layers of the SC (DesJardin et al., 2013) as well as the PAG, and this is hypothesized to be part of the sequencing elicited in Deep Brain Reorienting (Corrigan & Christie-Sands, 2020). The defense cascade model of Kozlowska et al. (2015) is a recent and helpful overview of the defensive response literature and the clinical implications although it does not include the SC and its contributions.

KB: The final section, "Therapeutic Applications of a Neuroscientific Understanding," offers several applications of understanding passive and active defenses, particularly when working with midbrain activation (Corrigan & Christie-Sands, 2020).

...

Th: "Bring your full attention to the tension, especially in your arms, chest, and head."

[After two minutes of silence:]

Th: "Describe what you feel."

Pt: "My arms are wanting to be protective, tighten down, get through the fear. It's just threatening."

Th: "Remember, tension is muscles contracting. Muscles contracting is movement that wants to happen. As you feel into the tension, what movement wants to happen?"

[My understanding that muscle tension is an action wanting to happen comes from Sensorimotor Psychotherapy (SP) (Ogden et al., 2006). Psychoeducation was used to help Isaac observe his bodily response with interest rather than fear and shame.]

...

FMC: The tension preparatory to the defensive responding is driven by the deep layers of the SC and the PAG in the brainstem. This is below the "reptilian complex" level of the triune brain—and below the cognitive level of the neocortex.

KB: Isaac now observed what occurred automatically and previously outside conscious awareness. Shame was reduced by Isaac's being "here and now" *and* "there and then," and opening to new meanings, for example,

"My body was trying to protect me" rather than "I was shamefully overwhelmed and powerless." Do you agree that may be one potential side benefit of my approach? Is it your view this operates within the domain of preconscious neurophysiology rather than neurophysiology *and* mindful psychology?

FMC: I do see the most significant perspective shift as that occurring in the upper brainstem as it assimilates all the information that flows down from cortex through the efference cascade (Merker, 2013). It is the output from the colliculus that is then significant for the body's response.

...

Pt: "Wants to get away. Or at least hide. Get away and hide."

[Isaac's flight reaction, i.e., to get away and hide, is an appropriate five-year-old response to a threatening father. Hiding is fueled by fear and/or shame, with shame often associated with covering over and making oneself small.]

...

FMC: I have argued for the urge to hide being the characteristic defensive response that accompanies shame—perhaps through activation of the dorsomedial column of the PAG (Corrigan, 2014). Hiding is often the safest defensive response when afraid and here it goes with fear: "get away and hide" equals flight and hide. Cowering may involve the deep layers of the SC (Dean et al., 1989) and has been more associated with fearful response to a looming stimulus (Li et al., 2018) than to shaming humiliation which, as you have pointed out, stimulates the urge to curl up to disappear. Gilbert (2002) notes the potential for shame to be linked to rapid onset of submissive behaviors, but I am generally working with impulses and tensions occurring before more organized behaviors.

KB: Interestingly, "cowering in *fear*" is often viewed later by patients as *shameful*. Understanding that cowering is an automatic reaction to avoid looming stimuli, such as an adult perpetrator standing over a six-year-old boy, can help patients appreciate the evolutionarily adaptive function of cowering, thus reducing shame, and enhancing pride. (For additional ways of understanding how neuroscience benefits therapy, see Benau, [2021a, 2021b].)

...

Th: "Imagine yourself moving that way. Breathe into the place in your body that holds the tension ... The thin white line, buzzing, what do you notice there now?"

Pt: "No, it's not active anymore."

...

FMC: This "it's not active anymore" may be because his PAG has shifted from shame to terror and Isaac has been able to step into both and breathe through them so that they are cleared. Although not all affective states have been studied separately it is fairly safe to assume that all distressing affects arising in trauma psychotherapy are activating the sympathetic nervous system. Slow exhalations bring in parasympathetic downregulation of this activation (Kozlowska et al., 2015). The prefrontal cortex and the PAG are key structures for control of breathing (Faull et al., 2015).

KB: "Slow exhalations," via the parasympathetic nervous system (PNS), downregulate fear/terror, also seem to reduce shame. How do you explain that PNS activity associated with slow exhalations reduces fear/terror *and* shame, when terror requires downregulation of arousal, and shame may call for upregulation?

FMC: I argue that shame which has traumatic origins involves activation of the sympathetic nervous system. More benign forms of shame in which positive affects are gently downregulated are not what I see clinically. It can be a disservice to patients suffering from peritraumatic shame to construe it as a parasympathetic downregulator of some other feeling. Shame as a peritraumatic affect is a painful state of activation which can be diminished by parasympathetic breathing.

KB: Frank, we agree "traumatic shame states" (your "shame as a peritraumatic affect") are "painful state(s) of activation." We also agree neurophysiologically differentiating "shame states" from "shame as emotional process" (Chapter 2) is essential in psychotherapy with RT. Your view that traumatic shame is sympathetically activating and not downregulating, as Tomkins (1963) and Schore (2003) suggested, is also useful. In Chapter 2, I posit traumatic shame states are *both* upregulating (hyperarousing) *and* downregulating (hypoarousing) at the same time or alternately (Lanius, 2018, personal communication). Initially, the shock of shame is activating. The activation of "shock" is so intense and painful the mind/brain/body often overcorrects, precipitating rapid downregulation, that is, "shutting down," and/or LT (Chapter 2 and Chapter 3) caused by hyperarousal and/or hypoarousal.

...

Th: "And the tension?"

Pt: "The tension is less, if I [Adult Isaac] stay in connection with the five-year-old."

[I had two competing thoughts: (1) Adult and Young Isaac's secure bond helped Young Isaac feel safer in the face of his father's threat to their bond, and processing of traumatic memory was proceeding well; or (2) Isaac backed away from trauma processing and was insufficiently, intrarelationally resourced. I was hoping the former, but did not yet know for sure.]

Th: "Allow your attention to move, like a pendulum, between the tension you feel in your arms, chest, and head, and the connection you feel Adult Isaac with five-year-old Isaac. Move back and forth, like a pendulum, at your own pace."

[Isaac focusing inward, silently, for two minutes:]

Pt: "[The tension is the ...] physical aspect of that fear. Fear of being hurt, physically."

[Isaac's "fear of being hurt, physically" grabbed my attention. Isaac had previously expressed fear and shame in response to his father's attacking words but never physical threats. Of course, he could have feared emotional attacks would become physical. Almost a year later, we learned Isaac's fear was also associated with his older brother physically hurting and restraining him.]

Th: "Where in your body do you feel that fear of being hurt, physically?"

Pt: "My arms are trying to protect myself from being hurt physically by my father, on my right side."

...

FMC: This indicates a further activation at the deep SC/PAG level where the muscular tension preparatory to the defensive movements would be initiated. CRM focuses on the pre-defensive tension and the associated affects rather than attending to the movements recruiting subcortical circuits through the basal ganglia (McHaffie et al., 2005). Switching focus to the defensive movements may take processing to the organized action level above the basic affective and defensive responding.

KB: In my view, what matters most is "What works?" If somatically processing defensive movements, for example, "arms trying to protect," as in Sensorimotor Psychotherapy (SP) (Ogden et al., 2006), proves effective, then that is sufficient. However, if the patient did not experience sustained relief, then working with SC/PAG, pre-defensive tension and pre-affect as in DBR (Corrigan & Christie-Sands, 2020) would be indicated. In addition, some patients take to one approach better than another.

...

Th: "Allow your attention to orient toward the threat of your father hurting you, and then come back to your bond with the five-year-old. Again, like a pendulum, at your own pace, allow your attention to shift from seeing your father threatening to hurt you, and back to your bond, five-year-old and Adult Isaac. Now breathe into where you felt the tension, and notice what movement wants to happen, now."

Pt: "I [five-year-old Isaac] want to protect myself. Arms over my head, so my head is protected."

[Isaac demonstrated putting both arms up over head on his right side as he turned his head toward his left side, away from the imagined blow coming from above and to his right side.].

Pt: "Arms up. If I can protect myself, with my hands. Maybe this [i.e., being hit by father] won't happen. He [five-year-old Isaac] wants to stay connected [with Adult Isaac]. He [five-year-old Isaac] doesn't want to move. I cower."

[Notice five-year-old Isaac both "wants to stay connected" with Adult Isaac, and "doesn't want to move ... cower(s)." Isaac was in a transitional phase between the present, secure attachment bond and the past, alone, immobilized, and cowering.]

...

FMC: The cowering response comes from the deep layers of the SC in response to a threatening stimulus looming over him (e.g., Li et al., 2018). This activation comes in before the PAG comes online (Evans et al., 2018) with the terror—possibly the delay is in fractions of seconds.

The SC have separate areas for approach behavior (Comoli et al., 2012) which can be seen as part of an innate connection system (Corrigan & Christie-Sands, 2020). Here you are attenuating the effect of the fearful looming stimulus memory by maintaining an awareness of the connection of the different self-states.

KB: Isaac's father repeatedly "installed" two contradictory and impossible to satisfy messages: "*Never* be 'weak' and submit to anyone's threatening behavior, and *always* submit to *my* dominance." Six months earlier, Isaac's conscious awareness of the many ways six-year-old Isaac tried to physically protect himself from the sexual perpetrator, diminished Isaac's shame and enhanced both good enough me pride and pro-being pride (Chapter 2; Benau, 2021a). With "cowering" preceding "fear," an automatic, neurophysiological reaction precedes fear affect and adaptive action. This finding suggests psychoeducation, that is, conscious, non-judgmental awareness of how automatic "cowering" once served survival, can reduce shame, but would not process shame states completely.

…

Th: "Who cowers? Five-year-old Isaac or your Adult Self?"

[As the reader will see, my asking Isaac "Who cowers?" helped him realize his five-year-old self was smaller than his father, while Adult Isaac was now bigger than his father. I wanted to reduce Isaac's shame by helping him realize that, as a child, he was much smaller than and completely dependent upon his father and now, as an adult in relation to his father who was long deceased, Isaac no longer needed to be afraid. This dramatically showed how trauma memory casts a very long shadow.]

Pt: "I'm bigger than my father … I'm flushed with fury."

…

FMC: Now active defensive response of fight with associated rage coming in through PAG/hypothalamus activation of thalamo-cortical systems.

KB: A traumatic, shame state-informed therapist will be prepared for patient rage when shame no longer dominates the neurophysiological landscape (Benau, 2021b). (See Chapter 2 discussion of shame and humiliation, and Chapter 7, where this shame-rage connection is further explored.)

…

[Young Isaac had felt intense fear, perhaps terror in the face of a looming, actively shaming father. Adult Isaac, realizing he was no longer "just" Young Isaac, could feel and express embodied anger and fury.]

[Ten months after this session, Isaac observed that his "fury" was reactive rather than reflective, that is, dissociated (Benau, 2021b). Although Isaac's traumatic memory processing was progressing, most important therapeutically was whether he could embody and express rather without becoming dysregulated and dissociative, leaving his optimal window of arousal (Siegel, 1999; Ogden et al., 2006).]

Th: "Where do you feel flushed with fury in your body?"

[I sought to help Adult Isaac embody rather than dissociate from his protective anger in a fit of fury/rage. I also wanted to help Isaac experience himself (Isaac's young self with his adult self) and me (both Isaac's young self with my adult self), to remain self-regulated and co-regulated and fully feel and express his anger toward the sexual perpetrator and his father.]

Pt: "The right side of my face got hot."

...

FMC: The hypothalamus acts with the PAG in active defensive responses and their associated affects and likely mediates such temperature changes. In CRM the usual approach would be to "fire breathe" through this emerging rage.

KB: Fire breathing would have been helpful, here. Fire breathing, for those unfamiliar with the CRM (Schwarz et al., 2017), is a guttural growl with each outbreath that empowers patients, helping them process unfettered anger without feeling overwhelmed or shamed.

...

Th: "Is there tension there?"

Pt: "No ... Adult fury. I'm so fucking angry at him [father]!"

[Isaac's "fury" appeared part of an adaptive action tendency. If true, "fury" referred to a protective, rage response that wanted to happen when Isaac was young but could not because he was so little and alone, no one helping him with his father's angry shaming.]

[Both shame and fury are often displayed in a flushed, red-hot face. Shame is a fight self and fight other reaction. In both instances, the face is flushed with increased arousal and blood flow. When feeling shame, a flushed face signals to the shaming other "I'm no threat," that is, a submit response, whereas a flushed face in fury/rage displays a protective, fight response. Perhaps the absence or presence of eye contact and baring of teeth, respectively, communicate "I'm no threat!" (shame) versus "I'm a threat!" (rage).]

Th: "Check to see how the five-year-old is with your becoming angry."

[I wanted to ensure Young Isaac was not frightened by Adult Isaac's anger/fury, and that five-year-old Isaac remained safely attached with and co-regulated by Adult Isaac throughout this rage portrayal.]

Pt: "He's [the five-year-old is] okay. He's pleased."

[Hearing that Isaac's five-year-old was "pleased" relieved a young, anxious part of me so I felt freer to continue this exploration. Therapists with an RT history often reactivate their own trauma memories when working with survivors. "Re-experiencing" benefits therapy only when the therapist can observe and process their reactivity, finding their way back to empathic, "present" receptivity. (Chapter 5, on patient-therapist shame state *reactivity* versus *responsivity*.)]

Th: "Where does he feel 'pleased' in his body?"

Pt: "His [five-year-old's] whole body. He doesn't want to cower. He wants to stand up and stay connected."

Th: "How does that feel, to stand up and stay connected?"

Pt: "Really good. Strong. Powerful. Full of energy."
  [Note that Young Isaac's secure bond with Adult Isaac, and Adult Isaac's better regulated protective fury, enabled Young Isaac to stand up and face his father's physical threat and rejection. From the perspective of therapeutic MR (Ecker et al., 2012), "isolated and alone while cowering in fear and shame" was now experientially juxtaposed with "standing up, staying connected, and empowered."]

...

FMC: A nice physiological mismatch.
KB: Yes, experientially juxtaposing "cowering" and "standing up" offers a dramatic, neurophysiological mismatch. Given that meanings are embodied (Lakoff & Johnson, 1999), I believe *both* physiology and implicit meanings were juxtaposed. The words associated with Isaac's new, emotional truth might have been: "When accompanied by a trusted adult, including myself, I can stand up to bullies, vanquishing fear and shame." Another therapist might have drawn Isaac's attention to this explicit-implicit mismatch. In my view, suggesting Isaac say that at the time would have weakened the power of the moment.

...

Th: "Where in the five-year-old's body does he feel full of energy?"
Pt: "From his feet, his legs, though his entire body. [The energy is] pulsing."
Th: "Feel into this pulsing, while five-year-old Isaac is connected with Adult Isaac ... Is it okay to return to Adult Isaac?"
  [I asked Isaac if he was okay with shifting attention back to Adult Isaac, fearing I might interrupt five-year-old Isaac's triumphant, de-shaming moment. As Barral & Meares (2019) observed, Janet's discussion of post-traumatic acts of triumph "have nothing to do with grandiosity; they are victories over obstacles ... It [an act of triumph] requires effort and *results in a sense of pride that is a form of joy and heals shame*" (Barral & Meares, 2019, p. 121, my emphasis), referencing the works of Janet (1935, pp. 64–65). From what followed, it seemed I had not abandoned Young Isaac's anger by turning toward Adult Isaac's reassurance.]
Pt: "He [five-year-old Isaac] is taller. The fury was the whole right side of my head, head and brain. Everything."
  [Isaac's right side, previously "tense" in reaction to traumatic activation, was now filled with adaptive fury and strength.]
Th: "Is there a color to the fury on the right side of your head and brain?"
Pt: "Black heat. But the heat is gone, now. It's a feeling of fury."
  [The heat *may have* dissipated as Isaac's hyperaroused, fight response settled and his intense anger was expressed rather than inhibited. Still, I wanted to ascertain whether heat "gone" reflected affect avoidance.]
Th: "What does that feel like, physically?"
Pt: "Focus."
Th: "Intense focus?"
Pt: "Yes, behind my eyes. In my brain, behind the eyes."

[Isaac had observed brain activation behind his right eye many times. This was the first time it was associated with Isaac orienting toward the threat of his father hitting him on his right side and responding with "fury" toward his father. Isaac's orienting was shifting from a defensive to adaptive and protective response. This was even clearer later in the session.]

...

FMC: The narrowing of the attentional focus is an important part of defensive responding as it allows increased awareness of what is salient for goal-directed activity such as that favoring survival. The locus coeruleus in the upper pons is part of an innate alarm system (Liddell et al., 2005; Terpou et al., 2019) which promotes arousal and attention to salient stimuli.

KB: This "narrowing of attention", described in Chapter 3, characterizes one aspect of the phenomenology of shame and dissociation. In that chapter, another clinical vignette with Isaac using DBR (Corrigan & Christie-Sands, 2021) demonstrated therapeutic movement from narrow (reactive) to wide (reflective) attention.

...

Th: "Is five-year-old Isaac connected with Adult Isaac?"
Pt: "Yes."
Th: "Bring your attention to the intense focus, behind your right eye and in the brain behind your right eye."
Pt: "It's very familiar."
Th: "What is 'it'? The intense focus?"
Pt: "Yes, I've felt this, I'm used to it, many times. At work. In sports. In study."
 [Previously, Isaac's "focus" cost him, for example, when he became too argumentative with co-workers. Here, Isaac's intense focus was adaptive, directed toward his father, the source of his trauma.]
Th: "Focus that intensity on your father."
Pt: "Bringing father back takes away the positive nature of the focus. Becomes anger. I feel a desire to punish [my father]."
Th: "Where in your body do you feel that desire to punish your father?"
Pt: "My jaw tightens up. The focus shifts in my brain, farther away from the right side, more centered."

...

FMC: Back to the active defensive response of the PAG (Bandler et al., 2000). Jaw tightening is a good sign of this—perhaps because of our pre-weapons past when snarling, growling, and biting were needed more than they are now in armed conflicts. Awareness of tension in the jaws is usually a part of an angry, active defensive, or fight response.

KB: Interestingly, Isaac's snarling, growling, or biting did not frighten him. Given the benefit of his meditation practice, Isaac mindfully observed sensations, movements, and imagery from a well-regulated and well-resourced place intrarelationally, Young Isaac with Adult Isaac, and implicitly interrelationally, Adult and Young Isaac with me.

...

[I thought the center or midline of Isaac's brain might be linked with Isaac developing a more integrated self (Van der Kolk, 2014). I now wonder whether my understanding of the brain's midline helped Isaac and me stay within our midlines, that is, our better regulated, integrated "selves."]

...

FMC: The midline systems of the self may well have their deepest level in the area between, or encompassing, the deep layers of the SC and the PAG (Panksepp, 2003).

There is a requirement for the body maps provided in response to sensory stimuli by the SC and for the value-generating apparatus of the PAG (Panksepp, 2003). Action tendencies in response to stimuli—and the affective loading on them—may form the core of the self's interaction with the world, well "below" the levels of thought and language.

...

Pt: "Closer to the middle, and thinner. It feels thinner, and dark."
Th: "What are the physical sensations you're noticing, there?"
Pt: "Sharp."
Th: "Is sharp a physical sensation?"
Pt: "Yes."
Th: "Bring your full attention there, to that sharp sensation in your brain. See what comes as your attention shifts, like a pendulum, from the sharp sensation in your brain to focusing on your father."
Pt: "I want to tell him, he's an asshole. He's 45."
Th: "What's your age when he's 45?"
Pt: "Eight."
Th: "Can you see him?"
Pt: "He's wearing a wife beater. Pants. Wild hair. Crazy. Big moustache. He's on the phone, talking."
Th: "Return your attention to the center of your brain."
Pt: "I feel protective of myself." [Presumably, Adult Isaac felt protective of Young Isaac]. Being angry. Want to keep him [father] out."
Th: "Out of where?"
Pt: "Out of myself. My brain. My body."

[Earlier this session, Isaac observed a buzzing sensation associated with an "installed," trauma memory. Here, Isaac wanted to expel his father's installation of fear and shame.]

Th: "How do you want to do that?"
Pt: "Take him [Isaac's father] outside. Reduce the memory."

["Reduce the memory" followed a protocol borrowed from the Developmental Needs Meeting Strategy (DNMS) called "switching the dominance." When switching dominance, memories of previously internalized, malevolent others, that is, introjects, are externalized and auto-hypnotically altered in size, shape, color, sound, etc., reducing their hegemony over the patient's internal world (Schmidt, 2009, pp. 62–69). The benefits of this mental action are temporary, however, as many other dissociative parts will keep intact the father introject and installation. Having "switched the dominance" many times before, Isaac needed no prompting from me.]

Th: "Do that first. Then notice what's happening in your body ... What did you do with him [your father]?"

Pt: "I made him into a picture, and put him into a jar?"

Th: "And the jar?"

Pt: "On the left side of the cave, in the desert."

[Isaac had placed a two-dimensional, shrunken image of his father into a desert jar several times before. As a young adult, Isaac visited Israel, perhaps contributing to archetypal imagery reminiscent of the Dead Sea Scrolls. This was the first time, however, Isaac specified placing the jar on the *left side* of the cave—the opposite side of Isaac's eye/brain trauma and father "installation." Not wanting to interrupt Isaac's process, I kept these musings to myself.]

Th: "Bring your attention back to the center of your brain."

Pt: "The anger on the right side and the anger in the center are now connected."

[Consistent with our discussion about brain midline and sense of self, Isaac's imagery showed movement toward "integration." "The anger on the right side," associated with Isaac's traumatic activation and defensive, fight response was now "connected" with adaptive anger associated with the "center of [his] brain." In addition, connecting the right and center of Isaac's brain brought together past-trauma alone with present-safe connection, free from fear and shame, all indicative of another experiential "mismatch" facilitating MR (Ecker et al., 2012, p. 57).]

Th: "What happens now that they're connected?"

Pt: "There's more space, to let it happen."

Th: "Now?"

Pt: "There's more room, to be different. Room for connectivity with the five-year-old."

Th: "There's more room in your brain to connect Adult Isaac with your five-year-old. How do you feel that in your body?"

Pt: "My Adult Self is relaxed."

Th: "And in the five-year-old's body?"

Pt: "He's bringing his head up and exploring around, to see if it is safe."

Th: "Let him look around, 360 degrees."

...

FMC: Nice orienting to the environment that no longer holds a prominent threat and instead feels safe. It is possible that there is a different sense of safety or safeness derived from the PAG when active defensive responses have cleared. When the PAG activation, the basic affective state, is positively valenced then the therapist knows that the session is concluding successfully.

KB: Your understanding of Isaac's brain activity fits with my view of Isaac's psychology. Attachment theory predicts that with greater safety within

(Adult Isaac with Young Isaac) and between (Isaac with me and the external world), a more integrated Adult and Young Isaac is freer to explore internal and external landscapes. In asking Young/Adult Isaac to look around, I encouraged Isaac's adaptive exploration. From previously dissociated fear/terror, anger/rage, and shame, Isaac now moved into a state of curiosity and enlivened engagement with himself and others. Attachment theory predicts with secure attachment comes exploration, consistent with "SEEKING," one of seven basic, affective systems (Panksepp & Biven, 2012, p. xi).]

FMC: The brainstem theoretical perspective is that there is a more fundamental orienting without defensive responding when the SC are not eliciting PAG activation.

KB: Does thinking in terms of "attachment" (KB) versus "safe orienting" (FMC) alter how a therapist responds? Does knowing the neurophysiology, that is, the structure and function of the PAG, lead to a different therapeutic response?

FMC: Attachment theory is often unclear as to which areas of the brain are likely to be involved with particular relational patterns. That is one of the reasons that we have described a basic connection system in the midbrain as an important substrate for more complex forms of attachment (Corrigan & Christie-Sands, 2020).

KB: Working directly with the brainstem as in DBR (Corrigan & Christie-Sands, 2020) offers therapists greater specificity in understanding and therapeutically processing these auspicious developments.

…

Pt: "It's safe. He's out of the house. In front, on the street."

  [Isaac referred to his house when very little. Out "front, on the street" suggested Young Isaac felt freer to play outside, in the world, and inside, in his imagination, less immobilized by fear and shame (Benau, 2021a, 2021b)].

Th: "Notice what is happening in the five-year-old's body as he knows it's safe, and with his connection with you, Adult Isaac."

  [My language intended to strengthen Isaac's secure attachment within and with others. Isaac was sexually molested when he was six by a stranger in a park, on a day he was excited to play with friends. In addition, Isaac's playfulness was compromised by his father's actions *before and after* the sexual molestation, repeatedly humiliating Isaac, his siblings, his mother, and strangers. Here, Isaac reclaimed some of his native curiosity and playfulness, both expressions of pro-being pride. Isaac was increasingly able to "delight in being himself, while delighting in others delighting in being themselves, with him."]

Pt: "He [five-year-old Isaac] is able to feel his body completely differently. Fill up his body, with nature."

  [Isaac loved being in nature both as a little boy and an adult. This was another marker of Isaac reembodying his extrarelational, pro-being pride (Chapter 2).]

Th: "As you bring your full attention to the body of five-year-old Isaac, in nature, and to Adult Isaac relaxed, what is your new truth, now?"

[My remarks came from the CRM protocol (Schwarz, 2014–2017), where the patient's new truth, following traumatic memory processing, is named, deepened, and processed more fully.]

Pt: "We can do this?"

Th: "Do what?"

Pt: "Be more alive, awake. More able to take care of myself."

…

FMC: The SEEKING system is no longer dominated by threat and the associated defensive responses—it has become positively valenced. The PAG may be active through CARE/Nurturing directed towards the self rather than through the basic affects associated with adversity—fear, rage, grief, and shame.

KB: Frank, are you saying that neurophysiologically the PAG moved from "threat response" to "safe, nurturing response"? Is that akin to Porges' (2011) polyvagal theory and description of movement from flight-fight-freeze (Sympathetic Nervous System) to the Social Engagement System (SES)? Would Panksepp's view have led to a different therapeutic response than mine, informed by polyvagal theory and attachment theory (Bowlby, 1969)?

FMC: Some therapists prefer to work with the evolutionary perspective. My interest in the PAG goes back to the early 1990s (e.g., Bandler & Shipley, 1994; Zhang et al., 1990) and in 2000 there was an important paper on "neglected contributions of the periaqueductal gray" by Watt (2000, p. 91). I then found that Panksepp (1998) was describing in detail from laboratory work affective systems that made sense to me of what I was seeing clinically during, for example, sessions of EMDR (Shapiro, 1995). I did not find the later packaging of the defensive response research into an evolutionary theory (Porges, 2011) helpful clinically as it largely ignored the controls in the prefrontal cortex and PAG. The wiring of the speedometer is not necessarily the most significant part of a car in motion with a driver at the wheel. Also, a preoccupation with engagement at the subtly changing interpersonal level can be to the detriment of processing at a deeper level. My view is that clinically it is more helpful to try to understand what is happening in the basic machinery for orienting, affective, and defensive responding rather than to be preoccupied with an advanced form of relational communication and how it impacts on the autonomic nervous system. My interest is in attuned connection rather than social engagement in therapy, as I believe it keeps therapist involvement to an effective minimum. Therapist interventions designed to maintain social engagement can get in the way of the natural healing process which the therapist is there to facilitate. Silence (Frankel et al., 2006) that allows emotional experience and reflection while remaining interactional may be beneficially representative of a secure attachment. However, I know that these are minority views.

KB: Your "minority views," Frank, are worthy of consideration. In my view, "processing at a deeper level" and the therapist's "attuned connection rather than social engagement" reflects a matter of emphasis rather than absolute difference. At our best, therapists "quietly accompany" trauma processing, especially when the patient needs little direct help. At the same time, when processing midbrain activation, there are always intrarelational (i.e., self with self), and interrelational (i.e., self with other, such as the therapist) experiences at play, even when the latter is not made explicit. Even within DBR that privileges self-with-self processing, there are times when a patient's dissociation, for example, calls for active therapist intervention, at least until the patient is sufficiently psychologically present and embodied. Whether the emphasis is on self-with-self (i.e., more your view) or self-with-self *and* self-with-other/therapist (i.e., my view), and whether the therapist is more receptive versus active, depends upon their assessment of what the patient needs and does not need, at that time.

…

Th: "Where are you, now, with spending money on yourself?"

["Spending money on himself" was Isaac's presenting problem, with Young Isaac feeling unworthy of investing in his physical care. Given RT processing, did Isaac feel less frightened of and shamed by his father and greater self-worth?]

Pt: "I don't care about money. Money is just money. Money is not a punisher."

["Punisher" referred to Isaac's father withholding money, leaving Isaac feeling dominated and shamed.].

Th: "What about five-year-old Isaac's worth?"

Pt: "He's [five-year-old Isaac] worth every penny."

[A profound transformation had transpired, from terror and shame to self-love and self-valuing].

Pt: "It's not about money. It's about love. It's about being happy."

Th: "Does your Adult Self agree?"

Pt: "Yes."

Th: "The new truth is, 'We can do this. It's about love. It's about happy.'"

[Following the CRM protocol (Schwarz, 2014–2017), the next series of questions is designed to help Isaac strengthen and embody his "new truth," now and forward into his extra-therapy life.]

Th: What is the color of this new truth?"

Pt: "Bright, yellow."

Th: "What is the shape, the sacred geometry of your new truth?"

Pt: "A big circle, a sphere."

Th: "What is the tone of your new truth?"

[Isaac toned a resonant, mid-range tone.]

Th: "As you tone the tone of your new truth, 'We can do this. It's about love. It's about happy,' bring the bright, yellow sphere of your new truth, 'We can do this … It's about love. It's about happy' into every cell of your body and being, from your toes up to your head."

[Isaac had used this method to embody his new truth many times. For the next few minutes, Isaac "toned" while imagining his new truth entering into every cell of his body and being.]

Th: "Now find the eye position that corresponds with your strongest connection, in your body, to your new truth, 'We can do this. It's about love. It's about happy.'"

[Within seconds Isaac nodded to signal he found his eye position.]

Pt: "Okay."

Th: "Now, thank five-year-old Isaac for showing up, for being so brave, and for sharing with us in a way that was so helpful, helping us to understand him. And tuck him away, safely, in your body now."

[Isaac quickly nodded, letting me know five-year-old Isaac was tucked away].

Th: "Keep your eye position on your new truth, that you can return to when meditating on this. It's We can do this, it's about love, it's about happy." Now, take five earth breaths and five ocean breaths and return to the room here with me."

[Isaac's earth and ocean breaths enabled him to remain grounded, embodied, and present with me, now (Schwarz, 2014–2017; Schwarz et al., 2017).]

[I had written on the back of my business card Isaac's new truth, handing it to him as he opened his eyes. I was making explicit that I stood firmly with Isaac feeling safely connected, loved, and happy, using my card to symbolize our secure bond beyond this session. Rereading the card would also facilitate MR (Ecker et al., 2012).]

[Eyes now open, Isaac and I briefly reviewed the session.]

Pt: "That was such a difficult and sweet experience. It was really hard to sit with that moment of that much fear. And really sweet to be connected, to be connected with the five-year-old after that experience [i.e., of terror and shame]. The five-year-old can be in the world. He's not experiencing incredible fear. It's amazing the amount of weight in that [i.e., fear]. There's no way to manage that [i.e., when very little]. I couldn't go to my older brother."

Th: "You couldn't go to anyone. The very person you would need to go to—your father—is the very person who terrified you.

[My comment intentionally referenced Isaac's disorganized attachment (Liotti, 2004) with his father.]

Th: "When emotions are processed, when you're not alone anymore, you can move through the emotions, from fear and terror to completion, the feeling is always 'good', or in your words 'sweet', when processed to completion."

[Gendlin (1981) observed that processing traumatic memory in the end always feels good: "Another major discovery is that the process of actually changing feels good. Effective working on one's problems is not self-torture. The change process we have discovered is natural to the body, and it feels that way in the body. The crucial move goes beneath the usual painful places to a bodily sensing that is at first unclear. The experience of something emerging from there feels like a relief and a coming alive … One of the chief new principles is that the change process feels good" (p. 8). "Coming alive" is also consistent with Janet's (1935, cited in Barral & Meares, 2019 in Craparo et al., Eds., 2019) act of triumph that "requires effort and results in a sense of pride that is a form of joy and heals shame" (p. 121). Isaac's triumph reflected his movement from a traumatic shame state to the restoration of pro-being pride.]

...

FMC: In the Complex Integration of Multiple Brain Systems (CIMBS; Sheldon & Sheldon [2022]) see Safeness/Safety as a PAG-derived state. When it is a positive affective state, I think that this is likely to be the case. That is, clearing the fear, rage, and shame activations of his PAG leaves a sense of safeness and worth beyond the simple absence of the negative affects.

KB: We strongly agree. The goal of therapy is not only the absence of threat, but rather the presence of safety and, beyond that, pro-being pride. I know we do not yet know what parts of the brain are activated during pro-being pride, but my intuition, based upon lived experience as therapist and person, tells me it is a well-integrated, part brain-with-part brain, brain-with-body, and self-with-others, and the world experience.

FMC: The idea that clearing negative affects allows more cortically-based states such as pride to be experienced is supported by some neuroimaging studies. For example, viewing pictures related to achievement and status is associated with activation in the posterior cingulate cortex rather than the PAG (Simon-Thomas et al., 2012).

KB: Can you say anything about the functions of the anterior cingulate as relates to the adaptive pride I call good enough pride?

FMC: If pride in the achievements of others can be a guide, then an area of posteromedial cortex which includes the posterior cingulate is likely involved (Immordino-Yang et al., 2009).

...

ISAAC: "The five-year-old is now free. He probably wants to play."
Th: "Of course he does! He's five!"
  [Our session ended with Isaac's five-year-old free to play again, a natural consequence of secure attachment. Joyful, exuberant play provided further evidence that Isaac's embodied, pro-being pride had been restored.].

...

FMC: One of the positive affects of the PAG is PLAY/Joy (Panksepp, 1998)— for which there is space now that the negative affects are cleared.

KB: PLAY/Joy is closer to the affective experience of what I term pro-being pride. It is the joy in being oneself with others en-*joy*-ing being themselves with you. Frank, do we know anything about the brain in "PLAY/Joy"?

FMC: The neocortex is not essential for play whereas the parafascicular area of the thalamus appears to be required (Panksepp, 1998). Nevertheless, play has powerful effects on the programming of the cortex so may positively energize experiences of pride although the neurochemistry is largely undefined. Watt (2000) emphasized the relational underpinning of joy and other basic positive affects, and expressed surprise that their contribution to attachment was often ignored.

KB: Play and joy, vital aspects of pro-being pride, take the patient beyond alleviation of shame toward enlivenment, self-with-self, self-with-others, and with the larger world.

...

Therapeutic Applications of the Neuroscientific Understandings: The Third Perspective

Some argue knowledge of the neuroscientific correlates of complex, psychological/emotional phenomena in psychotherapy with survivors of RT does not inform nor, more importantly, advance our therapeutic methods. In contrast, this final perspective explores how neuroscientific understandings might have guided and enhanced psychotherapy in this session, and more generally with RT survivors.

Trauma therapists work best "bottom-up," subcortical to cortical processing. I privileged clinical phenomena associated with Isaac's limbic activation, for example, fight, flight, freeze, and submit reactions and related, implicit beliefs/schema, and "emotional learnings" (Ecker et al., 2012, p. 14). Frank's work with DBR (Corrigan & Christie-Sands, 2020) focuses on preaffective, midbrain (brainstem) activation. In either case, therapeutic effectiveness is limited only by understanding subcortical activity and creatively applying this understanding to the work.

Frank's understanding of shame affect as relates to the midbrain to limbic activation included three components, a visceral sensation, often outside conscious awareness (midbrain); a defensive, somatic response, often outside of conscious awareness (midbrain); and an emotional response, often conscious and associated with implicit and explicit meanings and beliefs (limbic). When therapists work with shame affect at the level of conscious feelings and explicit beliefs, such as Isaac not feeling "worth" spending money on physical therapy, they neither transform implicit emotional and somatic, limbic realities, nor preaffective and somatic, midbrain processes (Corrigan & Christie-Sands, 2020).

Working subcortically and bottom-up is essential when encountering, as with Isaac, traumatic shame states showing different degrees of dissociation (Chapter 2 and Chapter 3). While Isaac recalled being shamed and witnessing shaming by his father, he also lived with the effects of preverbal and nonverbal shaming. Later in therapy, we explored his father's failure to recognize and nurture Isaac's pro-being pride, that is, his creativity, sensitivity, playfulness, and love of nature; his mother's implicit shaming when emotionally pulling for Isaac to take care of her, and her failing to provide food and emotional nourishment; and his older brother's implicit, pervasive threat to dominate and humiliate Isaac. The most damaging and difficult to reach shame state effects are subcortical and, lacking specialized approaches, are neither felt nor articulated.

Traumatic shame states not yet therapeutically processed are recursively replayed (Scheff, In press) in mind and body. Following Frank's view, preverbal, preaffective roots of repetitive shame states begin in the midbrain of the brainstem; send signals up to the limbic brain where patients are more conscious of emotional and somatic correlates of shame, yet typically remain unaware of implicit, shame-driven schema; and then send activation and information to the neocortex where explicit narratives of shame states coalesce. If working with verbal narratives and conscious mental schema (cortically), and/or implicit, emotional survival reactions and meanings (limbically) (Ecker et al., 2012) fail to help the patient interrupt recursive self-shaming, then processing preaffective, somatic correlates of shame-induced, midbrain activation is indicated (Corrigan & Christie-Sands, 2020).

Frank observed that Panksepp's (1998) CARE/Nurturance system is a PAG-based affect. As Isaac felt safer intrarelationally, that is, traumatized, Young Isaac felt accepted and loved by Adult Isaac, shame affect was met with CARE rather than FEAR systems. When RT therapy succeeds, shame and FEAR are replaced by PLAY, as seen toward the end of Isaac's session.

Whether seen through the lens of attachment theory (Chapter 1), or Panksepp (1998) and a midbrain perspective (Corrigan & Christie-Sands, 2020), several therapeutic applications are shared. Shame affect takes patients away from connection with themselves and others. Self-alienation and social isolation (DePrince et al., 2015; Dorahy et al., 2017) are frightening and painful, contribute to mind/body detachment (Dorahy et al., 2021) and SD (Van der Hart et al., 2006; Chapter 3), further intensifying feelings of shame, psychosocial withdrawal, and dissociation (Dorahy et al., 2017; Wu et al., 2020).

To heal shame states, interpersonal (Kaufman, 1996/1989) and intrapersonal bridges, initially unconscious and preaffective (Corrigan & Christie-Sands, 2020), must ultimately be consciously nurtured and strengthened. As seen with Isaac, only then will patients feel safe enough (i.e., diminished FEAR) within and between to PLAY (Panksepp, 1998). Therapists working with traumatic shame states are wise to attend to the *quality* of the relationship (self with self, self with other, including the therapist), fear, shame, and dissociation, and privilege signs of healing evidenced by play, joy, and probeing pride. A midbrain-informed understanding of shame states (Corrigan & Christie-Sands, 2020; Panksepp, 1998) may offer greater therapeutic specificity than attachment (Bowlby, 1969) and polyvagal theories (Porges, 2011), going beyond safe-enough relating toward midbrain transformation.

Frank observed "respiratory patterns are often disrupted by traumatic experience" either involuntarily to "regulate the distress," or "as an expression of the sympathetic nervous system activation that accompanies the basic affects" (Kreibig, 2010). He added conscious breath control via the prefrontal cortex's top-down processing of the PAG modulates the traumatic response, including shame affects. Patients like Isaac also benefit from mindfully observing somatic-affective correlates of traumatic shame, creating psychological distance between a "present, wise, adult self" and "past, traumatized, young self" (Chapter 4, #12, Psychological Distance). "Observing" while "reexperiencing" shame events is needed in all RT therapies to facilitate MR (Ecker et al., 2012). Breathing patterns reveal somatic markers of shame-induced distress and, coupled with nonjudgmental observation, offer additional healing resources.

Frank suggested "shame and sadness are two distinct forms of the pain of separation distress (Corrigan & Elkin-Cleary, 2018)" and their healing leads to "the resolution of distressing affects associated with the traumatic experiences." Healing also leads to the patient's authentic pride and even pro-being pride. Several therapeutic applications include:

- With the premature, traumatic separation of child and caregiver, both shame and sadness (grief) typically follow. The patient may *believe* "I'm bad" (e.g., "Why else would my caregivers abandon me?") yet *feel* "I'm sad" (i.e., grieving the loss of caregiver). Patients often notice feeling "sad" before recognizing shame. Shame states must be sufficiently processed before a patient can grieve the caregivers they never had, and years lost living in the shadow of shame. (See Chapter 7 and Isaac's grief following therapeutically processing shame states and pro-being pride.)

- Whenever shame is at play, be it conscious or unconscious and dissociated (Chapter 2 and Chapter 3), separation from self and others (e.g., caregivers and other adults) is inevitable. Even when the patient is mostly oriented self-to-self, as was Isaac in this session, or attending to the somatic correlates of midbrain activation (Corrigan & Christie-Sands, 2020), the therapist implicitly and explicitly bears witness to the patient's suffering. In contrast to shame states, the therapist's presence communicates to their patient, "You are not alone" and "Your subjective experience is real and matters. Therefore, *you* matter."

Our views diverged with respect to traumatic and transformative "meaning." At the time of this session, my understanding of "subcortical processing" was limited to limbic learnings (Ecker et al., 2012). I was later introduced to DBR (Corrigan & Christie-Sands, 2020), based upon an understanding of midbrain/brainstem functioning. Frank argued that transformation in DBR, and specifically MR (Ecker et al., 2012) and updating of traumatic experience, reflects a mismatch between old and new neurophysiological realities. As Frank observed, therapy "transform(s) the trauma memory held in the body." This view suggests the transformation of "meaning" and "implicit schema" follow the neurophysiology rather than are the driver of change.

We agreed deep transformation occurs subcortically via bottom-up processing and MR (Ecker et al., 2012). Following Ecker (2020, personal communication), I argued "meaning" is not limited to cortical activity. "Meaning" emerges out of significant changes in "memories" correlated with neocortical, limbic, and midbrain/brainstem activity. "Meaning" and "memory," broadly defined, reflect responses or reactions indicating changes within a particular domain of the brain. Thus, meanings and memories correlated with higher, neocortical activity are very different from "limbic" or "midbrain" meanings and memories. Using DBR (Corrigan & Christie-Sands, 2020), I have observed patients sometimes spontaneously become aware of physiological (midbrain), emotional (limbic), and narrative (neocortex) changes associated with shame states, in that order.

While Frank and I agree MR (Ecker et al., 2012), requiring the experiential juxtaposition of old (traumatic) and new (evolved, adaptive) realities, is necessary for deep transformation of shame states, we differ about where MR occurs in the brain. In my view, MR, regardless of therapeutic focus, never occurs just physiologically. Since the mind/brain/body and environment are aspects of a complex, dynamic system, I believe MR occurs within each brain region, even when changes originate within the limbic system or midbrain.

Do our conceptual differences have therapeutic implications? Perhaps only that all successful therapies with RT survivors generally and shame states specifically transform meaning, although the domain where the therapist focuses their attention, for example, explicit beliefs and memories—neocortical; implicit schema and affect—limbic; and/or precognitive/preconceptual, preaffective, somatic experience—midbrain/brainstem, depend upon patient need and receptivity to different therapeutic approaches at any moment in time. Again, we agree transforming traumatic shame states always requires subcortical to cortical, bottom-up processing.

Frank's attention to midbrain functioning alerts therapist and patient to specific physiological markers of active defenses in response to being shamed/humiliated that might otherwise go unnoticed. For example, tension around the eyes and forehead is often associated with a heightened focus on salient, social stimuli that are safe versus unsafe. The locus coeruleus in the upper pons is part of an innate alarm system (Liddell et al., 2005; Terpou et al., 2019) and promotes arousal and attention to salient stimuli evoking fear and/or shame. Jaw and mouth tension are often associated with inhibited snarling, growling, and biting, and reflect PAG's active defense (Bandler et al., 2000) reactions to fear and/or shame.

"Pure affects" registered as "nonconceptual stimuli" within the midbrain also manifest as specific physiological states of activation and defense. Shame affects may be "simple" (e.g., "shame") or "compound" (e.g., "shame and fear" or "shame and sadness"). Understanding that each affect is associated with unique somatic, exteroceptive gestures (e.g., shame as "curling in," fear as "bracing of the torso") and interoceptive sensations helps therapists observe and intervene with greater specificity and effectiveness.

With regard to feeling worthless, Isaac shared, "It's in my lower stomach, gut. Fear." Frank attributed this to midbrain activation of the PAG, coupled with dread in the gut (Mobbs et al., 2007). Knowing this helps therapists understand that "gut dread" may be a harbinger of and/or accompany traumatic shame states. Likewise, knowing somatic correlates of shame states helps therapists identify common interoceptive and behavioral responses such as catching one's breath, and/or becoming hyperaroused and/or hypoaroused while frozen or immobilized (Benau, 2021a, 2021b). Catching one's breath and high freeze reactions fit with a five-state model of shame, especially State 2: Surprise or Shock, State 4: Shame Proper, and State 5: LT and/or SD (Chapter 2).

Isaac's active, somatic defenses in reaction to his father's shaming also showed how somatic awareness informs therapeutic action. When I asked Isaac, "Where in your body do you feel that desire to punish your father?" he responded "My jaw tightens up. The focus shifts in my brain, farther *away from the right side, more centered.*" Van der Kolk (2014) suggests a sense of "self" is associated with midline brain activity. Frank added, "the midline systems of the self may well have their deepest level in the area between, or encompassing, the deep layers of the SC and the PAG (Panksepp, 2003)," "well below the levels of thought and language." Understanding the import of midline brain activation helps therapists recognize a patient's movement toward integration.

Frank's description of active defensive responses (fight/flight) and passive defensive responses (hypotonic collapse) in two different regions of the PAG, that is, lateral and dorsolateral, and ventrolateral, respectively, was consistent with Porges' (2011) description of active and passive defenses, but added specificity with regard to midbrain activation. Interestingly, Isaac's tonic immobility as seen in his high freeze response (Chapter 4, #15, Shame and Pride: Prototypical Parts), reflected both active and passive defenses responses, with neurophysiologically active (hyperarousal) and passive (hypoarousal) reactions consistent with "deer in the headlights" phenomena.

Frank observed that when defensive activation occurs within the PAG, the patient may have difficulty accessing their preaffective and precognitive experience. In these instances, patients may benefit from DBR (Corrigan & Christie-Sands, 2020), purportedly working within the midbrain. In this session, Isaac successfully processed his shame affects presumably within the limbic region. If he had not, DBR or another approach targeting sublimbic, midbrain activation would be indicated.

Frank's model suggested preparatory muscle tension preceding gross motor movement indicates midbrain activation of the SC/PAG. He argued working with these predefensive tensions as contrasted with defensive, behavioral actions gets at the roots of shame states and their therapeutic amelioration. In my view, what most matters is, "What works?" Isaac mindfully observed his nascent, actively defensive, gross motor movements following a Sensorimotor Psychotherapy (SP) approach (Benau, 2021a; Ogden et al., 2006). If that had not afforded Isaac lasting relief, then working with SC/PAG predefensive tension would be indicated (Corrigan & Christie-Sands, 2020).

Therapists sharing with patients their understanding of the subcortical origins of shame states, via psychoeducation, may be shame reducing (Benau, 2021a), although insufficient for complete processing of shame states. For example, the reflex to cower in the presence of looming stimuli (SC) precedes, perhaps by seconds, fear and shame affect (PAG), that in turn precede automatic, defensive reactions. As Frank explained, cowering originates in the midbrain before organized, physical defenses and conscious awareness and volition. For some patients, knowing this helps them view automatic, behavioral reactions, such as cowering, with acceptance and compassion. At minimum, understanding subcortical brain processes helps patients create psychological space (Chapter 4, #12, Psychological Distance) between themselves and their shame state. This makes possible thinking about unwanted reactions in new ways. Mindfully observing the body's self-protective measures in the face of looming threat further engenders patient pride.

Whether the shame we observe when working with RT survivors activates the sympathetic nervous system (i.e., Frank's view), downregulates via the parasympathetic nervous system (Tomkins, 1963; Schore, 2003), or both (i.e., my view) remains an intriguing question. One way to understand these divergent positions is to consider that shame as downregulator of arousal and affect (Tomkins, 1963; Schore, 2003) reflects shame as an emotional process, whereas shame as upregulator (i.e., Frank's view) and mixed hyperarousal and hypoarousal (i.e., my view) indicate traumatic, shame state activation common in RT survivors.

Frank suggested slow, deep, diaphragmatic breathing lessens the stress of shame states. In my view, when a person is shamed, deep breathing may quiet the initial shock and heightened arousal flooding the mind/brain/body system. Deep breathing and related methods of downregulation, however, do not always bring relief, as excessive downregulation of shame states can cause neurophysiological shutdown and/or dissociation. In addition, for a patient living with dissociative parts, some parts may need downregulation whereas others may remain hypervigilant in order to avoid future shame attacks. The therapeutic implications concern what the therapist anticipates, that is, up, down, or combined arousal, and what to do therapeutically, that is, decrease activation (i.e., Frank's view), increase activation (Tomkins, 1963; Schore, 2003), or modulate arousal both down and up as needed (i.e., my view). Each approach seeks to help patients return to their optimal window of arousal (Siegel, 1999; Ogden et al., 2006), such that shame states are processed and pro-being pride restored (Chapter 2). However, given the complexity of intrarelational and interrelational dynamics with respect to traumatic shame, no one size fits all.

Frank and I agreed successful psychotherapy with shame states, including the "clearing [of] the fear, rage, and shame activations of [the] PAG leaves a sense of safeness and worth beyond the simple absence of the negative affects" (FMC). Greater self-worth moves patients toward good enough me pride and, with proper therapeutic attention, pro-being pride.

While we do not know where conscious, adaptive pride originates within the brain, viewing pictures related to one's own achievement and status were associated with activation in the posterior cingulate cortex rather than PAG (Simon-Thomas et al., 2012), and pride in others' achievement involved an area of posteromedial cortex that included the posterior cingulate (Immordino-Yang et al., 2009). I predict pro-being pride, a psychobiological state of integration, that is, self with self and self with others, would involve subcortical and cortical regions of the brain situated along the midline (Northoff & Panksepp, 2008). Interestingly, Isaac reported midline brain activity (this session) and elsewhere right/left brain activation when in mind/body states indicative of pro-being pride (Benau, 2021a).

Along with a felt sense of safety and pride interrelationally and intrarelationally, a greater capacity to play follows processing of shame states. As Frank noted, positive affects of the PAG include PLAY/Joy (Panksepp, 1998). In my view, play and joy move patients beyond good enough pride toward pro-being pride (Chapter 2). As Isaac's shame affect lessened, intrarelational and interrelational safety, play, good enough me pride, and movement toward pro-being pride occurred. As Isaac shared toward the session's end, "five-year-old [Isaac] is now free. He probably wants to play." Isaac's freedom to embody his playful, joyful self where previously immobilizing fear and traumatic shame dominated reflected his reclamation of pro-being pride, the ultimate goal of psychotherapy with shame affects.

Conclusion

The third perspective suggested that with greater observational specificity, particularly of somatic experience accompanying (i.e., limbic) and preceding emotional awareness (i.e., midbrain), therapeutic applications of neuroscientific findings when working with shame states are many. Avenues for healing shame states and enhancing states of pro-being pride will likely increase as neuroscientific understanding expands.

This chapter's three perspectives, which included reflections on a psychotherapy session with Isaac, a survivor of RT; the neuroscience that correlates with observable clinical phenomena; and brain science applications, were illuminating in distinct and interrelated ways, like three strands of a complex braid. Psychotherapy with RT, shame, and pride will benefit from similar explorations.

References

Bandler, R. & Shipley, M. T. (1994). Columnar Organization in the Midbrain Periaqueductal Gray: Modules for Emotional Expression? *Trends Neuroscience*, 17(9), 379–389. https://doi.org/10.1016/0166-2236(94)90047-7.

Bandler, R., Keay, K. A, Floyd, N., & Price, J. (2000). Central Circuits Mediating Patterned Autonomic Activity during Active vs. Passive Emotional Coping. *Brain Research Bulletin*, 53(1), 95–104. https://doi.org/10.1016/S0361-9230(00)00313-0.

Barral, C. & Meares, R. (2019). The Holistic Project of Pierre Janet: Part Two: Oscillations and Becomings: From Disintegration to Integration. In G. Craparo, F. Ortu, & O. Van der Hart, Eds., *Rediscovering Pierre Janet: Trauma, Dissociation, and a New Context for Psychoanalysis* (pp. 116–129). New York: Routledge. https://doi.org/10.4324/9780429201875.

Beck, J. (2021). *Cognitive Behavior Therapy: Basics and Beyond (3rd Edition)*. New York: Guilford Press.

Benau, K. (2021a). Shame to Pride Following Sexual Molestation: Part 1: From Traumatic Immobilization to Triumphant Movement. *European Journal of Trauma & Dissociation*, 5(4), 100198. https://doi.org/10.1016/j.ejtd.2020.100194.

Benau, K. (2021b). Shame to Pride Following Sexual Molestation: Part 2: From Pro-being Pride to Retaliatory Rage, Adaptive Anger, and Integration. *European Journal of Trauma and Dissociation*, 5(4), 100194. https://doi.org/10.1016/j.ejtd.2020.100194.

Benau, K. (2020). From Shame State to Pro-being Pride in a Single "Session." *The Science of Psychotherapy*, 20–39.

Bovin, M. J., Ratchford, E., & Marx, B. P. (2014). Peritraumatic Dissociation and Tonic Immobility: Clinical Findings. In U. F. Lanius, S. Paulsen, & F. M. Corrigan, Eds., *Neurobiology and Treatment of Traumatic Dissociation: Towards an Embodied Self* (pp. 51–68). New York: Springer.

Bowlby, J. (1969). *Attachment. Attachment and Loss, Vol. 1: Loss*. New York: Basic Books.

Comoli, E. das Neves Favaro, P., Vautrelle, N., Leriche, M., Overton, P. G., & Redgrave, P. (2012). Segregated Anatomical Input to Sub-regions of the Rodent Superior Colliculus Associated with Approach and Defense. *Frontiers in Neuroanatomy*, 6(9), 1–19. https://doi.org/10.3389/fnana.2012.00009.

Corrigan, F. M. (2014). Shame and the Vestigial Midbrain Urge to Withdraw. In U. F. Lanius, S. Paulsen, & F. M. Corrigan, Eds., *Neurobiology and Treatment of Traumatic Dissociation: Towards an Embodied Self*. New York: Springer, 173–192. https://doi.org/10.1891/9780826106322.0009.

Corrigan, F. M. & Christie-Sands, J. (2020). An Innate Brainstem Self-Other System Involving Orienting, Affective Responding, and Polyvalent Relational Seeking: Some Clinical Implications for a "Deep Brain Reorienting" Trauma Psychotherapy Approach. *Medical Hypotheses*, 136, 109502. https://doi.org/10.1016/j.mehy.2018.07.028.

Corrigan, F. M. & Elkin-Cleary, E. (2018). Shame as an Evolved Basic Affect—Approaches to It within the Comprehensive Resource Model (CRM). *Medical Hypotheses*, 119, 91–97.

Corrigan, F. M. & Hull, A. M. (2018). The Emerging Psychological Trauma Paradigm: An Overview of the Challenge to Current Models of Mental Disorder and Their Treatment. *International Journal of Cognitive Analytic Therapy and Relational Mental Health*, 2, 121–146. Craparo, G., Ortu, F., & Van der Hart, O., Eds. (2019). *Rediscovering Pierre Janet: Trauma, Dissociation, and a New Context for Psychoanalysis*. New York: Routledge. https://doi.org/10.4324/9780429201875.

Dean, P., Redgrave, P., & Westby, G. W. (1989). Event or Emergency? Two Response Systems in the Mammalian Superior Colliculus. *Trends in Neuroscience*, 12,(4) 137–147. https://doi.org/10.1016/0166-2236(89)90052-0.

DePrince, A. P., Huntjens, R. J. C., & Dorahy, M. J. (2015). Alienation Appraisals Distinguish Adults Diagnosed with DID from PTSD. *Psychological Trauma: Theory, Research, Practice, and Policy*. 7(6), 578–582. Doi: https://doi.org/10.1037/tra0000069.

DesJardin, J. T., Holmes, A. L., Forcelli, P. A., Cole, C. E., Gale, J. T., Wellman, L. L., Gale, K., & Malkova, L. (2013). Defense-Like Behaviors Evoked by Pharmacological Disinhibition of the Superior Colliculus in the Primate. *Journal of Neuroscience*, 33(1), 150–155. https://doi.org/10.1523/JNEUROSCI.2924-12.2013.

Dorahy, M. J., Gorgas, J., Seager, L., & Middleton, W. (2017). Engendered Responses to, and Interventions for Shame in Dissociative Disorders: A Survey and Experimental Investigation. *The Journal of Nervous and Mental Disease*, 205(11), 886–892. Doi: 10.1097/NMD.0000000000000740.

Dorahy, M. J., Schultz, A., Wooler, M., Clearwater, K., & Yogeeswaran, K. (2021). Acute Shame in Response to Dissociative Detachment: Evidence from Nonclinical and Traumatised Samples. *Cognition and Emotion*, 35(6), 1150–1162. Doi: 10.1080/02699931.2021.1936461.

Ecker, B. Personal communication, August 18, 2020.

Ecker, B., Ticic, R., & Hulley, L. (2012). *Unlocking the Emotional Brain: Eliminating Symptoms at Their Roots Using Memory Reconsolidation*. New York: Routledge. https://doi.org/10.4324/9780203804377.

Evans, D. A., Stempel, A. V., Vale, R., Ruehle, S., Lefler, Y., & Branco, T. (2018). A Synaptic Threshold Mechanism for Computing Escape Decisions. *Nature*, 558, 590–594. https://doi.org/10.1038/s41586-018-0244-6.

Faull, O. K., Jenkinson, M., Clare, S., & Pattinson, K. T. (2015). Functional Subdivision of the Human Periaqueductal Grey in Respiratory Control Using 7 Tesla fMRI. *NeuroImage*, 113, 356–364. https://doi.org/10.1016/j.neuroimage.2015.02.026.

Fosha, D. (2000). *The Transforming Power of Affect: A Model for Accelerated Change*. New York: Basic Behavioral Science.

Frankel, Z., Levitt, H. M., Murray, D. M., Greenberg, L. S., & Angus, L. (2006). Assessing Silent Processes in Psychotherapy: An Empirically Derived Categorization System and Sampling Strategy. *Psychotherapy Research*, 16(5), 627–638. https://doi.org/10.1080/10503300600591635.

Gendlin, E. T. (1981). *Focusing*. New York: Bantam New Age Paperbacks.

Gilbert, P. (2002). Body Shame: A Biopsychosocial Conceptualisation and Overview with Treatment Implications. In P. Gilbert & J. Miles, Eds., *Body Shame: Conceptualisation, Research and Treatment* (pp. 3–54). Abingden, England: Brunner-Routledge, Hove.

Grand, D. (2013). *Brainspotting: The Revolutionary New Therapy for Rapid and Effective Change*. Boulder, CO: Sounds True.

Hopenwasser, K. (2008). Being in Rhythm: Dissociative Attunement in Therapeutic Process. *Journal of Trauma & Dissociation*, 9(3), 349–367. https://doi.org/10.1080/15299730802139212.

Immordino-Yang, M. H., McColl, A., Damasio, H., & Damasio, A. (2009). Neural Correlates of Admiration and Compassion. *Proceedings of the National Academy Sciences*, 106(19), 8021–8026. https://doi.org/10.1073/pnas.0810363106.

Janet, P. (1935). *Les Debuts de L'Intelligence*. Paris: Flammation.

Kaufman, G. (1996/1989). *The Psychology of Shame (2nd Edition): Theory and Treatment of Shame-Based Syndromes*. New York: Springer.

Kozlowska, K., Walker, P., McLean, L., & Carrive, P. (2015). Fear and the Defense Cascade: Clinical Implications and Management. *Harvard Review of Psychiatry*, 23(4), 263–286. https://doi.org/10.1097/HRP.0000000000000065.

Kreibig, S. D. (2010). Autonomic Nervous System Activity in Emotion: A Review. *Biological Psychology*, 84(3), 474–487. https://doi.org/10.1016/j.biopsycho.2009.11.004.

Lakoff, G. & Johnson, M. (1999). *Philosophy in the Flesh: The Embodied Mind and its Challenge to Western Thought*. New York: Basic Books.

Lanius, U. (March 22, 2018). Personal communication, ISSTD Annual Conference, Chicago, IL.
Li, L., Feng, X., Zhou, Z., Zhang, H., Shi, Q., Lei, Z., Shen, P., Yang, Q., Zhao, B., Chen, S., Li, L., Zhang, Y., Wen, P., Lu, Z., Li, X., Xu, F., & Wang, L. (2018). Stress Accelerates Defensive Responses to Looming in Mice and Involves a Locus-Coeruleus-Superior Colliculus Projection. *Current Biology*, 28(6), 859–871. https://doi.org/10.1016/j.cub.2018.02.005.
Liddell, B. J., Brown, K. J., Kemp, A. H., Barton, M. J., Das, P., Peduto, A., Gordon, E., Williams, L. M. (2005). A Direct Brainstem-Amygdala-Cortical "Alarm" System for Subliminal Signals of Fear. *NeuroImage*, 24(1), 235–243. https://doi.org/10.1016/j.neuroimage.2004.08.016.
Liotti, G. (2004). Trauma, Dissociation, and Disorganized Attachment: Three Strands of a Single Braid. *Psychotherapy: Theory, Research, Practice, and Training*, 41(4), 472–486. https://doi.org/10.1037/0033-3204.41.4.472.
McHaffie, J. G., Stanford, T. R., Stein, B. E., Coizet, V. & Redgrave, P. (2005). Subcortical Loops through the Basal Ganglia. *Trends in Neurosciences*, 28(8), 401–407. https://doi.org/10.1016/j.tins.2005.06.006.
Merker, B. (2007). Consciousness without a Cerebral Cortex, a Challenge for Neuroscience and Medicine. *Behavior Brain Science*, 30(1), 63–134. https://doi.org/10.1017/S0140525X07000891.
Merker, B. (2013). The Efference Cascade, Consciousness and Its Self: Naturalizing the First Person Pivot of Action Control. *Frontiers in Psychology*, 4, 501. https://doi.org/10.3389/fpsyg.2013.00501.
Mobbs, D., Petrovic, P., Marchant, J. L., Hassabis, D., Weiskopf, N., Seymour, B., et al. (2007). When Fear Is Near: Threat Imminence Elicits Prefrontal-Periaqueductal Gray Shifts in Humans. *Science*, 317(5841), 1079–1083. https://doi.org/10.1126/science.1144298.
Northoff, G. & Panksepp, J. (2008). The Trans-Species Concept of Self and the Subcortical–Cortical Midline System. *Trends in Cognitive Science*, 12(7), 259–264. ttps://doi.org/10.1016/j.tics.2008.04.007.
Ogden, P., Minton, K., & Pain, C. (2006). *Trauma and the Body: A Sensorimotor Approach to Psychotherapy*. New York: W.W. Norton. Panksepp, J. (2003). The Neural Nature of the Core SELF. In T. Kircher & A. David, Eds., *The Self in Neuroscience and Psychiatry* (pp. 197–213). Cambridge: Cambridge University Press.
Panksepp, J. (1998). *Affective Neuroscience: The Foundations of Human and Animal Emotions*. Oxford: Oxford University Press.
Panksepp, J. & Biven, L. (2012). *The Archaeology of Mind: Neuroevolutionary Origins of Human Emotions*. New York: W.W. Norton.
Porges, S. W. (2011). *The Polyvagal Theory: Neurophysiological Foundations of Emotions, Attachment, Communication, and Self-regulation*. New York: W.W. Norton.
Real, T. (1997). *I Don't Want to Talk About It: Overcoming the Legacy of Male Depression*. New York: Simon & Schuster.
Richardson, P., Williams, S. R., Hepenstall, S., Gregory, L., McKie, S., & Corrigan, F. M. (2009). EMDR Treatment of a Patient with Posttraumatic Stress Disorder: A Single-Case fMRI Study. *Journal of EMDR Practice and Research*, 3(1), 10–23. https://doi.org/10.1891/1933-3196.3.1.10.
Scheff, T. J. (In press). *A Social Theory and Treatment of Depression*. http://scheff.faculty.soc.ucsb.edu/main.php?id=62.html. Accessed December 28, 2019.

Schmidt, S. J. (2009). *The Developmental Needs Meeting Strategy: An Ego State Therapy for Healing Adults with Childhood Trauma and Attachment Wounds.* San Antonio, TX: DNMS Institute.

Schore, A. N. (2003). *Affect Regulation and the Repair of the Self.* New York: W.W. Norton.

Schore, A. N. (2001). The Effects of Relational Trauma on Right Brain Development, Affect Regulation, and Infant Mental Health. *Infant Mental Health Journal,* 22(1–2), 201–269. Doi: 10.1111/j.1749-6632.2009.04474.x.

Schwarz, L. (2014–2017). *CRM (Comprehensive Resource Model) Practitioner Booklet.* CRM LLC.

Schwarz, L., Corrigan, F., Hull, A., & Raju, R. (2017). *The Comprehensive Resource Model: Effective Therapeutic Techniques for the Healing of Complex Trauma.* New York: Routledge. https://doi.org/10.4324/9781315689906.

Shapiro, F. (1995). *Eye Movement Desensitization and Reprocessing: Basic Principles, Protocols and Procedures.* New York, NY: Guilford Press.

Shaw, D. (2014). *Traumatic Narcissism: Relational Systems of Subjugation.* New York: Routledge. https://doi.org/10.4324/9781315883618.

Sheldon, B. & Sheldon, A. (2022). *Complex Integration of Multiple Brain Systems in Therapy.* New York: Norton.

Siegel, D. J. (1999). *The Developing Mind: How Relationships and the Brain Interact to Shape Who We Are.* New York: Guilford.

Simon-Thomas, E. R., Godzik, J., Castle, E., Antonenko, O., Ponz, A., Kogan, A., & Keltner, D. J. (2012). An fMRI Study of Caring vs Self-focus during Induced Compassion and Pride. *SCAN,* 7(6), 635–648. https://doi.org/10.1093/scan/nsr045.

Steuwe, C., Daniels, J. K., Frewen, P. A., Densmore, M., Pannasch, S., Beblo, T., Reiss, J., & Lanius, R. A. (2014). Effect of Direct Eye Contact in PTSD Related to Interpersonal Trauma: An fMRI Study of Activation of an Innate Alarm System. *SCAN,* 9(1), 88–97. https://doi.org/10.1093/scan/nss105.

Terpou, B. A., Densmore, M., Thome, J., Frewen, P., McKinnon, M. C., Lanius, R. A. (2019). The Innate Alarm System and Subliminal Threat Presentation in Posttraumatic Stress Disorder: Neuroimaging of the Midbrain and Cerebellum. *Chronic Stress,* 3, 1–13. https://doi.org/10.1177/2470547018821496.

Tomkins, S. (1963). *Affect, Imagery and Consciousness: The Negative Affects, Vol. 2.* New York: Springer.

Van der Hart, O., Nijenhuis, E. R. S., & Steele, K. (2006). *The Haunted Self: Structural Dissociation and the Treatment of Chronic Traumatization.* New York: W.W. Norton.

Van der Kolk, B. A. (2014). *The Body Keeps the Score: Brain, Mind, and Body in the Healing of Trauma.* New York: Viking.

Vogt, B. A. & Laureys, S. (2009). The Primate Posterior Cingulate Gyrus: Connections, Sensorimotor Orientation, Gateway to Limbic Processing. In B. A. Vogt, Ed., *Cingulate Neurobiology and Disease* (pp. 275–308). Oxford: Oxford University Press.

Watt, D. F. (2000). The Centrencephalon and Thalamocortical Integration: Neglected Contributions of the Periaqueductal Gray. *Consciousness & Emotion,* 1(1), 91–114. https://doi.org/10.1075/ce.1.1.06wat.

Winnicott, D. W. (1971). *Playing and Reality.* London: Tavistock.

Wu, C., & Dorahy, M. J., Johnston, C. M., Näswall, K., & Hanna, D. (2020). Shame, Personality Orientation, and Risk in Intimacy: Direct and Estimated Indirect Pathways. *Current Psychology*, 1–9. https://doi.org/10.1007/s12144-020-00966-z.

Zhang, S. P., Bandler, R., & Carrive, P. (1990). Flight and Immobility Evoked by Excitatory Amino Acid Microinjection within Distinct Parts of the Subtentorial Midbrain Periaqueductal Gray of the Cat. *Brain Research*, 520(1–2), 73–82. https://doi.org/10.1016/0006-8993(90)91692-A.

7 Shame State to a Core Way of Being

Beyond Pro-being Pride to Radiant Joy, Grief, Integration, and Oneness

Introduction

This chapter continues my work with "Isaac" (Chapter 6), an adult survivor of childhood relational trauma (RT) (Schore, 2001), by studying complete transcripts of two psychotherapy sessions and excerpts of two more. I was surprised to discover metatherapeutically processing (Fosha, 2000) pro-being pride takes some RT survivors beyond pro-being pride into joyful states of oneness or unity consciousness. These states were followed by grief that comes with recognizing the lifelong costs of RT, and ultimately deeper, psychological integration and oneness within and with the world.

Pro-being Pride

As detailed in Chapter 2, pro-being pride embodies the most powerful antidote to traumatic shame and pride states. My short definition of pro-being pride is, "I delight in being me, delighting in you delighting in being yourself, with me" (self with other); and "I delight in being me, delighting in me delighting in being myself, with me" (self with self). I derived the concept of pro-being pride from the Latinate word origin of "proud," "prodesse," where "prod" = "for," and "esse" = "to be" or, for our purposes, a person's "being," "essence" or "essential self" (Proud, word origin). Pro-being pride is neither hubristic pride (Tracy, 2016), not me pride (i.e., dissociated aspects of self) nor no me pride (i.e., whole self dissociated), all consequences of RT (Schore, 2001). Nor is pro-being pride a *feeling* or *categorical emotion*. Rather, pro-being pride is an intermittently accessed, enduring state of joy-in-being one's whole self and with that of others. "Joy" and "delight" do not mean "always happy." For example, pro-being pride can be experienced when people gather to grieve the death of a loved one. Pro-being pride refers to the organismic pleasure of being alive within oneself and with others and the world. This organismic aliveness was beautifully conveyed in Whitman's (2007–2013/1855) poem, "I Sing the Body Electric" (pp. 109–116).

Introducing Isaac

What follows are four sessions with Isaac, a man in his 60s, and survivor of childhood RT that included sexual, emotional, and physical abuse, psychological terrorizing and humiliation, emotional nonattunement, and neglect. At six-years-old, Isaac was sexually molested once by a man he did not know in a park where he enjoyed playing, unsupervised by his parents. Isaac described his father as narcissistic, domineering, emotionally abusive, neglectful, and chronically shaming. Isaac's older brother was intermittently physically abusive and controlling. This brother also psychologically terrorized Isaac, leaving him with a pervasive sense he could be assaulted or humiliated at any time, even when his brother was not around. Isaac's parents divorced when Isaac was seven-years-old. His mother was a psychologically fragile woman who pulled for Isaac to take care of her emotionally, both as a child and an adult. She was sometimes so overwhelmed she was unable to provide Isaac and his siblings enough food. Isaac's beloved younger sister, "Mary," was developmentally delayed and died when she was two and a half and Isaac seven. Mary was the only family member Isaac felt loved by as a child, and who received his love unconditionally. The RT Isaac experienced at the hands of his father, mother, and older brother preceded and followed, for many years, the incident of sexual abuse.

Overview of Four Psychotherapy Sessions with Isaac

Isaac graciously gave me permission to share details of our psychotherapy sessions. He hoped therapists and patients alike would learn and benefit from his psychotherapy and life experience.

Session 1 and Session 2 are transcribed in their entirety, and Session 3 and Session 4 offer selected excerpts. All four sessions follow several sessions, previously described (Benau, 2021a, 2021b), of Isaac's movement from immobilization within a traumatic shame state ("shame state") to a state of pro-being pride.

Isaac's psychotherapy focused on the intrarelational and interrelational sequelae of sexual abuse, physical abuse, emotional neglect, and RT. The first of four sessions, Session 1, occurred three years, seven months into weekly psychotherapy with Isaac, three weeks following a previously documented session that closed with Isaac deepening into his experience of pro-being pride (Benau, 2021b). Session 1 powerfully demonstrated that transformative, depth psychotherapy with survivors of sexual and RT can transcend the alleviation of shame states. Given an appropriate conceptual framework and therapeutic approach patients can, at times, progress beyond pro-being pride and enter the realm of core self where, in Isaac's words, a felt sense that "all is connected" and "radiant joy" is realized.

Session 2 took place two and a half months after Session 1, three years, nine and a half months into Isaac's psychotherapy. Session 2 showed that after the RT survivor accesses pro-being pride and beyond, grief, sorrow, and regret for life unlived often follow.

216   *Beyond Pro-being Pride*

Session 3 occurred almost three and a half months following Session 1, 3 years, ten and a half months into Isaac's therapy. In Session 3, Isaac identified more specifically what he lost and grieved as a consequence of RT.

Session 4 occurred three and a half months after Session 1, three years, ten and a half months into weekly psychotherapy. Processing his grief allowed Isaac to move toward a place of greater integration, renewed freedom, and "joy of being," all emblematic of pro-being pride.

Caveat to the Reader

Isaac was particularly well-suited for shame and pride-informed psychotherapy. An active meditator for over ten years, Isaac excelled at mindfully observing his inner-experience that included chronic trauma memories, without becoming dysregulated or dissociative. Isaac was also adept at contacting his imagistic, emotional, and somatic experience, enabling us to work with preverbal and not yet verbalized experience. A lover of literature, Isaac described his internal experience eloquently and at times poetically. Finally, despite his RT history, Isaac had earned secure attachments (Pearson et al., 1994; Roisman et al., 2002) with his wife, adult children, friends, family members, and former co-workers. While I was an important relational resource for Isaac, I was not alone.

Given his unique personal and interpersonal strengths, Isaac's transformation will not be achievable for all patients or patient-therapist dyads. Nonetheless, this chapter offers the reader a roadmap for what may lie "beyond pro-being pride."

Session 1: From Pro-being Pride to Core, Radiant Joy (Three Years, Seven Months of Weekly Psychotherapy)

This first session took place via video conferencing (VSee) as Isaac was recovering from foot surgery and unable to navigate the flight of stairs to my office. All sessions lasted 80 minutes. Longer sessions allowed Isaac to do deep work in a semihypnotic state that responded best to nonrushed spaciousness within himself and between us. Session 1 occurred two weeks after Isaac had accessed a state of pro-being pride that followed processing fears associated with his being physically restrained by the sexual perpetrator (Benau, 2021b). Only later did we learn Isaac's immobilization anxieties were also strongly associated his older brother's pervasive physical entrapment of and psychological threat toward Isaac throughout his childhood.

All four sessions provided close to verbatim transcripts. "Th" refers to me, the therapist, and "Pt," Isaac, the patient. Brackets [ ] both clarify Isaac's communications and provide some of my reflections upon and intentions during each session.

Session 1 began with Isaac explaining his decision not to come to my office, yet. Isaac recognized he was engaging in "better self-care" and experienced "increased flexibility in [his] thinking." I commented Isaac was more in "attunement" with his physical and emotional state.

In the past, Isaac would "berate [him]self as weak and soft" for not pushing himself physically and psychologically. I mentioned a therapist (Real, 2002, 1997) who wrote about how boys are enculturated by age three, before they have many words, to not be "weak wusses like girls." Isaac agreed, adding that societal messages were powerfully reinforced by his father who viewed all vulnerability as weakness that others would exploit. Isaac also learned, beginning at a very young age, that he had to override physical and emotional pain lest he be cruelly shamed by his father and older brother.

Intentionally wanting to challenge Isaac's beliefs about "weakness" as a man, I praised Isaac for *not* coming into my office today and for doing "the opposite" of his training.

I next invited Isaac to focus on his mind/body experience of "openness" to a new way of treating himself. Isaac remarked that "powering through my pain" was no longer happening. I repeated, "The old way is not happening, now." Isaac added, "Why do that?"

I typically asked Isaac to attend to his somatic experience, particularly new, life-enhancing, emotional and relational truths, to help make them more real and sustaining rather than abstract and intellectual. This way of working is consistent with my training in somatic psychotherapy (Ogden et al., 2006; Bowen website). In addition, narrative therapy and solution-focused approaches oriented me toward future growth more than past suffering (White & Epston, 1990; O'Hanlon, 1999). While privileging transformation, I did not ignore painful experience requiring trauma processing.

Therapist (Th): "Where do you feel that knowing in your body, Isaac?"
Patient (Pt): "The pain in my back is my teacher. The behavior [i.e., choosing to power through pain] brought me more pain, after the previous [foot] surgery. I have a physical memory of that pain, there [i.e., in my back]. The second surgery [showed me] my worth. I'm valuable. I have nothing to prove. There's a deeper feeling of relaxation."
Th: "Where, in your whole body?"
Pt: "Yes. In my legs, torso, back … I have physical access to a deeper relaxation. A whole physical feeling. I tighten up when I push through [my pain]."
Th: "There's a whole-body relaxation and a body memory of pain."
Pt: "Two of the same places that work with … value. Both are relaxed feelings, both very young."
Th: "There's a contrast between 'value' and 'pain.'"
   [I made explicit the previously implicit contrast between Isaac's "body memory of pain" and old belief, "I have little value. I must be strong and push through the pain, no matter what!" and his "whole body relaxation" and new belief, "I have value. Listening to my body teaches me to take care of myself." This juxtaposition of old and new meanings, held somatically, is one step toward lasting, memory reconsolidation (MR)

218 *Beyond Pro-being Pride*

(Ecker et al., 2012). Simultaneously holding in Isaac's awareness this new, now explicit, self-valuing and old, previously implicit, self-shaming, moved him toward a transformation of archaic beliefs about himself and relationships.]

Pt: "Valuing has to do with pro-being aliveness."

[I typically do *not* discuss my concept of pro-being pride. In a prior session, however, I had explained to Isaac how I thought about the relationship between pro-being pride and our work, as it helped him reflect upon and modulate his traumatic reactions. (See Chapter 4, #12 and #13, on the benefits of *shared consciousness* and *psychological distance*.)]

Pt: "Valuing: Being in nature, the smells, breeze, fresh. The 15-year-old's [one of Isaac's younger part's] pain: It's anger-fueled. Not listening, an aggressive part, moves me more than my thinking about why I'm moving."

Th: "Moves where in your body?"

Pt: "On the right side of my head and eyes. It's dark. From the [right] collarbone, up through my neck to my head. With the first one [i.e., "valuing"], I feel physically very connected. The second one is a not physically connected place in my head."

[Isaac's feeling valued reflected good enough me pride, and his lifelong love of being in nature a marker of emergent, pro-being pride. The 15-year-old's "anger-fueled" pain was linked with dissociated, not me shame, and a self-protective intrareaction (Chapter 5) mimicking his father's indoctrination that Isaac must never be vulnerable to attack. Isaac alluded to this dissociation when he said valuing "was physically very connected," that is, embodied and well-integrated, yet devaluing was a "not physically connected place in my head," that is, disembodied and dissociated. I knew from our previous work (Benau, 2021b) that Isaac's "anger-fueled" rage followed his feeling shamed and/or humiliated (Lewis, 1971, 1992), and was dissociated from his body. (See Dorahy, 2017; Benau, 2021b; and Chapter 1 on shame, humiliation, and impotent rage.)

Th: "Can you go inside and contact the first one [feeling valued] and then slowly approach the second one [the pain of being devalued, that is, shamed and/or humiliated]? Can you move, slowly, like a pendulum, between 'the feeling connected you' and 'the feeling disconnected you'?"

[The concept and method of pendulation, that is, shifting mindful attention between two somatic experiences, is derived from Levine's (2010) Somatic Experiencing (SE). SE's pendulation was designed to foster somatic regulation of traumatic, body memories. Here, I was not trying to help Isaac regulate neurophysiologically nor quiet his rage. Rather, I remained focused on facilitating a somatic-emotional juxtaposition between Isaac's belief about being valued versus devalued, in order to augur MR (Ecker et al., 2012).]

Pt: "As I come up to the edge [of the rage-fueled pain], I feel lots of grief and sadness."

[I was not certain whether Isaac's "grief and sadness" was a self-protective reaction against feeling humiliated and rageful toward his family and the molester, or what lay below the rage that needed to be processed, so I suggested he attend to what was emerging.]

Th: "There's more within you. See what comes up. Play with that edge [between valued and devalued]. See what comes up in relationship with the grief."

Pt: "There's a kernel at the center [of my pain and rage]. Beneath the anger. A kernel of fear. There's a really young, scared part of me. Beneath the aggressiveness."

Th: "Are you able to step, to let the 'aggressiveness' step aside?"

[My asking Isaac's self-protective strategy, that is, "aggressiveness," to "step aside" was borrowed from Accelerated Experiential Dynamic Psychotherapy (AEDP) (Fosha, 2000). I used the passive "*let*" rather than active, agentic "*put*" because I was unsure whether Isaac's aggressive, self-protective part was ready to allow other, more vulnerable mind/body states to come forward.]

[Another therapist might have elected to focus on Isaac's rage reaction to being humiliated by his father and brother (Dorahy, 2017). From that perspective, Isaac's fear would be viewed as inhibiting his direct experience, expression, and processing of rage. At the time, I thought Isaac's rage was blocking access to his fear and followed his lead. In retrospect and given my own RT history, this may have reflected avoiding Isaac's humiliation-rage cycle (Dorahy, 2017).]

Pt: "Yes, with vigilance."

[Isaac's "vigilance" was a well-worn, mental habit intended to inhibit his aggression and thwart future attacks by the perpetrators who bullied, abused, shamed, and humiliated him.]

Pt: "There's a lot of shame there. The five–six-year-old [part]. Very young. He's [the five- or six-year-old] being told not to be a certain way. 'Don't be who you are.'"

[Celebrating "who you are" reflects quintessential pro-being pride, something Isaac learned to suppress before age five. Here pro-being pride is peeking out, like a tender green shoot breaking through springtime soil.]

Th: "The shame is a covering. Is that true?"

[Linking "shame" with "covering" comes from the word origin of shame. The Proto-Indo-European (PIE) "kem" means "to cover" (Shame, word origin).]

Pt: "Yes."

Th: "Let the shame step aside."

Pt: "Yes."

Th: "Notice what you are feeling, in your whole body, beneath the aggression and its cover. Shame is a cover of _____?"

[After a minute or so:]

Pt: "It's me. There's *a radiance* to it … A little, really vulnerable center" (my emphasis).

220 *Beyond Pro-being Pride*

[Isaac had never before used the word "radiance." It immediately captured my attention as a portal to his pro-being pride. I next made explicit that Isaac's "radiance" was intrarelational, within him, and interrelational, between Isaac and myself, and that I welcomed his "radiance." In my work with RT survivors, I always privilege our individual and shared pro-being pride.]

Th: "My radiance and your radiance finds you all the time."

Pt: "There's *a deep connection with everything*" (my emphasis).

Th: "Yes! You with you. You with me and us. And you with all that is … This is a whole body, your experience. Radiant you. Just notice."

[Isaac's radiant, pro-being pride extended beyond himself and our relationship and again in Session 4. I think of this "deep connection with everything" as an expression of extra-relational, pro-being pride.]

[Isaac focused silently inward. After two minutes:]

Pt: "*It's like the core, the radiant … is very slowly stepping into the light. I feel a pulsing part of me*" (my emphasis).

[Isaac had contacted his core, essential self. Here, I tried to gently encourage rather than direct or interfere with Isaac's emergent, transformative process.]

Th: "Stay with that. We don't need to talk. *The radiant you stepping into the light, the whole body you*" (my emphasis).

[Isaac sighed. Another two minutes passed, silently.]

Pt: "It's a relief … Really happy like two little boys. Arms around each other's shoulders. They're jumping up and down. So happy. Both feel really young. Young, but also here … Not the way it was, and is … I'm not sure I had this in the past."

Th: "It could be it's happening for the first time."

[Isaac's parents were incapable of attuning to his emotional and relational needs, to truly see, feel, and recognize him. For some RT survivors, their experience of *shared* joyful, pro-being pride occurs for the first time in psychotherapy.]

[Many would argue Isaac did not have a core self until recently. Alternatively, I believe all people have a core self or at least nascent protoself from birth if not earlier (Chapter 2).]

Pt: "Incredible. It's heartening, that I can be like this in the world."

Th: *"Ask your body, not your mind, if this is integration? Your whole [self] with differentiation [of parts].* Ask your body, yes or no?" (my emphasis).

["Ask your body not your mind" was taken from the Comprehensive Resource Model (CRM) (Schwarz et al., 2017; Schwarz, 2014–2017), a therapeutic approach working with early, often preverbal RT memories. While I wanted to facilitate psychobiological integration of previously dissociated parts, I suggested Isaac "ask" his body to ensure I was not getting ahead of him. "Asking the body" helps bypass the patient's conscious thought *and* therapist's agenda.]

Pt: "Yes … It feels like that."

Th: "Let your whole body and your radiance come together. Whole, and what each bring to the whole."

[I gave Isaac plenty of time, in silence, to allow this integration of his whole body/mind and radiance to come together. At three minutes, Isaac sighed, then a moment later smiled and tilted his head back, up and to his left side, with his mouth slightly open. I thought "up" might reflect Isaac's hope and possibility, and "to the left side" his healing potential, as his right side was *always* associated with traumatic memory. I kept these thoughts to myself. After another four minutes in silence, Isaac spoke:]

Pt: "It's like there's *four … circles radiating out from my body*" (my emphasis).

[Isaac's four, concentric circles of transformation and healing reminded me of and offered a powerful contrast to Dante's (Alighieri, 2002/1320) concentric circles of degradation and Hell. For the reader's clarification, not Isaac's, I number each circle.]

Pt: (1) "The most internal one, closest in, is joy. (2) The next one, security. (3) The next one, openness. (4) The next one, love. *Out there [in the world, love is possible] because of the three beneath them. Looking back, to the radiant kernel, to my head and the center of my body* … Looking at the vigilant, angry, and shame part—they're still there, but much lighter and further away … While the other expansiveness is happier" (my emphasis).

[I thought but did not say that Isaac's innermost circle was congruent with pro-being pride, that is, "I delight in being me, delighting in you delighting in being yourself, with me." Isaac's core, pro-being pride (#1) radiates out toward others in the world (#4).]

[Previously dissociated parts that Isaac had developed in response to chronic RT, that is, "vigilant," "anger/rage," and "shame[d]" parts, were now "much lighter and farther away." In my experience, "expansiveness" in the chest is often associated with both adaptive pride subtypes, good enough me pride (i.e., the pride of achievement) and pro-being pride (i.e., the pride of being and relating). I believed Isaac was becoming more accepting of shame and rage as *aspects* of his whole being that no longer dominated his consciousness. I said none of this to Isaac.]

Pt: "The security piece was big."

Th: "The whole. Joy, security, openness, love, plus anger, and shame … Shame often leads to [protective] aggression, whether you were shamed in the past [as was Isaac] or not."

Pt: "It [shame] is a long way, away. *I push them [shame and aggression] outside the larger circle, they're supposed to be in it.* There's an area between them [i.e., between joy, security, openness, and love within the larger circle, and shame and aggression outside the larger circle]. A lot of the time, I thank that part [I assumed Isaac was referring to shame and aggression] for [protecting] me [in the past]. They're a part of me. I thank them. They got me here" (my emphasis).

[I became concerned "shame and aggression" were being banished outside the circle of Isaac's core being and thus, once again, being shamed and dissociated. I thought we should work toward bringing shame and aggression closer for his more complete integration. Still, I did not want to get ahead of nor dictate Isaac's process:]

Th: "I don't know if you are ready to bring them [shame and aggression] closer. What is your body saying?"
Pt: "It feels like such a well-worn groove. It's scary to bring them [shame and aggression] closer. I'm fearful I'll drop into it."
[In order to work toward an integration of "shame and aggression," I needed to help Isaac regulate his fear. I told Isaac his fear was not all of him. In my view, his fear represented a previously dissociated part (Van der Hart et al., 2006). I next suggested Isaac mindfully attend to only one aspect of his somatic rather than emotional experience. Following SP (Ogden et al., 2006) and Deep Brain Reorienting (Corrigan & Christie-Sands, 2020), observing somatic, preaffective experience mitigates the grip of overwhelming, trauma-based fear. This also reflected one benefit of narrow lens attending as described in Chapter 3.]
Th: "The part of you that is fearful is not the whole of you. Where in your body is it located?"
Pt: "Same place. Same fear. Within the body [is] shame, guilt, and aggression."
[I assumed this "same place" was behind Isaac's right eye, in the right side of his brain, where Isaac always held somatic memories of his complex RT.]
Th: "A part of you is afraid it [the shame, guilt, and aggression] will take over."
Pt: "It was happening in the past."
Th: *"Approach the fear, with your whole-body radiant joy, security, openness, and love"* (my emphasis).
[I believed that when well-resourced (Chapter 4, #11) within his "radiant" self, Isaac's strength and wisdom would guide him to determine what was best for the young part afraid of falling into the trauma vortex of shame, guilt, and reactive aggression.]
[Isaac went inside and remained silent for another minute. Trusting his process, I remained silent.]
Pt: "That part—the fear, shame—got thinner. Wasn't … Less solid … Thinner. There's a deep message [i.e., from the fear and shame] behind that … *I'm not good. I'm not okay*" (my emphasis).
[The italicized words were the voice of shame. Next, notice how quickly Isaac began to grieve the terrible cost of being shamed as a little boy.]
Pt: "There's a sad part. I approach with a ton of empathy … For that little boy, at four or five years old. He was wrong."
Th: "More than 'not good'?"
Pt: "*Joyful exuberance*—wrong, not good. *The joy of living*—not good" (my emphasis).
Th: "*The joy of you being you* [implicitly referencing pro-being pride] was [treated as] not good … It [the shame, 'not good,' and reactive anger] doesn't take over, it gets thinner" (my emphasis).
[What the perpetrators treated as "wrong, not good" was Isaac's unique way of being alive in relationship with himself and others, his pro-being pride.]

Beyond Pro-being Pride 223

[I said Isaac's shame "doesn't take over" because he had just remarked "the fear, shame—got thinner." Rather than predicting Isaac's future healing, I trusted his and our process. Several years of working together, rather than blind faith in Isaac, made that possible.]

Pt: "True."

Th: "Just notice that ... The whole you—joy, security, openness, love, whole body radiance, is not diminished at all. Love is more powerful [than shame, 'not good,' and aggression]. It [shame and aggression] doesn't overpower you."

[I made explicit that Isaac's radiance was not diminished when he brought closer body memories of shame and aggression. Isaac's "radiant joy," his pro-being aliveness, directly contrasted with Isaac's internalized shame and reactive aggression that, a moment earlier, Isaac feared he would "drop into." Suggesting Isaac "approach the fear" conveyed my confidence in present-day Isaac who then comforted his five-year-old self. Isaac's new interrelational and intrarelational process stood in direct contrast to Isaac's father and older brother engendering and enforcing chronic, trauma-induced fear and shame.]

Pt: "It's happening. I'm able to thank the parts of my body, my self. My habits of mind."

Th: "Yes, the cauldron [of your relational history] ... made it unsafe to be you."

Pt: "I feel closer [to those younger parts that held shame, aggression, and fear] ... I can have them. Those habits of mind ... I needed [in the past but not now]."

Th: "That was your protection, the fear keeps out [your radiant joy]."

Pt: "Yes, it [my joy in being] was there the whole time."

[Isaac's comment, "there the whole time" fits with my belief that pro-being pride, or more accurately its potential, like acorn to oak, exists from the beginning of conception or birth.]

Th: "Yes."

Pt: "[In the past] I had different ways of contacting [my joy]. Drinking, singing, dancing ... sex."

Th: "Drinking, singing, dancing, sex ... all ways to express your joy, and other ways."

Pt: "I did not feel at ease. Yes."

Th: "Contacting your joy, but also fighting."

Pt: "There's aggression [in those activities]."

Th: "Because ...?"

Pt: "My attempt to contact [my joy], but no contact. For example, singing, I was connected with the deep past."

[Isaac's paternal grandfather was a cantor who came from a long line of cantors and rabbis. Cantors are the singing, spiritual leaders of the Jewish tradition. Isaac was not Jewish by birth, as his mother was Christian and father a nonpracticing Jew. Session 4 revealed more about Isaac's and his father's conflicted relationship with Judaism].

Th: "Yes, and no. It [singing] was not part of the whole."
Pt: "I was not free ... getting closer to anger and shame. Freedom. Previously, I was aggressive—an attempt to connect. I was not free."
   [On the basis of things Isaac had shared in previous sessions about living away from home as a young adult, I now realized his "aggressive," rage and shame-fueled drinking, singing, dancing, and sexual activity were done compulsively, somewhat failed attempts to more fully connect with his own and others' aliveness.]
Th: "To connect within and with others ... Relational to the whole, and your whole to your whole."
Pt: "I am accessing a part of my heart, but it wasn't braced. *A part of me felt deeply emotional, with a tinge of sadness. From my head to my heart ... Not the same as my core of radiant joy.* A sad heart. It felt really different, one much deeper [radiant joy] than the other [deeply emotional, with a tinge of sadness]. *In touch with your heart, not core radiance*" (my emphasis).
   [Isaac's "sad heart" confirmed what RT therapists know well, that with self-transformation and liberation come deep grief over life unlived. We see this again in Sessions 2 and 3.]
Th: "[The sadness] is beckoning. The wisdom of core radiance loves the attempt [to connect]. It needs to be accompanied. This is not a solo act."
Pt: "There's anger, shame [Th: 'and fear'] of the solo act."
Th: "The solo act is of the past. It is no longer needed."
Pt: "Yeah."
   [Trauma involves being overwhelmed, unbearably alone (Fosha, 2000). Healing, here of shame and fear, is always relational, both within the survivor (intrarelational) and between them and welcoming others, including the therapist (interrelational).]
Th: "Feel into that."
Pt: "First thing that came up ... I believe it."
Th: "You believe what?"
Pt: "*I'm believing it's, all is connected. Everything—I don't have to be alone*" (my emphasis).
   [Shame and humiliation breed isolation (DePrince et al., 2015), reflecting a lack of secure attachment within and between (Bowlby, 1969). In contrast, Isaac was entering a state of oneness, self with self and self with other, that went beyond pro-being pride and toward a transcendent state of unitive consciousness (Wilber, 1998). This was again evident in Session 4].
Th: "Attachment doesn't work that way [i.e., as a solo act.]"
Pt: "Yes, it's a good feeling."
   [With less than 10 minutes remaining in this session, I wanted to help Isaac further strengthen his new, mind/body state, "all is connected." As we had done many times, I instructed Isaac to find the eye position that would help him anchor and build upon this transformative experience in his extra-therapy world. My therapeutic use of eye positions came from the Comprehensive Resource Model (CRM) (Schwarz et al., 2017), a method originating in Brainspotting (Grand, 2013).]

Th: "Find the place in your body that holds that knowing, [i.e., "all is connected"].
Pt: "Okay."
Th: "Find the eye position most strongly connected with that knowing in your body."
[Finding his eye position, Isaac nodded.]
Th: "From the eye position [eyes closed], then see me [eyes open]. Then back to the eye position [eyes closed]. Stay no longer with me than you choose."
[Isaac accessed his eye position, eyes closed, then opened his eyes while maintaining his eye position, and repeated this process several times. Maintaining an eye position with eyes closed was common for Isaac. I wanted Isaac to experience his connection with me while also remaining connected with himself in his state of radiant joy and oneness. In prior sessions, Isaac and I learned it was harder for him to remain in an open, vulnerable state while remaining connected with me. This may have been because his young, traumatized parts still equated openness and intimacy with psychological and physical danger. Maintaining a connection with himself and me while facing his archaic fears gave Isaac another opportunity for MR. That is, by juxtaposing simultaneously two contrasting realities, that is "Never trust others, especially when you are being your true self" (old) and "Connection with oneself and others when vulnerable is both possible and beneficial, at least some of the time" (new).]
Pt: "It's hard. Being open [here, in relation to you] and staying with it. Trusting, connecting in this really deep way … I like it. There's more happiness with it. In past—being open—staying with it. Trusting and connecting in this really deep way. In the past, I heard the message 'Don't do that.' Noise. Trying to do it. It doesn't feel like trying."
[Parts of Isaac welcomed deeply connecting with me while other parts remained anxious. I believed the "don't do that" message from his past represented his internalized father's voice. While Isaac felt the tug of past mistrust, it did not prevent him from feeling warmly connected within himself and with me.]
Th: "The whole you, with community, and with others."
Pt: "Yes, I've been doing that, already. Now I'm considering a job at the ___ ____ [where Isaac had worked before retiring]. I'll bring this [new way of being and relating] here [to work]."

Session 2: Anger and Grief Follows Radiant Joy (Three Years, Nine Months of Weekly Psychotherapy; Two and a Half Months after Session 1)

Session 2 took place, via Zoom videoconferencing, approximately one month after the worldwide COVID-19 pandemic hit northern California, where Isaac and I live.

Pt: "I've been walking and meditating, [meditating] longer each day. Up to 45 minutes one day. Jacob [one of Isaac's two young adult sons] got a job interview. The quarantine has been good for our family. I've been having some conversations with Jacob."

[Jacob had developmental challenges as a child, so conversations were rarely easy.]

[Three months prior, Isaac required a second surgery for unremitting pain in one of his toes. The second toe Isaac referred to was in his other foot].

Pt: "My other toe, a different foot, has been hurting. Arthritis. I'm going to need surgery at some point. I'm not happy about that [as it takes several months of limited mobility to recuperate], but I'll deal with it as soon I can" [when no longer sheltering-in-place]. Last week I was good at it [meditation] because I love it. It helps with the narrative, 'I'm not good at anything.' It's not true. In the Middle Ages there were craft guilds. There was nothing wrong with being a journeyman. I hammer myself [for being less than excellent, that is, "only" a journeyman].

["Hammering oneself," that is, self-shaming, is always born in relationship.]

Th: "Where and with whom did you learn to hammer yourself."

[Having worked with this theme many times, I assumed Isaac was referring to his father. Still, I wanted to remain open to whatever we discovered.]

Pt: "My parents. [Now] there's some air, some breath around it. ["It" referred to Isaac's implicit belief he must shame himself for those things he did not do well.] It's [the air around the hammering] has been helpful. I can accept my talents [more]. I'm less interested in them, what …"

Th: "What, and how?"

Pt: "The [old] narrative. For example, I don't understand technology well enough. I'm not really interested in technology. [Yet, the old narrative insists …] I should be able to do it. 'You're not good at this. You should be. Everyone else does it. How come you're not?'"

Th: "And the breathing around it?"

[My question was intended to better understand how much Isaac remained in the grip of traumatic shame, as contrasted with being able to "breathe" and think about the self-punishing voice (Howell, 2020). As is typical, I acknowledged Isaac's pain while privileging growth.]

Pt: "There's a young part [of me] that got the message, very early. I wasn't good at operational [activities], such as using scissors, learning dance steps, art."

[For over 40 years I have worked with children and adults with various learning and developmental challenges in both school settings and psychotherapy. Trained also in neuropsychological testing, I now view these difficulties not as individual, brain disorders but rather as ecological "mismatches" between brain differences and environmental expectations, including what is being asked of the brain at that time—in Isaac's words, operations.]

Th: "It sounds like you had some fine motor, visual-motor, and possibly gross motor challenges."

[I wanted to normalize Isaac's struggles, to convey I knew something about this, and to show empathy as an alternative to "hammering." Despite having worked with Isaac for almost four years, I had never before heard of his visual-motor struggles. Fairly often new layers of shame appear when a patient's intrarelational and interrelational landscapes deem it safe enough. These shame states can be understood as pockets of memory/experience previously dissociated. A young part of Isaac was unsure whether or not I would abandon and shame him, while present-day Isaac trusted me enough for his younger, shamed part to come forward. My acceptance of learning differences, something Isaac had witnessed earlier when I helped him understand the developmental challenges of his adult child, undoubtedly enabled Isaac to share another traumatically shaming experience.]

Pt: "When I was five-years-old [in Kindergarten], we were making flowers out of construction paper. I couldn't coordinate my hands, and cut around the circle to make the flower."

[I allowed myself to empathically imagine how excited I would have felt when I saw a beautiful flower I wanted to make with my peers. I then felt how rapidly my excitement dropped into shame following this abrupt interruption of my authentic aliveness, my pro-being pride.]

Th: "You must have felt so alone. I bet no one knew how frustrated and alone you felt. You couldn't have expressed all that."

[Mine was a fair guess: (1) By age five, Isaac had already been shamed repeatedly by his parents and older brother, particularly when brainwashed to never appear "weak"; (2) When in the grips of shame, most people dare not share their pain, consciously and unconsciously fearing more shame, rejection, and abandonment; and (3) Isaac was only five years old, so he would not have known he was not the only child struggling to make the flower. I told Isaac that approximately 20% of all students have some learning, developmental, and/or social-emotional challenge.]

Pt: "There was so much more. The fine motor skills. My fear of going home, not making it [the flower]. My father and brother mocking and shaming me. 'What's wrong with me? Help!'"

Th: "You learned to punish, to pummel yourself."

Pt: "I'd already been hurt [many times]."

Th: "Why do you think you did that [i.e., pummel or hammer yourself?]"

[Rather than seeking insight, I wanted to help Isaac better understand the function of self-shaming. That is, to think compassionately about how hammering himself fit within implicit and explicit demands of past relationships, particularly with his father and brother, and with internalized demands between different parts of self, such as "I'm in pain" and "I must push through my pain and never appear weak." By our mindfully observing Isaac's habitual self-punishment, I hoped to weaken the grip of his shame states and, together as adults, bear witness to the memorialization of Isaac's RT.]

228 *Beyond Pro-being Pride*

[Instead of posing a "why" question, it would have been better if I asked, "*What* made it necessary to hammer yourself when you were little?" or "*With whom* did you learn to hammer yourself when you were little and didn't know how to do something?" These wordings might have prompted less intellectualization and brought Isaac closer to his attachment wounds and the roots of his shame state.]

Pt: "You tell yourself [the self-shaming messages] in order to be prepared for an attack in advance."

[Isaac's understanding made sense. I also wanted to help Isaac realize his self-shaming may have been motivated by love, with "love" defined here as preserving attachment bonds with his father and brother. Learning that self-punitive behavior may also be motivated by a desire for connection can be intrinsically de-shaming.]

Th: "You loved your father and brother. [By shaming yourself] you're trying to get it [your father's and brother's love] back. What do you think your [self-] hammering is about?"

[While I believed my interpretation had merit, as soon as I spoke I wanted to back up and explore *Isaac's* experience, which is why I said, "What do you think ...?" Doing so first would have invited greater curiosity and been more respectful, empowering, and potentially less shaming.]

Pt: "I'm like a nail that sticks up."

Th: "And if you're a nail that sticks out ... then what?"

Pt: "If you do it—be it."

Th: "You were hammered for being [you]?"

[Being hammered for being your true self, for embodying your pro-being pride, lies at the heart of RT and shame states. It is most damaging when "the hammerers" are primary attachment figures the person depended upon for their physical and psychological survival.]

Pt: "Daily. Multiple times [each day]. [I was taught] I shouldn't be like that."

[Given my own RT trauma, I resonated with what it was like to be hammered by others one depends upon. Isaac and I were now in the realm of the intergenerational transmission of trauma and the interplay of patient and therapist trauma memories. While I could have reacted self-protectively and avoided my own and Isaac's pain in many ways (Chapter 5), I believed I responded with empathy. My next words needed to convey both the disintegrating power of the shame of existing (Wille, 2014; DeYoung, 2015), with my vitality affects (Stern, 1985) matching the unbearable pain of being treated, "multiple times each day" as though "I shouldn't be."]

Th: "You shouldn't *be*!" (my emphasis).

Pt: "It was really awful. How can you do that to a child?!"

[Aided by my empathy, Isaac moved from self-shaming to self-compassion, exclaiming his fierce, protective love of his five-year-old self: "How can you do that to a child?!" Isaac was beginning to repair another early, attachment wound.]

Th: "How are you feeling, now?"

Beyond Pro-being Pride   229

[I intentionally slowed down our process. I wanted Isaac to feel the full effect of his/our words; to feel me accompanying his Adult Self caring for five-year-old Isaac; and to ensure Isaac was not dysregulated by his shame state.]

Pt: "Really sad. Exhausted. Sad … It feels really true. The thought that it should be like that."

Th: "Yes, it should *never* be!" (my emphasis).

[I wanted Adult Isaac and five-year-old Isaac to know viscerally I stood resolutely with them so that this time he was not unbearably alone (Fosha, 2000). My vitality affects more than my words conveyed the power and meaning of my conviction about Isaac's experience. Stern (1985) described vitality affects as the *how* rather than the *what* of behavior: "Vitality is ideally suited to be the subject of attunement, because it is composed of the amodal qualities of intensity and time …" (p. 157). Isaac's feeling "Really sad. Exhausted," an unfolding of his grief, suggested five-year-old Isaac felt accompanied by me. In retrospect, however, I was so vehemently focused on the injustice of the hammering of Isaac's "being" that I was insufficiently attuned to his grief. I believe this said more about where I stood with respect to my RT than where Isaac was most at this point in the session.]

Pt: "Yes, really bad."

Th: "Hammer to nail. You don't get to *be*."

Pt: "Wouldn't it be so freeing to be a nail."

[I had not realized, at the time, that Isaac's describing himself as "the nail" suggested a part of him still viewed himself from the perspective of the perpetrators who included Isaac's father, brother, and later sexual violator. "Wouldn't it be freeing to be a nail" may have meant Isaac was transitioning psychologically from seeing himself through the eyes of the perpetrators toward his Adult eyes, "freeing" him of their projections.]

[Given my understanding now, I would have said, "The problem isn't the nail, it's the hammer and the hammering." What I *did* say showed empathy for Little Isaac who "chose love," the trauma bond (Van der Kolk, 1989), over unbearable aloneness (Fosha, 2000).]

Th: "You were trying desperately to be loved."

Pt: "In order to preserve my self."

Th: "And to love and be loved."

Pt: "The nail, hammered, it still exists in my mind. I pressure myself, which is safer than being hammered."

[Isaac identified with the self-protective aspect of self-shaming, that is, "Do it to myself before it is done to me," and shame's self-regulatory function. I still emphasized the traumatic attachment bond. I hoped to help Isaac see the interrelational origins of his intrarelational "solution," in part to mitigate shaming himself for shaming himself. Gradually, I became more attuned, identifying the paradox of Isaac protecting himself by shaming himself before being shamed. Even when a therapist is misattuned, the strength of the therapy bond combined with the

230 *Beyond Pro-being Pride*

patient's resilient, pro-being pride, make it possible for them to hold onto their subjective truth until the therapist "catches up."]
Th: "Or not being seen."
Pt: "Take care of my self. Of not-being."
Th: "Don't be less than. Don't be. *An act of destruction, in an effort at preservation*" (my emphasis).
Pt: "Yes, some way preserving myself. Ensuring that there was [my] core [self]. Taking …"
Th: "Not hammered."
Pt: "Not visible … to you [i.e., dissociated from other aspects of Isaac's self-experience]."
Th: "Until you are …"
Pt: "Safe enough … to do what we are doing."
 [I was struck by Isaac's remark, "some way preserving myself" until "safe enough to do what *we* are doing." While not in my notes, I described here something I learned many years ago at a workshop with David Scharff, object relations couple and family therapist. Scharff talked about states of mind/body (the concept, then, was internalized object relations) that preserve harmful aspects of a patient's early relationships with caregivers, as well as authentic, pre-trauma aspects of self, what Isaac named his "core." According to Scharff, a valued, nondamaged self sometimes reemerges many years post-trauma when the patient, often outside conscious awareness, deems the intrarelational and interrelational landscapes safe enough to feel and express their "core self" within more hospitable, relational environs.]
 [Isaac next described some reasons why and ways of being he could more freely express himself. These included self-recognition, self-compassion, and creativity.]
Th: "Why [is this preserved aspect of self, visible] now?"
Pt: "I'm more aware. I recognize. It's free to come forward."
Th: "Why else [does your core self come forward], now?"
Pt: "I'm more able to be kind to myself. I have areas of interest. I've always loved art. I received really early [destructive] messages, for example, about art."
Th: "This is a new development, the result of all your and our work, together."
Pt: "I feel spacious, freer to think about all kinds of things. For example, about the hammering. I'm more free to think about positive things, my creative impulses, and to enjoy them."
Th: "There's the [embodied] memory of what didn't happen [that should have], that contributes to the memory of being hammered, of the hammering."
Pt: "I need accompaniment when that happens. Welcoming it [the five-year-old part of me that was hammered, that is, shamed]. Do this together."
Th: "That is, I remember your ways."
Pt: "I'm *remembering* to sit with it."
Th: "And what are you feeling as you sit with it?"

Pt: "Dismissed as a person."

["Dismissed as a person" is a painfully apt expression of traumatic shame states.]

Pt: "I need to identify it as a memory. Not make it go away. When the time comes, put it in a cave."

["Put it in a cave" referred to something Isaac had done many times during therapy, using his visual imagination to alter his relationship with an abusive, shaming father introject. Here, Isaac spontaneously accessed my modified version of a protocol called "switching the dominance" (Schmidt, 2009, pp. 62–69). I was concerned, however, that if Isaac "put … in a cave" not only his father introject but also a shamed, younger part of himself, then parts of him might once again feel dismissed and shamed. I did not say anything about my concern.]

Th: "It [the you that is dismissed as a person] is not you. It reflects the hammered, and the hammering. You shouldn't be."

[Stating that Isaac was treated as though he "shouldn't be" hit him extremely hard, and he was stunned by an emotional truth. The "…" in the following transcription depicts Isaac's pausing, several times, to reflect upon having been treated, by his own father, as though he "shouldn't be." This is comparable to premeditated soul murder (Shengold, 1991)].

Pt: "That's so painful! A terrible thing … I need to sit with it … It makes me angry … I need to sit with that."

Th: "Is your anger a defense? [i.e., avoidance of some deeper pain], or does your anger express—or is an expression of—your being."

[I was inviting Isaac to wonder aloud, with me, whether his anger was "defensive" or a powerful affirmation of his right "to be," to exist (Wille, 2014). I now realize it could have been both, and much more.]

Pt: "The anger is suppressing—a way not to feel the pain. It's very painful. There's pain."

[Since Isaac indicated this anger served a protective function, I worked to help him soften his affect-avoidant reaction]

Th: "Where in your body is the pain?"

Pt: "In my head, right head behind my eyes—my eyes—are sad."

[As observed many times, the right side of Isaac's right head and behind his right eye consistently held traumatic, body memories of his father's and brother's abuse, and the sexual molestation. The latter was also experienced physically in his groin and sphincter.]

Pt: "Oh, fuck!"

Th: "Now that?!"

Pt: "I've gone a long way … So many layers. Further and further … Part of me felt I turned a corner. Part of me felt, 'Oh, this is a whole nother layer. Part of me thought—we were done. Oh fuck, we're not done.'"

Th: "And that makes you feel very sad."

Pt: "Yeah, very sad. In therapy, it feels like grief. My joy-in-being, and the pain of nonbeing. Grieving, the pain and grief of nonbeing."

[Given that Isaac's painful, unfinished business and grief arose at the close of this session, I wanted to leave him with something to reflect upon between sessions. I sought to encourage present-day Isaac to accompany a young, emerging Isaac, while remaining connected to me and our work.]

Th: "Write this down: *"The joy-in-being, and the pain and grief of nonbeing"* (my emphasis).

[Isaac endorsed my summary, adding:]

Pt: "What feels right. The grief and pain of nonbeing. It doesn't feel scary."

Th: "It's not scary. *Your joy-in-being can't be taken from you*" (my emphasis).

Pt: "Yes. I have confidence, and substance. It doesn't feel overwhelming. It doesn't feel threatening. That's because I do have joy-in-being, in ways I have. [My] right to celebrate something, to enjoy."

Th: "That's part of being, and part of grieving."

[Isaac and my reflections, particularly those italicized, speak to his relationship with his "joy-in-being" that captures experientially my concept of pro-being pride. Since I believe a person's pro-being pride always was, is, and will be, I told Isaac it "can't be taken away from you."]

As seen in this Session 2, when a person reconnects or connects for the first time with their pro-being pride, grief often follows. This includes the grief that accompanies the patient's growing realization of life unlived, as a result of chronic effects of RT. More will be revealed about grief and its processing explicitly in Session 3 and implicitly in Session 4.

Session 3: Grief Never Has the Last Word: Toward Integration (Three Years, Ten Months into Weekly Therapy; One Month Following Session 2, and Three and a Half Months after Session 1)

Having experienced a state of oneness, one might predict Isaac would feel some loss after returning to a quotidian sense of self as more separate from the external world. In fact, the grief in Session 3 was even more arresting, harkening back to Isaac's childhood and the lifelong costs of RT. Isaac's losses were existential, a painful, growing awareness of life unlived.

RT survivors invariably experience grief soon after embodying the fullest flowering of pro-being pride. The more deeply Isaac experienced the joy in being himself with others, the more he realized how profoundly his life had been diminished by growing up in an emotionally and physically punishing and depriving family. As Isaac observed in Session 2, "[Being is necessary] to get to grief and pain [of nonbeing]."

In Session 3, Isaac described with specificity personal losses over 60 years of his life.

Th: "Death can be equated with losses. What losses are you grieving?"

Pt: "Loss of my self. Loss of possibility, who I could've been. More, deeper, loss of loving trust with people, not being able to trust. Loss of being separated away from my own feelings. For example, large deaths, as an adult. I couldn't feel it [the adult deaths] fully, loss of childhood, loss of freedom, loss of my self."

[Isaac was moved to tears. I gently accompanied him.]

Th: "Sit with all of that."

[After a minute of silence:]

Pt: "So much insecurity … because of this. I had to [try to] behave in ways that would provide me security."

Th: "And that was impossible."

Pt: "Impossible to be secure. I didn't take chances, because I was scared I wouldn't be secure."

Th: "What chances?"

Pt: "I sang in a band in _____ [a foreign country Isaac lived in as a young adult]. I loved it. Here [after returning to the United States], I never sang again. In college, I wanted to be a disc jockey. I was too scared that I wouldn't make a living doing that. Now, there is a disc jockey, a woman on _____ [a radio station in the SF Bay Area where Isaac lives], to whom I recommend a song each day, that she and others really enjoy … [Being a disc jockey] was something I really wanted to do ever since I was 18, 19 years old. Lots of areas. I wanted to write more. At work, I had the opportunity to do things. It grieves me. I'm [now in my 60s] … I'm profoundly sorry, I was so mean at work, I lost friends. Unaccepting. I have lots of regrets about that. Had I been allowed to be myself [by my father and brother], I could've had a very different life."

[The more Isaac processed his grief over specific losses, the more these could be incorporated within his growing sense of self, and as part of broader meanings of his life narrative. In Sessions 3 and 4, Isaac moved toward greater psychological integration.]

Pt: "I took a different job, in order to make more money, leaving a job and people I loved."

[Isaac changed jobs primarily to pay for private schooling for his learning challenged child. Isaac now recognized his desire to make more money also reflected yet another reaction to his father's shaming messages, including injunctions to dominate and defeat others.]

Th: "If you loved too long [the people at your former place of work], you turned later toward domination."

[Describing the effects of the implicit message Isaac's father "installed":]

Pt: "If I act with love, I can't continue. My ego. I had to be more successful."

[I next wanted to see if two previously dissociated aspects of Isaac's personality, that is, his capacity to love himself and others and his installed drive to dominate others, could be brought into experiential contact with each other. MR and deep transformation are achieved by juxtaposing experientially trauma-induced beliefs and behavior with new, life-enhancing ways of being and relating (Ecker et al., 2012).]

[Isaac was familiar with our working this way. When asked to locate somatically these two different ways of being, Isaac identified the right side of his body with the drive to dominate others, and the left side with his ability to love and connect authentically.]

Th: "Love is on the left side. Love people at work, your children. Driven by love. On the right side, you having to be the best [i.e., dominate and win over others]."

Pt: "Two disparate feelings. Always in flux [throughout my life]."

["In flux" referred to two, previously dissociated parts in constant tension and competition but never interacting with awareness. Isaac was now in the early phases of working intentionally with this "flux" that had previously prevented movement toward integration.]

Th: "Two different ways of being" (Chefetz, 2015).

Pt: "One was heightened, then the other. Back and forth [throughout my life]."

[Summarizing our recent work together, as described in Session 1, Session 2, and now Session 3, I wanted to point toward a yet unknown possibility of self-discovery.]

Th: "Love of self, equivalent to loving the world … love fails. Love of self, led to loss. Who do you get to be and become?"

[Thinking about "love" and "domination," I shared an excerpt of a poem by Martin Buber (1967):]

"We cannot avoid
Using power,
Cannot escape the compulsion
To afflict the world,
So let us, cautious in diction
And mighty in contradiction,
Love powerfully."

Session 4: Renewed Pro-being Pride, Integration, and Unity Consciousness (Three Years, Ten Months into Weekly Psychotherapy; Three and a Half Months Following Session 1, and One Week after Session 3)

Toward the end of Session 4, Isaac shared how further processing his grief (Sessions 2 and 3), and movement toward greater integration (Session 3), opened space internally to reconnect more strongly with his joy-of-being, his pro-being pride.

In Session 4, we explored Isaac's understanding of his father's conflicted, confusing, and dissociated relationship with Judaism. For example, Isaac's father identified as an Orthodox Jew yet never practiced Judaism. Likewise, his father went to a Rabbi to have young Isaac designated Jewish, yet refused to perform the simple ritual ceremony prescribed.

As we worked with Isaac's father's irresolvable contradictions, both within himself and in communications with Isaac, something profound ensued. Isaac decried his father as "an insidious monster" and then, with eyes closed, observed something that stunned us both:

Pt: "All that energy ['black' energy emanating from his father's incongruent beliefs regarding Judaism and other things, held in Isaac's body] is flowing through me, out of me. [Isaac paused for less than a minute.] And returning to my body in a different way. The touch, feel, [my] core a relaxed, secure, confident feeling. Down deep in me. Love of me—really fine. All that [black energy pouring out of my body] doesn't scare me. [It's just] energy. Just to watch it. It's not bad, even if it's hard. There's nothing scary about it. For years it was scary. But at my core, I knew this [my father's energy, installed in me] was happening. I knew it was wrong."

Th: "It didn't take over your mind completely, even if it did, some."

[After a minute of silence:]

Pt: "It takes a lot out of me."

[Since we were working with two types of energy, one Isaac identified as black, toxic, and linked with his father abusing and brainwashing him, and another, life-affirming energy, I said:]

Th: "It's [black, toxic] energy expelled, and then there's energy in the circle of life."

Pt: "The circle [of energy] is on both sides [of my body]. Up through the body [on Isaac's right side, associated with Isaac's RT and his father's toxic installation], out [of the right side of Isaac's head/brain], and back through the body [on Isaac's left side]. The energy is on both sides."

[The old, pathogenic energy was leaving Isaac's right side and new, healing energy entering his left, as though a circular flow of Isaac's life force was being cleared of traumatic residues.]

[After remaining silent for another minute, Isaac shared that he first thought he would have to figure what to do with the black, energy stream. Isaac quickly realized:]

Pt: "I don't need to know what is happening."

Th: "You can know without words."

[Isaac continued to release himself of any expectation he had to be better than everyone else, another father-installed belief. For example, Isaac recognized he need not be "super-mindful" during meditation.]

Pt: [I'm] … "[I'm] narrating my transformation. It's happening in real time. It's a relief to have a way to approach this, my father's installation. My father was so dominant, for so many years. It's a relief to release it. I don't need it [i.e., the dark, toxic energy, and installed beliefs]. It's a relief, feel into my body feeling. Sitting with it."

[As I considered my next response, I was concerned Isaac might think he had "to do" something to please me. I cautiously suggested Isaac might strengthen and anchor his deeper connection with this release of his father's toxic beliefs and energy by finding an eye position corresponding with his strongest, bodily connection with this new, transformative state. Isaac thought this would be helpful.]

[Once again, eye positions were used to solidify Isaac's relationship with a new, liberating, mind/body state. This approach is taken from the Comprehensive Resource Model (CRM) (Schwarz, 2014–2017; Schwarz et al., 2017) and originally developed in Brainspotting (Grand, 2013).]

[Isaac remained silent for three minutes, eyes closed and focused on the eye position linked with his transformation. As in Session 1, I next asked Isaac to open his eyes to ensure he could experience his transformation both inward, with himself, and outward, in relation to me and others outside of therapy. Isaac opened his eyes and, per my instruction and the CRM protocol, retained his eye position.]

[Isaac observed the black energy still moving out of him and felt no need to make something happen.]

Pt: "It's continuing to do its own thing. Continuing to [expunge my father's] installation. Out of my brain [on the right side]. Pumping it out. I don't need to examine it."

Th: "You don't need to know what it means."

Pt: "It's so much. So many years [of my father's abuse and brainwashing]. Pumping out sludge. Different areas of my life, for example, as a Jew but lots of others [i.e., aspects of my life] that I haven't talked about."

[Returning to the idea that there were two manifestations of one energy, I observed Isaac's father's toxic "sludge" leaving his right side and Isaac's cleared "life force," that I believed was an expression of Isaac's pro-being pride, pouring in on his left side. Based upon my belief that a person's life force or pro-being pride is present from birth until death, I suggested:]

Th: "Your life force was, is, and always will be. You're discovering an old [original, core] way of being."

Pt: "There's more room for joy, on the right side of my forehead."

[Notice "joy" was entering Isaac's right side of his head where previously traumatic memory was held. Adopting the language of pro-being pride, I stated:]

Th: "The joy of being oneself."

Pt: "Joy-of-being."

[Referring to Isaac's former, traumatic shame state:]

Th: "In the past, your being was covered over."

[I intentionally chose "covered" as the word origin of "shame" is from the Proto-Indo-European (PIE) word "kem," "to cover" (Shame, word origin). Rather than a "covering," Isaac experienced the suppression of his joyful being as immobilizing (Benau, 2021a, 2021b).]

Pt: "[Being] bound. Wrapped up and bound. [Being] not available to me."

Th: "You couldn't be it, feel it [your core, joyful self, your pro-being pride]."

Pt: "I couldn't celebrate it."

Th: "What do you feel in relation to your core, now?"

Pt: "It feels unbound."

[Once again, to strengthen Isaac's connection with his core way of being:]

Th: "Repeat, 'I'm unbound, I'm free.'"

Pt: "I'm unbound, I'm free."

[I suggested Isaac locate another eye position linked with his strongest, physical connection with this new belief, "I'm unbound, I'm free." I then asked Isaac if this eye position was the *same* or *different* from the eye position associated with feeling the relief accompanying his deepening transformation.]

Pt: "Different."

[Coming to the close of Session 4, I noticed but chose not to comment on Isaac's gentle smile, his head and eyes directed straight ahead and slightly upward, a posture consistent with adaptive, authentic pride (Tracy, 2016) and pro-being pride (Chapter 2).]

Pt: "Waves flow back through my body. Relaxed. Letting go—all kinds of tension."

[To ensure Isaac's pro-being pride was available to him in relation to himself, eyes closed, and with me and others, eyes open, I suggested Isaac open his eyes while maintaining the eye position somatically linked with his belief, "I'm unbound, I'm free." Isaac opened his eyes:]

Pt: "Happens with eyes open, too. Very deep connection to the world. That's what it feels like. To the natural world."

[Notice Isaac's "Very deep connection to the world" suggested he again experienced, as in Session 1, a felt sense of oneness within himself and between himself and the world, from a more integrated place. This was also an expression of Isaac's extra-relational pro-being pride.]

[Session 4 closed with my recommending that Isaac, during the coming week, access several times daily the eye position associated with feeling "unbound," "free," and at one with himself and the world. I thought of this as connecting Isaac's pro-being pride and unity consciousness.]

Pt: "That's gonna be fun."
Th: "You get to play with it."
Pt: "See you next week."

Discussion

Session 1 displayed the power of metaprocessing (Fosha, 2000) Isaac's pro-being pride. Isaac and I discovered, to our shared surprise and delight, that sustained interest in Isaac's pro-being pride took us beyond strengthening pro-being pride, into what Isaac called "radiant joy," and a state of oneness elsewhere described as unity consciousness (Wilber, 1998) or unitive experience (Stace, 1960).

A state of oneness may grow out of a dedicated, spiritual practice (Goleman, 1972) or be facilitated by select, mind-altering drugs (Weil, 1986). My work with Isaac showed unity consciousness can also be achieved in psychotherapy, given the right psychological preparation and relational milieu.

How might we understand Isaac, a survivor of RT that included chronic emotional, physical, and sexual abuse, and pervasive nonattunement, moving from a chronic, traumatic shame state to an enlivened state of pro-being pride and unity consciousness?

While we can never really know with certainty, I propose specific principles, attitudes, and concepts that help us better understand Isaac's transformation. These include the concept of pro-being pride and its relationship with Janet's act of triumph and Spinoza's pleasure in distinctness; pro-being pride as an antidote to traumatic, shame states; the relationship between "integration" and "unity consciousness"; and "beyond pro-being pride," that is, therapeutically metaprocessing pro-being pride as a pathway toward unity consciousness.

The Concepts of Pro-being Pride, Janet's "Act of Triumph," and Spinoza's "Pleasure in Distinctness"

Most researchers and psychotherapists say little about the role of pride in psychotherapy with RT (Dearing & Tangney, 2011). When they do, they often point to harm caused to patients and their loved ones by maladaptive, hubristic pride, my better me pride. This pride subtype is common in narcissistically wounded individuals. Less discussed is chronic, maladaptive pride dissociated in differing degrees, that is, not me pride and no me pride.

The most significant lacunae in the literature about psychotherapy with survivors of RT is what I have named pro-being pride. (See Benau, 2021a, 2021b, 2020a, 2020b, 2020c, 2019, 2018 for exceptions.) As explored throughout this book, my abbreviated definition of pro-being pride is, "I delight in being me, delighting in you delighting in being yourself, with me" (self with other); and "I delight in being me, delighting in me delighting in being myself, with me" (self with self).

Descriptions of the phenomenological experience of pro-being pride predate me. Two examples, from the work of French psychologist Pierre Janet (1859–1947) and philosopher Baruch Spinoza (1632–1677), follow.

Pierre Janet was an historically prominent and until recently oft neglected French psychologist. In the four sessions described, Isaac experienced what Janet called an act of triumph (l'acte de triomphe). An act of triumph, the result of processing inhibited action to completion (Janet, 1925, 1919; Ogden, 2019; Ogden et al., 2006), follows successful integration of traumatic memory. Consistent with Isaac's proclamation in Session 4, "I'm unbound. I'm free," acts of triumph are evidenced when RT survivors transition from traumatic immobilization to freedom of movement, emotion, and thought (Benau, 2021a, 2021b).

Janet's act of triumph approaches my concept of pro-being pride. Both acts of triumph and pro-being pride directly contrast with hubristic or better me pride (Chapter 2; Tracy, 2016). As Barral and Meares (2019) observed, Janet's understanding of post-traumatic acts of triumph *"have nothing to do with grandiosity; they are victories over obstacles … It* [an act of triumph] *requires effort and results in a sense of pride that is a form of joy and heals shame* [(Barral & Meares, (2019, p. 121, my emphasis); referencing the work of Janet (1935, pp. 64–65)]. Janet's "pride that is a form of joy [that] heals shame" is congruent with pro-being pride (Chapter 2).

In his treatise on *Ethics*, 17th-century philosopher Baruch Spinoza (2006/1677) offered the following, Proposition, Number 53: "When the mind regards itself and its own power of activity, it feels *pleasure*: and that *pleasure* is greater in proportion to *the distinctness wherewith it conceives itself and its own power of activity*" (p. 134, my emphasis). As part of his proof of this proposition, Spinoza (2006/1677) argued,

> A man does not know himself except through his modifications of his body, and the ideas thereof ... *When, therefore, the mind is able to contemplate itself, it is thereby assumed to pass onto a greater perfection, or to feel pleasure; and the pleasure will be greater in proportion to the distinctness, wherewith it is able to conceive itself and its own power of activity.*
>
> (p. 134, my emphasis)

Spinoza's ideas fit well with the concept of pro-being pride and my work with Isaac:

- The more a person reflects upon their self-experience, and the more they recognize their experience as uniquely theirs, "distinct" from others, the more they feel pleasure. In this instance, my word for "pleasure" is "delight." Spinoza's description is closer to the intrarelational aspect of pro-being pride, "I delight in being me, delighting in me delighting in being myself, with me" than its interrelational counterpart, "I delight in being me, delighting in you delighting in being yourself, with me."
- This "pleasure" includes an activity of the mind and the body. Spinoza makes explicit here and throughout *Ethics* that, unlike his contemporary DesCartes, the mind and body are one, two ways of experiencing the whole (Nijenhuis, In press).
- Pleasure involves the person perceiving and experiencing their uniqueness, including the power of their idiosyncratic way of being in the world, their "activity." Pro-being pride is pleasurable because it is empowering, involving action and interaction with oneself, others, and the world. The more a person embodies their distinct way of being in the world, the more they are able to be and become who they are in relation to themselves and "others," animate and inanimate, that constitute "the world."

Spinoza viewed mind and matter, including mind and brain, as two attributes of a singular substance he called Nature or God. According to Nijenhuis' (personal communication, March 21, 2020), Spinoza (2006/1677) argued, "Nature consists of 'an infinity of attributes or properties of which each one expresses an eternal and infinite essence' (Proposition X, p. 16)." As a species, we experience and know two of these: matter and mind. The brain, parts of the brain, and other material structures are in this perspective not substances, but ways Nature is.

Given that pro-being pride reflects a unique expression of one's aliveness, and integration of previously dissociated aspects of self a common goal of trauma-informed psychotherapy generally and with RT survivors specifically, pro-being pride and psychobiological integration can be conceived as two sides of the same coin. Spinoza's philosophy argued brain and mind were expressions of the same substance, "Nature." Integration, pro-being pride, and a sense of one's wholeness or oneness with self are all part of the same, healing experience. This gives us one way of understanding how Isaac's growing integration of previously dissociated memories of shaming abuse and neglect led to his sense of oneness with himself. It also led to Isaac's subjective experience of oneness with all things. (See below, "psychobiological integration and unity consciousness" and "metaprocessing pro-being pride.")

Pro-being Pride as an Antidote to Shame States

Throughout this book, I have argued pro-being pride is the most powerful antidote to maladaptive shame, both as an acute emotional process and traumatic mind/body state. Extending beyond Janet's act of triumph (Barral & Meares, 2019), pro-being pride is not only the result of a patient overcoming the harmful effects of trauma. Pro-being pride also reflects the patient's *return to their natural way of being and being with others* that had been occluded by the effects of trauma. If shame states represent an occlusion of being and being with, then pro-being pride reflects the patient's reconnection with their unique aliveness, a restoration and reclamation of their birthright.

When a therapist keeps forefront an understanding of pro-being pride, both as concept and intrasubjective and intersubjective experience, then the overarching goal of therapy with RT survivors includes the alleviation of suffering due to traumatic shame and pride states, *and* the restoration of the patient's intrinsic and interpersonal aliveness. In the language of pro-being pride, this entails a celebration of the patient being and becoming their unique self in relation to others and the world.

On the Relationship between "Psychobiological Integration" and "Unity Consciousness"

If mind and body are considered one (Spinoza, 2006/1667), does it follow that self and other and by extension self and environment are also one? While we do not always *feel* at one with the world any more than we always *feel* integrated, the unity of self/other/world is a subjective, experiential reality achievable through various means, including shame and pride-informed, depth psychotherapy with RT survivors.

Conceptualizing a unified self and environment is consistent with the theory of some contemporary psychologists who, following Spinoza, find both differentiation and unity within "self" and "environment." While this takes us into epistemology, the study of what we know, and ontology, the study of being and reality, it enriches our understanding of Isaac's experience of oneness with himself and the world, that is, unity consciousness.

The following four quotes are from Ellert Nijenhuis (Nijenhuis, 2015; personal communication, March 21, 2020). Nijenhuis is a psychologist who has studied extensively Spinoza and related philosophies on the nature of mind and reality. Nijenhuis' (2015) observations point toward a better understanding of the relationship between "RT," "an integrated self," and "oneness with all things."

- "To live life efficiently and effectively, *organisms must appreciate which environmental bodies and ideas tend to promote their power of action and their power of existing, that is, their power to preserve their existence. In this sense they [organisms] must also reach a conclusion as to which other bodies and ideas might endanger them, that is, diminish, if not ruin, these powers*" (p. 71, my emphasis).

- "The order of causes is therefore an order of composition and decomposition of relations, which infinitely affects all of nature. But as conscious beings, we never apprehend anything but the effects of these compositions and decompositions: *we experience joy when a body encounters ours and enters into composition with it, and sadness when, on the contrary, a body or an idea threatens our own coherence*" (p. 72, my emphasis).

- "*The crucial point is that an event does not exist in isolation of an experiencing and knowing individual. Rather, it constitutes a perception and/or conception of an individual whose brain is embodied, and who is a biopsychosocial whole, a whole living system, intrinsically embedded in an environment*" (Järvilehto, 2001a, 2001b, 2000a, 2000b, 2000c, 1999, 1998a, 1998b; Fuchs, 2010, 2008; Northoff, 2003; Schopenhauer, 1958/1844/1818; Spinoza, 1996/1677; Thompson, 2007)" (p. 119, my emphasis).

- "Consciousness thus begins with ideas of affections of the body. In this conscious awareness, *the subject (i.e., the conscious organism) and the object (i.e., the thing that the subject perceives) become* **linked but also differentiated** *('I am not the thing that affects me')*" (p. 188, my emphasis).

- "*Individuals are co-dependently and co-constitutively related to events, some of which can injure and traumatize them as a living system*" (p. 119, my emphasis).

- "*Organisms and environments are co-occurrent, co-dependent and co-constitutive* such that it is better to say that organisms are part of their world, the world they co-create" (Nijenhuis, personal communication, March 21, 2020, my emphasis).

I take from Nijenhuis several things:

- We are all unified mind/bodies that exist in relation to environments that can only be known through our interaction with, and perception and experience of, those environments.
- A person and his environment are co-constituted. We cannot have one without the other.
- Humans must and do determine what in their environment, including other humans, threaten, injure, and traumatize them as contrasted with enhance their healing, thriving, integration, and sense of oneness.
- Our sense of "oneness" within ourselves, with others, and with our environment include ways we are "united" and the ways we are "differentiated."

Another way of describing the relationship between "differentiation" and "unity" is found in the work of Otto Rank (1978/1929). Rank described two life forces in dynamic relationship, life fear and death fear. Life fear refers to existential anxieties associated with separation and individuation. Death fear refers to existential anxieties associated with merger with and being undifferentiated from the parent. When in balance, Rank suggested there is a sense of oneness within and between the person and environment.

Following my work with Isaac, integration within one's self and between one's self, others, and environment, allow us to know that, following Walt Whitman's (1965/1855) poem "Song of Myself," we all "contain multitudes" (p. 88). Discovering and welcoming our complexity, including our suffering and joys, enriches our sense of a unique, differentiated self *and* the more we know ourselves as individuals, the more we feel at one with other unique beings and an infinitely variegated, wonderous world.

Beyond Pro-being Pride: Metaprocessing Pro-being Pride as One Pathway toward Unity Consciousness

With others, I believe unity consciousness is an innate, human potential people often lose contact with as they develop. Following certain psychological and spiritual practices, including the use of certain psychoactive substances, individuals can sometimes reconnect with an unitive experience of the world (Goleman, 1972; Weil, 1986; Wilber, 1998; Stace, 1960). As demonstrated with Isaac, particularly in Session 1 and Session 4, one pathway toward achieving unity consciousness in psychotherapy is by metaprocessing a patient's experience of pro-being pride.

Therapeutic metaprocessing (Fosha, 2000) refers to the patient and therapist intentionally reflecting upon and working with a *positive, growth enhancing* outcome of therapy, analogous to processing traumatic experience. At the start of Session 1, I was unsure how to effectively metaprocess pro-being pride, having never done so before. I decided to use an approach informed by the CRM (Schwarz, 2014–2017; Schwarz et al., 2017), a method developed to work with complex, developmental trauma, and apply it to Isaac's experience of pro-being pride.

In Session 1, Isaac's pro-being pride was brought into direct, experiential contact with pro-being pride intrarelationally, Isaac with himself, and interrelationally, Isaac with my pro-being pride. Said another way, Isaac's pro-being pride activated my pro-being pride and vice versa. While metaprocessing our individual and shared experience of pro-being pride, Isaac and I were afforded an unexpected gift I now think of as exponential pro-being pride. Together we observed a powerful expansion of Isaac's pro-being pride that evolved toward "radiant joy" (Session 1) and beyond pro-being pride toward "deep connection with everything" (Session 4), unity consciousness.

Following my discussion of Janet and Spinoza, pro-being pride is a natural outgrowth and expression of psychobiological integration. Integration refers to previously dissociated aspects of self experientially coming together such that what were once distinct "parts" are now experienced part of a larger whole, what Isaac called his "core." It follows that personal integration, under optimal psychological and relational conditions bringing the patient's and therapist's full attention to their individual and shared pro-being pride, leads to a felt sense of oneness with the world. If pro-being pride can be thought of as a birthright, my work with Isaac suggests a sense of oneness is an innate, human potential at times gifted to patient and therapist alike.

Summary: From Unity Consciousness and Radiant Joy, to Grief, and a Return to Integration, Joy, and Oneness

During a recent webinar on MDMA (3, 4-Methyl enedioxy methamphetamine)-assisted psychotherapy, also known as Ecstasy, researchers described a process whereby participants/patients experienced the drug-induced state as mind and heart opening (Mithofer et al., 2021), and that this openness led to deep feelings of loss and grief. The psychotherapy process following MDMA sessions facilitated an integration of these experiences of grief and oneness.

Although Isaac took no drugs during this process, having been a recovering alcoholic for 30 years who eschewed alcohol and drugs, our work followed a similar process: enhanced openness (including, in my view, pro-being pride)→ unity consciousness→ grief→ integration and unity consciousness. Contrary to this schematic, Isaac's actual therapeutic process was not linear. His experiential process included openness, unity consciousness, grief, and integration as part of a complex, nonlinear, dynamic system. At the same time, the similarities between MDMA-assisted psychotherapy and Isaac's shame and pride-informed psychotherapy point toward a universal process of transformation and healing.

As Sessions 2 and 3 showed, just as psychotherapy with RT does not end with the alleviation of the sequelae of chronic trauma, it also cannot end with a sense of radiant joy and oneness. As patients feel more of who they truly are and, in my view, have always been, they invariably become painfully aware of what they have lost. The patient's grief is part of what Rank (1932) referred to as an awareness life unlived. Isaac reflected upon his *losses* from a position of *gain*, that is, from the perspective of pro-being pride. Isaac grieved many things including, in his words, "Loss of my self, loss of … who I could've been … loss of loving with people … [and] loss of being separated from my own feelings." Isaac went on to add the loss of "security," of feeling safe within and in relation to others. Finally, Isaac mourned the years he felt disconnected from his creativity. As Isaac's therapy progressed beyond these sessions, he gradually reclaimed other forms of self-expression, including writing short stories and poems.

Some describe therapy with survivors of complex, RT as one step forward and two steps back. I prefer to think of this work as a pendulation between and often co-occurrence of life-distorting or denying forces and life-enhancing energies that promote evolution and growth. In Session 4, Isaac experienced the former visually, emotionally, and somatically as "dark energy" linked with his father's toxic installation of shaming beliefs and behavior. By extension, dark energy included Isaac's RT at the hands of other family members and a sexual predator. Therapeutically processing dark energy, emanating from Isaac's right side and out the right side of his head, harkened a return of healing, enlivening energy I associate with pro-being pride, circling "back through [Isaac's] body" on his left side. This gave Isaac a renewed, embodied sense of integration, "energy on both sides."

How might we explain Isaac releasing traumatic, dark energy on his right side and receiving healing energy on his left side? This was certainly not anything Isaac had ever experienced, nor anything I had witnessed personally nor as therapist. Neither of us "made" any of this happen. Indeed, we agreed to observe this powerful process without needing to, in Isaac's words, "examine" nor in my view "explain" it. In retrospect, it appears we co-created conditions that released transformative life forces larger than us both.

My work with Isaac continued a few years after these sessions, taking us deeper into previously uncharted terrain of RT at the hands of his mother and later older brother. As Isaac's trauma processing and healing progressed, he reported feeling more and more whole and joyful to be alive. At the same time, Isaac always reminded himself and me that this did not mean he was always happy. I believe this was his way of saying that to be fully alive is to experience deeply both pain and joy.

I can think of no more fitting ending to a book about psychotherapy with shame, pride, and relational trauma than pro-being pride: The delight we take in being ourselves, with others delighting in being themselves, sharing our unique ways of being alive with each other and the world.

References

Alighieri, D. (2000/1320). *Inferno* (R. & J. Hollander, Transl.). New York: Anchor Books.

Barral, C. & Meares, R. (2019). The Holistic Project of Pierre Janet: Part Two: Oscillations and Becomings. From Disintegration to Integration. In G. Craparo, F. Ortu, & O. Van der Hart, Eds., *Rediscovering Pierre Janet: Trauma, Dissociation, and a New Context for Psychoanalysis* (pp. 116–129). New York: Routledge. Doi: https://doi.org/10.4324/9780429201875.

Benau, K. (2021a). Shame to Pride Following Sexual Molestation: Part 1: From Traumatic Immobilization to Triumphant Movement. *European Journal of Trauma & Dissociation*, 5(4), 100198. https://doi.org/10.1016/j.ejtd.2020.100194.

Benau, K. (2021b). Shame to Pride Following Sexual Molestation: Part 2: From Pro-being Pride to Retaliatory Rage, Adaptive Anger, and Integration. *European Journal of Trauma and Dissociation*, 5(4), 100194. https://doi.org/10.6092/2282-1619/mjcp-2155.

Benau, K. (2020a). Shame, Pride and Dissociation: Estranged Bedfellows, Close Cousins and Some Implications for Psychotherapy with Relational Trauma Part I: Phenomenology and Conceptualization. *Mediterranean Journal of Clinical Psychology*, 8(1), 1–35. Doi: https://doi.org/10.6092/2282-1619/mjcp-2154.

Benau, K. (2020b). Shame, Pride and Dissociation: Estranged Bedfellows, Close Cousins and Some Implications for Psychotherapy with Relational Trauma Part II: Psychotherapeutic Applications. *Mediterranean Journal of Clinical Psychology*, 8(1), 1–29. Doi: https://doi.org/10.6092/2282-1619/mjcp-2155.

Benau, K. (March, 2020c). From Shame State to Pro-being Pride in a Single "Session." *The Science of Psychotherapy*, 20–39.

Benau, K. (2019). Catching the Wave. *The Neuropsychotherapist*, 7(4), 4–13.

Benau, K. (2018). Pride in the Psychotherapy of Relational Trauma: Conceptualization and Treatment Considerations. *European Journal of Trauma & Dissociation*, 2(3), 131–146. https://doi.org/10.1016/j.ejtd.2020.100198.

Bowen, B. www.relationalimplicit.com/bowen/. Accessed August 1, 2021.

Bowlby, J. (1969). *Attachment. Attachment and Loss, Vol. 1: Loss*. New York: Basic Books.

Buber, M. (1967). *A Believing Humanism: My Testament, 1902–1965*. New York: Simon and Schuster.

Chefetz, R. (2015). *Intensive Psychotherapy for Persistent Dissociative Disorders: The Fear of Feeling Real*. New York: W.W. Norton. Doi: 10.1080/00332747.2016.1237710.

Corrigan, F. M. & Christie-Sands, J. (2020). An Innate Brainstem Self-Other System Involving Orienting, Affective Responding, and Polyvalent Relational Seeking: Some Clinical Implications for a "Deep Brain Reorienting" Trauma Psychotherapy Approach. *Medical Hypotheses*, 136, 109502. https://doi.org/10.1016/j.mehy.2018.07.028.

Craparo, G., Ortu, F., & Van der Hart, O., Eds. (2019). *Rediscovering Pierre Janet: Trauma, Dissociation, and a New Context for Psychoanalysis*. New York: Routledge. https://doi.org/10.4324/9780203759981.

Dearing, R. L. & Tangney, J. P., Eds. (2011). *Shame in the Therapy Hour*. Washington, DC: American Psychological Association. https://doi.org/10.1037/12326-000.

DePrince, A. P., Huntjens, R. J. C., & Dorahy, M. J. (2015). Alienation Appraisals Distinguish Adults Diagnosed with DID from PTSD. *Psychological Trauma: Theory, Research, Practice, and Policy*, 7(6), 578–582. Doi: https://doi.org/10.1037/tra0000069.

DeYoung, P. (2015). *Understanding and Treating Chronic Shame: A Relational/Neurobiological Approach*. New York: Routledge. https://doi.org/10.4324/9781315734415.

Dorahy, M. J. (2017). Shame as a Compromise for Humiliation and Rage in the Internal Representation of Abuse by Loved Ones: Processes, Motivations, and the Role of Dissociation. *Journal of Trauma & Dissociation*, 18(3), 383–396. Doi: 10.1080/15299732.2017.1295422.

Ecker, B., Ticic, R., & Hulley, L. (2012). *Unlocking the Emotional Brain: Eliminating Symptoms at Their Roots Using Memory Reconsolidation*. New York: Routledge. https://doi.org/10.4324/9780203804377.

Fosha, D. (2000). *The Transforming Power of Affect: A Model for Accelerated Change*. New York: Basic Behavioral Science.

Fuchs, T. (2010). *Das Gehirn–ein Beziehungsorgan: Eine phänomenologisch-ökologische Konzeption* (3. aktual.underw.Auflage) [The Brain—A Relational Organ: A Phenomenological-Ecological Conception, 3rd Updated and Extended Edition]. Stuttgart: Kohlhammer.

Fuchs, T. (2008). *Leib und Lebenswelt: Neue philosophische-psychiatrische Essays* [Body and Life-World: New Philosophical-Psychiatric Essays]. Kusterdingen: Die Graue Edition.

Goleman, D. (1972). The Buddha on Meditation and States of Consciousness Part 1: A Typology of Meditation Techniques. *Journal of Transpersonal Psychology*. 4(1), 151–210.

Grand, D. (2013). *Brainspotting: The Revolutionary New Therapy for Rapid and Effective Change*. Boulder, CO: Sounds True.

Howell, E. (2020). *Trauma and Dissociation-Informed Psychotherapy: Relational Healing and the Therapeutic Connection*. New York: W.W. Norton. 0.4324/9780203888261.

Janet, P. (1935). *Les Debuts de l'Intelligence*. Paris: Flammarion.

Janet, P. (1925). *Principles of Psychotherapy*. London: Allen & Unwin. https://doi.org/10.1037/13452-000.

Janet, P. (1919). *Psychological Healing*. New York: Macmillan.

Järvilehto, T. (2001a). Feeling as Knowing, Part 2. Emotion, Consciousness, and Brain Activity. *Consciousness & Emotion*, 2(1), 75–102. https://doi.org/10.1075/ce.2.1.04jar.

Järvilehto, T. (2001b). The Self and Free Will in the Framework of the Organism-Environment Theory. Karl Jaspers Forum, Target Article 36b. www.kjf.ca/36B-TAJA.html.

Järvilehto, T. (2000a). Theory of the Organism-Environment System: IV. The Problem on Mental Activity and Consciousness. *Integrative Physiological and Behavioural Sciences*, 35, 35–57. https://doi.org/10.1007/BF02911165.

Järvilehto, T. (2000b). Consciousness as Cooperation. *Advances in Mind Body Medicine*, 16(2), 89–92; discussion, 97–101.

Järvilehto, T. (2000c). Feeling as Knowing. *Consciousness & Emotion*, 1(2), 53–65. https://doi.org/10.1075/ce.1.2.04jar.

Järvilehto, T. (1999). The Theory of the Organism-Environment System: III. Role of Efferent Influences on Receptors in the Formation of Knowledge. *Integrative Physiological and Behavioural Sciences*, 34, 90–100. https://doi.org/10.1007/BF02688715.

Järvilehto, T. (1998a). The Theory of the Organism-Environment System: I. Description of the Theory. *Integrative Physiological and Behavioural Sciences*, 33, 321–334. https://doi.org/10.1007/BF02688700.

Järvilehto, T. (1998b). The Theory of the Organism-Environment System: II. Significance of Nervous Activity in the Organism-Environment System. *Integrative Physiological and Behavioural Sciences*, 33, 335–342; discussion 343. https://doi.org/10.1007/BF02688701.

Levine, P. A. (2010). *In an Unspoken Voice: How the Body Releases Trauma and Restores Goodness.* Berkeley, CA: North Atlantic Books.

Lewis, H. B. (1992). *The Role of Shame in Symptom Formation.* Hillsdale, NJ: Lawrence Erlbaum Associates.

Lewis, H. B. (1971). *Shame and Guilt in Neurosis.* New York: International Universities Press.

Mithoefer, M., Doblin, R., Wolfson, C., Carhart-Harris, R., & Penn, A. (May 27, 2021). *The Use of Mind-Altering Substances for Treating PTSD and Other Mental Distress.* Boston: 32nd Annual Boston International Trauma Congress.

Nijenhuis, E. R. S. (In press). Steps towards an Ecology of Dissociation of Mind and Matter in the Context of Trauma. In P. Dell & J. O'Neil, Eds., *Dissociation and the Dissociative Disorders: Past, Present, Future.*

Nijenhuis, E. R. S. (2015). *The Trinity of Trauma: Ignorance, Fragility, and Control: Volume II, The Evolving Concept of Trauma/The Concepts and Facts of Dissociation in Trauma.* Bristol, CT: Vandenhoeck & Ruprecht LLC. https://doi.org/10.13109/978366 6402470.

Northoff, G. (2003). *Philosophy of the Brain: The Brain Problem.* Amsterdam/ Philadelphia: John Benjamins. https://doi.org/10.1075/aicr.52.

Ogden, P. (2019). Acts of Triumph: An Interpretation of Pierre Janet and the Role of the Body in Trauma Treatment. In G. Craparo, F. Ortu, & O. van der Hart, Eds., *Rediscovering Pierre Janet: Trauma, Dissociation, and a New Context for Psychoanalysis* (pp. 200–209). New York: Routledge. https://doi.org/10.4324/9780429201875.

Ogden, P., Minton, K., & Pain, C. (2006). *Trauma and the Body: A Sensorimotor Approach to Psychotherapy.* New York: W.W. Norton.

O'Hanlon, B. (1999). *Do One Thing Different: Ten Simple Ways to Change Your Life.* New York: William Morrow.

Pearson, J. L., Cohn, D. A., Cowan, P. A., & Cowan, C. P. (1994). Earned- and Continuous-Security in Adult Attachment: Relation to Depressive Symptomatology and Parenting Style. *Development & Psychopathology*, 6, 359–373. https://doi.org/10.1017/S0954579400004636.

Proud, word origin: www.etymonline.com/word/proud. Accessed March 21, 2021.

Rank, O. (1932). *Art and Artist: Creative Urge and Personality Development* (C. F. Atkinson, Transl.). New York: Agathon Press.

Rank, O. (1978/1929). *Will Therapy* (J. Taft, Transl.). New York: W.W. Norton.

Real, T. (2002). *How Can I Get Through to You?: Reconnecting Men and Women.* New York: Fireside (Simon & Schuster).

Real, T. (1997). *I Don't Want to Talk About It: Overcoming the Secret Legacy of Male Depression.* New York: Simon & Schuster.

Roisman, G. I., Padron, E., Sroufe, A., & Egeland, B. (2002). Earned-Secure Attachment Status in Retrospect and Prospect. *Child Development*, 73(4), 1204–1219. https://doi.org/10.1111/1467-8624.00467.

Schmidt, S. J. (2009). *The Developmental Needs Meeting Strategy: An Ego-State Therapy for Healing Adults with Childhood Trauma and Attachment Wounds.* San Antonio, TX: DNMS Institute LLC.

Schopenhauer, A. (1958/1844/1818). *The World as Will and Representation, Vol. 1 (1818) and Vol. 2 (1844)* (R. B. Haldane & J. Kemp, Transl.). Clinton, MA: Falcon's Wing Press.

Schore, A. N. (2001). The Effects of Relational Trauma on Right Brain Development, Affect Regulation, and Infant Mental Health. *Infant Mental Health Journal*, 22(1–2), 201–269.

Schwarz, L. (2014–2017). *CRM (Comprehensive Resource Model) Practitioner Booklet.* CRM LLC.

Schwarz, L., Corrigan, F., Hull, A., & Raju, R. (2017). *The Comprehensive Resource Model: Effective Therapeutic Techniques for the Healing of Complex Trauma.* New York: Routledge. https://doi.org/10.4324/9781315689906.

Shame, word origin: www.etymonline.com/word/shame. Accessed April 1, 2021.

Shengold, L. (1991). *Soul Murder: The Effects of Childhood Abuse and Deprivation.* New York: Ballantine.

Spinoza, B. (2006/1677) (R. H. M. Elwes, Transl.). *The Ethics (Ethica Ordine Geometrico Demonstrata): Parts 1–5.* Charleston, SC: BiblioBazaar. https://doi.org/10.1524/9783050050218.1.

Spinoza, B. (1996/1677) (E. Curly, Ed. & E. Curley, Transl.). *Ethics.* London: Penguin.

Stace, W. T. (1960). *Mysticism and Philosophy.* London: St. Martin's Press. 10.2307/2217211.

Stern, D. N. (1985). *The Interpersonal World of the Infant: A View from Psychoanalysis and Developmental Psychology.* New York: Basic Books.

Thompson, E. (2007). *Mind in Life: Biology, Phenomenology, and the Sciences of Mind.* Cambridge, MA: Belknap Harvard.

Tracy, J. (2016). *Take Pride: Why the Deadliest Sin Holds the Secret to Human Success.* New York: Houghton Mifflin Harcourt.

Van der Hart, O., Nijenhuis, E. R. S., & Steele, K. (2006). *The Haunted Self: Structural Dissociation and the Treatment of Chronic Traumatization.* New York: W.W. Norton.

Van der Kolk, B. (1989). The Compulsion to Repeat the Trauma: Re-enactment, Revictimization, and Masochism. *Psychiatric Clinics of North America*, 12(2), 389–411. https://doi.org/10.1016/S0193-953X(18)30439-8.

Weil, A. (1986). *The Natural Mind: An Investigation of Drugs and Higher Consciousness (Revised Edition).* Boston: Houghton Mifflin.

White, M. & Epston, D. (1990). *Narrative Means to Therapeutic Ends.* New York: W.W. Norton.

Whitman, W. (1965/1855). *Leaves of Grass (Poem: "Song of Myself," Lines 1324–1326).* (H. W. Blodgett & S. Bradley, Eds.). New York: New York University Press.

Whitman, W. (2007–2013/1855). *Leaves of Grass (Poem: "I Sing the Body Electric").* (J. Manis, Ed.). Hazelton, PA: Electronic Classics Series.

Wilber, K. (1998). *The Essential Ken Wilber.* Boston: Shambhala.

Wille, R. (2014). The Shame of Existing: An Extreme Form of Shame. *International Journal of Psychoanalysis*, 95(4), 695–717. https://doi.org/10.1111/1745-8315.12208.

Index

absence 10, 13, 28–9, 41, 43–5, 48–9, 87, 120, 147, 158–9, 161, 192, 201, 207
abuse 2, 6, 10, 13, 15, 23–5, 27, 39, 55, 62, 75, 80–2, 87–90, 101, 105, 114–6, 121, 131–3, 146, 149–50, 165, 174, 215, 231, 236–7, 240
ACES 29–30
act of triumph 3, 25, 46, 54, 68, 80, 103, 150, 193, 238, 240
Adam and Eve 12
adaptive pride 143
affect; and emotion 13, 30, 73
Alighieri, D. 222
Alix, S. 27
Andrews, B. 146
annihilation, perceived 44
anti-symptom position (ASP) 126
anticipatory shaming 64
Apparently Normal Parts of the Personality (ANP) 74, 132
attachment 9–11, 18, 24, 27, 29, 37, 41–46, 51, 79, 86, 88, 102–6, 135, 138, 140–2, 145–7, 153, 156, 165–67, 170, 176, 179–80, 183–6, 190, 196–8, 200–3, 209, 211–2, 216, 224, 228–9
attach part 135–6
attention, 6, 82–50; directionality 82–5, 88–9; phenomenology of 88–9; quality, 85–9; with wide or narrow lens 86–90

Bach, S. 29
Bandler, R. 187, 194, 198, 205
Barach, P. 114
Barral, C. 3, 25, 46, 54, 80, 87, 170, 193, 201, 238, 240
Barrett, L.F. 30
Beck, J. 195
Beebe, B. 8, 28, 84

being-in-relationship 112
Bekoff, M. 11
Benau, K. (author) xi–xii, 12, 15, 25, 39–40, 57, 59, 75, 87, 92, 101, 103, 113, 121, 126, 130, 135, 147–9, 158, 160, 164, 180, 188, 191, 197, 206, 208, 215–6, 218, 236, 238
Bergson, H. 50
Berne, E. 104, 136
better me pride 45, 47; vignette: "Mary and Jack" 47–48
Bierer, L.M. 53
Bovin, M.J. 187
Bowen, B. 114, 129, 141, 217
Bowen, M. 120
Bowlby, J. 15, 40, 85, 90, 125, 136, 147, 149, 153, 165, 176, 198, 203, 224
Brach, T. 95, 123
brain function 239–40
Broucek, F.J. 14, 16, 119
Bromberg, P. 2, 10, 42, 48, 58, 98, 115, 117, 144–5, 158
Brothers, L. 1
Brown, D. 51, 120
Buber, M. 115, 253
Buchman-Wildbaum, T. 24

Calhoun, L.G. 50
caregivers 10, 43–4
"Carla" 80–2
Caretti, V. 26, 59, 63, 74, 148, 151
Chefetz, R. 9, 135
children, behavior of 146
Christie-Sands, J. 53, 60–1, 91, 118, 121, 177, 185–7, 190–1, 194, 197, 202–6, 222
Clearwater, K. 76
clinical observation 28
Cloitre, M. 28
Co-consciousness 130–2

Coherence Therapy (CT) 47, 122
Comoli, E. 191
Complex PTSD 27
Comprehensive Rescue Model (CRM) 105–6, 114, 121, 130, 176, 179–80, 183–4, 190, 192, 198–9, 220, 224, 226, 242
Corrigan, F.M. 6, 53, 60–1, 79, 81, 91, 118, 121, 174, 179–207
countertransference 143
COVID-19 pandemic 225
Craparo, G. 25, 164, 201
Csikszentmihalyi, M. 59

Daedalus 12
Dalenberg, C.J. 26, 115, 125, 142, 144
Damasio, A. 1, 53
"Dan" 114–5
"dark energy" 244
Dean, P. 188
Dearing, R.L. 25, 37, 113, 127, 143–4, 163, 238
Deep Brain Reorienting (DBR) 61, 81, 91–3, 121, 185, 190, 194, 197, 199, 202, 204–6, 212; vignette "Isaac" 204–6
delight 1, 12, 52, 239
depersonalization/derealization (DP/DR) 27, 29, 44, 57, 59, 63–4, 67, 74, 78, 151
DePrince, A.P. 27, 75–8, 95, 100, 150, 203, 224
devalue 1, 12
DeYoung, P. 39, 143, 228
death fear 242
Delafield-Butt, J.T. 52–3
delight 52, 239
Descartes, R. 239
DesJardin, J.T. 187
Developmental Needs Meeting Strategy (DNMS) 114, 129–30, 195
Dickinson, E. 94
disembodied SD and LT 78
dissociation and dissociative disorders xii, 5, 9–10, 26–29, 63, 74–5, 87, 151; see also Structural Dissociation (SD)
Dissociative Identity Disorder (DID) 9, 29
Dorahy, M. xi–xiii, 17, 75–8, 100, 134, 150, 203, 219
drop 61, 66
drop and spike 66
drug-taking 243
Dutra, L. 28

Ecker, B. 47, 81, 89, 96, 98, 103, 116, 122, 124–27, 130, 136, 153, 175, 181–5, 193, 196, 200, 202–5, 218, 233

Ecstasy (MDMA) 243
Ekkekakis, P. 13, 30, 33, 50, 73, 93
Elkin-Cleary, E. 60–1, 78, 81, 118, 121, 175, 184, 186, 204
Ellison, W.D. 29
"Ellen" 133–4
Elliott, D. 51, 120
embodied shame and pride processes and states 80, 120–2, 127
emotion 13–16, 62–6, 73–4, 142–4
enlivened/enlivenment 4, 5
Epston, D. 87, 89, 98, 217
Erozkan, A. 10
Evans, D.A. 190
evolutionary survival 117–18
experience-distant and experience-near perspectives 5, 57
explicit and implicit shame 145
Eye Movement Desensitization and Reprocessing (EMDR) 129

Felitti, V. 29
Ferrante, E. 24
fight part 134
fight/flight reactions 60
fighting 134, 149
Firestone, R.W. 125, 134
Firth, C.D. 1
Fischer, K.W. 13, 24, 47, 75, 119, 144
Fisher, J. 6, 148–51
Fisher's Parts Model 149
flight part 136
Fosha, D. 7, 97, 99, 118, 120, 122, 184–5
Frankel, Z. 198
Frederick, A. 129
freeze-high and freeze-low 135
Freud, S. 18, 102, 146
"Frieda" 41
Functional Coherence (FC) 96, 113, 124–5; Vignette: "Karl" 124–5.

Gallese, V. 147
Gangopadhay, N. 1, 52–3
gaze/gazing 83, 94–106; absenting 97; celebratory 96, 99; disintegrative and destructive 97; evaluative 96–7; heart/slant vs. eye/goal-oriented 94–5, 97–8; mindful 95–6; phenomenology of 97–106; quality of 94–5, 98–9
Gilbert, P. 14
going on being 57
good enough me pride 25, 29, 37, 45; vignette: "Kristina" 46
good enough me shame 17, 19, 37–40; vignette: "Laura" 40

Goldman, A. 146
Goleman, D. 51, 55, 237, 242
Gloria Films 123
Grand, D. 176, 224, 236
"Greg" 55–6
grief 4–7, 41, 52, 80, 86, 91–3, 97, 118, 162, 174, 198, 214–9, 224–5, 229, 231–4
guilt 5, 9, 14, 17–21; adaptive 17; punitive and reparative 18, 20, 73

Hahn, W.K. 120
Hansard, G. 115
happiness 4
"Harold" 165–70
Herman, J.L. 12, 24, 27–8, 39, 134
Hicks, D. 25, 26, 43, 46, 53, 74, 89, 135, 155–6
Howell, E. 29, 63, 73, 134, 149–50, 226
Hoppenwasser, K. 159, 175
hubris 47; *see also* pride, hubristic
Hull, A.M. 181
humiliation xi, 5, 9, 21–3
hyperarousal and hypoarousal 26

Icarus 12–13, 47
Immordino-Young, M.H. 201, 207
integration 82, 93, 182, 196, 206, 214, 216, 221–2, 232–4, 238, 240
intra- and inter-relational shame 3, 4, 9, 142, 152–61
internal working model 15
inter-actions and intra-actions 143–45
intra- and inter-subjective experience 240
intrarelational and interrelational resourcing 127–8
introversion 146
invisibility, feelings of 49
"Isaac" 6, 90–3, 174–208; *passim*, 214–37; *passim*, 242–4

"Jack" 47–8
"Jacob" 99
Janet, P. 3, 25, 46, 54, 62, 80, 87, 89, 103, 164, 170, 193, 201, 238, 240, 243
Jarvilehto, T. 241
Johnson, M. 193
joy 3–4, 25, 46, 51–4, 96, 170, 193, 201–3, 208, 214–6, 221–5, 230–8, 241–4

Kabbalah 104–5
Kaplan, B. 128
"Kara" 48–9
"Karl" 42, 124–5

Kaminer, T. 28
Karman's Drama Role Model 151
Karpman, S.B. 6, 142, 148, 151
"Kathy" 105–6
Kaufman, G. 167, 179, 182, 203
"Kendra" 126–7
"Kerry" 115–6
Kohut, H. 29
Kozlowska, K. 183, 187–8
Kreibig, S. 183, 203
"Kristin" 20–1
"Kristina" 46

Lachmann, F. 28, 84
Lakoff, G. 193
Lanius, U. 26
Lanius, R. 151
"Laura" 40, 45, 49–50
Laureys, S. 183
Leask, P. 22–3
leave taking (LT) 5–6, 26, 28–9, 57, 59, 63–4, 74, 78, 159
Levine, P. 59, 129–30, 149, 218
Lewis, H.B. 120, 146, 156, 218
Lewis, M. 14
Li, L. 185, 188
Liddell, B.J. 194–5
Liotti, G. 170
Lyons-Ruth, K. 28, 120

McKeogh, K. 75–6
"macro" perspective 36–7, 57
maladaptive shame and pride 24, 54–5
maladaptive shame 37; as micro process 57
Marsh, R.J. 77, 119
"Mary" with "Isaac" 215
"Mary and Jack" 47–8
McHaffie, J.G. 190
Meares, R. 3, 25, 46, 54, 80, 87, 170, 193, 201, 230, 238
Memory Reconsolidation (MR) 89, 103, 113, 116, 125–7, 130, 181, 183–5, 193, 196, 200, 204–5, 210, 211–2, 217–8, 225, 233; defined 125–6; vignettes: "John Walker" 103–4; "Kerry" 115–6; "Kendra" 126–7
Merker, B. 53, 183, 208
metaprocessing, therapeutic 242
"micro" perspective 36–7
Middleton, W. 29
Miller, A. 153
mind, human 239–40
mind/body organisation 83, 100–1
Mobbs, D. 176, 205
models, conceptual 6

Mollon, P. 13
Multiplicity of Parts 132–4

narcissism 13
narrative layers xi
Nathanson, D. 6, 14–15, 18, 119, 148–51
Nathanson's Shame Defence Model 150–1
neglect 10
neuroception, concept of 60, 149
neuroscience 6, 53, 174; therapeutic applications of 202–8
Nijenhuis, E.R.S. 50, 52, 59, 63, 74, 84, 239, 241
no me pride 45, 49; vignette: "Laura" 49–50
no me shame 38–9, 43–5; vignette: "Laura" 45
Northoff, G. 208
not good enough me shame 38, 40–1; vignette: "Frieda" 41
not me pride 45, 48; vignette: "Kara" 48–9
not me shame 38–9, 41–2; vignette: "Karl" 42
Nouwen, H.J.M. 147

Ogden, P. 40, 58, 61, 65, 80, 103, 120–1, 127, 131, 178, 183, 186–7, 190–1, 206–7, 213, 217, 222, 238
O'Hanlon, B. 217
"oneness", sense of 7, 56, 214, 224–5, 232, 237, 240–3
ontology 241
organismic pleasure 3
organization of mind/body 6, 83, 100–1
"overwhelming" abuse 10

Panskepp, J. 53, 179–80, 182, 195, 197–8, 201, 203, 206, 208
Pearson, J. 216
Papousek, H. 119
Papousek, M. 119
Parasympathetic Nervous System (PNS) 61
pathogenic shame 40
patient attacks 152–7
patient, origin of 11
patient flight 157–8
patient freeze 159
patient withdrawal 157
periaqueductal gray (PAG) 53
pleasure 239
polyvagal theory 60
Porges, S. 26, 44, 47, 59–63, 84, 95–6, 120, 135, 149, 159–60

Premack principle 83
pride xi–xii, 1–5, 9, 11–17, 24–6, 29; action/interaction 17; authentic/genuine 2, 6, 25; better me pride 47–8; characteristics 13–17; good enough me pride 46–7, 50, 65; emotional process 11, 12, 16, 46–7, 66–7; hubristic and adaptive 11–17, 24–6, 29, 238; maladaptive 2, 13, 16; no me pride 49–50; not me pride 48–9; physiology 16–7; subtypes 45; thoughts/beliefs 15–6; traumatic state 48, 67; *see also* shame and pride
pride states xii, 3–5, 26–9, 54–5, 117; and the body 121
pro-being pride xii, 3–7, 11–12, 25–6, 29, 38, 45, 48–50, 73, 112, 119, 122, 128, 164, 191, 214–5, 227–8, 232–4, 238–44; act of triumph vignette: "Isaac" 242–3; antidote to shame states/"thrival" 53–5; vignettes: "Greg" 55–6; "Jacob" 99; "John Walker" 101–4; "Sam" 118–9; "Harold" 164–170, 241; "Isaac" 201, 204, 207–8, 215–6, 218–24; beyond 6, 214, 216, 242; CARE/PLAY systems 180–1, 184; vignette: "Isaac" 197, 202; definition of 3–4, 52, 214–15, 238; "exponential" 242; expressed delight/joy 51, 85–6, 112; vignettes: "Kerry" 115–6; "Isaac" 232; extrarelational 51; intrarelational 51; interrelational 51; metaprocessing vignette: "Isaac" 242–3; no technique/be real vignettes: "Dan" 113–4; "Isaac" 230; psychodynamic relationship to shame, LT, SD 77–82; unity consciousness and integration vignette: "Isaac" 234, 231, 237, 243–4
pro-symptom position (PSP) 126
"protoself" concept 1, 52–4
"proud", word origin 3, 50, 214
proud people 15
psychoactive substances 242
psychological distance 128–30
psychological influences 145–6
psychopathology 75
psychotherapy 2–7, 17, 24, 27, 30, 112; applications of 80–2

Radical Inquiry, Radical Empathy, Radical Acceptance and Radical Reflection 112–13
radical, word origin 122
rage 67
Rank, O. 242, 244

reactivity 6; shame-induced 62, 161–4
Real, T. 195
recognition between therapist and patient 2, 10, 115
reflective responses and responsivity 6, 142–3
relational trauma (RT) xi–xii, 1–11, 21, 23–30, 36–8, 41, 48–50, 53, 57, 64–7, 95, 106, 112–13, 134, 142, 144, 174, 214, 216, 232, 238, 243–4; defined 2, 9–11; legacy of 4
relationality 14, 116–17
Representations of Interactions that have been Generalized (RIGs) 15
resourcing 127–8
responsivity 62
Retzinger, S.M. 24
Rodin, A. 16
Rogers, C. 50, 123
Roisman, G.I. 103, 170, 216
Ross, C. 95
Russell, J.A. 30
"Ryan" 126

"Sam" 118
Sapolsky, R.M. 1
"Sarah" 91
Scaer, R.C. 30
Schimmenti, A. 26, 59, 63, 74, 85, 104, 120, 134, 142, 174, 177, 189, 207, 214–5
Schmidt, S.J. 88, 90, 114, 130, 170, 195, 231
Schopenhauer, A. 241
Schore, A.N. 2, 9–11, 36, 40, 74, 112, 118, 120, 134, 142, 149, 174, 177, 189, 207, 214–5
Schwartz, R. 38, 129, 132
Schwarz, L. 85, 114, 121, 130, 176, 179–80, 183, 192, 198–20, 212, 220, 224, 226, 242
self, sense of 2–3
self-consciousness 12
self-experience 239
self-organization and self-reflective capacity 38
self-protective responses and reactions 62–7, 142–3; models of 147–52
self-righting shame 40
self-shaming 63, 146
seven deadly sins 13
shame xi–xiii, 1–5, 9–27, 73; adaptive and maladaptive 37–8, 112, 117; defensive strategies in response to 18, 62–63; as an emotional process 2, 6, 12, 16, 38–9, 61–2, 143–4; external or internal 14–15; good enough me shame 40; and guilt 17–20; and humiliation 21–4; origin of 21; no me shame 41–43; not good enough me shame 40–1; not me shame 41–43; patient-therapist shame dynamics 152–161; proneness to 142, 145–6; research into shame and dissociation 74–7; relationship with pride and SD 77–80; shame reaction model 147–52; state shift model of 57–8; subtypes of 5, 39; and trauma 24; well-regulated 17
shame-inducing events 142
shame and pride 13–17, 25–7; actions and interactions connected with 17; adaptive types 117; body 113, 120–22; development in first year of life 119; dissociation 112, 117; as embodied states 77–9; feelings and emotions about 16; general characteristics 13–17; knowledge of 143; phenomenology with dissociation 82–106; ; physiology of 16–17; prototypical parts 119, 134–6; psychodynamics with dissociation 77–81; psychotherapy, *generally* 24–5; psychotherapy *specifically* with relational trauma 25–30; relational nature *116–17*; relations between 37; subtypes of 36–7, 45, 144; "techniques" 112–6; thought/beliefs about 15–16; working with 136; *see also* Embodied; Functional Coherence (FC); Radical Inquiry, Radical Empathy, Radical Acceptance, Radical Reflection
shame states 2–5, 12, 27–9, 39, 42, 117, 142–5; and the body 121; challenges for 144; Three Therapist Phases and associated Tasks 161–6
shame, word origin 21, 219, 236
Shapiro, F. 129, 185, 198
"Shara" 131–2
shared consciousness 130–2
Shaw, D. 29, 129, 133, 136, 178
Sheldon, A. & B. 181
shift model of pride 64–7
shock 58
Shook, N.J. 117
Shore, A. 2, 9–10
Siegel, D. 40, 58, 66, 120–1, 127, 178, 183, 191, 207
Simon-Thomas, E.R. 201, 207
Social Engagement System (SES) 60, 160, 198–99

social withdrawal 63
Sohms, M. 53
Spinoza, Baruch 13, 50–1, 238–43
Steiner, J. 29, 47, 93
Stern, D. 15, 44, 59, 99, 136, 228–9
Stern, S. 113–14
still-face research paradigm 119, 160
structural dissociation (SD) 5–6, 20, 26–29, 39, 42, 44, 56–9, 63–4, 67, 73–90, 94–106, 132, 135, 148–50, 162, 165, 213, 226; as shards of light 104–6
subjective experience 2, 5
surprise 58
submit part 136, 149, 159–61
superior colliculi (SC) 53
surprise and shock 58–60, 65

Tauber, Y. 168
talk therapy 121
"techniques" 113–16
Tangney, J.P. 13, 24–5, 27, 37, 47
Tedeschi, R.G. 50
Terpou, B.A. 194–5
Terrizzi, J.A. 117
therapy, goal of 144
"thrival" functions 113, 117–18
Tomkins, S. 61
toxic shame 40
Tracy, J. 12–16, 24–5, 30, 46–7, 50, 114, 116, 119, 214, 237–8
Tronick, E. 119, 160
transformative pride 50
transtheoretical stances 6, 112, 136, 161
trauma: origin of the word 11; reactions to 142
traumatic states 36, 48, 61–2
Trevarthen, C. 1, 24, 119
Twain, M. 12

"underwhelming" neglect 10
unity consciousness 7, 51, 55, 214, 234, 237–8, 240–3

value 5, 12
Van der Hart, O. 38–9, 42, 44, 48–9, 57–9, 61–4, 68–9, 74, 77, 79, 82–3, 87, 89–90, 101, 103, 105, 132, 148–51, 164–5, 175, 203, 232
Van der Kolk, B. 30, 62
Van Nuys, D. 51
vehement emotions 62
vignettes 6, 40–50, 55, 80–1, 90–1, 99–105, 114–19, 124–6, 131–3, 142, 164–70
Vogt, B.A. 59

Walker, J. 101–4
Watkins, J. & H. 132
Watt, D.F. 198, 201
Weil, A. 51, 55, 224, 227, 242
Werner, H. 128
White, M. 87, 89, 98–9, 217
Whitman, W. 214, 242
Whittaker, C. 114
Wilber, K. 51, 55, 224, 227, 242
Wille, R. 12, 16, 23, 43–5, 64, 79, 118, 144, 228, 231
"window of optimal arousal" model 40, 65, 127, 178, 183, 191, 207
"window of tolerance model" 58–60, 66, 120–1, 178
Winnicott, D.W. 4, 36, 40, 44–5, 54, 58, 79, 179
Woodman, M. 51

Yehuda, R. 53

Zhu, P. 26